Max Weber and the Idea of
Economic Sociology

Max Weber and the Idea of Economic Sociology

RICHARD SWEDBERG

PRINCETON UNIVERSITY PRESS

PRINCETON, NEW JERSEY

Library of Congress Cataloging-in-Publication Data

Swedberg, Richard.
Max Weber and the idea of economic sociology / Richard Swedberg.
p.   cm.
Includes bibliographical references and index.
ISBN 0-691-02949-0 (alk. paper)
1. Economics—Sociological aspects.   2. Weber, Max, 1864–1920—
Contributions in economic sociology.   I. Title.
HM35.S95   1998
306.3—dc21   98-5129

CONTENTS

5/01

ACKNOWLEDGMENTS

MANY PEOPLE have helped me in writing this book, but I am in particular debt to two people: Peter Dougherty, publisher at Princeton University Press, who gave extremely good advice about how to improve this book, and Ralph Schroeder, who read the manuscript as I wrote it and commented on all of it. Single chapters were read by friends and colleagues—Karl-Ludwig Ay, Bernard Barber, Bruce Carruthers, Sven Eliaeson, Neil Fligstein, Edith Hanke, Ulf Jonsson, Timur Kuran, Arthur Stinchcombe, Keith Tribe, Charles Tilly, Stephen Turner, Lars Udehn, and Sam Whimster—and I am grateful for all of their comments and critiques. Special thanks should also be extended to Johannes Winkelmann, who answered my first queries about Weber's economic sociology and *Sozialökonomik* in 1985, a few months before his death; Harry Dahms for discussions of German social science terminology; Wilhelm Hennis, who kindly loaned me some Weber documents; Gordon Marshall for conversations about *The Protestant Ethic;* Robert K. Merton, who tried to make me distinguish between Weber's ideas and my ideas, and who also taught me how to trace a social science concept; Mark Granovetter for discussions on Weber and network theory; Friedrich Wilhelm Graf and Martin Riesebrodt for information about Weber's religious terminology; Guenther Roth for generously sharing his knowledge of Weber; and Wolfgang Schluchter, who provided answers to some questions about *Economy and Society* that only he knows.

A large number of people kindly answered questions or helped me in other ways: Ola Agevall, Patrik Aspers, Harold J. Berman, S. N. Eisenstadt, Sven Eliaeson, Franziska Feulner, Torsten Gårdlund, Francisco Gil, Gary Hamilton, Peter Hedström, Michael Hechter, Søren Jagd, Fredrik Liljeros, Helga Moersberger, Apostolis Papakostas, Yuichi Shionoya, Georg Siebeck, Johan Söderberg, John M. Spalek, Dietlind Stolle, Katsuyoshi Watarai, and Michael Woolcock. I also received great help from the staff at a number of libraries, especially the University Library at Stockholm University, the Harvard University Archives, and the Widener Library at Harvard University. A few librarians and archivists went out of their way to track down information for me, and I would especially like to single out Carmen Herdenstatt at the library of the New School for Social Research, Mary Osielski at the State University of New York at Albany, Dr. Wolgast and Mrs. Hunerlach at the Ruprecht-Karls-Universität Heidelberg Universitätsarchiv, Dr. Kurt Mühlberger at the Archive of the University of Vienna, and Ronald Bulatoff at the Hoover Institution Archives. A number of items from the Talcott Parsons Papers are quoted with permission of the Harvard University Archives.

I spent the summers of 1995–1997 at the Minda de Gunzberg Center for European Studies at Harvard University in Cambridge, Massachusetts, and I especially want to thank Charles Maier and Abby Collins for their hospitality. I also want to thank the masters of Pforzheimer House (formerly North House) at Harvard University and especially Sharon Holt.

For financial assistance I am most grateful to the Swedish Council for Research in the Humanities and Social Sciences (HSFR) and the Foundation of Magnus Bergvall at S-E-Banken, both in Stockholm.

Beth Gianfagna and Janet Schilling Mowery patiently and skillfully transformed the manuscript into a book.

I dedicate this book with fondness and love to Cecilia Gil-Swedberg, my wife—and also the author of two works on Weber.

Stockholm, November 1997

ILLUSTRATIONS

Max Weber and the Idea of
Economic Sociology

INTRODUCTION

DURING the twentieth century, mainstream economists have focused exclusively on the role of interests in explaining economic behavior, while sociologists have tended to emphasize the role of social interaction and social structure. Good reasons exist for both of these analytical strategies, and much important work has been produced by economists and by sociologists. However, there are also some economists and sociologists who believe that progress in the understanding of certain economic phenomena can be made only if interests and social structure are *combined* in one analysis. Max Weber, I argue in this work, attempted such an integration, and he was successful in eliminating several of the obstacles. His efforts are highly interesting and deserve to be discussed by economists as well as by sociologists—something that has yet to happen. Most sociologists and economists know *The Protestant Ethic* and a few other writings by Weber, but they are still unfamiliar with his economic sociology and with his work in economics more generally.

The central theme of this book is Weber's attempt to integrate the idea of interest-driven behavior with the idea of social behavior in one and the same analysis. We know, for example, from Amartya Sen's work how insufficient an economic analysis that is grounded exclusively in interest can be. Sen cites Edgeworth's statement in *Mathematical Psychics* (1881) that "the first principle of Economics is that every agent is actuated only by self-interest." Sen adds the following comment to Edgeworth's remark: "This view of man has been a persistent one in economic models, and the nature of economic theory seems to have been much influenced by this basic principle."[1] Similarly, sociologists have from early on tended to see people's behavior as shaped mainly by their social dimension. *Homo sociologicus,* Ralf Dahrendorf wrote in a famous essay from the 1950s, is a being whose behavior is totally determined by his or her roles. A few years later, Peter Berger and Thomas Luckmann coined the phrase "the social construction of reality," which also expresses the tendency to reduce human behavior to interaction, roles, and social structure.[2] That people have interests, and that these interests play a crucial role in determining their behavior, has all too often been ignored by sociologists, or at least pushed into the background.

More recently, in economics as well as in sociology, efforts have been made to bring interests and social behavior together in one and the same analysis. In economics, this development started in the mid-1970s and has resulted in a series of interesting works by such people as Gary Becker, Albert O. Hirschman, Douglass North, Thomas Schelling, Oliver Williamson, and more generally "new institutional economics."[3] In sociology a similar development—sometimes referred to as "new economic sociology"—was initiated a few years later and has engaged other talented people, such as Neil Fligstein, Mark Granovetter, Arthur Stinchcombe, Harrison White, and Viviana Zelizer.[4] While the economists have started out from the idea of interests and tried to develop a way of taking social behavior into account, sociologists have typically done the opposite and developed various ways to "embed" economic action and interests in the social structure.

These efforts have produced some very suggestive ideas, by economists as well as by sociologists. There are, for example, Thomas Schelling's tipping models and Mark Granovetter's ideas on the role of social networks in economic life. There is also James Coleman's attempt, nearly singlehandedly, to bring about a synthesis of rational choice theory and sociology—what is known as rational choice sociology. Coleman started in this direction in the 1960s, but his main work in this respect is *Foundations of Social Theory* (1990). Many of Coleman's ideas, as I will show, are considerably closer to what Weber tried to accomplish than much of what goes under the heading of *Verstehen* in contemporary sociology.

Weber's attempt to unite interest-driven behavior and social behavior constitutes the major theme in this book, and it is followed through an examination of two of his main projects: to develop a distinct *economic sociology* and a new overall conception of economics—"social economics" or *Sozialökonomik*, as Weber called it. "Social economics" was a term that had emerged in the mid- to late nineteenth century that some economists, including Weber, felt was a good replacement for "political economy," which was seen as outmoded around the turn of the century. Weber argued that social economics should be a broad science and include several social sciences, especially economic theory, economic history, and economic sociology. Depending on the problem at hand, the analyst would then draw on whichever of these three sciences was the most suitable. It should be noted that Weber had great respect for economic theory and viewed it as indispensable for the understanding of economic phenomena, both in the form of a separate analysis and as a support for economic sociology and economic history. It is in economic theory, according to Weber, that the interest-driven type of analysis comes to its clearest expression among the social sciences.

To get an accurate picture of how Weber regarded (social) economics, his view of interests must also be explained. First, the three main branches of economics—economic theory, economic history, and economic sociology—were all what Weber called "cultural sciences," and by this term he meant that they dealt with phenomena that involve meaning. Only in the natural sciences could the analyst dispense with taking meaning into account. In other words, for an interest to become an interest, it has to be invested with a distinct meaning by the actor. Second, and equally important, Weber divided the category of interests into two types: *material interests* and *ideal interests*. Both of these can propel the actor into action. Ideal interests include such things as status, nationalism, ethnic honor, and what Weber calls "religious benefits,"—that is, a desire for salvation, a better position in the next life, and the like. In economic analysis material interests count most, but Weber was also extremely interested in what happens when those who pursue ideal interests look after their material interests, when the two types of interests collide, when ideal interests reinforce or block material interests, and so on. Some of Weber's most important works explore these issues historically, such as *The Protestant Ethic* and *The Economic Ethics of the World Religions*. Finally, Weber also argued (unlike modern economists) that not only interest but also tradition and emotions drive the behavior of the individual. The result was a very flexible and social version of interest theory, reminiscent of the great works of Hume and Tocqueville.[5]

Most of this book is devoted to Weber's economic sociology: how it evolved and, more important, how Weber tried to develop it into a practical and efficient type of analysis. Very early in his career Weber thought it natural to include a social dimension in his analysis of economic phenomena, but at that stage of his thinking he was not very interested in developing a distinct sociology or in theoretically working out how a social type of analysis could be integrated with an interest-driven one. "At the turn of the century," one commentator notes, "sociology meant for Weber an inflated approach, vainly claiming the status of a master science."[6] Some years later, however, when Weber was in his early forties, he set out to lay a solid conceptual foundation for sociology and to attempt this integration. These efforts resulted first in a general sociology and some time later in what Weber called his economic sociology, or *Wirtschaftssoziologie*.

At first, Weber applied his new type of sociological analysis only to the relationship between the economic sphere and other spheres in society, such as politics and religion. Much of what he wrote as part of this effort can be found in Part 2 of *Economy and Society* and in other writings. During the last few years of his life, however, Weber also applied his new sociological perspective *directly* to economic phenomena and thereby created an economic sociology in the more strict sense of the word. The result of this last effort can be found mainly in chapter 2 of Part 1 of *Economy and Society*, "Sociological Categories of Economic Action."

One particularly suggestive quality of Weber's economic sociology is the way that he conceptualized economic action and attempted to introduce a social dimension into the analysis of economic behavior. According to Weber, all the cultural sciences (not only sociology, in other words) analyze phenomena that are constituted through the meaning that people invest in them. This applies to economic theory as well as to history and psychology. What sets sociology apart and makes it into a science of its own is consequently something other than meaning per se. Sociology focuses more precisely on the way that people's actions are *oriented to the behavior of others*. "Sociology," to cite Weber's famous definition in *Economy and Society*, "is a science concerning itself with the interpretive understanding of social action and thereby with a causal explanation of its course and consequences. . . . *Action is 'social' insofar as its subjective meaning takes account of the behavior of others and is thereby oriented in its course.*"[7]

When applied to economic phenomena, sociology looks at behavior that is driven mainly by material interests and also oriented to the behavior of others. In other words, economic *social* action, the basic unit in Weber's economic sociology, differs from economic action, the basic unit of analysis in economic theory, in that it not only is driven by material interests and directed at utility, but also takes the behavior of others into account.

Using this conception of *economic social action* as the foundation for his economic sociology, Weber developed a series of more complex concepts in *Economy and Society*, such as open and closed economic relationships, economic organizations, political and rational capitalism, and so on. He applied his new sociological perspective to economic phenomena as well as to the relationship between economic and other phenomena, such as religious, political, and legal behavior. Some aspects of the economic sociology that resulted from this is well known among sociologists, but little sustained attention has been devoted to Weber's economic sociology as a whole, either by sociologists or by economists.

The main body of this book is devoted to a presentation and critical discussion of Weber's economic sociology; the historical evolution of his thought on economic topics can be found in the appendix. In chapter 1 the reader is introduced to Weber's view of how the economy has evolved in the West, based on *General Economic History*. Chapter 2 discusses Weber's sociological analysis of the economy, as this is to be found in *Economy and Society*. The next three chapters deal with Weber's view of the relationship of the economy to other social phenomena: these chapters focus on the relationship between the economy and politics (chapter 3), the economy and law (chapter 4), and the economy and religion (chapter 5). Chapter 6 provides some complementary material on how Weber saw the relationship between the economy on the one hand, and science, technology, race, and a few other topics on the other. The last chapter also contains an assessment of the huge handbook in economics that Weber was editing in the 1910s (*Grundriss der Sozialökonomik*), and a comparison between Weber's economic sociology and contemporary economic sociology.

In discussing Weber's economic sociology I draw mainly on his later writings, meaning by this his work from the period 1910–20, such as *Economy and Society*, *The Economic Ethics of the World Religions*, and *General Economic History*. The reason for this is that it was during his last years that Weber decided to try to develop a new type of analysis of the economy, situated somewhere between theoretical economics and economic history.

The appendix at the end of the book is devoted to the evolution of Weber's thought on economics more broadly conceived (economic theory, economic sociology, and economic history). It also contains some biographical information on Weber (1864–1920) as well as a discussion of his most important works in economics, from his early writings in the 1890s to *Economy and Society*, which was part of his handbook in economics. How Weber's work has been viewed by economists, economic historians, and sociologists is noted in the appendix as well.

It is clear that Weber is one of the few thinkers in social science whose work must be taken seriously, and what he has to say on the relationship between economics and sociology is of interest to both sociologists and economists. Very little attention, however, has been paid over the years to Weber's economic sociology, and it is my hope that with this book Weber's work in economic sociology will finally receive the discussion it deserves.

CHAPTER ONE

The Rise of Western Capitalism

THERE EXIST a number of competing versions of how Western capitalism was born, from that of Karl Marx in *Capital* (1867) to that of Douglass North and Robert Paul Thomas in *The Rise of the Western World* (1973). While Marx emphasizes the role of revolutions and class struggle, North and Thomas look mainly at property rights and incentives. To Marx, the bourgeoisie succeeded in breaking the fetters of feudalism and thereby set the productive forces free. North and Thomas argue that in order for economic growth to occur the private rate of return and the social rate of return have to coincide; and when this happened on a large scale, modern capitalism was born. Finally, a huge number of scholars believe that the Industrial Revolution was much more important for the creation of the modern economy than the birth of capitalism. In other words, since the second half of the eighteenth century, what has mattered most is how technology has been used in economic production.

Max Weber took a very different stance on these issues, as anyone knows who is familiar with *The Protestant Ethic and the Spirit of Capitalism* (1904–5). In this famous work Weber tried to argue that religion—or more precisely, ascetic Protestantism—had helped to create a new type of economic mentality, namely rational capitalism. What is less known, however, is that Weber saw the emergence of modern capitalism as a gradual process, which had institutional as well as cultural dimensions and extended over several centuries. The influence of ascetic Protestantism is only an episode in this long process, albeit an important and particularly fascinating one.

That this is Weber's view is not easy to grasp from *The Protestant Ethic,* but it emerges with great clarity in *Economy and Society,* written in the 1910s, and even more so in a lecture course that Weber gave at the University of Munich in 1919–20 and that was later published under the title *General Economic History.*[1] In this work Weber covers the economic evolution of mankind from antiquity onward, paying particular attention to the factors that would eventually give rise to Western capitalism. Weber discusses not only the impact of ascetic Protestantism, but also the evolution of the shareholding corporation, the emergence of the modern state, the Industrial Revolution, and a host of other factors. In brief, in Weber's mind the birth of modern capitalism was an extremely complex process that included state building, the creation of many new economic institutions, the birth of a new economic mentality, the introduction of technology, and other innovations.

Weber intended *General Economic History* to be primarily a work in economic history, not in economic sociology.[2] Weber's economic sociology is instead to be found in *Economy and Society,* which was part of the giant handbook in economics that Weber was editing in the 1910s.[3] Much of the material in *Economy and Society* can be classified as economic sociology, especially chapter 2 in Part 1, "Sociological Categories of Economic Action." This chapter, which is the size of a small book (150 pages), was written around the same time that Weber gave his lecture course in Munich but is of a very different nature. For one thing, "Sociological Categories of Economic Action" has primarily a theoretical purpose, namely to lay the conceptual foundation for economic sociology; it is therefore full of definitions and contains few historical examples. Most commentators agree that this chapter contains the most important presentation of Weber's economic sociology, but it is also generally considered to be very tough reading.[4] Indeed, the main reason Weber gave the course in Munich was that the students found his lectures, which were based on the first two chapters in *Economy and Society,* so difficult to follow.

For this reason it would probably be too demanding for the contemporary reader to start directly with "Sociological Categories of Economic Action," and I have therefore decided to follow Weber and first present the content of *General Economic History.* I hope the reader will thus have an easier time with Weber's view of economic sociology and also become familiar with some of the historical material that Weber had in mind when he constructed his sociological categories.

There is one more reason for beginning an exposition of Weber's economic sociology with *General Economic History* rather than with chapter 2 in *Economy and Society.* By starting directly with the latter, the impression might inadvertently be given that in Weber's view all societies have a sphere called "the economy," which has its own internal dynamic as well as autonomy. The reason for this is that chapter 2 deals mainly with the economic sphere.[5] This, however, is not how Weber saw things. It is only in modern times, he argues, that it makes sense to speak of the existence of an "economic sphere," which is "in principle autonomous" and which interacts with the other spheres of society.[6] Most of history, he adds, has taken place in pre-capitalist times, and what we today call "the economy" or "the economic sphere" has in reality emerged very slowly.

I. GENERAL ECONOMIC HISTORY

Weber's course at the University of Munich was called "Outline of Universal Social and Economic History," and it was a huge success. Weber lectured in the largest auditorium of the university to some 600 people. He soon felt exhausted by the quick pace of the course, he wrote to a friend.[7] Adding to Weber's difficulties was the fact that he had not been able to concentrate on economic history during his last years; most of his energy had been devoted to the handbook of economics and a giant project on the economic ethics of different religions.[8]

After Weber's death, the Munich course was reconstructed using students' notes to produce the volume that we today know as *General Economic History.* Since law students in Bavaria had to know shorthand, a number of good sets of course notes could easily be located. The editors emphasized that Weber would never have published the work in this form and noted that "statements by him show that he regarded [the course] as an imposed improvisation with a thousand deficiencies."[9] Given that Weber was never in a position to check the text of *General Economic History,* a certain caution should no doubt be shown when it is used. The current text contains, for example, some factual errors and probably also some errors of transcription.[10]

General Economic History is structured in the following way. After a couple of introductory pages, which contain a conceptual discussion and may well represent Weber's first lecture, he proceeds to the empirical part of the course. The editors have divided the lectures with an empirical content, which constitute roughly 95 percent of the text, into four parts: social groups and pre-capitalist agriculture, pre-capitalist industry, pre-capitalist trade, and a section entitled "The Origin of Modern Capitalism."

To those who are not familiar with Weber's early work, it may also be pointed out that there are some interesting parallels between the Munich course of 1919–20 and a lecture series that Weber gave some twenty years earlier in Mannheim called "The Course of Economic Development" (1897).[11] Also, the latter series was divided into four parts, with the first three devoted to the pre-capitalist period and the fourth entitled "The Historical Situation of Modern Capitalism." Both lecture series give the distinct impression that what most interested Weber about economic history was the emergence and nature of modern capitalism.

II. GENERAL ECONOMIC HISTORY
PART 1: SOCIAL GROUPS AND PRE-CAPITALIST AGRICULTURE

Many of the historical issues that Weber touches on in *General Economic History* have been discussed at length by contemporary economic historians, something I will return to in the chapters to come. For now, I cite only what some economic historians of an earlier generation thought of his work, such as A. P. Usher and Eli Heckscher. Both were demanding scholars and had, on the whole, a high opinion of *General Economic History.* According to Heckscher, "*General Economic History* [is] invaluable through its richness of ideas"; and according to Usher, "[This work] is the most important single contribution that has been made in economic history for more than fifty years."[12]

The first of the four parts of *General Economic History* is devoted to agriculture in pre-capitalist societies. Weber's central concept here is "*Agrarverfassung,*" which literally means "agrarian constitution" but is perhaps more appropriately translated as "the social and economic organization of agriculture." Why *General Economic History* was termed "sociological" by Usher, Heckscher, and others quickly becomes clear when one realizes that Weber looks primarily at the evolution of agrarian structures throughout history in relation to social groups, especially the household and the clan.[13] Weber's initial approach to economic sociology in *Economy and Society,* it should also be noted, had been to analyze the economy in relation to social groups, and when Karl Bücher failed to deliver a satisfactory article on the stages of economic development, Weber responded by enlarging his section on this theme.[14] As will soon be seen, Weber's original approach to economic sociology works quite well for pre-capitalist society, because not much of an autonomous economic sphere had yet developed.

Instead of beginning his lecture course by discussing what had supposedly happened at the dawn of history, perhaps with a discussion of some archaeological findings, Weber starts by presenting an early type of social structure—more precisely, the agrarian constitution of a typical German village in the Middle Ages. According to Weber, one reason for not starting at the very beginning of history is that "we know nothing about the economic life of primitive man."[15] One also suspects that Weber wanted to make it easier for his students by using an example from Germany. In any case, the typical German village of Carolingian times is presented by Weber in a way that is reminiscent of von Thünen's famous figure in *The Isolated State* (1826) with its series of concentric circles, each representing a different kind of zone (see figure 1.1). In Zone 1 or the center of the early German village, Weber says, one could find the individual houses of the peasants, and outside of these, in Zone 2, their gardens. The fields were situated in Zone 3, outside the gardens, and beyond these there were areas for grazing (Zone 4), and, even farther out, the forest (Zone 5). Thünen had used his figure to illustrate how agricultural production in an "isolated state" would be situated in different zones, because of transportation and production costs, but Weber's aim was different, namely to portray the social structure. Because of the way the fields were laid out, the peasants had to help one another and coordinate many of their agricultural activities, he points out. At this stage of history the individual German peasant was consequently "bound to the group of villagers in all his acts." By the nineteenth century, however, so many changes had taken place in the agricultural map of Germany that the peasant was "forced [to live] an individualistic economic life."[16]

Weber does not discuss only the situation of German peasants in his course, even though he knew the agricultural history of Germany better than that of any other country. He uses examples from all over the world—China, India, Egypt, and elsewhere—in the section on pre-capitalist agriculture, illustrating the depth of his knowledge. What interested Weber most, however, was not so much the variety of agricultural life throughout the world as the role that a few universal social groups had played in agricultural life, and how these had changed during the course of history. The clan, for example, was very important at an early stage of agricultural life.[17] It sometimes owned land, but more important, no land could be sold without its permission. The clan was typically in charge of security and also responsible for fines; it was run by an elder who settled disputes and divided up the land, according to tradition. Over the centuries, the clan lost its power in the West, but it remained strong in other parts of the world, such as China. Weber says that two forces in particular helped to eliminate the influence of the clan: the state, whose power over its subjects was threatened by the clan, and Christianity, which resented the hold of the clan over the individual.

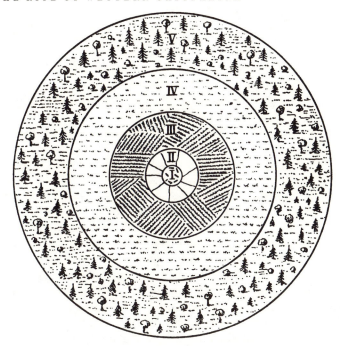

Fig. 1.1. A Typical German Village in Carolingian Times, according to *General Economic History* by Weber

A second social group that Weber analyzes in the section on agriculture is the household. A pre-capitalist household, Weber explains, could consist of one or of several families but always entailed consumption in common and sometimes also production in common. A household could own land but usually only movable means of production. An innovative feature of Weber's analysis of the household is that he pays much attention to the different economic roles of men and women. Far back in time, land belonged to women if it was cultivated; and it belonged to men if it had been conquered in war. Early in history, women worked continuously, while men only worked occasionally. Women were the ones who worked in the fields and were consequently "the first agriculturalists." The work was extremely hard, and "the woman was a field slave."[18] When the plow replaced the hoe, Weber says, men began to participate much more in agricultural work. Hunting, war, and agriculture eventually became male tasks, while women were in charge of the work around the house, including textile production.

In addition to looking at the internal structure of the household, Weber examines how households combined and changed over time. Several households, for example, might unite into a more communal form of social organization, such as the Zadruga or the communes in the Alps. They elected a head and engaged in common production as well as consumption. A very different type of development took place when one household expanded its power over other households. This could happen through conquest, the emergence of a military class, and in other ways; and the result was what Weber called seigniorial proprietorship.[19] In the West, the manor represents the classical form of this social structure. The lord had judicial power over his subjects, who were forced to pay the lord for various services. The payments were in kind and used for warfare or for the lord's household or were sold on the market. The lord was a military man, not a farmer, and typically wanted a steady income from his subjects. The result of seigniorial proprietorship was economic traditionalism as well as complex social and economic dependencies between the lord and his subjects.

The fact that no sharply separated spheres existed in early society also meant that political groups were central economic actors. The state, Weber says, could from a fiscal viewpoint be organized as either a "liturgical state" or a "tax state."[20] The former meant that the contributions to the state were in kind, that the subjects were typically servile, and that different social groups had different obligations. In the tax state, the subjects were formally free and treated as a source of taxation. Another important fiscal distinction that existed early in history has to do with the degree of centralization of administration: either the prince directly controlled and paid for the whole administration himself or land was granted to subordinates who, in their turn, controlled and paid for the administration. According to Weber, empires with political power resting on the control of water supplies tended to have a centralized fiscal administration. This happened especially in ancient Egypt and Mesopotamia. In the West, in contrast, which has a very different geography and climate, administration tended to be decentralized.

The section on agriculture in *General Economic History* ends with a discussion of the situation just before the breakthrough of modern capitalism. By this time, the key social groups had undergone deep changes: the clan had lost its importance in the West and the extended household was not any longer an important owner of land. Indeed, the principle of individual private property had been firmly established. The way the manorial system had been dissolved, Weber says, had important economic and political consequences. Peasants could emerge with or without property, and the ruling agricultural class could either lose its power, as it had in France, or remain an important actor, as the Junkers had in Germany. What undid the manorial system, according to Weber, was that the market had begun to dissolve the complex interdependencies that existed between the peasant and the lord. The bourgeoisie in the cities eventually also developed a power of its own and challenged the rule of the nobles.

III. *General Economic History*
Part 2: Pre-Capitalist Industry

After presenting the social and economic organization of agriculture, Weber proceeds to pre-capitalist industry in Part 2 of *General Economic History*. The notion of "industry" is given a technical definition as "[the] transformation of raw material."[21] The main focus of Part 2, however, is on the different ways this transformation has been organized, rather than on the evolution of technology. Weber first discusses the relationship between a few basic forms of social organization and industry, such as the household and the village; he then analyzes various economic organizations, especially the guild and the factory. Several of the commentators on *General Economic History* have praised the section on industry. A. P. Usher and Georg von Below, for example, found Weber's analysis of the guilds especially interesting.[22]

The first form of industry, Weber says, developed inside the household. Later, households started to produce for other households; village industries also appeared. Their products could be sold on the market or not. In certain circumstances, as in India, tribal industries could be frozen into a caste system, with each tribe fitting into an elaborate division of labor. But there was also the possibility of producing for the market, which entailed a very different dynamic from producing for the local lord or for one's village. When a household was in contact with the market, traditionalism was weakened. Or, as Weber phrased it, "The wall of the self-contained household economy was broken through, as it were, and a window opened up on the market."[23]

During antiquity there were also workshops in the cities (*ergasterion*), where slaves often would work. These operations demanded little fixed capital, and the workers typically stood side by side and produced the same item. During the Middle Ages slaves tended to disappear and were replaced by craftsmen, who grew in number and assembled in the cities. The markets of the Middle Ages were considerably larger than those in antiquity, and there was also a different consumption pattern among the population—two factors that called forth craftsmen. Various economic and political factors helped to undermine slavery during the Middle Ages; in particular, slaves became scarce and more expensive to buy. Slaves, in addition, were not easily motivated, except through harsh discipline; and they constituted risky investments since they could run away or die.

The next major forms of industrial organization were the guilds, the putting-out system, and the modern factory. Guilds did not exist in antiquity because they involved common rituals, which were impossible to have when slaves and freemen worked together, as they often did in the workshops of antiquity. Guilds did not become a predominant form of industrial organization in either China or India—in the former because of the clan economy and in the latter because of the caste system. The guilds triumphed only in the West, largely because of the role that the cities played in the Middle Ages. Schmoller was wrong, Weber noted, when he said that the guilds originated in the household of the lord. Their origin was clearly urban, though many details still were still missing from the records.

The Western guild was characterized, first and foremost, by internal regulation and the attempt to monopolize some form of economic activity. Its goal was to guarantee a certain lifestyle for its members, and in doing so it introduced measures that typically encouraged economic traditionalism. Only certain raw materials and techniques could be used, for example, while undercutting prices and other forms of competition between members were forbidden. As the number of potential guild members increased, the guilds tended to close themselves off, for example, by adapting measures that made it economically impossible to join. The division of labor within the guilds was not progressive, focusing on single objects rather than on individual moments of the work process. For example, one guild member would produce vests, another pants, and so on.

The guilds were replaced by the putting-out system, and what especially caused their downfall was their economic traditionalism. The putting-out system, Weber says, did not have its origin in the guilds but rather developed alongside, before overtaking them. This process was rapid in England, where the guilds were easily bypassed, but considerably slower in Germany, where the cities and the guilds had more power. The putting-out system often began as a monopoly on buying and then expanded to include monopolies on the raw material, the production process, the tools, and even whole stages of the work process. Though the domestic system existed outside of Europe as well—for example, in China and India—the last two stages—monopoly on providing tools and on parts of the work process—were rare.

The workshop system did not develop out of the domestic system but had its own tradition, starting with the *ergasterion* of antiquity and the giant workshops of Egypt. Two particular features distinguished the modern industrial workshop from the domestic system, according to Weber: the household was separate from the enterprise, and there was fixed capital—that is, capital far exceeding the value of a few simple tools. Again, it was only in the West that the factory developed; and while India, for example, had good technology, the caste system was an obvious hindrance, just as in China the clan constituted a serious obstacle.

While Weber regards the emergence of modern machinery as important to the development of the modern factory, he firmly rejects technological determinism and argues that "the modern factory was not called into being by machines."[24] What Weber sees as equally important as the machines themselves are such factors as capital, mass demand on the market, free labor, and the emergence of labor discipline. Together all of these made it possible to produce for a mass market by using systematic calculation; and the modern factory was a response to this whole development rather than some independently arising force. "Economically," Weber even says, "the significance of the machines lay in the introduction of systematic calculation."[25]

IV. *GENERAL ECONOMIC HISTORY*
PART 3: PRE-CAPITALIST TRADE

The third part of *General Economic History* is devoted to pre-capitalist trade and has been criticized by A. P. Usher for neglecting certain kinds of commerce and how interregional accounts were settled.[26] To these lacunae can be added that Weber says next to nothing about the law merchant, which is peculiar since he was very interested in the relationship between law and economics; and that we today know much more about, say, intercultural trade and medieval banking than was the case in Weber's day. Nonetheless, the section on trade in *General Economic History* is rich in information, and it contains some highly suggestive ideas about the emergence of economic institutions. As to the former, Weber succeeds in presenting not only the history of trade in goods (including their transportation), but also the history of trade in money (including banking), in a very small number of pages. And as to suggestive ideas, Weber argues that several features of the modern corporation have their origin in pre-capitalist trade practices, such as the ideas of capital accounting and separating corporate property from individual property.

In presenting the history of pre-capitalist trade, Weber begins by looking at the relationship between social groups and the economy, and he then proceeds to an analysis of economic organizations. Trade, Weber says, emerged historically in interactions between tribes and was consequently an "external phenomenon." Early forms of trade also included gift trade between rulers and seigniorial trade, which took place when there was a surplus on a lord's estate. Soon, however, trading became a distinct activity, with certain individuals, groups, or even whole communities making it their specialty. The Jews, for example, often chose trade as their occupation for religious reasons; it was much easier to follow the rituals of Judaism if one was a trader than an agriculturalist. While merchants early on were itinerant and had to accompany their goods, by the late Middle Ages it became possible for them to stay in one place and continue to trade. Weber also distinguishes "the alien trader" from "the resident trader," the former making a profit by covering huge distances and the latter by monopolizing some local market.[27] Merchant guilds reflected this distinction as well; domestic merchant guilds were created to guarantee the monopoly of some local merchants against foreigners, Jews, and people in the countryside; likewise, merchant guilds for foreigners had as their main purpose to legally protect their members from local merchants and authorities.

Weber also discusses some of the different kinds of markets that existed in pre-capitalist societies. Early on, special places were used as markets, and this is where trade had to take place. Markets could, for example, be held in designated city streets or some special place on a lord's territory. In the latter case, merchants often had to follow a particular road to get to the market, and once there, perhaps pay compulsory brokerage and other fees to the lord. Weber mentions at this point of his presentation the regulations concerning weights and measures, and that it might be obligatory also to use the crane of the lord. Markets where merchants dealt exclusively with other merchants were called fairs; and Weber briefly discusses the most famous of these, the fairs at Champagne where international accounts were settled. Presumably it is at this point that Usher wished Weber had supplied a fuller account.

Two key features of the modern corporation grew out of early trading practices, according to Weber. One was capital accounting, or the idea that one can measure profit by calculating the difference between the capital before and after business has been done. In a sea venture two parties would typically get together, with one supplying all or most of the capital (known as *commenda*), while the other party traveled with the goods to their destination and supplied none or a minor part of the capital. If the party who stayed ashore had invested all of the capital, he was entitled to three-fourths of the profit; if he had invested two-thirds, he received half the profit. "The characteristic feature of this business [the *commenda*]," Weber says, "was that capital accounting was employed for the first time."[28]

A second key feature of the modern corporation that has its roots in early trading practices is the separation of the property that belongs to the corporation from the personal property of its members. Originally, Weber says, the family was the trading unit all over the world, and in the family individual property and corporate property were not distinguished from one another. But as people other than family members began to be employed in the firm, and especially as the need for credit grew, it became increasingly necessary to separate the two. The first time this happened, Weber says, was in early fourteenth-century Florence, and the name for the property of the firm was *corpo della compagnia*.[29]

As already mentioned, Weber included not only the buying and selling of goods in his concept of trade but also the buying and selling of money. In early times, the reader of *General Economic History* is told, there existed many different kinds of money. Money could, for example, be beads or fur, and while one type of money was to be used for buying cattle, another was needed to buy, say, a bride. Coinage was invented in the seventh century, though it would be more than a thousand years before regular coins of even quality and value were produced. While the state controlled the production of coins in antiquity, during the Middle Ages local lords took over this task in order to make a profit through seigniorage and the debasement of coins. This typically resulted in "coinage irrationality," as Weber calls it.[30] Eventually, the state regained control over the production of money, and later it also developed a rational monetary policy—that is, a policy aimed at maintaining a well-functioning economy, rather than just making a profit by controlling the coinage.

One innovative feature of Weber's analysis of money and banking is his use of the difference between what goes on inside and what goes on outside a social group to explain different kinds of economic behavior. A certain kind of money, Weber says, was originally used inside a community, not outside of it. Only when "external money" began to overtake and meld with "internal money" did a general kind of money emerge.[31] Similarly, it was originally forbidden to charge interest to people who belonged to one's own community, Weber says, partly because one should not profit from their difficulties, but also because the members of a community must be able to afford to arm themselves and could therefore not be in debt. It was perfectly acceptable, however, to charge foreigners any interest whatsoever or otherwise cheat them. In other words, there were two separate sets of ethics—one internal and one external.[32] In connection with the discussion of interest, Weber also mentions that even though the Catholic Church forbade the taking of interest, it had to accept de facto that banks made a profit this way as early as the fifteenth century. The Protestants broke the ban on usury sometime later in Northern Europe.

V. GENERAL ECONOMIC HISTORY
PART 4: THE ORIGIN OF MODERN CAPITALISM

The fourth and last part of *General Economic History* is devoted to Weber's favorite topic, the origin of modern capitalism, and it also contains some controversial material. The reception of the final part was somewhat mixed among reviewers: Heckscher thought it was "vastly inferior" to the preceding material, while Usher and von Below found it "suggestive" (though the latter feared that it would be misunderstood, just as *The Protestant Ethic* had been).[33] More recently, Randall Collins has devoted an article in the *American Sociological Review* to the last part of *General Economic History,* arguing that it constitutes the only place in Weber's work where one can find a full theory of how Western capitalism has emerged. More than that, while *The Protestant Ethic* concentrates largely on "ideal factors," the final part of *General Economic History* gives us "the more fundamental historical and institutional theory" that Weber presented in his later works.[34] Collins himself also attempts to systematize and formalize Weber's argument, and he presents the reader with a model of "the Weberian causal chain."

While some minor objections can be raised to Collins's analysis, he is surely correct in arguing that the last part of *General Economic History* gives the reader a fascinating insight into Weber's view of the emergence of modern capitalism during the last few years of his life.[35] It is also clear that Weber was as eager to criticize competing theories of the origin of capitalism—especially that of Sombart—as he was to present his own theory of what he called "Western" or "(modern) rational capitalism."[36] In general, Weber was critical of the idea that one single factor could be held responsible for the birth of Western capitalism, be it population growth, the price revolution of the sixteenth and seventeenth centuries, or technological innovations. Some of the phenomena singled out in the one-factor theories had nonetheless played important roles in the developments that led to capitalism. As examples of this, Weber mentions Europe's geography (where forests and rains discouraged political centralization), the growth of war-related industries, and luxury industries. Finally, Weber also rejected the theories according to which it was the Jews or colonialism that had given birth to capitalism. Colonialism had led to an amassing of fortunes, Weber notes, but not to the introduction of market-oriented production, which is what characterizes modern capitalism. And while the Jews may have been skillful in trading with money, they had played no role in the creation of industrial capitalism and instead ended up by creating a kind of "pariah capitalism."[37]

At various points in *General Economic History,* Weber summarizes the factors that caused Western or rational capitalism to emerge, what its prerequisites were, and its general characteristics. All together, three summaries of this type

A. *Factors that "in the last resort . . . produced capitalism":*

    1. the rational (permanent) enterprise
    2. rational accounting
    3. rational technology
    4. rational law
    5. the rational spirit
    6. the rationalization of the conduct of life
    7. a rationalistic economic ethic

B. *"The most general presuppositions for . . . present-day capitalism":*

    1. rational capital accounting
    2. freedom of the market
    3. rational technology
    4. rational or calculable law
    5. free labor
    6. the commercialization of economic life

C. *"Distinguishing characteristics of Western capitalism and its causes":*

    1. a rational organization of labor
    2. no separation into internal and external economy
    3. the modern state
    4. rational law
    5. modern science
    6. a rational ethic for the conduct of life

Fig. 1.2. Western Rational Capitalism: Its Causes, Presuppositions, and Characteristics, according to *General Economic History* by Weber

Source: Max Weber, *General Economic History* (New Brunswick, N.J.: Transaction Books, 1981), pp. 354, 276–77, 312–14.

Comment: That there are a few discrepancies between these lists is probably explained by the fact that *General Economic History* is based on notes taken by Weber's students during one of his lecture courses and never checked by Weber himself. In his writings Weber also rejected the idea that any of the following factors by itself caused Western capitalism to emerge: population growth, technological advances, Judaism, the inflow of precious metals, demand created by the military, or demand for luxury items. In *Economy and Society* Weber enumerates a set of factors as essential to the "maximum formal rationality of capital accounting" that are very similar to these three lists (pp. 161–62).

can be found in *General Economic History*. Since Weber did not get an opportunity to go over the text of his lectures before they were published, these summaries do not match each other perfectly. They are nonetheless instructive, and they do give a sense of which factors Weber saw as critical in this context (see figure 1.2). On the whole, one can say that Weber believed there were three kinds of factors that had led to the formation of Western capitalism: economic, political, and religious factors

As economic factors, Weber singles out modern accounting, free labor, and the emergence of mass markets. To these should also be added the following, which he discusses in more detail: the emergence of the joint-stock corporation, rational speculation, the factory, and modern science and technology. The complicated history of the shareholding corporation is sketched in a few pages, which cover its beginning in state and city corporations in antiquity and the Middle Ages, as well as its popularization through the East India companies many centuries later. He also discusses the emergence in the sixteenth to eighteenth centuries of the modern exchange, where the merchants did not have to bring their goods and where they could speculate in futures or goods that did not yet exist. And finally, while Weber felt it was important to stress that the modern factory constituted a distinct social organization and not just some technical unit, he nonetheless felt that the emergence of rational technology—as well as its alliance with science—was central to the birth of modern capitalism. In the section on industrial technology, Weber also observes that unless it had been discovered that coal (and not only wood) could be used to produce iron in eighteenth-century England, capitalism might well have failed to develop any further.

The idea that the evolution of capitalism could have been stopped is also present in Weber's discussion of the second set of factors that helped to bring about modern capitalism, namely political factors. One of these is the notion of citizenship or the idea that the individual can belong to a political organization that is separate from such social units as the family and the clan. The idea that an individual could enter into a separate political community with other people, and break with the invisible barriers surrounding the family and the clan, was first developed in the Western city, Weber says, and would later be incorporated into the modern state. As the nation-state came into being, Weber adds, it is true that the independence of the cities was crushed and thereby also the original idea of citizenship. Because individual states competed with one another for capital, however, economic actors in the West were guaranteed a certain independence, and so were other groups. The "rational state" also developed a reliable bureaucracy, an advanced budget system, and a systematic economic policy. To this should be added a special legal system, which provided the economic actors with a predictable legal environment.

Weber had to go far back in history to properly account for the contribution of political factors to bringing about modern capitalism, and he had to go even further back to establish the role that the last of the three factors—religion—had played. Religion had helped to advance the cause of rational capitalism in primarily two ways, according to Weber. First, in early history, the hold of traditionalism on society was strengthened by the belief in magic. Judaism helped to break down traditionalism through its hostility to magic and also through prophecy. The most important contribution of Judaism to the emergence of rational capitalism was consequently not that the Jews had opposed the economic doctrine of the Catholic Church and thereby set free modern capitalism, as Sombart had argued;[38] it was that Judaism had turned religion in a nonmagical and to some extent also nontraditional direction.

The second major contribution that religion had made to the birth of rational capitalism was to help eliminate the negative attitude of the Catholic Church toward economic affairs, especially the idea that methodical economic activity as a goal in life was something negative. This change took place primarily through the introduction of the concept of vocation, or the idea that systematic work, including profit-making, had a religious value. Originally, Weber says, there were two kinds of economic ethics in all communities: an "internal ethic," according to which you must not make a profit from your fellow members, and an "external ethic," which said that foreigners were fair game for any economic behavior, however exploitative.[39] Gradually these two economic ethics began to merge in the West, but the result was an uneasy compromise, since the Catholic Church was suspicious of economic forces as well as the profit motive. The ascetic Protestants, however, succeeded in bringing the two together because they believed that systematic work and honest profit-making were legitimate ways of honoring God and that all human beings should be treated the same way. The result was that profit-making was freed from the old disapproval of the Church and that foreigners and members of one's own community were treated alike in economic matters.

The unintended result of all these different strands of development was the emergence of an economic system, which Weber called Western or rational capitalism. Earlier forms of capitalism had typically been some kind of political capitalism—that is, a form of capitalism that was directly connected to the political system. Although Weber does not define exactly what he means by rational capitalism or state precisely how it came into being in *General Economic History,* in his lectures he does suggest how he thought about these matters. Rational capitalism thus presupposes a society in which traditionalism has lost its hold on people and where the prevalent value system is favorable toward profit-making. It also presupposes a political state in which the legal system is predictable and economic activities are guaranteed their own semi-autonomous area in society. And in economic terms, rational capitalism means that the economy is organized in rational enterprises, which produce for mass markets and calculate profit using capital accounting. Rational technology is used and labor is formally free.

●   ●   ●

One can say that *General Economic History* contains an extremely rich account of the economic evolution of the West, including the rise of modern capitalism. Weber's work is filled with new ideas and concepts, many of which have never been explored. It is also clear that Weber had his own unique view of the evolution of Western capitalism, which deserves to be taken seriously and to become part of the current debate on economic development. As things stand today, only a few economic historians and sociologists seem to take *General Economic History* seriously.

It is true that a certain care has to be taken in referring to *General Economic History* since Weber never got a chance to inspect the text himself. But one can check many of the arguments in *General Economic History* against *Economy and Society,* which tells the same story as the lecture course from a different angle. This angle is that of *economic sociology,* and we are now in a position to proceed directly to the crucial chapter 2 in Part 1 of *Economy and Society,* "Sociological Categories of Economic Action."

Basic Concepts in Weber's Economic Sociology

GENERAL ECONOMIC HISTORY had been an attempt from Weber's side to make it easier for his students to understand the concepts that he had worked out in *Economy and Society*. The course was probably a success in this respect since *General Economic History* even today gives the reader a vivid sense of Weber's view of the economy, from early on until the birth of rational capitalism in the West. The general purpose of *Economy and Society* was different, however, namely to show how sociology, as a distinct perspective among the social sciences, can be used to analyze socio-economic phenomena and thereby introduce a social dimension into an interest-oriented analysis. This purpose infuses all of *Economy and Society*, but especially the chapter in which the basic concepts of economic sociology are presented, "Sociological Categories of Economic Action."

Economy and Society does not start with a discussion of economic sociology—this comes first in chapter 2—but with a presentation of general sociology and its basic categories. In hindsight, it seems obvious why this should be the case: it was not possible for Weber to develop the sociological approach to the economy without first presenting the sociological approach itself. The decision to begin with a chapter in general sociology had nonetheless been a difficult one for Weber; and in 1913 he had, for example, decided to publish a draft in general sociology as a journal article rather than save it for *Economy and Society*.[1] What made Weber change his mind later and decide to include a general chapter on sociology in the final version of his work is not known, even if it is plausible that Weber's decision to devote a chapter to a sociological analysis of the economy made it hard to exclude a discussion of what is distinctive in the first place about the perspective of sociology and how it differs from that of economics.

I. ON THE RELATIONSHIP BETWEEN ECONOMIC THEORY AND SOCIOLOGY IN GENERAL

Chapter 1 of *Economy and Society* ("Basic Sociological Terms") is usually read and discussed as if it contains only a general presentation of sociology and its main concepts. This is fine as far as it goes, because this was one of Weber's intentions with this chapter. What tends to be forgotten, however, is that it also contains a discussion of what distinguishes sociology from economic theory, and that chapter 1 in *Economy and Society* has the additional purpose of setting the stage for the presentation of economic sociology in the following chapter. Because there is so much confusion about how Weber saw the relationship between economic theory and sociology, a discussion of this issue is in order.

Weber's view of the principles of sociology and an introduction to its basic concepts is developed in the first chapter of *Economy and Society*. His famous definition of sociology is the following one:

> Sociology (in the sense in which this highly ambiguous word is used here) is a science concerning itself with the interpretive understanding of social action and thereby with a causal explanation of its course and consequences.[2]

The importance attached to the actor's understanding (*Verstehen*) is immediately clear from this definition; understanding is central to sociology, as to other social sciences, and it is also part of its main explanatory mechanism.[3] A social phenomenon is constituted through the meaning it has for the actor, and different actors may share an interpretation of this meaning. The same is true for social actions of an economic nature, for which the element of meaning is just as central.[4] An adequate explanation in sociology, according to Weber, is one that can explain the actual social action through the understanding of the actor. Weber's type of causality can be called interpretive; and it differs from functional and mechanical types of explanation.

The basic unit in sociology is the individual, or more precisely, the social actions of the individual. Just like economic theory, in other words, sociology starts its analysis with the individual and the meaning that the individual attaches to his or her behavior (methodological individualism).[5] The individual is driven primarily by his or her interests, which can be ideal as well as material; habits and emotions often play a role as well. What first and foremost distinguishes sociology from economic theory, however, is that the action of the individual also has to be *social*. This last point is crucial, according to Weber, who defines "social action" in the following way: "Action is 'social' [only] insofar as its subjective meaning *takes account of the behavior of others* and is thereby oriented in its course."[6] While economic theory, in other words, analyzes economic action in general, sociology only analyzes economic action that is also oriented in its meaning to the behavior of others (see figure 2.1).

Weber's analysis of interests also gets an interesting twist in chapter 1 of *Economy and Society* through Weber's typology of social action. According to Weber, the four major types of social action are: "traditional," "affectual" "value-rational," and "instrumentally rational." Value-rational social action is typically driven by ideal interests, just as instrumentally rational action is typically driven by material interests. The other two types of social action—affectual and traditional—complement Weber's analysis and add complexity to it: social action can be driven by habit (tradition) and by emotions, as well as by interests; most often, perhaps it is driven by all three. Weber's typology of social action has been much discussed in the secondary literature on his sociology, and its relevance for Weber's economic sociology will become increasingly clear as this book

A. Economic Theory
   (economic action)

B. Sociology
   (social action)

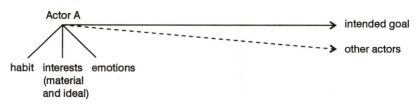

C. Economic Sociology
   (economic social action)

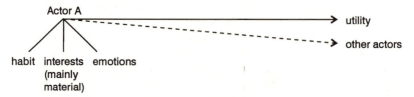

Fig. 2.1. Economic Action, Social Action, and Economic Social Action, according to Weber

Source: Max Weber, *Economy and Society* (Berkeley: University of California Press, 1978), pp. 1–24, 63–69.

Comment: In his sociology Weber attempts to combine an interest-driven analysis with one that takes social behavior into account. Economic theory, in his view, analyzes situations in which the actor is driven mainly by material interests and aims at utility but does not take the behavior of other actors into account (*economic action*). Sociology looks at action that is driven by ideal as well as material interests and that is also oriented to the behavior of others (*social action*). Economic sociology focuses on *economic social action*—that is, action that is driven mainly by material interests, is oriented to utility, *and* takes other actors into account. Social action and economic social action can also be driven by habit (or tradition) and emotions, typically in combination with interests.

proceeds. For reasons of space, however, the four types of social action cannot be discussed in detail here, and the reader who wants a discussion of this type is referred to the standard works on Weber's sociology.[7]

Weber defines sociology in the first half of chapter 1 and presents its basic concepts in the second half. Starting from individual (social) action, Weber increases the complexity step by step and discusses "social relationships" (two or more individuals who interact), a repeated number of actions (such as in "custom" and "usage"), and various types of "organizations" (such as "the enterprise," "the church" and "the state"). Some of the concepts Weber presents have become very influential in social science, such as his definitions of the state and of power. Chapter 1 also contains some general sociological concepts that are central to Weber's economic sociology, especially "struggle," "competition," "open" and "closed social relationships," and "uniformities determined by self-interest." The last, awkward-sounding term refers to a type of social action that is central to the modern economy, especially in the form of prices. It is defined as action driven by self-interest that becomes part of a social configuration together with other actions of the same type, even though it is not oriented to any specific norm. More will be said later on about these "uniformities determined by self-interest" as well as the other concepts in chapter 1 that are relevant to economic sociology.

In his discussion in chapter 1 of "convention" and "legitimate order," Weber comes close to the concept of norms in current sociology. The last of these two concepts is defined as "a social relationship . . . oriented toward determinable 'maxims' [for behavior]"; and for such an order to be valid or legitimate, these maxims must furthermore be experienced by the actor as "obligatory or exemplary."[8] Weber stresses that an order is always more than mere uniformity, caused by custom or self-interest; and he defines "convention" as an order where deviations from expected behavior are met with disapproval. Conventions of this type can exist in the market, Weber says, and they also play a key role in his concept of "economic ethic" (see chapter 5).

As mentioned earlier, an important purpose of chapter 1 in *Economy and Society* is to differentiate economic theory from sociology. Quite a bit of confusion exists on this issue in the secondary literature, with some people arguing that Weber constructed his sociology on "marginalist foundations" and others asserting that Weber wanted to "supplement" economic theory with an analysis of economic institutions.[9] These opinions actually address two different questions—the first concerns the relationship of economic theory to Weber's sociology in general, while the second has to do with the relationship of economic theory to Weber's economic sociology. Since the former question is discussed in chapter 1 of *Economy and Society* and the latter in chapter 2, it is appropriate to start with the former.

To state that Weber constructed his sociology on "marginalist foundations" (or, even stronger, that his sociology represents "a generalization of marginalist economics")[10] is erroneous and superficial. The notion of "marginal utility" plays next to no role in his general sociology, although it is mentioned in the context of instrumentally rational social action.[11] It is true, however, that Weberian sociology and economic theory (which Weber tends to equate with marginal utility theory of the Austrian kind in *Economy and Society*) do have something in common. What this is can easily be established if one takes a close look at what Weber actually says about the relationship between economic theory and sociology in chapter 1. He here advances three propositions, which taken together provide the answer: (1) economic theory, unlike sociology, takes only rational behavior into account; (2) economic theory, unlike sociology, takes only behavior with purely economic goals into account; and (3) sociology looks exclusively at social action or action that is oriented to the behavior of others. The first two propositions go together in the text:

> The concepts and "laws" of pure economic theory . . . state what course a given type of human action would take if it were strictly rational, unaffected by errors or emotional factors and if, furthermore, it were completely and unequivocally directed to a single end, the maximization of economic advantage.[12]

If we take this statement about economic theory and confront it with our previous knowledge that sociology deals with rational as well as with nonrational types of social action, and that these can have exclusively economic as well as not exclusively economic goals, then we are in a position to decide both what economic theory and sociology have in common, and what separates the two. What unites sociology and economic theory has to do with their *subject area*. Sociology deals with a much larger variety of actions than economic theory, but the two also have one type of action in common, namely rational action with exclusively economic goals (see figure 2.2).

The relationship between economic theory and sociology in general is more complicated, however. Weber says that although sociology deals only with action

	RATIONAL ACTION	NONRATIONAL ACTION
EXCLUSIVELY ECONOMIC GOALS	economic theory/ sociology	sociology
NOT EXCLUSIVELY ECONOMIC GOALS	sociology	sociology

Fig. 2.2. The Subject Areas of Economic Theory and Sociology (Part 1)

Source: Max Weber, "Basic Sociological Terms," pp. 9, 21 in *Economy and Society* (Berkeley: University of California Press, 1978).

Comment: Economic theory deals only with rational action that has exclusively economic goals; sociology deals in addition with nonrational action and with rational action with other than exclusively economic goals. See also figures 2.3 and 2.4 for further specification of the differences and similarities between economic theory and sociology.

that is social, "economic action as such need not be social action."[13] He defines economic *social* action as follows:

> The economic activity of an individual is social only if it takes account of the behavior of someone else. Thus very generally it becomes social insofar as the actor assumes that others will respect his actual control over economic goods. Concretely it is social, for instance, if in relation to the actor's own consumption the future wants of others are taken into account and this becomes one consideration affecting the actor's own saving. Or, in another connexion, production may be oriented to the future wants of other people.[14]

It should be noted that Weber nowhere says that economic theory does *not* deal with social behavior; nonetheless, it is clear that if economic theory should happen to touch on social action, it does not do so in a deliberate and systematic manner. This allows us to further specify the relationship between economic theory and sociology in general. The conclusion that imposes itself is that sociology and economic theory overlap to some extent, and that this overlap covers rational behavior with exclusively economic goals, or more precisely, rational behavior with exclusively economic goals that is also oriented to others. It is also clear that economic theory deals with both social and nonsocial action (see figure 2.3).

To bluntly assert that Weber's sociology in general is "based" on economic theory is consequently wrong, although the two approaches do overlap to some extent. More precisely, they overlap in the area of rationality, and one can conse-

	SOCIAL ACTION	NONSOCIAL ACTION
RATIONAL ACTION	economic theory/ sociology	economic theory
NONRATIONAL ACTION	sociology	"behavior" (reactive behavior, some psycho-physical processes)

Fig. 2.3. The Subject Areas of Economic Theory and Sociology (Part 2)

Source: Max Weber, "Basic Sociological Terms," pp. 4, 7, 22 in *Economy and Society* (Berkeley: University of California Press, 1978).

Comment: Both sociology and economic theory deal with rational action that is social, though the latter does not explicitly take the social dimension into account in the analysis. In other words, economic theory treats economic social action simply as economic action. It also deals with nonsocial rational action— that is, rational action that is not oriented to the behavior of others—such as cultivation of land or production in a narrow sense. Neither economic theory nor sociology deals with acts to which the actor does not attach any meaning ("behavior" in Weber's terminology). I am grateful to Lars Udehn for suggesting this table.

quently say that rationality is a topic that is of interest to both economic theory and sociology from Weber's perspective.

It is also true that both economic theory and sociology draw on rationality as a *method*. Even when one suspects that the behavior to be studied is not rational, Weber says, one should start the analysis by constructing a rational ideal type:

> For the purposes of a typological scientific analysis it is convenient to treat all irrational, affectually determined elements of behavior as factors of deviation from a conceptually pure type of rational action. For example a panic on the stock exchange can be most conveniently analysed by attempting to determine first what the course of action would have been if it had not been influenced by irrational affects; it is then possible to introduce the irrational components as accounting for the observed deviations from this hypothetical course.[15]

To conclude, Weber's sociology is not based on "marginalist foundations" in any meaningful sense of this expression. And Weber makes no analytical use whatsoever of the notion of declining utility in his general sociology. What economic theory and sociology have in common in Weber's scheme is something else, namely that they both study rational economic action and that they both use rationality as a tool of analysis. In other words, economic theory and sociology share a deep interest in rationality, according to Weber, just as they both use "ideal types" and start out from methodological individualism.

II. On the Relationship between Economic Sociology and Economic Theory

Even though chapter 2 ("Sociological Categories of Economic Action") has been largely ignored in the secondary literature on Weber, there are a few exceptions.[16] Talcott Parsons's introduction to the 1947 translation of *Economy and Society* is the pioneer among these as well as the one of highest quality.[17] Parsons's writings on Weber are in general solid and insightful, and the section of his introduction from 1947 that is devoted to chapter 2 ("Weber's Economic Sociology") is no exception. Nonetheless, a reassessment of Weber's analysis in this chapter—as well as of his economic sociology more generally—is long overdue.

Chapter 2 begins with a discussion of what constitutes "economic action," which clarifies the relationship of economic sociology to sociology as well as the relationship of economic sociology to economic theory. Economic action, as Weber constructs it, differs from social action through its much more narrow focus on a specific kind of activity, though it constitutes the foundation for both economic theory and economic sociology.[18] Weber does not attempt a radically new interpretation of what economic action is, but presents a rather standard version: "Action will be said to be 'economically oriented' so far as, according to its subjective meaning, it is concerned with the satisfaction of a desire for 'utilities.'"[19]

The concept of utility is central to Weber's concept of economic action, as in most economic theory, and covers objects (goods) as well as human behavior (services). The way Weber defines utility is less common, however. First, Weber uses a rather special German term for utility to make clear that it is not so much some inherent quality of an object that is important as the use one can make of an object.[20] Second, Weber says that it is preferable to use the concept of utility rather than "satisfaction of wants" as the basis for economic action, because it is broader in scope and also includes profit-making.[21] People's earliest economic activities, Weber says, may well have consisted of an instinctive search for food, but this stage soon passed.

A third and important dimension to Weber's concept of utility is that it emphasizes the element of "economic opportunity" and uncertainty in economic activities—what Weber calls *Chance*. This concept is central to all of Weber's economic sociology, but it also plays a role in his discussion of utility.[22] Economic action is always oriented to *opportunities* rather than to certainties, Weber says, and this deeply influences its character. The same is true of profit-making and the satisfaction of needs. Economic action is, of course, driven by the scarcity of means (or more precisely, by people's perception that something is valuable and usually also scarce), but there is also an element of uncertainty to each economic action in the sense that it is directed at an *opportunity* for utility, rather than at utility itself.[23] In other words, I may acquire an item in the hope that it will be useful to me (for profit-making or for the satisfaction of my needs), but what I get is in reality only an opportunity to use it in a number of ways. Part of having acquired an opportunity to use something, it may be added, is that one can then exclude others from such opportunities. Economic life, as Weber sees it, is to a large extent about appropriating, and preferably monopolizing, opportunities: opportunities for profit-making, market opportunities, and others. In so doing, one prevents others from using them.[24]

Weber's discussion of economic action in chapter 2 of *Economy and Society* also makes it easier to understand what differentiates his economic sociology from economic theory and to address the question whether Weber's economic sociology indeed "supplements" his economic theory, as some claim. In figure 2.2, the subject areas of economic theory and sociology were compared and found to overlap. Using the same categories, but replacing Weber's concept of "action" with "economic action," we quickly realize that the subject areas of economic sociology and economic theory also overlap to some extent (see figure 2.4). The topic that both economic theory and economic sociology deal with, more precisely, is rational economic action with exclusively economic goals. To this, as we know, must be added a qualifier, namely that it has to be *social* rational action of this particular type. One can, of course, discuss the extent to which this type of rational action is common in society, and it should also be pointed out that economic sociology has a much wider area of application than economic theory. Both of these issues are discussed later in this chapter. Nonetheless, economic theory and economic sociology *do* have an overlapping area of interest, and asserting that economic sociology simply supplements economic theory does not capture their relationship particularly well.[25]

	RATIONAL ECONOMIC ACTION	NONRATIONAL ECONOMIC ACTION
EXCLUSIVELY ECONOMIC GOALS	economic theory/ economic sociology	economic sociology
NOT EXCLUSIVELY ECONOMIC GOALS	economic sociology	economic sociology

Fig. 2.4. The Subject Areas of Economic Theory and Economic Sociology

Source: Max Weber, "Basic Sociological Terms," pp. 9, 21 in *Economy and Society* (Berkeley: University of California Press, 1978).

Comment: Economic sociology covers a much larger area than economic theory, but they have one topic in common: economic action that is social and rational and has exclusively economic goals. In addition, economic theory studies rational action with exclusively economic goals and that is not social. The most important example of nonrational economic action is traditional economic behavior. Weber's term for economic action that does not have exclusively economic goals is "economically oriented action" (see figure 2.6).

III. Major Theme #1: The Different Types of Economic Action

Chapter 2 in *Economy and Society* is a minor book in its own right; it is 148 pages long and divided into forty-one paragraphs of definitions, followed by dense explanatory comments. Weber begins by outlining what social economic action is and proceeds—as in chapter 1—to describe more complicated forms of social economic action, such as economic relationships, economic organizations, and whole economic systems. He states that his goal with this chapter is to work out a "sociological typology" and not to supply concrete historical explanations.[26] Since Weber's typology is complex and difficult, I have chosen his most important concepts plus those that I think will be particularly useful for today's economic sociology.

Weber begins by discussing a few different types of *economic social action* (henceforth referred to simply as economic action). The most basic distinction among them is unquestionably the one between "householding" and "profit-making," which has been part of economics since antiquity.[27] Aristotle spoke, for example, of "the art of household management" (*oekonomia*) and "the art of money-making" (*chrematistike*), and Weber—like Marx and Polanyi—believed that this conceptual pair was central to economic phenomena.[28] Householding, he says in *Economy and Society,* is mainly about consumption, while profit-making typically means the effort to expand one's control over new goods and services. Householding appeared earlier in history than profit-making, and it has been the dominant type of economic action for most of the time.

Throughout chapter 2 Weber refers to the distinction between householding and profit-making. There is, for example, the *oikos,* an economic unit that was common in antiquity and oriented mainly to self-sufficiency and to producing for the lord and his people.[29] The *oikos* consequently is a form of householding, even though some of its surplus was often sold on the market. The modern "enterprise" is more or less the antithesis of the *oikos* and is oriented to production for the market; it constitutes, in Weber's terminology, a form of continuous profit-making.[30] Similarly, "wealth" differs from "capital" (as "rent" does from "profit") in that it is used for the satisfaction of one's wants, not to gain control over additional goods and services.[31]

Weber also introduces two further typologies of economic action in chapter 2, which help to make the distinction between householding and profit-making even more useful. There is first the idea that economic action must be either "rational" or "traditional," and this goes for profit-making as well as for householding (see figure 2.5).[32] The *oikos* represents a traditional form of householding; the modern household is more rational, especially if it uses a budget. And just as there were once traditional money-exchange and money-related services, there is today rational banking. The traditional type of economic action was the predominant one for a long time in history, and Weber notes that in ancient Greece monetary wealth and capitalist exchange were like "islands in a sea of traditionalism."[33] One of the great themes in Weber's economic sociology is, as we know, how this "economic traditionalism" was broken down and replaced by more dynamic forms.[34]

The second typology of economic action that adds further complexity to the distinction between householding and profit-making is that of "economic action" and "economically oriented action."[35] The name for the latter of these two types of action may seem confusing since Weber now uses the word "orientation" for

	TRADITIONAL ECONOMIC ACTION	RATIONAL ECONOMIC ACTION
HOUSEHOLDING	the traditional household; the *oikos*	the modern family; socialist economies
PROFIT-MAKING	old-fashioned money-making; traditional manufacturing	modern banking; the modern firm

Fig. 2.5. The Two Fundamental Types of Economic Action: Householding and Profit-Making

Source: Max Weber, "Sociological Categories of Economic Action," pp. 86 ff., 90 ff. in *Economy and Society* (Berkeley: University of California Press, 1978).

Comment: Like Aristotle and Marx, Weber makes a distinction between economic actions that are oriented to the satisfaction of wants (householding) and those that are oriented to profit-making. Wealth and income are the two basic categories of householding, and capital and profit those of profit-making. Householding and profit-making, according to Weber, can be traditional as well as rational.

	VIOLENCE NOT USED	VIOLENCE USED
MAIN GOAL IS ECONOMIC	economic action	economically oriented action
ECONOMIC CONSIDERATIONS ARE TAKEN INTO ACCOUNT	economically oriented action	economically oriented action

Fig. 2.6. Economic Action and Economically Oriented Action, according to Weber

Source: Max Weber, "Sociological Categories of Economic Action," pp. 63–65 in *Economy and Society* (Berkeley: University of California Press, 1978).

Comment: "Economic (social) action" and "economically oriented (social) action" are two important concepts in Weber's economic sociology. In economic action, violence is not used and the orientation is primarily to economic ends. In economically oriented action, either the goal is economic but violence is used, or the goal is not economic but economic considerations are taken into account. Economic sociology deals with economic action as well as with economically oriented action; economic theory deals only with the former.

a second time in his conceptual scheme. The first time, to recall, was in the concept of "social action," which Weber defines as action that is oriented to the behavior of others. What Weber has in mind this time, however, is to highlight two types of economic action that do not qualify as full forms of "economic action" but that nonetheless are of much interest. There are, first, those actions that are not primarily oriented to economic goals but that still take economic considerations into account; and there are, second, those actions that are directly oriented to economic goals but that use violence to reach them. To call these two categories "economically oriented actions" allows Weber to incorporate a number of important phenomena of the economic world into his economic sociology, even if they do not constitute its core (see figure 2.6). Many of the actions of the modern state, for example, often have a political goal as well as an economic dimension. One example would be the decision to safeguard a nation's independence by investing in defense equipment. It is also obvious that many kinds of social action have an integral element of violence to them, such as looting, mugging, and "protection" of the kind that the mafia engages in.

Violence is alien to normal economic activity, according to Weber, and he says that "the use of force is unquestionably very strongly opposed to the spirit of economic activity in the usual sense."[36] The statement that economic activity usually does not include violence, should not, however, be understood to mean that economic actions, in Weber's opinion, are always free and voluntary. On the contrary, Weber viewed the empirical economy as an arena where there is constant struggle (*Kampf*); indeed, the attempt to lay bare the structure of these conflicts constitutes one of the great themes in Weber's economic sociology. In one of his writings he refers, for example, to "that loveless and pitiless economic struggle for existence . . . in which not millions, but hundreds of millions are physically and spiritually crippled year after year."[37]

Weber also argues that struggles in the economy follow their own dynamic, and he introduces a couple of concepts in chapter 2 to express this phenomenon. One of these is "power of control and disposal," which is similar to economic power.[38] According to Weber, it is "essential" to introduce this concept directly into the sociological concept of economic action.[39] Weber does not explain why this is so, but the reason is presumably that once the social element—taking each other into account—is introduced into the analysis of the economy, the issue of power must also be raised. He furthermore notes that the power of control and disposal rests on a de facto foundation, and that law is not a precondition for its existence.[40]

To sum up, according to the introduction of chapter 2, the following three elements characterize the sociological concept of economic action: (1) there is a peaceful attempt to gain power of control and disposal; (2) this action is directed at something that provides an opportunity for utility (either to satisfy one's wants or for profit-making); and (3) the action is oriented to the behavior of others. In the rest of chapter 2 Weber constructs more complex sociological concepts, which consist of various combinations of economic actions of this type. A few of these higher-order concepts also constitute general sociological concepts.

The sociological concepts that Weber presents in chapter 1 of *Economy and Society* are of a general nature, as was earlier mentioned, but are also essential to understanding the structure of the economy. There is, first, the interesting fact that certain self-interested forms of social action tend to turn into forms of regular collective behavior that are very common in the economy and that Weber calls "interest-driven regularities."[41] One example that Weber mentions is price behavior. Interest-driven regularities are noteworthy in the sense that the individual actors are not forced to do the same thing; nor do they do the same thing because of a norm. Instead they follow their private interests, and the more rational the actors are, the more similar their actions will tend to be. Something else that is important about this type of social action—and this brings us back to the issue of power in the economy—is that actors who choose *not* to follow their self-interest will damage not only themselves but also other actors.

Another pair of concepts in Weber's general sociology that is of much interest to economic sociology is "communal" and "associative" relationships.[42] The former always entail a sense of belonging together, while the latter have to do with rational agreement, typically involving interests. This means that economic actions are mainly of an associative nature; and the market and voluntary associations of an economic nature constitute the "purest cases" of associative relationships. In a free market, buyers and sellers come into contact with one another for a brief moment, perhaps never to meet again. Nonetheless, Weber also says that "to some degree" most relationships—also associative relationships in other

words—have an element of belonging together in them: "No matter how calculating and hard-headed the ruling considerations in such an [associative] relationship may be—as that of a merchant to his customers—it is quite possible for
it to involve emotional values which transcend its utilitarian significance."[43]
What Weber is talking about is to some extent covered by the concept of embeddedness, especially as Mark Granovetter has developed it.[44] It is also clear
that economic theory deals only with associative relationships.

That the power issue is very much present in Weber's general sociology is clear
from his discussion of the following three kinds of relationships, which are all related to one another: struggle, competition, and selection. Struggle is defined as
a situation in which one party to a social relationship is prepared to fight in order
to get his or her way, regardless of what the other party wants.[45] Weber saw
struggles throughout the economy, and his analysis in *Economy and Society* is
filled with references to different types. There is, for example, always struggle
between the two persons who decide to enter into an exchange with one another
("struggle over the price") as well as between each of those persons and their
competitors ("struggle between competitors").[46] In general, there is a *"struggle
of man against man"* in the market, according to Weber.[47] All of these different
types of struggle have to be carried out through nonviolent means to qualify as
properly economic, according to Weber's scheme, and this is also true for his
concept of competition. "A peaceful conflict is 'competition,'" Weber explains,
"insofar as it consists of a formally peaceful attempt to attain control over opportunities that others are also interested in."[48] "Selection," finally, is said to constitute a kind of struggle in which the actors are antagonistic but not aware that
their actions are directed at each other.[49]

A few words need also to be said at this point about the concept of domination (*Herrschaft*) and its role in the economy since it is relatively close in meaning to struggle. Weber's well-known definition is as follows: "'Domination' is the
probability that a command with a given specific content will be obeyed by a
given group of persons."[50] Weber uses the concept of domination very little in
chapter 2, although it is at the center of the discussion in chapter 3 of *Economy
and Society*, which is mainly devoted to political sociology ("The Types of Legitimate Domination").[51] Every political system, Weber here points out, is based
on domination in some form, and because an economy is usually part of a political system, it tends to operate under some kind of political domination. The state
or the ruling political organization may either set the parameters for the economy (as in modern capitalism) or directly dominate it (as in many earlier societies). But domination is also present *within* the economy itself, to the extent
that obedience is the rule. Indeed, much of what goes on in an economy, broadly
conceived, consists of domination in this sense. This type of domination I refer
to as economic domination (as opposed to political domination), and it characterizes, first and foremost, relationships within economic organizations. One of
the conditions of maximum rational capitalism, for example, is precisely that the
economic organizations are organized as "systems of domination."[52]

Domination, as defined by Weber, is, however, *not* present in the market itself, which is where exchanges take place. For a while Weber toyed with the idea of also using the term "domination" for certain types of interactions in the market; and in one of his early manuscripts for *Economy and Society* he contrasts "domination by virtue of a constellation of [economic] interests" with "domination by virtue of authority."[53] As the most typical example of the former, Weber mentions actors, who by virtue of their monopolistic position in a market can influence the behavior of some other actors just as directly as if an order had been given. In the final version of *Economy and Society,* however, Weber explicitly rejects this terminology and says that the concept of domination will not be used for what goes on in the market.[54] In the market, in brief, there is in principle no domination; actors who possess "power of control and disposal" are, however, in an advantageous position.

Weber occasionally formulates his ideal types in the form of a general mechanism; and one example of this can be found in his analysis of "open" and "closed relationships." Weber attached great importance to the role of these two types of relationships in his economic sociology, and in an early version of *Economy and Society* he had included a section called "Open and Closed Economic Relationships."[55] According to Weber, a relationship is in principle open when anyone who wants to participate in it is allowed to do so; and it is closed when the opposite is the case. A relationship that is closed to outsiders can also be regulated internally, so that it is closed to some of the insiders as well.

That open and closed relationships are prevalent in the economy is evident, and among the many examples that leap to mind are those related to cartels, monopoly, property, professionalization, and internal labor markets. What is usually at issue here, to use some of the earlier terminology, is an attempt to appropriate and monopolize economic opportunities by excluding others from them. Weber also argues that "when the number of competitors increases in relation to the profit span, the participants become interested in curbing competition."[56] A more general formulation of this mechanism can also be found in *Economy and Society*: "If participants expect that the admission of others will lead to an improvement of their situation, they will have an interest in keeping the relationship open; but if they think that they can improve their situation through monopolistic tactics, they will favor a closed relationship."[57]

It should also be mentioned that the theory of open and closed relationships has been used quite a bit in stratification theory, where it is often referred to as "closure theory."[58] Frank Parkin, for example, has used Weber's ideas on this topic to criticize Marx and to develop new insights into the formation of status groups and classes by looking at "strategies of exclusion."[59] It is clear that statements like the following in *Economy and Society* lend themselves in a very suggestive manner to stratification theory:

Usually one group of competitors takes some externally identifiable characteristic of another group of (actual or potential) competitors—race, language, religion, local or social origin, descent, residence, etc.—as a pretext for attempting their exclusion. It does not matter which characteristic is chosen in the individual case: whatever suggests itself most easily is seized upon.[60]

IV. Major Theme #2: The Role of Rationality in Economic Life

It has already been pointed out that economic sociology, like sociology in general, studies rational economic action and uses a rationalist methodology. But rationality plays a much larger role in Weber's economic sociology than that, and as an indication of this one can cite his statement in the preface to the first installment of *Grundriss der Sozialökonomik,* which appeared in 1914: "The point of departure [for this whole handbook] is the view that the development of the economy must be understood as part of the general rationalization of life."[61] One of the tasks of economic sociology, in other words, is to study how rational economic behavior or "economic rationality" (as Weber sometimes phrases it) has evolved as part of a larger historical movement.[62] In chapter 2 of *Economy and Society* Weber discusses some aspects of this task and attempts to outline what is rational in the sphere of the economy. In other chapters of the same work, and in other studies from this period as well, Weber also discusses the role that noneconomic factors have played in this development (for the role of religion and politics in furthering economic rationality often inadvertently, see chapters 3–5 in this book).

Two aspects of Weber's use of rationality in particular set economic sociology apart from contemporary economics. There is first the fact that Weber views rational behavior as evolving historically or, to phrase it differently, that to Weber—unlike to today's economists—rational behavior is a variable, not an assumption.[63] As a consequence of this, Weber tried to develop a series of concepts and typologies to capture how rational behavior had evolved historically and how it varied during different periods. Rationality in the sphere of the economy, Weber makes clear, differs from rationality in the other spheres of social life; the economy can furthermore be rationalized from the viewpoint of many different interests.

The second aspect that differentiates Weber's approach to rationality from that of contemporary economics has to do with his distinction between "formal rationality" and "substantive rationality."[64] The key idea here is that formal rationality is centered on calculation, while substantive rationality is related to absolute values. By introducing this distinction, Weber gets to approach the relationship of economics to ethics from a very different angle than the one that characterizes mainstream economics today. While welfare economics sometimes attempts to extract ethical conclusions directly from formal economic exercises (as in the case of, say, Pareto optimality), Weber took a very different route by arguing that value-oriented action can be just as rational as formal economic reasoning. Both perspectives are well worth pursuing, but while Pareto optimality and similar approaches have been thoroughly discussed, no one has

seriously tried to explore Weber's ideas on substantive rationality to see how far
they go.

Formal rationality is characterized by the extent to which calculation is possible; and this constitutes a fairly straightforward criterion, according to Weber.
Briefly, the more precise an economic calculation is, the more formally rational
it is. According to Weber, there are three major types of calculation: "calculations in kind," "calculation with the help of money," and calculations in terms of
capital or "capital accounting."[65] Substantive rationality, in contrast, is "full of
ambiguities," Weber says, and it raises much more difficult theoretical problems
than formal rationality. At issue is, first, the extent to which "the provisioning of
. . . groups of people" is considered to be in accordance with certain absolute values, be they of a political, ethical, philosophical, or similar nature.[66] According
to Weber, it should also be realized that no economy can be 100 percent formally
rational; it always contains an element of formal irrationality or substantive rationality. He also argues that in some situations formal and substantive rationality may coincide—for example, in the provision of a minimum of subsistence for
a huge population—but that this is quite rare and typically does not happen.[67]
As will soon be seen, most types of formal rationality also presuppose the existence of certain social conditions, which are clearly irrational from a substantive
viewpoint.

More concretely, what does "economic rationality" look like, according to
Weber? In chapter 2, Weber begins by distinguishing between rational economic action and technology.[68] Weber's argument on this point, it should be
added, was innovative for his time and is still of interest.[69] Rational economic
action, he explains, is oriented toward a situation where there is scarcity of means
and involves a "prudent choice *between ends*."[70] Scarcity plays no role in technology, which always has a given end. In brief, what technology is all about is the
rational "choice of *means*" with a predetermined end.[71] In principle, costs do
not enter into the picture at all; and from a technological viewpoint it is as rational to build a machine of platinum as of iron. In reality, however, technology
usually takes costs into account, and can be characterized as a form of applied
economics.[72]

After making the distinction between rational economic action and technology, Weber outlines what he regards as the most basic and typical measures of
rational economic action. These can all be found very early in history, he says,
but they only become rational to the extent that they are "systematically" applied. They are the following: (1) saving, (2) the ordering of consumption in
terms of preferences, (3) production, and (4) exchange. Saving means allocating
utilities to the future and is integral to the very idea of an economy.[73] So is the
ordering of utilities according to one's preferences or, more precisely, according
to the principle of marginal utility. That there is no economy without production
is obvious enough, as is the notion that exchange is an organic part of most
economies.

In order for these four phenomena to become truly rational, however, they
must also to be systematic, according to Weber. In the case of exchange, two

more requirements are needed. To the general definition of exchange—"a formally voluntary agreement involving the offer [of utilities] in exchange for utilities"[74]; Weber adds that the price has to be reached by bargaining ("struggle over the price") in combination with competitive bidding ("struggle between competitors"). Rational exchange also differs from traditional exchange and conventional exchange in that it is not backed up by the sanctity of the past or by the threat of disapproval. A rational exchange, in other words, is (formally) voluntary.

A higher level of rationality is immediately reached, Weber notes, when money is introduced into economic life. Money is "from a purely technical point of view . . . the most 'perfect' means of economic calculation"; it is also "formally the most rational means of orienting economic activity."[75] When money is used throughout the economy, Weber continues, this has a number of consequences: everything having to do with the economy can in principle be evaluated in money: for example, expected opportunities can be evaluated in advance and then compared with what actually happened, and one can make ex-ante and ex-post estimations of expenditures.[76]

The use of money also makes it possible for a very special phenomenon to come into being, which Weber refers to as "capital accounting" or calculations in terms of capital. What makes this kind of calculation so important is that capitalism could not exist without it, especially in its modern form. Weber mentions double-entry bookkeeping as a typical and important example of this type of calculation, which is defined as "the [continuous] valuation of the total assets (goods and money) of the enterprise at the beginning of a profit-making venture, and the comparison of this with a similar valuation of the assets still present and newly acquired at the end of the process."[77]

Weber not only discusses what characterizes "calculation using money" and "capital accounting"; he also outlines the social conditions that are necessary for their existence. What Weber says on this point illustrates, most importantly, that certain noneconomic forms of rational action are usually needed for formal economic rationality to come into being, and also that this formal economic rationality conflicts directly with substantive rationality on a number of points. The noneconomic forms of rational action that Weber specifically mentions are "mechanically rational technology" and "formally rational administration and law."[78] Formal economic rationality, in other words, requires predictability not only in economic calculations, but also from machines, judges, and state officials.

Weber takes great care in outlining how and why formal rationality involving the use of money or capital necessarily leads to conflicts with substantive rationality; and the accusation that Weber's economic sociology represents some kind of justification of modern capitalism must be rejected as wrong.[79] Capitalism presupposes *the battle of man against man,* Weber emphasizes, and points out that a rational exchange takes place "when both parties expect to profit from it [but also] when one [party] is under compulsion because of his own need or the other's economic power."[80] In the lectures published as *General Economic History,* Weber makes the same point: in rational capitalism the worker often sells his labor because of "the whip of hunger."[81] What matters in capitalism, Weber says (following Adam Smith), is "effective demand" rather than existing demand or wants.[82] Furthermore, what is responsible for much of the conflict between formal and substantive rationality in the economy, Weber says, is the skewed distribution of income.[83]

V. Major Theme #3: The Social Structure of Some Economic Institutions (Property, Economic Organizations, the Market, and Money)

Weber does not use the term "institution" (or "economic institution") as part of his formal terminology in *Economy and Society*, but he does begin his analysis with various types of social and economic action; and he then proceeds to more complex versions, which for all practical purposes may be called "institutions."[84] One of these is "property," which Weber constructs on the basis of his notions of "appropriation" and "closed social relationship"; with the latter defined as a relationship that excludes or limits the participation of certain persons or otherwise subjects their participation to specific conditions. When actors in a closed relationship succeed in appropriating some economic opportunities, they acquire a "right"; and when these rights can be inherited, there is "property," according to Weber.[85] The concept of "appropriation," it should be emphasized, is very evocative and at the center not only of Weber's concept of property but of his economic sociology in general. Appropriation is defined as the permanent and more or less alienable monopoly of opportunities in a closed social relationship[86] The notion of appropriation, as mentioned, is central to the concept of right. There is, however, no mention of law in Weber's definition of property, which means that it can have a legal dimension but that this is not a necessary condition.

When Parsons published his translation of chapter 2 in 1947, he noted that "sociologists have neglected the institution of property"; and today—fifty years later—it can be added that the situation has not changed very much.[87] For this very reason, Weber's analysis of property is of extra interest, including his efforts to understand the different types of property that have existed throughout history. Weber makes room for this variety in several ways. The owner, for example, can be an individual or a group; some types of property can be transferred to other people through voluntary agreement, while others are not alienable at all; and so on. Both *General Economic History* and *Economy and Society* contain elaborate typologies of different kinds of appropriation and property that have existed throughout history in agriculture, industry, mining, and transportation.[88] Special mention should also be made of Weber's brief but interesting account of how the notion of the shareholding company has emerged. There is furthermore Weber's effort, especially in his early works, to account for the way that individual property in land evolved from various communal forms.

Another economic institution that Weber constructs on the basis of closed

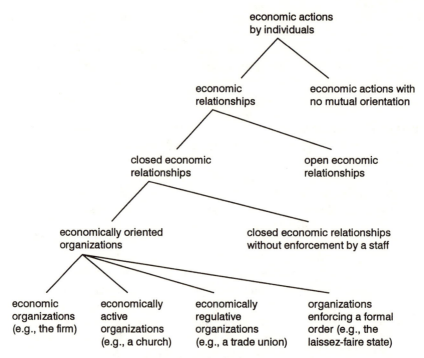

economic actions
by individuals

economic
relationships

economic actions with
no mutual orientation

closed economic
relationships

open economic
relationships

economically oriented
organizations

closed economic relationships
without enforcement by a staff

economic
organizations
(e.g., the firm)

economically
active
organizations
(e.g., a church)

economically
regulative
organizations
(e.g., a trade union)

organizations
enforcing a formal
order (e.g., the
laissez-faire state)

Fig. 2.7. How Economic Actions by Individuals Become Economic Organizations

Source: Max Weber, "Sociological Categories of Economic Action," pp. 48–50, 74–75, 340–43 in *Economy and Society* (Berkeley: University of California Press, 1978).

Comment: The figure illustrates how Weber constructs his concept of economic organization on the basis of economic (social) action. Economic organizations, like all organizations, consist of closed social relationships that are enforced by a staff. Although an economic organization is primarily based on economic action, in the three other types of organizations the economic element consists of a mixture of economic action and what Weber terms economically oriented action.

relationships is the economic organization (see figure 2.7). An organization, according to Weber's definition, consists of a closed relationship in combination with a staff or a person who enforces its regulations.[89] Organizations are in principle economic when they are oriented to the satisfaction of wants or to profit-making. If this orientation constitutes their main goal, they are "economic organizations." If they have a different primary goal but are still economically oriented, then they are "economically oriented organizations," in Weber's terminology. One example of this is a church; another is the state. Organizations like trade unions and employers' federations are "economically regulative groups" whose main activity is to regulate economic matters. A fourth and last type of economic organization is "the organization enforcing a formal order," which sees to it that other economic organizations are allowed the freedom to act and exist. An example of this type would be the laissez-faire state.

One feature of economic organizations that Weber pays much attention to is their division of labor. Or more precisely, what interests Weber is *the division and combination* of labor that goes on in them; for, following in the tradition of Friedrich List and Karl Bücher, Weber does not speak only about labor's being divided but also about its being combined.[90] Depending on the technical tasks of the organization, the "technical division of labor" will, for example, be structured in a certain manner.[91] Similarly, if the primary aim of the organization is to make a profit or to provide for wants, this will influence the "economic division of labor." The social structure of the economic group will affect the division and unification of labor as well. These "social aspects of the division of labor" are influenced by two important features: if the rules governing an economic organization are created on its own initiative or by outsiders, and if the chief and the staff are appointed according to the rules governing the organization or by outsiders. Weber's terms for the former are "autonomous" and "heteronomous," and for the latter "autocephalous" and "heterocephalous."[92] The division and unification of work in an economic organization is finally also connected, Weber says, to what kind of appropriation is involved. When the workers have been expropriated from the means of production, for example, this entails a certain division and unification of tasks.

The only economic organization throughout all of history, Weber says, that has been truly "*revolutionary*" is the firm or the capitalist enterprise.[93] This is because, first and foremost, the firm engages in a continuous type of rational economic action, which is oriented to profit-making by exploiting ever new opportunities. An important aspect of the firm's behavior in this context, Weber adds, is that it entails a continuous and systematic evaluation of how well it does by comparing its assets ex ante and ex post.[94]

What makes the firm so radical is clear enough: the idea of systematic and rational profit-seeking clashes with economic traditionalism and established modes of exploiting economic opportunities in the market. But capitalist firms with vested interests, Weber adds, may also have an interest in obstructing rational profit-making.[95] Though this tendency is decidedly less pronounced in contemporary capitalism than it was in the past, according to Weber, it nonetheless is a serious threat to the future of rational, dynamic capitalism.

Weber makes a distinction between the firm as a rational profit-making organization ("firm") and as a technical entity ("establishment"). He also gives a summary description of the internal organization of the typical capitalist firm. There are two types of people who work for a firm: the members of the administrative staff and the workers. The former tend to be rational in their behavior inside the firm; they are organized in the form of a bureaucracy; and they are motivated primarily by large incomes, ambition, and a sense of vocation.[96] The workers, in contrast, obey out of habit ("discipline"); their work tasks are organized, though not in the form of a bureaucracy; and they are motivated by the fact that if they do not work, they and their families will starve.[97]

Certain aspects of Weber's analysis of the administrative staff and the workers in the capitalist firm are still valid, while others have been questioned. That the members of the administrative staff have to be rational in their behavior at work has been affirmed by, for example, Arthur Stinchcombe; why workers are supposed to be less rational has, however, been questioned by, for example, James Coleman, who argues that the workers have their own rational interests, just as the administrators do.[98] Karl Polanyi and others have pointed out that Weber's argument means that only what the managers do qualifies as "economic action," not what the workers do.[99] Weber's theory of bureaucracy has also been challenged on a number of additional counts, especially his tendency to identify bureaucracy with efficiency.[100]

Another central economic institution that Weber discusses in his economic sociology is that of the market. The market is notoriously hard to define and has an "amorphous structure," as Weber puts it.[101] Nonetheless, he gives a precise picture of what constitutes a market from a sociological perspective. According to *Economy and Society*, a market has a social core and it can typically be found in a specific place.[102] An organization may or may not be in charge of the market. Its social core nonetheless consists of repeated acts of exchange—that is, of interactions that are simultaneously directed at *two* different types of actors. It is directed at one's exchange partner (with whom one bargains) and at one's competitors (who are outbid). The former presupposes direct contact ("struggle over the price"), while the latter form of relationship is indirect ("struggle between competitors"; see figure 2.8).

Dynamics can be introduced into Weber's basic model of the market through his idea of open and closed relationships. Some actors, in other words, may wish to close the market to outsiders, while others may wish to keep it open. In general, a market will be either open or closed, depending on the interests of the actors. In capitalism there is usually a tendency to close the market *and* to keep it open:

> Capitalist interests thus favor the continuous expansion of the free market, but only up to the point at which some of them succeed, through the purchase of privileges from the political authority or simply through the power of capital, in obtaining for themselves a monopoly for the sale of their products or the acquisition of their means of production, and in thus closing the market on their own part.[103]

In his analyses of the market in *Economy and Society* Weber also speaks of a phenomenon very similar to closed economic relationships, namely the different ways in which the freedom of a market can be regulated ("regulation of the market"). This regulation can come about in a number of ways: by law, by tradition, and by convention (the last, to recall, is Weber's term for an order that is maintained through social disapproval and is close to what is currently called norms). Another type of regulation, voluntary regulation, is interesting in that it

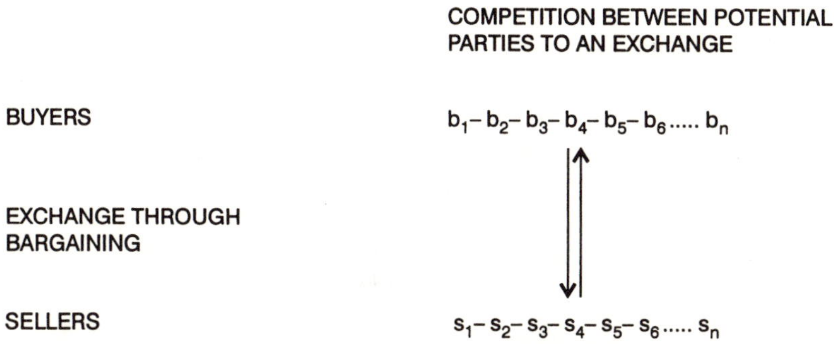

COMPETITION BETWEEN POTENTIAL
PARTIES TO AN EXCHANGE

BUYERS $b_1 - b_2 - b_3 - b_4 - b_5 - b_6 ..... b_n$

EXCHANGE THROUGH
BARGAINING

SELLERS $s_1 - s_2 - s_3 - s_4 - s_5 - s_6 ..... s_n$

Fig. 2.8. The Social Structure of Markets, according to Weber

Source: Max Weber, "The Market: Its Impersonality and Ethic," p. 635 in *Economy and Society* (Berkeley: University of California Press, 1978).

Comment: The heart of Weber's analysis of the market consists of the idea that its core is made up of one type of economic action—exchange—which is simultaneously oriented in *two* different directions: toward one's exchange partner ("struggle over the price") and toward one's competitors ("struggle between competitors"). Dynamics can be introduced into Weber's basic model through the idea that social relationships in the market can be either open or closed. Together with Alfred Marshall's famous chapter "On Markets" in *Principles of Economics* (1890), Weber's analysis represents a high point in the effort to understand the social structure of markets in the early economics literature.

can exist even if the market is formally free because of the presence in the market of strong actors. Typical examples of voluntary regulation are price cartels and quota agreements, both of which were common in Germany when *Economy and Society* was written.

Markets will typically break up "monopolies of status groups," according to Weber, since these resist market forces; but rational markets also may create their own "capitalistic monopolies."[104] What makes markets antagonistic to the idea of status groups, Weber says, is that they have no regard for personal qualities or for "honor"—all that matters is what is being exchanged. "The market and its processes do not take the person into account: 'impersonal' interests dominate it," Weber says, and concludes, "it knows nothing of 'honor.'"[105] For religion and other ethical doctrines, according to which people should treat one another as brothers and sisters, the kind of transactions that go on in a rational market are unacceptable. The market is in this sense "an abomination to every system of fraternal ethics."[106]

But the market is not only an outrage to religious and ethical systems in the sense that it breaks with their rules for how people should behave toward one another; the way a modern market operates also makes it difficult to influence from an ethical viewpoint. What should be done to the market, for example, when the demand for some item falls and the result is unemployment and mis-

ery for a number of people? No ready answer can be given from a religious or
ethical standpoint, according to Weber, who uses the term "impersonality" for
this phenomenon.[107] The fact that it is so hard to influence the market from a
moral viewpoint makes "impersonality" a characteristic of modern society.

Weber indicates in chapter 2 that he is not interested in supplying a theory of
price; this task belongs to theoretical economics rather than to economic sociology. Still, he also repeatedly points out that economic power struggles determine
what prices will be like. "Money prices are the product of conflicts of interest
and of compromises; they thus result from power constellations." At one point
Weber even writes that "prices . . . are instruments of calculation only as esti-
mated quantifications of relative chances in this struggle of interests."[108] How
are statements of this kind to be reconciled with Weber's desire to keep price
theory out of chapter 2, and more important, how can they be reconciled with
his many positive references to marginal utility theory throughout this text? No
answers to these questions can be found in chapter 2 or anywhere else in *Economy and Society*. However, in a private letter to Robert Liefmann, written while
Weber was working on chapter 2, Weber gives some indication of how he viewed
this issue.[109] Marginal utility theory follows its own distinct logic, just as math-
ematics; and it deals with prices exclusively on a *theoretical* level.[110] But when
real prices are to be calculated, it is what happens in reality and not in theory
that counts; and to understand this empirical process, economic struggles between the actors and similar elements of social action must be taken into account. When Weber wrote that "the theoretical insights of [economic theory]
should provide the basis for economic sociology," this type of argument was perhaps what he had in mind.[111]

Weber's analysis of money—another economic institution to which he devotes
much attention in chapter 2—presents some similar problems. Weber explicitly
says that he is not interested in developing a theory of money, and that he only
wants to present "the most general sociological consequences" of the use of
money.[112] These consequences include, for example, the fact that with money
one can suddenly exchange goods for an enormous range of other goods (indirect exchange). Other sociological consequences of the use of money include an
improved capacity to store values for future use, to calculate profit, and to calculate marginal utility. In a money economy, unlike in a natural economy, it is
also possible to transform control over economic opportunities into sums of
money.[113]

But Weber also asserts that "money is not a mere 'voucher for unspecified
utilities' which can be altered at will," and that it is rather a "weapon" in "the
struggle of man against man."[114] All of this might sound as if Weber attacked
conventional monetary theory in his economic sociology, but in my opinion this
is not the case. At one point in chapter 2, for example, Weber states that he more
or less agrees with the monetary theory of von Mises in *The Theory of Money
and Credit*.[115] Weber's attitude toward monetary theory was in all likelihood
similar to his view of price theory: a difference should be made between a purely

theoretical argument (as in marginal utility theory) and one that aims at explaining what happens empirically (as in economic sociology).

VI. Major Theme #4: Macro Structures, Including
Different Types of Capitalism

Weber also introduces a few concepts in his economic sociology in chapter 2 to capture what happens on a macro level. Every society, for example, has an "economic order," in the sense that there is a distinct distribution of economic power or, in Weber's terminology, a distinct distribution of "power of control and disposal" in the economy.[116] The economic order, Weber emphasizes, is in principle to be distinguished from the legal order, even if economic power in capitalist society is acquired through contracts.[117] Nonetheless, the economic order is more fundamental than the legal order because it is about "*de facto* recognition" of who controls what in the economy.[118]

Another important distinction in Weber's scheme on the macro level is that between "natural economy" and "money economy."[119] Throughout history, many societies have belonged to both types of economy. In a money economy, money is used and economic activities are oriented to the market with its prices in money. The concept of natural economy is more complex in the sense that it covers several different types of economies, Weber says. Most often it is simply used to denote an economy in which exchange takes the form of barter. This, for example, is how the concept was originally used by Bruno Hildebrand, who introduced the distinction between money economy and natural economy in the 1860s.[120]

Weber, however, was much more interested in a natural economy, where no exchange takes place at all and where calculation has to be made in kind, as in socialist society. Weber's deep concern with socialist economics is also central to another of his conceptual pairs on the macro level: "market economy" and "planned economy." A market economy is defined as an economy in which wants are satisfied using exchange in the market, while a planned economy ultimately depends on calculation in kind since its orientation is "*substantive.*"[121] In a planned economy economic actions are oriented to the activities of an administrative staff; they are also carried out according to a budget.[122]

Weber says very little in chapter 2 about how the economy develops from one stage to another, in part because he was skeptical of the evolutionary schemes popular in German economics. According to Gustav von Schmoller, for example, the economy goes through the following stages: village economy, town economy, territorial economy, national economy, and world economy.[123] Weber's position on this issue was that there exist no "economic laws" according to which the economy necessarily evolves from one stage to another, and that noneconomic factors would always have to be analyzed before one could enter into a discussion of economic stages. On the whole, Weber found schemes of the type that Schmoller advocated to be of little value. The notion of an economic stage, Weber says, was useful only if it was seen as an ideal type and as a heuristic tool.[124]

It has been suggested by Guenther Roth that Weber had his own evolutionary scheme, but that it was focused on his notion of "sphere" rather than the concept of stage.[125] This is an interesting idea, even if it remains to be seen how well it fits the different parts of Weber's economic sociology. It is, nonetheless, clear that those of Weber's macro-level concepts that have just been presented go rather well with the notion of economic sphere. A budding money economy and a market economy, for example, tend to constitute themselves as fairly distinct spheres in society. Whatever little that Weber has to say about business cycles in his writings can also be related to the idea that a relatively autonomous economic sphere at one point developed in the West. Business cycles, Weber thus says, emerged in the beginning of the nineteenth century; they are caused by rational speculation; and they occur roughly every ten years.[126]

Guenther Roth's suggestion that Weber's ideas on historical development are related to his concept of "sphere" also makes sense when it is applied to what is without doubt Weber's most suggestive typology on a macro level, namely the one that is devoted to the different types of capitalism and that can be found in §31 in chapter 2 ("The Principal Modes of Capitalistic Orientation of Profit-Making").[127] Instead of arguing that capitalism emerged at a certain historical point in time and eventually will be replaced by socialism and communism, as Marx does, Weber suggests that a number of different types of capitalism have developed parallel to one another, within one another, or after one another. Whether capitalism one day will be replaced by a new kind of economic system is not something that Weber speculates about in his economic sociology.

In §31 Weber says that there exist six principal, and distinct, modes of capitalism. The exact phrase that Weber uses is "principal modes of capitalist orientation of profit-making," and the link to his earlier discussion of profit-making as a special form of economic action (§11) is clear.[128] Neither here nor anywhere else in *Economy and Society* can one find a discussion or a formal definition of what constitutes capitalism in general, even if it seems clear enough that Weber identifies capitalism with organized forms of profit-making, often in combination with some kind of evaluation ex ante and ex post of the assets involved.[129] What distinguishes Weber's view of capitalism from other views—including that of Marx[130]—are primarily three things: the notion of capital accounting (or calculation ex ante and ex post), the emphasis on rationality (calculations can be more or less rational), and the idea that certain forms of capitalism existed long before modern commerce and industrialization. Of the six principal modes of capitalist profit-making that can be found in history, Weber says, two have appeared exclusively in the West, while three of the others constitute what he calls "politically oriented capitalism." I shall refer to the last category simply as "political capitalism," as is often done in the secondary literature, and to the former as "rational capitalism."[131] The sixth and remaining mode of capitalist profit-making I shall call "traditional commercial capitalism" (see figure 2.9).

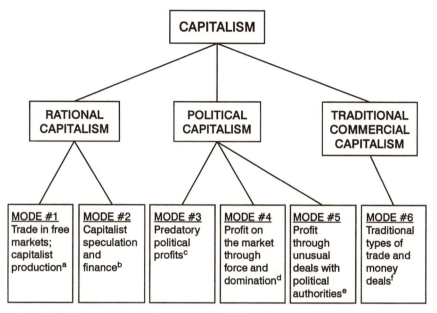

Fig. 2.9. The Main Types of Capitalism and the Principal Modes of Capitalist Orientation of Profit-Making, according to Weber (§31 in Chapter 2 of *Economy and Society*)

Source: Max Weber, §31. "The Principal Modes of Capitalist Orientation of Profit-Making," pp. 164–66 in *Economy and Society* (Berkeley: University of California Press, 1978).

Comment: Weber does not define capitalism in general in chapter 2 in *Economy and Society,* but talks instead of six "principal modes of capitalist orientation of profit-making" (§31). These six are then assigned to the categories rational capitalism, political capitalism, and what can be called traditional commercial capitalism. Different types of capitalism typically coexist and do so, for example, in modern capitalism, which is predominantly rational.

[a] Continuous buying and selling in free markets; continuous production of goods in capitalist enterprises.

[b] Speculation in standardized commodities or securities; continuous financial operations of political organizations; promotional financing of new enterprises by selling securities; speculative financing of new enterprises and other economic organizations to gain power or a profitable regulation of the market.

[c] Predatory profit can come, e.g., from the financing of wars, revolutions, and party leaders.

[d] Continuous business activity thanks to force or domination, e.g., tax and office farming, colonial profits (plantations, monopolistic and compulsory trade).

[e] No more information on this type of political capitalism is to be found in §31.

[f] Trade and speculation in currencies, professional credit extension, creation of means of payment, the taking over of payment functions.

Both political capitalism and traditional commercial capitalism, Weber says, have existed for thousands of years, while rational capitalism is much younger. *"Politically oriented capitalism"* or *"political capitalism"* is one of Weber's most interesting concepts, and although it is often referred to in the secondary literature, it has been little explored and even less used in substantive analyses.[132] Political capitalism typically emerges, Weber says, when political events and processes open up opportunities for capitalist profit-making.[133] He also has a theory of when it declines: when an area becomes pacified and dominated by a single empire, the state does not need to resort to the kind of money-raising activities that often feed political capitalism.[134] Political capitalism, Weber also makes clear, can be more or less rational or be allied to capitalism of a rational character.[135]

There are three distinct sub-types of political capitalism: (a) predatory political profit-making, (b) continuous profit-making made possible by the direct use of force or domination, and (c) profit-making due to unusual dealings with political authorities. As examples of predatory political profit-making, Weber cites the financing of wars, revolutions, and party leaders. What Weber means by financing is presumably that loans are given at high rates of interest or that they are extended against the promise of a share of the booty. Profit that is made possible by the direct use of force or domination, Weber says, includes tax farming, office farming, and colonial profit-making. By the latter term Weber primarily means plantations and trade, which is monopolistic and compulsory. Weber does not illustrate capitalistic profit-making attributable to unusual dealings with political authorities. One example, however, would perhaps be the bribing of an official to get a public concession.[136]

In *The Protestant Ethic* Weber uses the term "adventurers' capitalism" to denote an especially daring and ruthless form of capitalism; and he says that political capitalism is a typical example of this.[137] Some of the so-called "economic supermen" probably fall into this category as well.[138] When Weber gives examples of political capitalism, however, the case that he most often refers to is "capitalism in antiquity." The most thorough description of this type of capitalism can be found in *The Agrarian Sociology of Ancient Civilizations* (1909), which was written partly as a polemic against those who believed that capitalism in antiquity was similar to modern capitalism.[139] The kind of capitalism that existed in antiquity, Weber says, was not centered on commerce, which was viewed with disdain by the ruling strata. It was also very difficult in Greece and Rome to make money on the market through any kind of productive enterprise, among other reasons because slaves and political conditions made economic production unpredictable and difficult. Instead, Weber notes, "capitalism in antiquity was shaped by political forces [and was] only indirectly economic in character."[140] The largest capitalist enterprises in antiquity were the tax-farming companies in Rome, Weber says. Political capitalism reached its peak during the Roman Republic, but later vanished when the money economy began to dry up and was replaced by natural economy, especially in areas dominated by self-sufficient *oiki.*

The second type of capitalism that Weber outlines in §31 is *rational capitalism*. It consists of two different modes of capitalist profit-making: (a) one that is centered on modern trade and production, and (b) another that deals with capitalist finance. Modern trade is described as trade in a formally free (that is, non-traditional) market, while production is described as continuous production with some kind of procedure to evaluate the assets at regular intervals. Capitalist finance includes several kinds of activities, all having to do with finance, speculation, or a combination of the two. (More precisely, the following categories belong to capitalist finance: pure speculation in standardized commodities or in securities in enterprises; continuous financial operations of political bodies; promotional finance of new enterprises by the selling of securities; and speculative finance of capitalist firms to profitably control markets or otherwise gain power).

What is at the heart of all these different kinds of capitalist profit-making is the notion of rational capitalism, which is also central to Weber's economic sociology as a whole. In *General Economic History*, Weber discusses rational capitalism at great length, but since this work is based on students' notes, which Weber never got a chance to correct, his most authoritative statement on the topic is the one in §31 in *Economy and Society*.[141] The key actor in rational capitalism, Weber here says, is the rational capitalist enterprise. This type of enterprise presupposes the existence of a free labor force, a rational division of labor, and fixed capital. Labor can only be free, Weber points out, if there has been an expropriation of the means of production and a corresponding appropriation of these means by a group of owners. Rational capitalism also presupposes sophisticated money and capital markets, the possibility of investing in corporations via shares, and the existence of a rational monetary system that is operated by the state.

The third type of capitalism that Weber discusses in §31 is what I call *traditional commercial capitalism*. This type of capitalism is represented by a single type in his typology of profit-making modes, but covers several kinds of activities. These activities are commodity trade, speculation in currencies, professional credit extension, and the creation of means of payment.[142] As elsewhere in §31, Weber is extremely terse in his definition, and he gives no more details than this. Nonetheless, representative activities of this type of capitalism would presumably include traditional trade, usury, and early banking. What Weber calls "pariah capitalism" probably belongs to this category;[143] and in general one would assume that traditional commercial capitalism is fairly small-scale. While this type of capitalism once represented the heart of capitalism, today it represents one of its less central forms.

Since political capitalism and rational capitalism are the two most important categories in Weber's typology of capitalism, it may be of some interest to compare the two. First, it is important to note that Weber's discussion of different kinds of classes (in chapter 4 of Part I of *Economy and Society*) is connected to his distinction between political capitalism and rational capitalism. Political capitalism especially thrives in societies where there are "property classes," while rational capitalism can only exist in a society made up of "commercial classes."

Property classes include rentiers as well as "negatively privileged property classes," such as paupers; there also exist some middle classes, whose members support themselves through commerce, craftsmanship, and the like. Rentiers are mainly interested in rents, but might now and then get involved in some profit-making scheme—hence their attraction to political capitalism. In a society dominated by commercial classes, however, rational capitalism would be typical. The main classes in this type of capitalism consist of entrepreneurs and workers; there are also some middle classes, whose members are professionals, bureaucrats, and the like. In a society dominated by property classes there is considerably less dynamic than in one with commercial classes.

One might also go beyond Weber's own writings and try to establish a few more differences between political capitalism and rational capitalism. Depending on whether economic enterprises operate according to the principles of political capitalism or according to the principles of rational capitalism, they would presumably differ on the following issues: level of profit rates and interest rates, average duration of the enterprise, the role of personal contacts with the political elite, and whether there is access to an independent legal system. As to the profit rate, in political capitalism entrepreneurs often expect to make very high profits; the end result should also be more uneven over time than in rational capitalism. While a several-hundred-percent profit rate was not impossible for an enterprise in antiquity, modern corporations have considerably lower profit rates. The insecurity surrounding political fortunes would also push interest rates in a society with a strong political capitalism far above those in a society dominated by rational capitalism. Ventures in political capitalism are probably also shorter and more often limited to a specific time period than ventures in rational capitalism. Personal contacts with state administration many times are the key to success in political capitalism but are less important in rational capitalism. Finally, ventures in political capitalism are by definition less predictable than ventures in rational capitalism; and although in rational capitalism one typically has recourse to an independent legal system (which helps to ensure its predictability), this is often not the case in political capitalism.

Another important question is how Weber viewed modern capitalism or the capitalism that existed in his own time. Those who have touched on this question in the secondary literature often mention Weber's metaphor that modern capitalism is like an "iron cage," and thereby implicitly convey the impression that Weber saw capitalism as a relentlessly advancing machine. Weber's view, however, was much more complex than that. Modern capitalism, as he saw it, was predominantly rational but had its contradictions as well as its irrational elements. A hint of this complexity can be found in §31, where Weber notes that the modern forms of finance and speculation may have an irrational dimension.[144] He also points out that rational capitalism and adventurers' capitalism can exist side by side and that they "shade off into each other."[145]

Elsewhere in *Economy and Society* Weber touches on a similar point in a fascinating comment that has been overlooked by most commentators. Many economic systems—perhaps all—have a charismatic element to them, he says, and this includes modern rational capitalism. Weber even talks of *"the double nature of . . . the spirit of capitalism"* and means by this that modern capitalism is not only rational but that it also has some charismatic elements.[146] As an example of such an element in the capitalism of his own days, Weber refers to the "grandiose robber capitalism" of a certain Henry Villard.[147] This Villard, the reader is told, pulled off a successful takeover scheme in the nineteenth century by getting the public to supply him with funds without requiring any security from him. The public, in other words, was spellbound by Villard's reputation or charisma as a financial wizard. To this should be added that rational entrepreneurship also has some irrational elements, according to Weber. For one thing, the entrepreneur always "hopes" that he or she can make more money than the average rate of interest; the entrepreneur also relies heavily on his or her "business imagination."[148]

In his political writings Weber makes the observation that political capitalism had revived during World War I;[149] and this leads to the interesting question whether political capitalism also exists in modern society and is therefore more common than has usually been thought. If the answer is yes, modern capitalism would be considerably more unstable than what the "iron cage" metaphor indicates. It might also be interesting to see what parallels exist between Weber's idea of political capitalism and the concept of rent-seeking in modern economics.[150] Do not, for example, agricultural subsidies, tariffs, and public sector purchases also make possible modern forms of political capitalism?

Furthermore, modern rational capitalism—as Weber conceives it—contains a number of contradictions, caused by the existence of classes and status groups. Commercial classes typically fight one another as well as status groups. Commercial classes are fluid, anchored in production, and lead to change and development in society. Status groups, in contrast, are centered on lifestyle, honor, and consumption and thrive on stability.[151]

The idea that Weber saw modern rational capitalism as some kind of machine that goes through the same motion over and over again is consequently wrong. Modern rational capitalism, in Weber's view, can be characterized as dynamic and unpredictable, especially on the macro level. Weber, it should also be noted, was not at all sure that this dynamic type of capitalism would be able to last very long. Modern capitalism, as he viewed it, was threatened by a number of political and economic forces. Among the former, socialism was especially important. But there also exist economic forces—including capitalist interests—that might undermine modern capitalism. Individual capitalists, as mentioned earlier, do not hesitate to close a market once it is in their interest to do so. And if this tendency to turn capitalist profits into "rents" becomes general, Weber argued, the whole modern capitalist machine might come to a standstill because rents have a conservative impact on the economy, unlike profits, which lead to change.[152] The end result of this development would be an *oikos*-like traditionalistic economy with repressive features. In terms of Weber's class analysis, one can say that dynamic "commercial classes" (entrepreneurs, middle classes, workers) would be replaced by static "property classes" (rentiers, middle classes, the unfree).

Chapter 2 of *Economy and Society,* "Sociological Categories of Economic Action," is very rich and provides a solid foundation for economic sociology through its many concepts and typologies. It may at first seem unduly dry and impenetrable, but there is little point in dwelling on such a first impression if the analysis is of high quality. But a number of tasks remain to be tackled in relation to chapter 2. It is first imperative to locate the most promising concepts in Weber's economic sociology and to discuss these more extensively than has been done here. In my mind, Weber's typology of capitalism in §31 and his analysis of rationality are two of his most promising contributions. The underlying logical structure of chapter 2 also needs to be better understood. It is, for example, clear that many of Weber's concepts are linked to one another through certain key concepts—such as "opportunity," "struggle," and "power of control and disposal"—but exactly how this is done, and why, needs to be discussed. Single studies of individual concepts, such as speculation and appropriation, would also be illuminating.

To this should be added that today's economists and sociologists would be well served by better knowledge of the relationship between Weber's ideas on economics and the economic thought of his day. At a few points in the preceding pages I have tried to indicate how Weber was influenced by the economists and economic historians of his own time, but more needs to be known about the influence of Weber's contemporaries on his work. Finally, it would be interesting to find out how far one can integrate Weber's ideas on economic sociology with certain aspects of contemporary economics. There is, to repeat, a certain affinity between Weber's notion of political capitalism and the idea of rent-seeking, but to what extent these two approaches are truly compatible with one another is a different question. A similar affinity exists between Weber's concept of "orientation to others" and the idea that animates Thomas Schelling's work on tipping models. Finally, some of the things that Weber has to say about the relationship between economics and politics—which is the subject of the next chapter—are also of much interest to contemporary economics.

CHAPTER THREE

The Economy and Politics

THE ANALYSIS of the economic sphere in chapter 2 of *Economy and Society* constitutes the heart of Weber's economic sociology, but it is by no means all of it. Indeed, some of Weber's most original findings in economic sociology were due to his capacity to see a connection between something that happened in the economy and something that happened somewhere else in society, between, say, a material interest in one sphere and perhaps an ideal interest in another. Weber had always thought that economics should have a broad scope, a perspective that he later extended to his economic sociology as well. When he taught economics in the 1890s, for example, one part of his course was devoted to "the relationship between the economy and other cultural phenomena, especially law and the state." And when Weber sketched a program for social economics in his essay on objectivity from 1904, he noted that "the range of socio-economic phenomena is almost overwhelming." More precisely, what he called "social economics" was to cover not only economic institutions and events but also those parts of society that influence the economy ("economically relevant phenomena") and those parts of society that have in some way been influenced by the economy ("economically conditioned phenomena"). And, finally, Weber gave a very broad scope to the handbook of economics that he was in charge of, *Grundriss der Sozialökonomik,* and wanted it to include sections on the economy and geography, the economy and society, and so on. Weber's own contribution to this handbook covered such topics as the economy and the modern state, and the economy and law. Indeed, *Economy and Society* is so interesting precisely because it attempts to look at virtually all aspects of the kind of society that hosts the modern economy.[1]

In order to understand how Weber viewed the interaction between the economy and politics, it is useful to contrast his approach to that of Marx. Marx had claimed that the economy decisively influences most social phenomena, but Weber had a different opinion. For one thing, he argued, the causality may just as well work in the opposite direction; the economy may influence society, but, then again, noneconomic phenomena may equally well influence the economy. In addition, he said, economic phenomena may influence society, but not necessarily in a decisive manner. Weber stated his opinion on the interaction between economy and society in the following manner at a 1910 meeting of the German Sociological Society:

> I would like to protest the statement by one of the speakers that some one factor, be it technology or economy, can be the 'ultimate' or 'true' cause of another. If we look at the causal lines, we see them run, at one time, from technical to economic and politi-

cal matters, at another from political to religious and economic ones, etc. There is no resting point. In my opinion, the view of historical materialism, frequently espoused, that the economic is in some sense the ultimate point in the chain of causes, is completely finished as a scientific proposition.[2]

When one talks about the relationship between the economy and politics in very general terms, as I have done here, the impression may be given that these constitute two separate spheres in modern society. Weber's view, however, was that politics and the economy are closely interconnected and must often be analyzed together. In chapter 2 of *Economy and Society,* for example, several paragraphs discuss the relationship between the economy and politics. Quantitative measures may not constitute the most convincing arguments in this type of question, but the fact that one out of five paragraphs in chapter 2 is devoted to the role of the state in the economy should drive home the point. To eliminate the state from the analysis of economic phenomena might be appropriate in theoretical economics, Weber says, but not in economic sociology.[3]

I. THE SPECIFICITY OF THE POLITICAL, AND WEBER'S VIEW OF THE RELATIONSHIP BETWEEN THE ECONOMY AND POLITICS

Weber was passionately interested in politics all his life and several times contemplated becoming a professional politician. At one point he was considered for the position of envoy of the German Republic to Vienna and at another secretary of state for the interior. He advised several political parties and organizations; he helped to work out a new constitution after World War I; and he was included in the German delegation to Versailles in 1919 as an expert adviser. "Politics," as he once put it, "has always been my secret love."[4] Weber wrote profusely on political questions, in newspapers and elsewhere, and these writings have attracted a number of able commentators. The works of David Beetham and Wolfgang Mommsen have played an important role in mapping out Weber's opinions on a variety of political topics and also in providing a better overall view of how Weber regarded politics. One topic that has naturally attracted many comments is Weber's view of contemporary Germany, especially his notion that the German bourgeoisie had been kept politically weak and inexperienced ("Bismarck's Legacy"). In the chapter that follows, I will make more use of *Economy and Society* than of Weber's political writings, however, primarily because it is in this work that Weber presents the relationship of economics to politics in both the fullest and the most systematic manner, from a sociological viewpoint.

Before discussing how Weber viewed the relationship between economics and politics, a few words need to be said about his political sociology and its key concepts. In general, the concept of struggle—*Kampf*—is as central to Weber's view of politics as it is to his view of economics. At one point, for example, he states that "the essence of all politics is *struggle.*"[5] What differentiates politics from economics is in principle violence or the threat thereof. In the economy, struggles are typically settled through compromise, while in politics violence is used, even if only as a last resort. The political order consequently rests on violence, while in the economy one uses "(formally) peaceful means," as Weber puts it. Nonetheless, the economic order is ultimately guaranteed by the political order and, hence, "behind every economic order there is and must be the use of coercion."[6]

As part of his political sociology, Weber introduces and defines a number of important concepts such as "the state," "the nation," "the political party," and so on. Of these concepts, the state is by far the most important, and some of the others are defined in relation to it. The notion of "political organization" is nearly as central as the state, and can with some simplification be exemplified by the kind of ruling political organization that existed before there was a state. In other words, Weber's "political organization" is not what most people mean when they speak of political organizations; in Weber's terminology, a political organization is always a *ruling* political organization.[7] While a ruling political organization uses force or the threat of force to safeguard itself or its order within a certain territory, a state has monopoly on the legitimate use of force and a staff to administer this monopoly. The state is consequently a special type of ruling political organization.

Three items characterize a ruling political organization: it is somehow "more" than just an economic organization; it controls a territory; and it may threaten, or actually resort to, the use of violence. Of these three, Weber says, the latter two constitute the conceptual minimum for a ruling political organization, while the first is important for a fuller definition. That a ruling political organization is somehow "more" than just an economic organization means, according to Weber, primarily two things.[8] It means, first, that the ruling political organization regulates not only the economy, but also people's interactions in a specific territory. It furthermore means that the value system of the ruling political organization goes beyond purely economic matters.

As to control over territory—the second criterion for a ruling political organization—Weber notes that there have been times when no ruling political organization existed, such as when the economy was undifferentiated. Not until there was a need for permanent provision in a particular place did the institution of village chieftain appear. The authority of such a chieftain existed at first only in times of emergency, but was later extended to normal times. The village chieftain originally only had power over economic matters when there was peace. Weber further emphasizes that early in history many communities were terrorized by warrior bands, typically consisting of members of men's houses who supported themselves through violent raids and looting. In general, it took a long time for a political organization to emerge that was strong enough to maintain peace within its own territory. The effort to gain complete control over the territory and to eliminate private violence was supported by religious authorities as well as by certain economic interests. While the religious authorities felt that they could control their members much better under peaceful conditions, Weber says, groups with special "market interests" also supported the political authorities in their quest for public peace.[9] By groups with "market interests" in this particular case is meant not only the merchants but also the lords, with their interest in tolls of various kinds and, more generally, in the taxpaying capacity of their subjects.

The third and final item that characterizes a ruling political organization is violence. It has already been mentioned that while struggles in the economy are typically settled through compromise, according to Weber, struggles in the political arena are ultimately settled through violence or the threat of violence. In an earlier chapter it was also noted that Weber defines economic action as "[a] peaceful exercise of an actor's control over resources which is in its main impulse oriented towards economic ends"; he also argues that "the use of force is unquestionably very strongly opposed to the spirit of economic activity in the usual sense." To this should be added that, in Weber's mind, the very dynamics of economic phenomena typically differ from those of political phenomena. In the lectures on social and economic history that Weber gave during his last year, he says that politics and economics follow different "logics."[10]

One reason for singling out violence in this context, Weber says, is that it is impossible to define the state through its goals. States have had all kinds of goals throughout history, from being a robber state to being a welfare state; so the nature of the goal cannot be used as a criterium for what constitutes a state. But all states use the same means: in the end, they always resort to violence or the threat thereof. The fact that the members of a state are ready to die for it is also something that states often have in common. The "pathos" that such a sacrifice entails creates strong emotional foundations as well as common memories among the members of a state.

Weber's analysis of the relationship between the economy and the political realm is focused on the ruling political organization, especially the state, and it is summarized in §37 of chapter 2 in *Economy and Society*. Weber here enumerates, and briefly comments on, topics that are central to this relationship. Unfortunately, however, he had time to write more extensively on only three of these topics before his death.[11] All are discussed separately in the pages to come: the monetary system of the modern state; the financing of ruling political organizations; and the way different types of domination and their administrative staffs have been organized and financed throughout history (sections I and III). I have also included discussions of the relationship between the economy and politics in the city (section II) and the economic aspects of socialism (section IV).

II. POLITICAL DOMINATION AND FISCAL SOCIOLOGY

Weber's seminal contribution to political sociology, it is generally agreed, is to be found in his analysis of *Herrschaft* or domination, as presented in its final form in chapter 3 of *Economy and Society* ("The Types of Legitimate Domination"). This is where Weber proposes his famous typology of traditional, legal, and charismatic domination; he also works out what kind of administration and legitimation answers to each of them. What is rarely noted, however, is that there also exists an important *economic* dimension to Weber's analysis of domination. Each administrative type is paid for in different ways; it is staffed by individuals with different qualifications and interests; and it also affects the economy in different ways. Weber's analysis of the economic dimension of political domination can therefore be seen as falling partly in the field of fiscal sociology, if by this term we mean a sociological analysis of the finances of the state. This type of analysis has deep roots in the German tradition of economics as a *Kameralwissenschaft,* and about the same time that Weber was working on his analysis of domination, Rudolf Goldscheid popularized the notion of "finance sociology" and Schumpeter published his famous essay "The Crisis of the Tax State," which is in this genre as well.[12] That Weber himself attached great importance to the economic dimension of his analysis of domination is clear from his reference to chapter 3 in *Economy and Society* ("The Types of Legitimate Domination") as "Economy and Domination" in his correspondence with his publisher.[13]

Weber's contribution to fiscal sociology is of high quality and deserves to be as well known as Schumpeter's excellent study, from which it nonetheless differs on a number of points. For one thing, Weber's analysis covers much more territory than Schumpeter's; it also goes much further back in time than "The Crisis of the Tax State." Weber's fiscal sociology is, in addition, considerably more realistic than that of Schumpeter. It is true that Schumpeter approvingly cites Goldscheid's famous line, "The budget is the skeleton of the state, stripped of all misleading ideologies"; but it is also true that Schumpeter did not depict the brutality of the taxation system with the same intensity that Weber did. Take for example, the following passage from Weber's study of antiquity:

> We know how an Egyptian tax levy was made: the officials arrived unexpectedly, the women began to cry, and soon a general flight and hunt began; those liable for taxes were hunted down, beaten, and tortured into paying what was demanded by the officials, who were themselves held responsible for quotas based on the official cadaster. This was the guise in which the state appeared to the peasants in the Near East, and as it appeared in modern times to Russian peasants.[14]

And finally, unlike Schumpeter, Weber views the financing of ruling political organizations as part of the general rationalization of the West. Originally, states and similar organizations had no budgets and simply spent what was available at the moment. This was still true during the Middle Ages, and Weber points out that "the city, like the territorial lord, lived from week to week as is done today in a small household."[15] Various measures helped to increase the rational element in the financing of the state, especially tax farming. A truly rational administration of taxation, however, first appeared in the Italian cities and then spread to France, Germany, and other states.

The foundation for Weber's fiscal sociology is laid in chapter 2 of *Economy and Society,* which contains a typology of different ways of financing ruling political organizations (§38) as well as a brief analysis of the effects that these forms are likely to have on the economy (§39).[16] Weber emphasizes that *financing* constitutes "the most direct connection" between the economy and ruling political organizations.[17] His typology of the different ways of paying for these organizations is dry and formalistic but can be summarized as follows. The two most common forms of financing a state are through taxation and liturgies (obligations attached to privileges). Weber argues that financing can be temporary or permanent. Although it is possible to find a few examples of the former—pirate states, financed through booty, would be one—permanent financing is much more important.

Weber proposes the following typology to capture the phenomenon of permanent financing from a sociological viewpoint: (1) financing that takes place via productive units that belong to the ruling political organization; (2) financing that is organized via liturgies (obligations attached to privileges); and (3) financing when the ruling political organization has no productive units of its own and there are no liturgies. As examples of the first type Weber mentions *oiki,* feudal domains, and also state financing of its activities through commercial enterprises of different kinds, usually of a monopolistic nature. When the state is financed by its own productive units, it is usually through deliveries in kind or compulsory services in kind. When the financing of the state takes place without the state's having any productive units of its own, monetary contributions are much more common. The modern capitalist state, where taxes are paid in money and staff members get salaries, belongs to the latter category. Finally, liturgical financing—which, to recall, is one of the most common forms of financing, together with taxation—means typically that certain privileged groups have financial or other obligations. A group may, for example, be exempt from taxation but instead have a military obligation. Another example—discussed by Roman historian Paul Veyne—is how the rich in antiquity were obliged to pay for such things as public festivities and the defense of the city.[18]

How the state and other ruling political organizations finance their activities, Weber says, has "very important repercussions on the structure of private economic activity."[19] This is true not only for the different ways of financing in themselves—such as compulsory services in kind, money taxes, and so on—but also for the way that the financing is organized. The state can, for example, sell its rights to taxation in order to get a more steady income (tax farming); it can endow individuals with a right to an income for life in exchange for services (benefices); and so on. Depending, then, on the type of financing as well as on how the financing is organized, different types of capitalism are encouraged or discouraged in the economy at large (see figure 3.1). Only the modern system of taxation, Weber points out, constitutes a truly positive environment for rational market capitalism. Tax farming and most forms of liturgy encourage political capitalism but discourage market capitalism. Compulsory services, deliveries in kind, and benefices are bad for all kinds of capitalism. Finally, most ways of financing a state and other ruling political organizations are compatible with what Weber calls "speculative trade capitalism"; that is, they are compatible with a substantive trading of goods on the market, undertaken in the hope of realizing high profits.

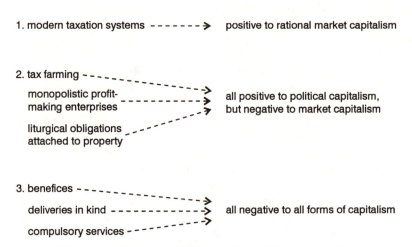

WAYS OF FINANCING THE STATE   IMPACT ON TYPE OF CAPITALISM

Fig. 3.1. Weber's Fiscal Sociology, I: Different Ways of Financing the State and Their Influence on Different Types of Capitalism

Source: Max Weber, "§39. Repercussions of Public Financing on Private Economic Activity," pp. 199–201 in *Economy and Society* (Berkeley: University of California Press, 1978).

Comment: Depending on how a state is financed, certain types of capitalism will be encouraged and others discouraged. There is no strict determinism involved in the relationship between type of financing and type of capitalism, only a general influence. Weber also notes that all ways of financing are compatible with speculative trade capitalism except for certain liturgical restrictions on trade.

Weber is careful to point out that the link between forms of financing and type of capitalism is rather weak; the reason for this, he says, is that so many other factors are typically involved. Religious attitudes, for example, may impede rational capitalism; firms and other economic organizations must also be "invented."[20] Weber explicitly states that there are instances when all fiscal obstacles to rational market capitalism have been absent but no rational capitalism has emerged anyway. The opposite is also true: rational capitalism has developed in circumstances that suggested the opposite outcome, given the way the state was financed.

Weber also approaches the problem of how financing affects the economy from a second perspective. What differentiates this part of Weber's argument from the one just discussed and summarized in figure 3.1 is that Weber was not only interested in understanding how different forms of financing tend to encourage or discourage different forms of capitalism, but he also wanted to find out how the state's degree of participation in economic life would affect the possibilities for capitalism. Figure 3.2 sums up the results of this second line of in-

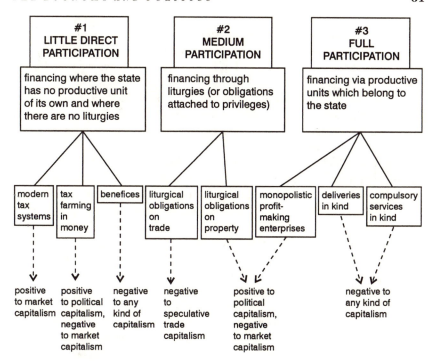

Fig. 3.2. Weber's Fiscal Sociology, II: The State's Degree of Participation in the Economy through Its Financing and the Effect of This on Type of Capitalism

Source: Max Weber, "§38. The Financing of Political Bodies," pp. 194–201 in *Economy and Society* (Berkeley: University of California Press, 1978).

Comment: No strict determinism is involved, only a general influence. Weber is talking of permanent ways of financing.

quiry and shows that the more directly a state has participated in the economy the less likely it is that there was a hospitable environment for market capitalism. States that get their resources through liturgies or through their own productive units tend to encourage either political capitalism or no capitalism at all. As is clear from figure 3.2, it is the use of money that allows the state to be less directly involved in the economy. Again, the influence that Weber speaks of is rather weak and no strict determinism is involved.

So far Weber's analysis of financing may seem somewhat dry to the reader, and it should therefore be emphasized that the best is yet to come. The most exciting and innovative part of Weber's fiscal sociology is no doubt his interpretation of the relationship between financing and type of domination. Domination in general, Weber says, is a phenomenon that pervades most types of social action, including economic and political relationships.[21] Domination in economic matters is often very similar to domination in political matters; that orders must be obeyed, for example, is as central to the smooth workings of the modern capitalist firm as it is to the state. As the reader may recall from the preceding chapter, Weber, however, does not want to extend the concept of domination to what goes on in the market (where instead "power of control and disposal" is applicable). Domination, he says in Part I of *Economy and Society,* will therefore be used only in the sense of power to command and duty to obey.[22]

Weber adds that domination in this sense can be strengthened in two ways: through legitimation and through an administrative staff. People will obey a command for a variety of reasons, such as habit, material interests, and the like, Weber says, but unless they also feel that the one who gives orders has a specific right to do so ("legitimation"), domination will be relatively unstable.[23] That the presence of an administrative staff makes domination more efficient is clear enough, but Weber also points out that the relationship between the chief and the members of the staff will vary, depending on how the latter are paid. The relationship between a chief and his or her staff members differs, for example, depending on whether the latter receive a salary or are rewarded in some other way. The legitimacy of the various ways of being paid is closely tied to the legitimacy of the chief, Weber adds, in the sense that if the legitimacy of the chief is challenged, the legitimacy of the staff may also be questioned.

Through his analysis of the economic dimension of the three major types of domination, Weber breaks new ground in fiscal sociology. He does this, more precisely, by showing how a specific form of administration answers to each type of domination, and how each of these administrations is staffed and paid for in different ways. Weber furthermore analyzes how the three forms of domination affect the economy, and he suggests that there is an ethos to each major type of domination that has a more general influence on the economy. There are a few differences in the way these themes are worked out in the various versions that exist of Weber's analysis of domination.[24] On the whole, however, a general pattern can be discerned; and it is this pattern that is primarily of interest here.

Legal domination—the first of Weber's three types of domination—rests on a belief in the legality of enacted rules and that those who have received a position of authority under those rules have a right to issue commands. It is not the person in command who is obeyed, but the law itself. Weber enumerates several features that are typical of legal domination, two of which are of special interest to fiscal sociology. One is that the incumbent in a position is not allowed to appropriate the office; there is in principle a sharp line between the position and the person who has been appointed. The second has to do with what Weber refers to as "the means of administration" and is similar to Marx's concept of means of production.[25] Just as the workers are separated from the means of production in rational capitalism, so are the officials separated from the means of administration in a rational state, Weber says.

The purest form in which legal domination can be administered is as a bureaucracy. Officials in a bureaucracy obey orders primarily because of appeals to their sense of status. They are specially trained, have an assigned sphere of competence, and develop a strong sense of duty in relation to their work. They have a career based on seniority and achievement, and they can only be terminated under certain circumstances. They are part of a hierarchy; they obey orders; and they carry out their work in a precise and impersonal way, with a minimum of feelings. A bureaucracy is unsurpassed, Weber says, in terms of efficiency, speed, and predictability.[26]

Officials are paid a fixed salary according to the rank of their office, rather than a wage for a specific amount of work; there is usually also a pension. The typical way to pay for a bureaucracy is through taxation, which presupposes a money economy. However, bureaucracies have also existed in natural economies, and Weber mentions the New Kingdom in Egypt as an example. But what made the New Kingdom into such a bureaucratic success—and for Weber, it represents *the* classical case of bureaucracy—was a series of unique historical circumstances. The only realistic alternative to a bureaucracy, if one wants people to do exactly what they are told, Weber says, is to use physical coercion. This, however, is only possible with slaves, and Weber mentions how owners of Roman latifundia preferred to have slaves as their money managers, rather than free men, because they could torture their slaves when they suspected something was wrong.[27] Nonetheless, it is difficult to produce consistent behavior over time through physical coercion, and Weber concludes that it is much more efficient to appeal to people's sense of status, as in a bureaucracy, than to use violence.

When Weber speaks of bureaucracy, he is thinking not only of the administration of a state, but also of the way that large capitalist firms and other, similar organizations are administered. Since this chapter, however, is devoted to the relationship between politics and economics, I shall limit the discussion to political bureaucracies (for the economic forms of bureaucracy, see note 28).[28] It also deserves to be pointed out that Weber may well have exaggerated the similarities between political and economic bureaucracies in his work. One reason for this, historian Jürgen Kocka argues, is that in Germany state bureaucracies developed well ahead of industrial capitalism, which meant that capitalist firms often were organized with state bureaucracies as their model.[29] Historical evidence, as Kocka shows, points in this direction; and salaried employees in German firms were, for example, originally called "private civil servants" (*Privatbeamte*). There was also a much sharper line between salaried employees and ordinary workers in Germany than, for example, in the United States.

A state bureaucracy, Weber says, is in many ways indispensable for the smooth working of rational capitalism. The modern firm with its capital accounting needs "complete calculability of the functioning of public administration and the legal order."[30] It is also true that the ethos of bureaucracy fits modern capitalism particularly well:

> Bureaucracy develops the more perfectly, the more it is "dehumanized," the more completely it succeeds in eliminating from official business, love, hatred, and all purely personal, irrational, and emotional elements which escape calculation. This is appraised as its special virtue by capitalism.[31]

But there also exists a tendency in the secondary literature on Weber's work to exaggerate how well modern bureaucracy and rational capitalism go together.

What drives state officials to perform so efficiently is ultimately their sense of status, but this search for status also makes them regard their positions as potential prebends or the right to a lifelong income of a private nature.[32] One can furthermore find an "abhorrence of the acquisitive drive" among bureaucrats, which is perfectly natural, Weber says, for someone who has a fixed income and who regards it as dishonorable to be swayed in his or her judgment by commercial considerations.[33] Weber also observes that it is this hostility to business that has made so many state officials positive to the welfare state. The same attitude would presumably also make bureaucrats into potential supporters of state socialism.

Charismatic domination—the second of Weber's three types of domination—is no doubt the most dramatic one. The charismatic personality is described as having an extraordinary or a superhuman quality that cannot be found in everyday life; and the followers or disciples regard it as self-evident that they shall obey the commands of the leader. Examples of charismatic personalities include prophets, warrior heroes, and great demagogues, all of whom have had a strong vision that things cannot go on as they are and that something has to be done ("It has been written . . . but *I* say unto you").[34] This emphasis on change makes charisma a radical element in society, and early in history it was *the* revolutionary force, according to Weber. He also notes that while powerful modern agents of change, such as bureaucracy and rational capitalism, make people adapt to outer circumstances, charisma influences the individual from within.

From this brief description of charisma, one might assume that economic matters play no role in it. This, however, is not so; and in fact, Weber refers repeatedly to economics in his analysis of this type of domination, especially to indicate what charisma is *not*. Charisma, according to Weber, can be characterized as an *"anti-economic force,"* and there is nothing it cares for as little as economic matters.[35] That charisma is anti-economic does not mean that it rejects the economy in all its manifestations; the charismatic warrior, for example, has his mind set on booty, and many charismatic movements accept donations and other forms of voluntary contributions. But what charisma cannot accept, under any circumstances, is the type of economic mentality that is typically found in everyday life. According to Weber, "What is *despised* . . . is traditional or rational everyday economizing, the attainment of a regular income by continuous economic activity devoted to this end."[36] While "everyday life [is] the setting of the economy," the very definition of charisma is that it is something that goes beyond everyday life.[37] This opposition to everyday life introduces a serious strain into the charismatic movement and makes it unstable; and sooner or later this strain has to be resolved by making peace with things as they are. This whole process—the famous routinization of charisma—is primarily driven by two forces. One of these has to do with finding a successor to the charismatic leader, and the other with the need to adjust to the economic forces of everyday life. The strongest of the two forces, Weber notes, is by far the latter, and no charismatic movement can escape it. "Every charisma," Weber writes in *Economy and Society*, "is on the road from a turbulently emotional life, which knows no economic rationality, to a slow death by suffocation under the weight of material interests; and every hour of its existence brings it nearer to this end."[38]

Some of the followers of the charismatic leader are part of what Weber refers to as "the charismatic administrative staff," even if he also expresses some doubt that the term "administration" is appropriate in this context.[39] The charismatic officials have been chosen not because of their proven capacity and training, as in a bureaucracy, but because of their devotion to the charismatic leader and the fervor with which they share his or her vision. There is no promotion, no career, no rule about terminating people or about anything else in a charismatic administration; all that matters is the vision of the charismatic leader and how it can be turned into reality. As routinization sets in, however, the nature of the charismatic administration changes: the line between the charismatic officials and the rest of the charismatic subjects becomes sharper, and there is a tendency for the staff to close itself off as a separate status group through demands of training and the like. Charisma becomes less pure, and it is typically transferred to some social group ("hereditary charisma") or to the organizational structure itself ("office charisma").

The financing of the charismatic administration goes through similar changes, as routinization sets in. At first, the members of the charismatic administration live in some kind of communism where everything is shared according to need. The leader is in charge of the resources and is accountable to no one for the way that he or she spends them. Since the charismatic movement is very suspicious of ordinary business activities, it finances itself through gifts, voluntary contributions, booty, and extortion. Followers and disciples typically feel it as their duty to help out with contributions, according to capacity and the need at the moment. But the members of the charismatic administration also want to have a steady income and normal family relations, both of which are incompatible with a state of pure charisma. As a result, staff members soon begin trying to introduce salaries, prebends, and the like, so that they can lead a more stable life— and the inexorable process of routinization is thereby set in motion, transforming the charismatic organization into some kind of prebendal, patrimonial, or feudal organization.

The impact of charismatic movements on the economy is "revolutionary," Weber says, but it clearly differs at different stages. When it first appears, charisma confronts economic traditionalism head on with its various demands. But as routinization progresses, the charismatic movement introduces a new kind of economic traditionalism, usually some form of patrimonialism or feudalism. One could characterize the impact of charisma on capitalism by saying that it is alien not only to rational capitalism but to any kind of capitalism, since it opposes all sustained attempts to make a profit. Although this statement is correct, it should be noted that a charismatic element is often present in capitalism, according to Weber. The case that Weber cites in this context (and which was mentioned in chapter 2) is that of Henry Villard, who got the U.S. public to back him in a famous deal around the turn of the century, just by virtue of his personality. But charisma is not only present in "grandiose robber capitalism" of this type, Weber says, but also in other forms of modern capitalism, including rational capitalism itself.[40] This, however, does not mean that some kind of "charismatic capitalism" is likely to emerge. Economic activities need to be repeated over time in order to become stable social structures, and charisma usually lasts only a short period.[41]

Traditional domination—the third of Weber's three types of domination—is more complex than either charismatic domination or legal domination; it also has something of a residual character to it, at least in Weber's early work. There exist, for example, different types of traditional domination, depending on whether there is an administrative staff and whether the ruler controls the means of administration. Most forms of traditional domination, however, have traits in common. First tradition is regarded as sacred—that is, commands are obeyed and legitimized with reference to the fact that this is how things have "always" been. Traditional domination also has two different spheres: one in which the ruler has to follow tradition, and one in which he is free to do whatever he wants. In certain types of traditional rulership, the former sphere predominates, while in others most matters are decided according to the ruler's discretion. The very notion of a fee, Weber points out, has its historical origin in the nontraditional sphere.

If there is no administrative staff at all, traditional domination takes the form of either gerontocracy or primitive patriarchalism. Both of these have a profoundly conservative impact on society, including its economy, because the ruler cannot do anything without the explicit approval of the community. Gerontocracy and primitive patriarchalism are soon surpassed in history by the most important form of traditional domination, namely patrimonialism. Weber's analysis of traditional domination is more or less centered on patrimonialism, which he defines as a regime in which the ruler regards all political and economic rights as his own personal rights. There is, in other words, no separation between the state's property and the ruler's personal property, as in a bureaucratic state. The ruler views the administration and the army as his personal tools, and he pays for them out of his own pocket. The ruler's private fortune is of crucial importance to his power, and he is constantly trying to enlarge it. He may try to encourage trade, found new cities, or do whatever it takes to bring in more money. The result is largely irrational: "The ruler's favor and disfavor, grants and confiscations, continuously create new wealth and destroy it again."[42]

In all but a few circumstances, the patrimonial ruler has full control over the means of administration.[43] At an early stage in history the ruler was assisted by just a few individuals, and there was no real administration. These household officials, as Weber calls them, ate at the ruler's table and were assigned elementary tasks. Crown offices from all over the world have their origin in this elementary type of household administration: the chamberlain (treasury and revenues), the intendant (clothing and armor), the marshal (the stables), and so on. Another early type of official was the political official, who was usually a favorite in patrimonial regimes; clerical and accounting officials appeared early on, when it was realized that it was difficult to rule effectively without their help.

When the number of officials became so large that they could not remain at the ruler's household, they were posted elsewhere in the empire. Their tasks, however, usually remained a mixture of stereotypical and ad hoc measures. Their primary allegiance was still to the ruler personally, and what mattered was loyalty, not impartiality as in a bureaucracy.

When the patrimonial officials stopped living off their master's table, they had to be paid in some other way—through benefices. These were originally in kind and later in money, perhaps in the form of fees. Benefices lasted in principle only for the recipient's lifetime, though in reality they often became hereditary; and they typically consisted of allowances from the lord's treasury or magazine, or of a piece of land. Patrimonial offices were paid by the ruler himself, usually from his hoard or treasury. The larger the ruler's resources, the larger his administration could be; and the general tendency in a patrimonial regime was consequently for the administration to grow.

The effect that patrimonial administration as well as patrimonialism in general tends to have on the economy, Weber says, is to discourage rational capitalism and to encourage traditional economic behavior as well as certain kinds of political capitalism, such as tax farming and office farming. A capitalist form of trading may also emerge because it can adapt itself to practically any conditions.[44] That rational capitalism cannot develop under patrimonialism has to do with its general atmosphere of arbitrariness; both the ruler and his officials have the freedom to do exactly what they want, outside the areas where they are bound by tradition. Industrial capitalism, however, is far too sensitive to irrationalities to survive under this condition. In addition, the ruler feels threatened by the kind of power that rational profit-making represents and consequently will not tolerate it. Political capitalism, in contrast, goes much better with the general atmosphere of arbitrariness, risk-taking, and quick money-making that is characteristic of patrimonialism. This is particularly true for sultanism, a form of patrimonialism in which the ruler is not bound by tradition in most of his decisions.

One type of domination that Weber has difficulty fitting into his scheme of legal, charismatic, and traditional domination is what he calls Western feudalism (simply feudalism from here on, though Weber also speaks of prebendal feudalism).[45] In the part of *Economy and Society* that Weber himself oversaw for publication, he suggests that feudalism is its own category, though it has both patrimonial and charismatic origins.[46] While someone like Marx defines feudalism primarily in economic terms, Weber regards the legal-social relationship between the lord and his vassal as more fundamental, even if he acknowledges that the manor was its typical economic unit. Feudalism exists, Weber specifies, where a lord and a vassal are tied together in a contract through which the vassal promises loyalty and personal service, mainly of a military kind, and through which he receives the right to a certain area in exchange. The contract is not an ordinary business contract; rather it is upheld through a sense of status honor, which is typical for feudalism as a phenomenon. The feudal army is by far the most important part of the feudal administration, and it consists of specially trained knights. Feudalism roughly emerged when military equipment became too expensive for the members of the popular peasant levy to arm themselves, and when they had to attend to their land continuously.

Feudal administration is characterized by the fact that its key administrators—the vassals—control the means of administration, and not the lord. This introduces a chronic instability into the relationship between lord and vassal, Weber says, because once the vassal is in charge of his land and has his own military force, there is little but his sense of loyalty to keep him from breaking away from the lord. The latter attempts to counteract this tendency in various ways, and for this reason (but also to take care of his personal affairs) he builds up his own administrative staff. On the whole, however, feudalism tends to minimize administration, Weber notes. Whereas in patrimonialism the ruler equates a large administration with more power for himself and new chances to expand the treasury, feudalism is much more conservative. One reason for this is that feudal administration is paid for through tributes and services in kind, a practice that makes the economic system inflexible as well as resistant to innovations.

In general, feudalism has a deeply stabilizing effect on the economy. Its economic structure—manors in combination with tributes and services in kind—obviously contributes to this. While patrimonialism, encourages trade, which leads to changes in the traditional distribution of wealth, this is not true of feudalism. Most important, however, the general ethos of feudalism is antagonistic to economic progress. The individual and his heroic deeds are celebrated in feudalism, while rational business demands impersonality and predictability to flourish. The feudal lord also displays a nonchalance in business that is typical of the aristocrat, to which should be added, Weber says, that "feudalism is inherently contemptuous of bourgeois-commercial utilitarianism."[47] As a result, neither rational capitalism nor political capitalism is encouraged, only economic traditionalism.

Even though feudalism does not fit well into Weber's typology, his analysis of domination nonetheless constitutes an important contribution to political sociology as well as to economic sociology. In a highly suggestive, clear, and systematic manner, Weber proposes a way to think about and analyze the relationship between type of domination, structure of administration, way of financing administration (including way of compensating the officials)—plus the effect that all of this has on the economy, particularly on the rise of rational capitalism (see figure 3.3).

But from the viewpoint of economic sociology, Weber's analysis contains more than this. For the different types of domination, Weber also looks at the relationship between domination, type of army (bureaucratic, patrimonial, and so on) and way of paying for the army.[48] He furthermore makes an analysis of the relationship between domination, type of law, and impact on the economy, a topic to which I return in chapter 4. Finally, in his analysis of patrimonialism Weber also sketches the relationship between early forms of the welfare state and the economy; the main argument being that the patrimonial ruler easily takes on the benevolent role of "father of the people," but that this makes it

	LEGAL DOMINATION	CHARISMATIC DOMINATION	TRADITIONAL DOMINATION: PATRIMONIALISM	CHARISMATIC AND TRADITIONAL DOMINATION: FEUDALISM
NATURE OF LEGITIMATION	obedience is to the law and to rules, not to persons	obedience is inspired by the extraordinary character of the leader	obedience is due to the sanctity of tradition; there is a corresponding loyalty to the leader	contract of fealty between lord and vassal; a mixture of traditional and charismatic elements
TYPE OF ADMINISTRATION	bureaucracy; the official is trained and has a career and a sense of duty	followers and disciples who later become more like normal officials as a result of routinization	from house-hold staff to more advanced officials with mostly ad hoc and stereotyped tasks	small-scale administration, similar to patrimonial staff but with a distinct status element to it; the vassal has especially military duties
MEANS TO PAY FOR THE ADMINISTRATION AND TO COMPENSATE THE OFFICIALS	taxation; the official gets a salary and possibly a pension	booty, donations, and the like pay for the needs of the "officials" before routinization leads to other forms of compensation	from the rulers' own resources or treasury; the official first eats at the ruler's table, then gets a benefice	tributes and services from the subjects; fiefs to the vassals, while the minor officials get paid as in patrimonialism
EFFECT ON THE ECONOMY, ESPECIALLY ON THE RISE OF RATIONAL CAPITALISM	indispensable to rational capitalism through its predictability; hostile to political capitalism	initially hostile to all forms of systematic economic activity; when routinized, usually a conservative force	hostile to rational capitalism because of its arbitrary element; positive to economic traditionalism and to political capitalism	the ethos of feudalism goes against all types of capitalism; deeply conservative effect on the economy

Fig. 3.3. Main Types of Domination and Their Relation to the Economy

Source: Max Weber, *Economy and Society* (Berkeley: University of California Press, 1978), pp. 212–301, 941–1211; Max Weber, "The Three Types of Legitimate Rule," pp. 6–15 in Amitai Etzioni, ed., *A Sociological Reader of Complex Organizations* (New York: Holt, Rinehart and Winston, 1969).

Comment: Weber's most important contribution to fiscal sociology is to be found in his analysis of the relationship between form of domination and way of financing the domination and what general effect this arrangement has on the economy. Figure 4.1 adds information on the relationship between law and the different forms of domination.

harder for rational capitalism to emerge because substantive justice tends to run counter to formal economic rationality.[49]

III. Economy and Politics in the City

One can find some further material on the relationship between political phenomena and the economy in Weber's studies of the city. The development and nature of the city was a topic that interested Weber from early in his career. When he taught economics in the 1890s he devoted a section to the city, and he lectured on such topics as the economic theory of the city, the economic policy of the city, and the "town economy" as a special stage in economic development.[50] In his economic and social history of antiquity from 1909, there is a section comparing the *polis* to the medieval city. The plan for his handbook of economics (*Grundriss der Sozialökonomik*) that Weber published in 1914 contains a section called "Non-Legitimate Domination: A Typology of Cities"; and when a huge manuscript on the city was found among Weber's belongings after his death, it was incorporated into *Economy and Society* ("The City"). Finally, as part of his course in 1919–20 on social and economic history, Weber also lectured on the city. These lectures were based on material that was very similar to "The City," but the focus was on citizenship rather than on nonlegitimate domination. As is clear from this overview, in Weber's early work he looked at the city primarily from an economist's perspective and also at its general role in economic history. In his later works Weber added a political focus: nonlegitimate domination (in the contribution for the *Grundriss*) and citizenship (in the course from 1919–20 on social and economic history).

Weber was, of course, well aware of the crucial role that the city had played in the evolution of Western capitalism; this was something that Marx—as well as a number of scholars after him, including Karl Bücher and Gustav von Schmoller—had emphasized. In his social and economic history of antiquity from 1909, Weber says, for example, that Western capitalism rests on a foundation of trade and industry laid by the medieval city. In his lectures from 1919–20, Weber pays much attention to the various economic organizations that emerged in the city, such as craft guilds and the *commenda*. In "The City," he notes that the city was certainly not "the carrier" of modern capitalism, but says that it is nonetheless "inseparably linked [to the rise of capitalism] as one of its crucial factors."[51]

But Weber was just as interested in the *political* contribution that the city had made to the rise of Western capitalism and to the process of rationalization in general. As part of his attempt to show the relevance of the city's political role, Weber made a sharp attack on the economic theory of the city as well as on the notion that the town economy constitutes a distinct stage in economic development.[52] Economic theories of the city, Weber argued, do indeed highlight important aspects of the city, such as the centrality of the market, the need to import agricultural products, and so on. Concepts such as "consumer city," "producer city," and "merchant city" are consequently useful. But Weber also believed that this approach was restrictive and that "the concept of 'the city' can and must be analyzed in terms of a series of categories other than the economic ones . . . namely, in terms of *political* categories."[53] In particular, it was important to realize that the typical city, besides being a market, also had been a fortress, and that a city constitutes a distinct community with special political and administrative institutions. Weber was even more critical of the attempt to view the town economy as a distinct stage in economic development. While the economic theories of the city needed to be complemented, he argued, the view of the city in theories of economic stages had a basic flaw. The error lay in confusing "purely economic categories" with "economic policy"; and part of what a stage theorist like Schmoller saw as typical of the city economy in general was in reality the result of a special economic policy.[54] More precisely, the relationship of the medieval city to the countryside was not inherent in the economic nature of the city, but the product of a conscious political strategy of certain groups in the medieval city to subjugate the countryside to their interests. This policy included such things as price control, restrictions on the establishment of rural industries, and regulations on where the peasants could sell their products.

In the following pages, Weber's view of citizenship and nonlegitimate domination will be sketched, together with an attempt to outline the role that economic factors have played in these two phenomena. Citizenship is defined by Weber as membership in a political community, typically the state, together with a sense of right connected to such membership. Citizenship has its origin in two very different periods of history; first in the city of antiquity or the *polis*, and then in the medieval city. It has not emerged outside the West because of two primary factors: economic-geographic conditions and competing social ties. When irrigation and river regulations were central to an economy, a strong and centralized state power emerged in the form of a royal bureaucracy ("'hydraulic' bureaucracy"), which also had full control over the means of warfare. This meant that cities in Asia, the Near East, and Egypt never got to rule themselves for any extended period of time because the military power of the ruler was overwhelmingly large. The second factor that has prevented the emergence of a sense of political community outside the West has to do with the existence of strong traditional social ties. In China, for example, the individual belonged first and foremost to the clan, and this attachment was supported by magical beliefs. And in India, each individual belonged to a caste, which meant that there were strict regulations about whom to interact with; it was consequently very difficult for a common sense of political identity to emerge.

The *polis* came into being primarily for military purposes: a few noble families gained their independence by uniting into a community for self-defense. They usually settled along the coast in order to have access to trade. Though each individual was still tied to powerful social organizations—typically the clan and some military organization—he now also became a citizen or member of a political cult community, where the inhabitants sacrificed and ate together. From Weber's description of the *polis,* it is clear that its motivating force was military and that its primary identity was political, not economic. The citizen of the *polis* was a *homo politicus,* Weber concludes.

But even if politics played the central role, Weber's portrait of this early and primitive stage of citizenship in the West contains a number of interesting observations on the interaction between economic and political phenomena. The warlike character of the *polis,* for example, made it prone to different forms of political capitalism, unlike rational capitalism, which can only exist in an atmosphere of peace. The *polis* prospered through warfare and the stealing of booty, and it was constantly at war with its neighbors. Its patricians looked down on trade and rational forms of money-making; they were greedy, but did not want to work for their riches (they were "honorable idlers").[55] The *commenda* was tailor-made for these patricians: they could invest in a cargo or a ship while somebody else did the work. The only equivalent in the *polis* to the peaceful medieval merchants, Weber says, were the freedmen. They, however, were not allowed to take part in the city's many forms of political capitalism.[56]

The autonomy of the *polis* with its rudimentary sense of citizenship disappeared together with the possibilities for political capitalism toward the end of antiquity. The type of citizenship that emerged in the medieval city was considerably more advanced and also had different causes. It was more advanced in the sense that the citizen no longer had any strong ties to groups that competed with the political community, something that Christianity had contributed to through its emphasis on the individual and its hostility to magic. The citizens were part of a special community, which was called *coniuratio* in Italy, but which also appeared elsewhere in the West. The medieval city, as opposed to the *polis,* had not come into being for military reasons; instead, a lord had usually founded the city to make money. Since the city encouraged trade and industry, it usually became a center for money-making activity. Unlike the citizen in the *polis,* Weber says, the citizen in the medieval Western city was a *homo economicus.*[57]

The interaction of political and economic elements in the medieval city is described by Weber in the following manner. Early on, patrician families controlled the city. Their attitude toward business was similar to that of their counterparts in the *polis*: they wanted to get rich quickly, but not through work, so the *commenda* suited them very well. As in antiquity, democracy spread in the medieval city mainly for military reasons, but it extended active citizenship to a larger number of inhabitants and it also spelled an end to the rule of the patricians. The bourgeois ethos of peaceful acquisition intensified and spread within the city. Business activities were not, however, allowed to spread to the countryside; and the reason for this was that the city wanted to control and regulate the countryside in ways that suited its own interests.

The second major political theme in Weber's later work on the city is what he termed *nonlegitimate domination.* In Weber's opinion, the medieval city in the West represented a unique kind of domination in that it was simultaneously autonomous and part of a larger political realm, which was ruled by a lord. The power of the lord was acknowledged, but it was not seen as legitimate in the city. The difference between nonlegitimate domination and illegitimate domination, where the subjects outright reject the authority of the ruler, is not very clear; and nonlegitimate domination is in many ways a difficult concept. For a while it seems that Weber tried to incorporate the concept of nonlegitimate domination into his typology of domination and legitimacy; and in a 1917 talk in Vienna, Weber, for example, spoke of the Western city as "a fourth type of legitimacy."[58] He later dropped the idea of a fourth type of domination, however, and never integrated his analysis of nonlegitimate domination with his general scheme of domination.

The only place Weber thoroughly discusses nonlegitimate domination is in his later studies of the city, where it is approached from several angles. Its origin, for example, is explained in the following way. A medieval lord would typically found a city in the hope of making money through rents, market fees, and the like. He would also prefer to be paid in money by his subjects, rather than in kind, and this constituted another motive for him to encourage city trade. From an economic viewpoint, Weber says, it is clear that the founding of a city led to a clash between two economic principles: the market, as represented by the city, and the *oikos,* as represented by the lord. But this clash of principles did not cause many conflicts in real life because the lord also had an interest in the spread of the money economy and the existence of a nearby market. What he did resent, however, was the growing political power of the medieval city and that it had a tendency to develop into a kind of liberated zone inside his own territory. The main reason the lord nonetheless left the city alone—again demonstrating the link between politics and economics—was that he needed money. "The financial strength of his urban subjects," Weber writes, "forced the lord to turn to them in a case of need and to negotiate with them."[59] But historical causality is usually complex, and in this particular case there was also a political reason for the strength of the city in its financial relationship with the lord. The lord would negotiate with a city in the first place, Weber says, only if the city had its own military power. Such power, Weber emphasizes, was possible only as long as the lord lacked a fully developed administrative machine; and once a well-working bureaucracy was in place, the medieval city gradually began to lose its autonomy and was eventually swallowed up by the patrimonial-bureaucratic state.

I hope that these two examples of citizenship and nonlegitimate domination are enough to convince the reader that Weber's studies of the city are of interest not only to urban sociology and historical sociology but also to economic sociology. I have only discussed "The City" and similar works from the viewpoint of the relationship between economics and politics, and even this in a rather cursory manner. If one also were to look at the purely economic institutions that existed in the city—such as craft guilds, markets, different types of entrepreneurship, and so on—the importance of these studies to economic sociology would become even more evident.

IV. Economy and Politics in the Modern State: Themes
from Weber's Unfinished Sociology of the State

According to Weber, the modern rational state has emerged only in the West. Its primary features are outlined in different places in Part I of *Economy and Society*: the legitimacy of the rational state is based primarily on legal authority; its resources come mainly through taxation; and its administration is typically organized in the form of a bureaucracy, which—like its legal system—has to be highly predictable in order for rational capitalism to thrive. Weber, however, had originally wanted to include a much more extensive and systematic political sociology in his contribution to the *Grundriss der Sozialökonomik*, and in several places in Part 1 of *Economy and Society* he refers to a "sociology of the state" that he never had the time to complete. Some of the material that Weber wanted to include here can, no doubt, be found in his early version of *Economy and Society* (Part 2 in the current English edition), but it is not as systematic or as conceptually sharp as Part 1. Weber's political writings also indicate that he had much more to say on this topic than he ever got around to covering in his scientific writings. For this reason, Weber's political sociology, as it exists today, is fragmentary, as is his discussion of the relationship between the state and the economy. Nonetheless, Weber's political sociology does contain some analyses that are of distinct interest to economic sociology. I have chosen to focus on the following three topics: (1) *the economic policy of the state;* (2) *the monetary policy of the state;* and (3) *the relationship between democracy, the state, and capitalism.*

Before presenting Weber's view on these topics, a few words should be said about the history of the rational state and the role of capitalism in this. Although both capitalism and the state have adopted the bureaucratic form of organization, they have very different social origins. The patrimonial state dominated most of the West until about the time of the French Revolution, after which the modern bureaucratic state took over. In some cases patrimonialism developed directly into the modern state, and in other cases it came into being via the *Ständestaat*. According to Weber, capitalism benefited immensely from the way that politics developed in the West, especially from the fact that the individual states were often at war with one another. Fighting between patrimonial princes and between the princes and the estates cost money and therefore encouraged the growth of capitalism. "This competitive struggle [between nation-states]," Weber points out, "created the largest opportunities for modern Western capitalism."[60] The mechanism at work in this process is referred to as "political competition" by Weber; and he notes that it also played a central role in the development of political capitalism in antiquity.[61] In general, Weber says, opportunities for all types of capitalism tend to open up when political units fight one another and need money for their wars. When political competition ends, on the other hand, and a single empire comes into being, capitalism is typically strangled. According to Weber, this happened in China and also in Rome.

The Economic Policy of the State

There exists no systematic treatment of the economic policy of the state in Part 1 of *Economy and Society*. Part 2, however, contains an interesting analysis of two concrete cases: mercantilism and imperialism.[62] Mercantilism was a much debated topic in Weber's days; and Schmoller, in particular, tried to counter Adam Smith's thesis that mercantilism had had a negative effect on the economy with the argument that mercantilism should rather be seen as a strategy for state building.[63] Weber, as usual, had his own angle and argued that mercantilism represented the first form of rational economic policy in the West. What was particularly important with mercantilism was that some states, such as England and France, began encouraging industry in a systematic manner, either through protection of their existing industries or through promotion of new industries through monopolies and investments. State support for industry was part of a more general attempt to increase the power of the state—for example, by developing a positive balance of trade (a concept that was developed around this time). While regulation of trade and industry had initially a rational impact on the economy, Weber notes, this later changed, and mercantilism was eventually abolished.

The second type of economic policy that Weber takes up in *Economy and Society* is imperialism, also a topic that attracted much attention in his day.[64] Weber views imperialism as a political rather than an economic phenomenon. There is a particular dynamic to political power, he argues, and "power prestige" can sometimes—but only sometimes—make a great power want to expand.[65] Economic interests would typically play "a weighty part" in the transition from a nonexpansive policy to an expansive one.[66] Throughout history, starting with Rome, there had also existed something that Weber calls "imperialist capitalism," which can be characterized as a form of political capitalism. Groups with an interest in this type of capitalism include tax farmers, suppliers to the state, and overseas traders with privileges from the state. Referring to what Aristophanes calls "industries interested in peace" and "industries interested in war," Weber argues that the latter tend to encourage imperialist capitalism, while the former prefer free trade.[67] Imperialist capitalism clearly was an irrational and ancient form of capitalism, but Weber also points to its revival in his own time; Germany and many other European nations were all trying to carve out a colonial empire before World War I.

A comparison of what Weber says on imperialist capitalism with other well-known theories of imperialism from about the same period makes it clear that Weber had developed an angle of his own. For example, Weber is much less categorical and deterministic in his approach than either Lenin or Schumpeter. While Lenin saw imperialism as directly caused by capitalism, and Schumpeter argued that imperialism was pre-capitalistic and irrational in nature, Weber viewed it primarily as a contingent, political phenomenon. The dynamics of power prestige *could* lead a great power to expand, and, if so, imperialist capitalism would probably accompany it.[68] In Weber's view, a socialist state could also be an imperialistic power.

The Monetary Policy of the State

Part 1 of *Economy and Society* contains a systematic treatment of the monetary policy of the modern state; in fact, some twenty-five pages in the central chapter 2 are devoted to this topic. Weber argues that a rational monetary system is a condition of modern capitalism and that such a system has appeared only in the West. A rational monetary system is especially important for efficient capital accounting and requires specific conditions to come into being. These conditions are the following: the state has a monopoly on issuing money; the state has a monopoly on the regulation of the monetary system; and monetary policy is informed by formal rather than substantive rationality.[69]

It is of some interest to note that much of what Weber wrote on monetary policy was influenced by his colleague G. F. Knapp, who in 1905 had published a treatise entitled *The State Theory of Money.* Knapp suggests that money should be viewed from a legal-statist perspective, and that this perspective can be used to analyze a series of important issues in monetary theory. "Money is a creature of law," the book begins, and Knapp later explains that this means that "money . . . is a creation of the legislative activity of the state."[70] Much of Knapp's work is devoted to an attempt to introduce a new and elaborate terminology, which reflected his legislative-statist viewpoint. That money is "chartal," for example, means that an authority has turned some material—say a piece of paper—into a legal means of payment by stamping or otherwise marking it, similar to the way that a postage stamp comes into being. In other words, the value of money does not reside in the physical material it is made of, but derives from the fact that the state has put its mark on it. Knapp's work became popular among German economists before World War I, and according to Weber, *The State Theory of Money* is a "masterpiece."[71] Other economists who have shared Weber's positive opinion include Knut Wicksell, according to whom Knapp's book "belongs to the pearls in the economics literature."[72] Wicksell, like Weber, was also enthusiastic about Knapp's effort to introduce a number of new terms.[73]

Quite a few economists, however, were annoyed by Knapp's avalanche of new and peculiar terms, and some also felt that his ideas were dangerous because they glorified the state. Von Mises was one of these critics, whose number grew as Germany and Austria experienced devastating inflation after World War I.[74] Weber himself was skeptical about certain aspects of Knapp's work, but his reaction differed from that of Mises and most other critics in two ways. For one thing, Weber felt that Knapp's ideas were formal and scientific rather than practical and that they had been used for partisan purposes, especially in Austria. Second, he argued that although Knapp had solved some difficult formal problems in monetary theory in a brilliant manner, his work needed to be complemented and made more realistic. Weber, in brief, took a more conciliatory attitude than Mises, whose ideas on monetary theory he otherwise shared.[75]

Weber rejects as misguided the notion that the state can decide through legislation what economic reality will look like. "In the future as in the past," Weber says, "it will be the 'interests' of individuals rather than the 'ideas' of an economic administration which will rule the world."[76] He also points out that Knapp had failed to understand that the value of money is determined by its relationship to other goods and not by proclamations of the state; similarly, money is not only a means of payment, as Knapp had argued, but also a means of exchange.[77] In Weber's mind, Knapp was correct in arguing that monetary policy around the turn of the century had been concerned mainly with how the value of one country's currency was related to the value of other currencies. But he believed that Knapp was wrong in thinking that stability was the only goal that a state could have for its monetary policy; a state could equally well be interested in using its monetary policy to stimulate the economy or to deliberately create inflation. The strategy of creating inflation, Weber adds, was of special interest to a country with huge foreign debts—a situation that Germany was going to be in after World War I. Knapp's failure to realize that a state might have other goals for its monetary policy than to stabilize its currency, points once more to his most important shortcoming, as Weber saw it—namely, Knapp's inability to realize that the value of money is set by a number of economic factors over which the state has little or no power.[78] Weber was also skeptical of Knapp's enthusiastic endorsement of paper money; having a metal standard, Weber says, would at least set a limit to the state's capacity to indulge in irresponsible monetary policy. Weber concludes his critique of Knapp by suggesting that a clear distinction must be made between "the formal validity of money" and its "substantive validity." The former refers to the value of a currency that a state attempts to impose, while substantive validity refers to the value that money has on the market, when it is exchanged against other commodities.

The Relationship between Democracy, the State, and Capitalism

Although Weber presented his ideas on monetary policy in a fairly systematic manner in *Economy and Society*, his analysis of the relationship between democracy and the economy is scattered throughout his scientific and his political writings. It is nonetheless clear that Weber attached special importance to the following two topics: the historical relationship between capitalism and democracy, and the more general relationship between money, democracy, and working as a politician.[79] That both of these topics are as relevant today as when Weber was active needs perhaps not be said.

As to the relationship between capitalism and democracy, Weber is firm: they have nothing in common; there is no "elective affinity" whatsoever between capitalism and democracy.[80] That modern society, with its capitalist economy, has come to be characterized by a certain individualism as well as by political democracy is merely a historical coincidence and the result of certain events that will not be repeated. Weber especially mentions Cromwell's army and the French Constituent Assembly in this context. Capitalists, he adds, are usually not very democratically inclined: they prefer to deal with a single authority behind the scenes than with a number of democratically elected officials.[81] As to the future, Weber was pessimistic: if economic and technical progress would begin to fail, or if rents would start to replace profits throughout the economy, the freedoms that exist today would quickly vanish.[82]

Weber also deals with the relationship between money and political behavior in the modern state in addressing how people who are active in politics get paid or otherwise finance their political activities. The most important concepts here are "economic availability" and "living off politics [in the economic sense of the word]" versus "living for politics."[83] Living off politics means that one gets paid to devote oneself to politics, while living for politics means that one views politics as a vocation. To be able to live for politics, one has to either be paid to devote oneself to politics or have private means. Weber points out that in a direct democracy, power tends to drift into the hands of those who can afford to be active in politics without being paid for it. But he also notes that only people who are wealthy can afford to be truly independent in their politics. Modern democracy, Weber concludes, is impossible without paying some people to devote themselves to politics: "Democracy has only the choice of being run cheaply by the rich who hold honorary office, or of being run expensively by paid professional politicians."[84]

Through the concept "economic availability" Weber attempts to capture a phenomenon that is similar but not identical to living off and living for politics, namely that only certain people can be active in politics without giving up their ordinary job or status position.[85] He points out that some categories of people, such as industrial workers, cannot devote any time at all to professional politics; others are busy only during certain months of the year, such as farmers; and some people work only occasionally, such as the medieval patricians who now and then got involved in some business deal. The average entrepreneur might look like a good candidate for political work, Weber says, but is usually so involved in what he is doing that he lacks the appropriate distance to politics. An additional dimension of being economically available is here revealed: the entrepreneur simply does not have "the *inner* availability . . . from the struggle of every day interests."[86]

V. ECONOMICS AND POLITICS IN SOCIALISM

Another important theme in Weber's writings on politics is socialism; and it was especially during the years after World War I—when revolutions were sweeping through Russia and Europe, including Germany—that Weber started to write more extensively on this topic. Parts of his analysis can be found in chapter 2 of *Economy and Society*, especially his assessment of the difficulties involved in having a planned economy (§§12, 14). His more general analysis of socialism, however, is mostly to be found in his political writings. What Weber had to say about economic planning in general, and about economic calculation in particular, is often brushed aside as passé, especially in view of what Oskar Lange had to say on this topic in the 1930s.[87] But, as I shall try to show, this is an erroneous view, which confuses Weber's *sociological* argument about the difficulties of economic planning in a concrete socialist society with the kind of analysis that is typically made in theoretical economics and that has been developed with capitalist society in mind. That Weber was indeed making a sharp sociological statement becomes even more obvious if one combines what he has to say about economic planning and calculation with his views of the general nature of socialist society, and asks the question, "What effect will this type of society have on the possibility of formulating accurate prices?"

One important consequence of the socialists' taking power in a country, Weber says, would be the merger of the political bureaucracy and the economic bureaucracy into one single bureaucracy. Such a merger would obviously increase the importance of bureaucracy throughout society; and it would also strengthen the power of the state by doing away with its most important competitor under capitalism. According to Weber, "State bureaucracy would rule *alone* if private capitalism were eliminated. The private and public bureaucracies, which now work next to, and potentially against, each other and hence check one another to a degree, would be merged into a single bureaucracy."[88] The result would not only be that the oppressive "iron cage" that is part of capitalism remained intact—rational socialism cannot do without large-scale industry, factory discipline, and bureaucracy—but also that the general situation got considerably worse. A person living in a socialist society, Weber says, would have no more power over his or her life than the average subject in ancient Egypt.

From an economic viewpoint, the introduction of socialism would mean an end to all independent economic behavior. That socialism would have this effect has to do with the power of its bureaucracy; and *"every* bureaucracy," according to Weber, has a tendency to "stifle the private economic initiative."[89] Workers would not improve their economic situation in a socialist society; they would still be separated from the means of production, and they would also have to face a much more powerful opponent than the individual capitalist, namely the socialist state. Capitalist entrepreneurs would naturally disappear in a socialist society—and with them the only force that could have brought some change and vitality to the economy. The triumph of socialism means the triumph of economic traditionalism, perhaps in combination with a socialist version of imperialism.[90]

Weber was also skeptical that altruism or some form of revolutionary ideology would have much effect on the way that the socialist economy operates. What drives the individual in economic matters in a capitalist society, he says, is his or her material and ideal interests—and "in an economic system organized on a socialist basis, there would be no fundamental difference in this respect."[91] The individual would try to work each economic situation to his or her advantage, in a capitalist as well as in a socialist society. In a socialist state, violent struggles would soon develop over a variety of economic issues, especially work and salary-related ones. These struggles would take place within the context of a socialist society; and the individuals would have to orient their actions to socialist managers, the agents of socialist repression, and so on.

At the time when Weber was writing on socialism in chapter 2 of *Economy and Society,* that is in 1919–20, very little thought had been given to what the economy of a socialist society would look like in reality. The fullest proposal had been made by Otto Neurath, an Austrian socialist and economist who claimed that it was perfectly possible to organize a socialist economy on the basis of calculations *in natura*—that is, without resorting to money. After World War I, Neurath's ideas were challenged by Ludwig von Mises in a now-famous article which, according to Hayek, was the first work to successfully state the central problem of socialist economics: namely, that it is impossible to formulate effective prices without recourse to a (capitalist) market. Hayek also points out that Weber "arrived independently at very similar conclusions."[92]

In *Economy and Society,* Weber expresses skepticism that it would be possible to run a full-scale socialist economy without using money. Neurath is probably correct in his argument about calculations *in natura,* he says, but only if the economy is very simple, centered on consumption, and restricted to a few, easily identifiable needs. Once, however, comparisons are involved—comparisons of different needs, of different uses of resources, and so on—calculations in kind become exceedingly difficult. The same is true when one goes from simple forms of consumption to industrial production, according to Weber. How, for example, does one determine what parts of an economic organization are doing poorly, or how much a factor of production has contributed to the value of a product, if one does not use money? The whole thing is impossible or close to impossible, Weber concludes. And he adds that there is very little stimulus for exact calculation in a socialist economy; people have no incentive to calculate the cost of alternatives because they do not exist.

Weber's critique of socialist economics is of a sociological nature and more convincing in my opinion than various formalist or logical arguments in defense of socialist calculation. To see what differentiates Weber's approach from that of Oskar Lange and others, the reader may recall what Weber says about the unitary power structure of socialist society; it is at the point where calculations become difficult in a socialist economy that social forces are likely to intervene in an effort to influence prices. It seems obvious enough that interest groups in socialist society will push for whatever solution benefits them the most. In discussing why efficient economic calculations are impossible in socialism, Weber mentions, for example, the problem of comparisons, and notes that it can only be solved in two ways: by following tradition or through "an arbitrary dictatorial regulation."[93] Similarly, in discussing the problems of calculation that are likely to develop within socialist enterprises, Weber points out that someone will have to settle on some kind of value, and that once this has been done, these values must be "policed."[94] That sociology is more relevant for analyzing this type of nonmarket price formation than theoretical economics (which has been worked out with a well-functioning capitalist society in mind) seems obvious enough.

There is, finally, also Weber's argument in response to those who believe that socialism is superior to capitalism because it entails a more efficient use of economic statistics. Some people argue, he says, that in a socialist society one can simply take everybody who has worked with economic calculations in capitalist society and gather them together in one big "Universal Statistical Office." The people in this giant office will then be able to solve all the problems of calculation in socialist economies because they have access to all the information that exists in the system. But this proposal misses the point of why economic statistics are gathered in capitalism in the first place, Weber says—namely, as part of an effort to make a profit. "This idea not only fails to take account of the fundamentally different motives underlying 'statistics' and 'business accounting,'" Weber says; "it also fails to distinguish their fundamentally different functions; they [consequently] differ just like the bureaucrat differs from the entrepreneur."[95]

That it is possible to find an interesting sociological analysis of the economic side of socialism in Weber's work is rarely mentioned in the secondary literature on his work; and the same is true for his more general attempt to analyze the relationship between economics and politics. That Weber himself was perfectly conscious of this dimension of his work in economic sociology is clear from the systematic manner in which he analyzes the interaction between economics and politics in chapter 2 of *Economy and Society* as well as elsewhere in this work. That Weber's interest in this aspect of economic sociology also extended to the one major area of politics that has not yet been discussed—law and the legal system—is shown in the next chapter.

CHAPTER FOUR

The Economy and Law

WEBER DEVOTES a great deal of attention to law in his economic sociology in part because he views law as central to a capitalist society. The modern state, according to Weber, has five basic functions, and three of these are directly related to the legal system: "the enactment of law (legislative function)," "the protection of vested rights (administration of justice)," and "the protection of personal safety and public order (the police)."[1] There is furthermore, in Weber's mind, a strong tendency in Western societies for legitimation to be legal in nature; political leaders are obeyed primarily because they have received and exercise power in accordance with law. Law also plays a key role in the modern economy, owing mainly to the contract: "Present-day economic life, rests on opportunities acquired through contracts." All contracts are in principle guaranteed by "the threat of legal coercion," which is administered through the state.[2] In general, there is a need for calculability in the modern economy, and this includes the legal system. One of the presuppositions of Western rational capitalism, according to Weber, is "rational, that is calculable, law."[3]

A second reason why Weber pays so much attention to law in his economic sociology probably has to do with his interest in and vast, comparative knowledge of the subject. Weber excelled in several academic disciplines, but he was better trained in law than in any other subject. Most of the courses he took at the university were in law, and so were his two dissertations; he trained as a barrister, and his first academic appointment was as a lecturer in law at Berlin University. In particular, Weber was attracted to commercial law, which he studied with the great Levin Goldschmidt in Berlin.[4] Throughout his life Weber wrote on legal topics and, in one way or another, law tended to be an integral part of his works.[5] Furthermore, Weber knew several of the greatest legal minds of his time, and Germany had a highly developed legal culture in the nineteenth century. Producing a new legal system had become an important national enterprise for Germany, and several substantial codifications came into being during the 1800s. These include a new commercial code from 1861 as well as a whole new civil code, the famous *Bürgerliches Gesetzbuch* from 1900. The latter legislation was preceded by a huge debate between those who wanted to draw exclusively on the Germanic legal tradition and those who favored Roman law.[6] The first draft, which was presented in 1888, was rejected for being too Roman; a second draft was presented in 1896 and went into effect some time later. One result of all this interest in different legal traditions, Weber noted, was that legal historiography in his day had reached a level "never achieved in any other country."[7]

Weber's work in the sociology of law has been interpreted in a few different ways in the secondary literature. According to Talcott Parsons, for example, the very "core" of Weber's sociology is not to be found in his sociology of religion or in his analysis of domination, but rather in his sociology of law.[8] The reason for this, Parsons says, is that law mediates between ideals and reality, and thereby constitutes the heart of the normative order of society. A recent work similarly suggests that Weber's work in law is central to an understanding of his sociology, but here the argument is that Weber took some concepts in jurisprudence and transformed them into the basic categories of his sociology.[9] Weber's notion of causality, for example, has its origin in legal methodology. A few commentators have also proposed that Weber's work on law should be seen as part of his more general analysis of Western culture; the evolution of law is part of the general rationalization of the world, and this accounts for much of Weber's fascination with law.[10] Usually, however, the more modest claim is made that Weber's work is a contribution to the sociology of law as well as to sociology in general.[11]

That Weber's work on law also contains an important contribution to economic sociology is rarely mentioned; and, when this is done, it is not elaborated upon. Talcott Parsons, for example, has noted that Weber's sociology of law represents "an essential key" to the understanding of his economic sociology—only to say no more. Similarly, Anthony Kronman has noted that Weber's analysis of the relationship between law and economy constitutes "a kind of connective tissue" in Weber's sociology of law—but he does not elaborate on this statement. Johannes Winkelmann, finally, has argued that it would be to belittle Weber's analysis of law to state that it deals only with the relationship between law and economy.[12]

Most of those who have commented on the relationship between law and economy in Weber's work have done so by referring to the so-called England Problem, while ignoring the rest of his economic sociology. The England Problem refers to the contradiction that supposedly exists in Weber's work between his general thesis that modern capitalism can only be served by a highly formalistic kind of law, and the fact that such a law (according to Weber himself) never existed in England, where capitalism had its breakthrough. The question then becomes: is there a flaw in Weber's general understanding of the relationship between law and capitalism? Or is the England Problem fictitious and based on a misreading of Weber's work?

There is today a growing literature on the England Problem, which is discussed later in this chapter. The main thrust of this chapter is different, however. More precisely, I argue two points: (1) that Weber's sociology of law has a microfoundation in his concept of social action, driven by ideal and material interests; and (2) that his work contains a sophisticated middle-range analysis of the relationship between law and economy, which fills a void in today's economic sociology and also represents a healthy challenge to the hegemony of the "law and economics" literature.[13] This middle-range approach is very much present in Weber's analysis of specific legal institutions, such as the contract, the notion of juristic personality, and the legal profession. There are furthermore many middle-range reflections in what Weber has to say about different kinds of law, including Roman law, medieval law, and canon law. All of these topics, plus

Weber's analysis of the relationship between law and capitalism, are discussed in this chapter.

I. THE RELATIONSHIP BETWEEN LAW AND ECONOMY

It no doubt constitutes an important task to show exactly how Weber's views on the relationship between law and the economy evolved over time, from his earliest writings to the works produced just before his death in June 1920, but it will not be undertaken here. Instead I primarily discuss how Weber viewed law and economy in the sociology that he produced during his last decade, 1910–20 because it was during those years that Weber developed both his sociology of law and his economic sociology. My major focus is on Weber's contribution to the *Grundriss der Sozialökonomik*—that is, on *Economy and Society*. I begin by showing how Weber looked at the relationship between law and economy from a sociological viewpoint; and I then discuss how he viewed this relationship in the major types of law that have existed throughout history. In structuring the presentation in this manner, I have taken my cue from Weber's description in 1910 of one of his contributions to the *Grundriss*: "The Economy and Law (1. Their Fundamental Relationship, 2. Epochs in the Development of Present Conditions)."

One way of approaching the first topic would be to review *Economy and Society* for what Weber has to say about the general relationship between law and economy from a sociological viewpoint. But an easier way to proceed, which might also bring us closer to Weber's own approach, is to focus on two particular writings in which Weber discusses this particular question. One of these is a chapter found among Weber's belongings and which was later included in *Economy and Society* under the title "The Economy and Social Norms."[14] A more accurate title, given its contents, would perhaps have been "The Economy and Law: Their Fundamental Relationship." The second text is Part 1 of *Economy and Society*, which Weber himself had approved for publication and which the reader was supposed to work through before approaching the more elaborate discussion of law and economy later in the work. Since it was in Part 1 that Weber first provided a detailed account of economic sociology, what he has to say on the relationship of law to the economy in this work is of special interest.

Weber's famous definition of law can be found in Part 1 of *Economy and Society*. It is possible to construct a kind of continuum of recurrent social action, Weber says, on which such phenomena as "usage," "custom," "convention," and "law" can be placed.[15] When people perform some social action regularly it is called "usage"; and when this has been done for a long time it becomes a "custom." When there is a "convention," deviations from a certain pattern of social action will be met with disapproval, while a "law" presupposes that there is "a *staff* of people," whose members will use "physical or psychological coercion" if some action deviates from the prescribed course. For Weber, the distinguishing mark of law is consequently the existence of a staff, which includes people such as judges, lawyers, and police officers. If someone breaks the law, "the people with the spiked helmets" will appear, as he used to put it more colloquially.[16]

In presenting his definition of law in Part 1 of *Economy and Society*, Weber does not comment on its possible links to the economy. But given what we know about the financing of administration (from Weber's analysis of domination), one such link is obvious. Like any administration, the legal staff must be paid; and the ruler or state has to get the money from somewhere. A legal staff can be paid, for example, through resources from benefices, booty, or rational taxation. It is also clear that the staff will be structured in different ways. Legal professionals who work for a modern state, for example, will become part of a public bureaucracy with all that this entails, while private law firms are usually more decentralized as well as less formal.

A quick look at Weber's definition of law may give the impression that it is identical to Austin's famous definition of law as the command of the sovereign. Though some parallels no doubt exist, there are also important differences between the two. That Weber's definition is both broader than Austin's and more flexible is clear from Weber's analysis of the different types of domination in Part 1 of *Economy and Society*. In a strongly traditional society, for example, law tends to be identified with tradition, and legal innovations have to be presented in the guise of tradition or they will automatically be rejected. A charismatic leader, in contrast, breaks with traditional law and distrusts legal norms because these are by definition applicable to a number of cases and not to what is unique. Charismatic justice typically takes the form of revealed justice and is inherently individual and irrational. Legal domination, finally, means that a ruler is obeyed because he or she acts in accordance with law, and also has acquired the power in a legal manner. The type of law that answers to legal domination has been intentionally created and can be characterized as a consistent system of abstract rules.

From the analysis in chapter 3 of this book we also know that different types of domination tend to influence the economy in certain ways: charismatic domination is hostile to all forms of established economic order until it has become routinized; the patrimonial version of traditionalism cannot coexist with rational capitalism because of its arbitrary element; and so on. What role, then, does law play in these processes? Weber does not answer this question directly, but the following is clear. No direct causality can be established between type of law and kind of economy, be it from law to the economy or the reverse. Instead, a certain type of law fits into a certain constellation of domination; and this constellation coexists more or less well with different types of economies (see figure 4.1).

But there is also a much more direct relationship between law and economy, according to Weber. In Part 1 of *Economy and Society* he gives three examples, the first of which can be said to constitute the micro foundation for Weber's analysis as a whole. Economic actions, he notes, are often oriented simultaneously to some actor and to the legal order. "The actor in his choice of economic procedures," Weber says, "naturally orients himself [not only to some other

	LEGAL DOMINATION	CHARISMATIC DOMINATION	TRADITIONAL DOMINATION: PATRIMONIALISM	CHARISMATIC AND TRADITIONAL DOMINATION: FEUDALISM
NATURE OF LEGITIMATION	obedience is to the law and to rules, not to persons	obedience is inspired by the extraordinary character of the leader	obedience is due to the sanctity of tradition; there is a corresponding loyalty to the leader	contract of fealty between lord and vassal; a mixture of traditional and charismatic elements
TYPE OF ADMINISTRATION	bureaucracy; the official is trained, has a career and a sense of duty	followers and disciples who later become more like normal officials as a result of routinization	from household staff to more advanced officials with mostly ad hoc and stereotyped tasks	small-scale administration, similar to patrimonial staff but with a distinct status element to it; the vassal has especially military duties
LEGAL SYSTEM	law constitutes a consistent system of abstract rules that have been intentionally established	justice is made through revelation in the concrete case; there are no legal traditions or abstract legal principles	juxtaposition of legal traditionalism with arbitrary decisions by the ruler creates an unstable legal situation	the contract between lord and vassal permeates society and creates a stable legal situation
EFFECT ON THE ECONOMY, ESPECIALLY ON THE RISE OF RATIONAL CAPITALISM	indispensable to rational capitalism through its predictability; hostile to political capitalism	initially hostile to all forms of systematic economic activity; when routinized, usually a conservative force	hostile to rational capitalism because of its arbitrary element; positive to economic traditionalism and to political capitalism	the ethos of feudalism goes against all types of capitalism; deeply conservative effect on the economy

Fig. 4.1. Major Types of Domination and Their Relation to the Legal System, Type of Administration, and Form of Economy

Source: Max Weber, *Economy and Society* (Berkeley: University of California Press, 1978), pp. 212–301, 941–1211; Max Weber, "The Three Types of Legitimate Rule," pp. 6–15 in Amitai Etzioni, ed., *A Sociological Reader of Complex Organizations* (New York: Holt, Rinehart and Winston, 1969); for law, see also *Economy and Society,* pp. 1041, 1082, 1099, 1115.

Comment: The influence of law on the economy differs according to the type of domination involved: legal, traditional, charismatic, or some mixture of these. For information on means of paying for the administration, see figure 3.3.

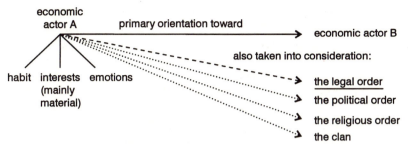

Fig. 4.2. The Micro Foundations for Weber's Analysis of Law and Economy, from a Sociological Perspective

Source: Max Weber, *Economy and Society* (Berkeley: University of California Press, 1978), p. 33.

Comment: In the modern market economy, the economic actor typically orients his or her action to another economic actor and at the same time to the legal order. The orientation to the legal order increases the likelihood that a certain economic action will take place. In other types of society, economic action may also be oriented to the clan, the political order, and the religious order.

economic actor but] *in addition* to the conventional and legal rules which he recognizes as valid, that is, of which he knows that a violation on his part would call forth a given reaction of other persons."[17] This dual orientation, so to speak, is by no means unique to economic phenomena that involve the legal order; when a party receives money in a transaction, for example, he or she also assumes that other actors will accept it in future transactions. The effect of being oriented not only to another economic actor but also to the legal order, Weber notes, is that an economic action is more likely to take place as intended. This, of course, is the heart of the matter: thanks to law, promises will be kept more often and property will be better defended (see figure 4.2).[18]

Weber brings up a second form of direct relationship between law and economy in his discussion of what he calls "the power of control and disposal." Each economic order, he notes, entails a certain de facto distribution of control over economic resources, and each economic action affects this distribution. In a market economy the control of these resources is typically transferred through contracts—and this is where law and economy come into direct contact with one another. The transmission of "power of control and disposal" through contracts, Weber says, "is the principal source of the relation of economic action to the law."[19]

A third type of direct connection between law and economy is also to be found in Part 1 of *Economy and Society*—namely, in Weber's discussion of the conditions necessary for maximum formal rationality in capital accounting. Of the eight conditions enumerated, two bear directly on law. First, there has to be "substantive freedom of contract," by which Weber means that there should exist no substantive or (formally) irrational regulation of consumption, production, and prices. Second, there must be "complete calculability of . . . the legal order and a reliable, purely formal guarantee of all contracts by the public authority."[20] Quite a bit can be said about each of these two conditions. What they have in common, however, is that they make the legal order more predictable and thereby more attuned to rational capitalism.

The second place where Weber discusses the general relationship between law and economy is, as earlier mentioned, in an article entitled "The Economy and Social Norms." He points out that jurisprudence and the sociology of law are concerned with different aspects of law: while jurisprudence is in principle concerned with what *should* happen, the sociology of law is concerned with what *does happen.* The basic function of law in economic life, viewed from the perspective of sociology, is described in the following manner: "The empirical validity of a norm as a legal norm affects the interests of an individual in many respects. In particular, it may convey to an individual certain calculable chances of having economic goods available or of acquiring them under certain conditions in the future."[21]

Several interesting implications follow from looking at law as a way of increasing the probability that some action will indeed take place. For one thing, businessmen may dispense with legal forms, if they feel sure that the transaction will take place anyway (as they often do, Weber adds).[22] This confidence also explains why new forms of economic behavior may come into being long before there is any relevant legislation. In addition, it is not at all assumed in Weber's argument that people do something primarily because they wish to obey the law; in many economic situations, for example, the main reason people engage in a certain behavior is self-interest rather than obedience to authority.[23] Finally, Weber also points out that it is admissible in economic theory to disregard the legal environment (as well as other norms) in its models. All that matters to economic theory, Weber says, is that some behavior indeed takes place—not the various reasons why it does (usage, custom, convention, law, self-interest, and so on). This last argument—that "economic theory . . . properly disregards the character of the [legal] norms to some extent"—is usually not mentioned in discussions of Weber and economics, but it represents an important clarification of why economic theory can ignore the impact of law in its arguments.[24]

A large part of "The Economy and Social Norms" is devoted to a critique of Rudolf Stammler's famous work on the relationship between law and economics in Marxism.[25] One of Stammler's primary errors, Weber says, is to argue as if sociology and jurisprudence deal with the same issue, namely the normative validity of law. Another error is to assume that law determines economic life, in the sense that the legal structure of a society constitutes its "form" and the economy its "substance." To argue that law in this sense can shape the content of the economy is wrong, according to Weber. Equally untenable, he adds, is the reverse argument of the Marxists, namely that the economy determines the superstructure, including law. In Weber's view, the relationships that do exist between law and economy are complex; there are no one-to-one correlations, and causality does not go only one way, as Stammler and the Marxists claim.

At the end of "The Economy and Social Norms" Weber supplies a short catalogue of what he calls "the most general relationships between law and economy."[26] These six points are meant as correctives to the simplistic ideas of people like Marx, Stammler, and their followers.[27] (1) Weber points out that law tends to protect economic interests, since important social groups usually have important material interests. (2) Law, however, defends not only economic interests, but also a variety of other interests, such as honor, religious authority, and personal safety. (3) Economic relations in society can also undergo a radical transformation, Weber notes, without there being any corresponding change in the legal system. (4) But just as it would be wrong to see law exclusively as the product of economic forces, Weber says, the opposite argument is also wrong, namely that the economy is the product of legislation by the state. There are definite limits to how much the state can influence the economy through legal interventions. (5) It is also clear that legal protection of important economic phenomena can be provided by agencies other than the state. (6) Finally, Weber says, an economic phenomenon can be given a new legal interpretation or classification without this having any practical consequences for the economy.

II. Law and Economy in Major Legal Systems throughout History

Weber's most important contribution to the sociology of law is generally considered to be a book-length manuscript found among his literary effects and later incorporated into Part 2 of *Economy and Society* under the title "Sociology of Law (Economy and Law)." Weber probably wrote this manuscript during the years 1911–13 but did not have time to revise it for the new edition of *Economy and Society* he was preparing at the time of his death. While the emphasis in Part 1 of *Economy and Society* and in "The Economy and Social Norms" is on the general relationship between law and economy, in the unrevised manuscript it is on law and economy from a historical perspective. Weber, it seems, was primarily interested in two questions: What role has the economy played in the general evolution of law? And what can different legal systems, such as Roman law, canon law, and others, teach us about the relationship between law and economy?

The first of these two questions—how has law evolved throughout history, and what role has the economy played in its evolution?—can best be approached by looking at Weber's general scheme of how law has developed. This scheme is presented toward the end of Weber's manuscript and sums up much of his analysis.[28] According to Weber, legal history can be divided into four stages for heuristic purposes. Early in history, he says, there was "legal revelation through 'law prophets'" (Stage 1). This was followed by "empirical creation and finding of law by legal honoratiores" (Stage 2); and later by "the imposition of law by secular and theocratic powers" (Stage 3). The modern legal situation is characterized by "the systematic elaboration of law and professionalized administration of justice by people who have received legal training in a learned and formally logical manner" (Stage 4).

The formal qualities of law, Weber says, have grown stronger throughout history, and one can speak of a general tendency for law to become ever more systematized, specialized, and logical. Weber in particular emphasizes the central role that various types of legal experts, such as legal honoratiores and professionals with a formal legal education, have played in this process. As to economic forces, he makes a distinction between bourgeois groups on the one hand, and economic factors or conditions on the other. The influence of the latter has primarily been "indirect"; "economic conditions have . . . everywhere played an important role, but they have nowhere been decisive alone and by themselves."[29]

Bourgeois groups have played a more active role in the evolution of law, according to Weber, and have especially pushed for a rationalization of the law, insofar as this has meant a more "calculable law."[30] Economic interest groups cannot, however, create legal concepts at will and, in this sense, their impact has been "indirect" as well. Weber puts the last point in the following way:

> Like the technological methods of industry, the rational patterns of legal technique to which the law is to give its guaranty must first be "invented" before they can serve an existing economic interest. Hence the specific type of techniques used in a legal system or, in other words, its modes of thought are of far greater significance for the likelihood that a certain legal institution will be invented in its context than is ordinarily believed.[31]

In order to clarify what he means by the increase of rationality during the course of legal history, Weber introduces a series of distinctions that are central to his sociology of law and of interest for his analysis of law and economy as well. From an ideal-typical point of view, he says, law can be either formally rational or formally irrational.[32] Law is formally rational when the general characteristics of a particular case are taken into account; and it is formally irrational when the legal reasoning is not controlled by the intellect. An example of the latter would be when an oracle is used to decide a case. Law can also be either substantively rational or substantively irrational. The former means that nonlegal norms are introduced into the legal process and influence the formal legal reasoning, and the latter that each case is decided differently using nonlegal norms for guidance.

It is sometimes noted in the secondary literature that Weber's four ideal types roughly correspond to his four stages in the historical evolution of law. The legal prophets, for example, who are found early in history, produced a type of law that was formally irrational and not controlled by the intellect (Stage 1). Gradually, the legal process became substantively irrational or more empirical, but was still very much influenced by nonlegal norms (Stage 2). Patrimonial and theocratic powers tended to impose a systematized form of law, which was deeply influenced by nonlegal values and hence substantively rational (Stage 3). And finally, in modern times a formally rational type of law has emerged, thanks mainly to the legal professionals (Stage 4).

It is also clear that each of Weber's four ideal types of law is more or less compatible with different forms of capitalism. Substantively rational law, for example, is compatible with all forms of political capitalism and speculative trade cap-

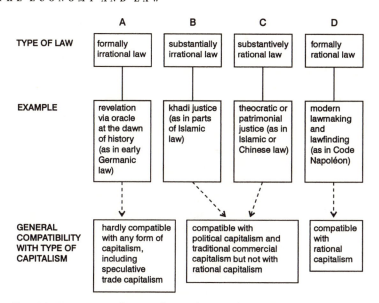

Fig. 4.3. Law, Form of Rationality, and Type of Capitalism

Source: Max Weber, *Economy and Society* (Berkeley: University of California Press, 1978), pp. 164–66, 656–58; Max Weber, *General Economic History* (New Brunswick, N.J.: Transaction Books, 1981), pp. 340–41.

Comment: According to Weber there is a certain compatibility between law, its form of rationality, and type of capitalism. Only formally rational law is compatible with rational capitalism; formally irrational law is not compatible with any kind of capitalism. Both substantively rational and substantively irrational law are incompatible with rational capitalism.

italism, but not with rational capitalism; formally rational law is compatible only with rational capitalism; and so on (see figure 4.3). It must, however, not be forgotten that Weber introduced his four ideal types of law for heuristic purposes and not to summarize concrete historical processes. The scheme in Figure 4.3 should be used in a similar spirit.

But Weber was not only interested in the general evolution of law; he also looked at a number of concrete legal systems and analyzed their relationship to the economy. In studying different legal systems from this angle, Weber cast his net very wide, both geographically and in time. He looked, for example, at Indian law, Chinese law, and Roman law and even mentions the regulation of economic affairs according to Mesopotamian law.[33] Since one of the problems he was most interested in was the role that law has played in the evolution of Western capitalism, he drew a rough line between legal systems that have helped such a capitalism to emerge and those that have not. The three most important legal systems to have obstructed the emergence of rational capitalism were in Weber's mind Indian law, Chinese law, and Islamic law.

Indian law was to a large extent controlled by the Hindu priesthood, and there existed no special stratum of specially trained jurists.[34] As a result, law was sacred and its formal-juristic qualities were not well developed. Religious values infused most of the legal system, and these values often ran counter to economic rationality. At one point Weber notes, for example, that "a ritual law in which every change of occupation, every change in work technique, may result in ritual degradation is certainly not capable of giving birth to economic and technical revolutions from within itself, or even of facilitating the first germination of capitalism in its midst."[35] But this does not mean that Indian law always favored religious values over economic values when the two clashed; and in certain cases where caste law ran counter to strong economic or personal interests it was simply changed. When it came to having servants, for example, it did not matter according to caste law whether they were impure or not; and different castes that ordinarily would not have had any contact with one another were similarly allowed to mix in the workshop.[36]

In describing the state of Indian law in the Middle Ages, Weber says that it was astonishingly poorly developed and characterized by a mixture of irrationality and magic. The law regulating economic affairs tended, however, to be in better shape. Heirs inherited the debts of relatives, but only for a few generations. At the same time, there were no legal rules about joint liability of business partners, and unconditional credit was given only to relatives. The legal concepts of corporations and other economic associations were also poorly developed.

Summing up the situation in India sometime later in history, Weber says that even if the law allowed commerce to take place, it did not actively promote trade. The reason for this was that Hinduism prevented the development of a more positive attitude toward capitalism, including capitalist legislation. For a long time, for example, a creditor who had difficulty getting paid would go to the debtor's home and there either hang himself or sit at the threshold of the house and slowly starve himself to death. Through these measures the creditor hoped to force his clan to intervene on his behalf and thereby increase the pressure on the debtor.

Chinese law has also constituted an obstacle to rational capitalism. Although it was not religious in character, it nonetheless has some important parallels to Indian law. [37] In China, there existed, for example, neither an independent stratum of jurists nor a tradition of formal justice. The mandarins feared that written laws would encourage insubordination among the population and tended therefore to avoid formal legislation. The few collections of Chinese laws that do exist, Weber says, consist to a large part of ethical rules and testify more to the high literary culture of the mandarins than to their legal skills. Much of the economy was controlled by two very resilient forces that have dominated Chinese society throughout history: the clan and the patrimonial state, with the emperor at the head. The strong position of magic in Chinese society also prevented legal rationality from emerging.

In general, legal institutions were poorly developed in China, and the ones that did exist, Weber says, typically lacked stability and security. There was private property in goods, but it had taken a very long time to develop. Land, however, could only be sold on condition that the clan had the right to buy it back. A partner in an economic partnership could not make a deal for which the other partners were also responsible; and it was not possible for a partner to limit his economic responsibility to a particular sum of money. The legal forms of business enterprises were on the whole poorly developed. What ultimately prevented Chinese law from developing in a more formal and pro-capitalistic direction, Weber says, was its patrimonial character. The ruler and his mandarins had tremendous power, and their only competition was the clan. The main influence of the patrimonial state on the legal system, Weber argues, was to make Chinese law formless and give it an economically irrational character. If someone, for example, sold a house to another person, the seller could show up many years later, when he had become poor, and demand to live in the house. He would then be accepted as a nonpaying border because of fears that the ancestral spirits would otherwise be disturbed. Weber comments: "Capitalism cannot operate on a basis so constructed. What it requires is law which can be counted upon, like a machine; ritualistic-religious and magical considerations must be excluded."[38]

Islamic law was similar to Indian law in that it was a sacred law, but it differed in that Islam early developed a written code and also had a stratum of trained jurists.[39] Formally, all law was based on the Qu'ran, but in reality it had been developed by jurists. Sacred values thoroughly infused Islamic law, however, and made it lifeless and difficult to apply. Legal experts often had to be consulted for its interpretation in concrete cases, but because they did not have to state their opinions those opinions tended to be unpredictable and to resist systematization. Islamic law, in brief, did not encourage rational capitalism because of several factors: the law was sacred or substantively rational; the legal system was at the mercy of patrimonial rulers; and the legal experts did not have to state their opinions when consulted.

Islamic commercial law, Weber says, was secular and innovative and played a progressive role in the legal development of capitalism. From the various legal techniques that existed in late antiquity, commercial legal institutions were created, several of which were later taken over by the West. What stopped this innovative spirit from further developing and spreading to the rest of the law, Weber says, is that it lacked official protection. Islamic merchants had to police the law themselves, a little like their Western counterparts with the law merchant. Unlike the merchants in the West, however, the Islamic merchants did not have the backing of powerful city states and were easily dominated by the patrimonial ruler.

That the combination of patrimonial rule and sacred law would result in a law that was formally irrational was not much of a surprise to Weber. One aspect of Islamic law that fascinated him, however, was that it also had a third source of irrationality: the judge, or *quadi,* whose task it was to interpret the law and determine its meaning in concrete cases. The *quadi* only handled cases that were covered by religious law, such as marriage, divorce, and inheritance; and he decided these in an extremely formalistic manner. It should be noted, however, that Weber tended to use the concept of *"quadi* justice" in a wider and somewhat different meaning than the kind of justice that was made by the local Islamic judge. To Weber the concept of *"quadi* justice" embodied a very special attitude to law that could be found all over the world. More precisely, it meant that judgments were made according to the judge's own sense of equity in the particular case and with no regard for formal rules.[40] While political capitalism and speculative trade capitalism might be able to coexist with such a type of justice, it was definitely "uncongenial" to rational capitalism.[41]

Judaism has helped in indirect ways to prepare the road for Western capitalism, according to Weber, but not through its legal system.[42] Jewish law, for example, did not have a high degree of formal rationality. Weber also took pains to refute the argument that the Jews had invented some of the most important legal institutions of capitalism, as Werner Sombart claimed. There was no proof, for example, that instruments payable to the bearer or modern securities had their origin in Jewish law. Instruments payable to the bearer existed already in early Babylonian law and modern securities drew heavily on medieval procedural law. In Weber's mind, not one legal institution that was central to capitalism could be traced back to Jewish law. At the most, the Jews had helped transmit certain forms of business enterprise from the Orient to the West—but not even that was certain.[43]

Weber not only investigated the relationship between Jewish law and the evolution of capitalism; he also looked at the relationship between law and economy on a more everyday level in Jewish culture. *Ancient Judaism* (1918–20), especially, contains a wealth of information on early Jewish law. Weber here notes that an important legal dimension to Judaism was the concept of *"berith"* or covenant; the Jewish people had a special oathbound or contract-like agreement with God, which profoundly affected their lives. Jewish piety was deeply legalistic, and the beginnings of a social legislation existed in Israel, with economic protection for widows, servants, and slaves. The idea of a sabbatical year was also part of the social legislation and had a number of important economic consequences for agriculture, land ownership, and debt prisoners.

According to Weber, collections of law such as the Book of the Covenant and Deuteronomy contain a wealth of information about social and economic development. Legal collections of this type indicate what kind of conflicts over property were likely to occur, how debts were to be regulated, and much more. Weber draws particular attention to one legal institution that was later to be decisive for the economic role of the Jews in capitalism, namely that an Israeli must not take interest from another Israeli. This prohibition, Weber says, went back to the old neighborhood ethics, according to which one must help a brother in need. However, it also allowed the Jews to collect interest from non-Jews and thereby contributed to the development of a strongly dualistic economic ethic in Judaism.

Canon law—by which is meant the body of legal rules of the Roman Catholic and Orthodox churches—was rationalistic and formalistic in spirit and differed in this respect sharply from Jewish law.[44] There were many reasons why canon law had become so rationalistic, according to Weber, and the most important had to do with the influence of Roman law on Christianity. The early Church admired Roman law; it also absorbed and reproduced aspects of Roman law through its own very rational organization, the Catholic Church. Canon law influenced the economy in three ways, Weber says: it recognized informal contracts; it advocated the freedom of testation (for easily understood reasons); and it helped to introduce a religious concept of public corporation, which later influenced the secular concept of the enterprise. Weber also mentions the legal prohibition against usury and notes that it was present in all the major religions.[45] For a variety of reasons, however, the Church itself helped to diminish the effectiveness of this prohibition, and the medieval merchants also devised a number of ways to circumvent it. In general, Weber concludes, canon law had very little influence on economic realities, and its special place in the history of law is mainly due to its high level of legal formalism.

As Weber saw it, only the West had developed a thoroughly rational and predictable kind of law, and *Roman law* represents its finest achievement as well as its foundation.[46] Roman law was secular in nature and became rational in stages. There was first the Republic, during which law was empirical; then came the Empire, during which the administrative machinery helped to initiate a considerably more formal kind of law; and finally there was the Reception of Roman law during the Middle Ages, when the formal and rationalistic qualities of Roman law burst into full bloom. But despite its many qualities, Roman law was not the source of any of the major legal institutions on which modern capitalism rests. Commercial legislation was quite primitive during the Republic as well as the Empire. Agency was next to impossible; there were no negotiable instruments; and the concept of the private corporation practically did not exist. The only way to limit one's liability, for example, was through a legal institution called *peculium,* which allowed a slave to do business on behalf of his master and lose no more of his master's money than the original investment. Weber concludes, "Ancient Roman commerce apparently could and had to get along without . . . technical devices, which seem indispensable to us today."[47]

It was not until the Reception in the Middle Ages that the formalistic and rational qualities of Roman law were fully developed. A number of basic legal concept were worked out, such as the notions that law is a gapless system and that a legal concept is applicable in different circumstances. The famous Roman concept of *dominium* or ownership also comes from this period and not from antiquity. The Reception of Roman law had, first of all, political and administrative reasons; kings and princes wanted Roman law, among other things, for prestige and because it increased the efficiency of their administrations. Jurists played a key role as well, especially the Italian notaries who had kept Roman law alive after the fall of the Western Empire. Economic forces, however, did not play much of a role in the Reception, Weber says.

Medieval law—especially medieval commercial law—was not much influenced by Roman law, according to Weber.[48] One reason was that economic institutions were so poorly developed in Roman law, and another was that it was not always to the advantage for businessmen to use the formally most rational type of law. "The consequences of the purely logical construction," Weber notes, "often bear very irrational or even unforeseen relations to the expectations of the commercial interests."[49] Weber also points out that certain "backward" elements in medieval law had actually turned out to be very helpful in economic affairs. The examples he mentions are: readiness to recognize separate funds in a variety of contexts; the idea that it is possible to hold whole groups responsible for something; and the use of instruments in writings, which draws on the magic attributed to certain objects in archaic law.

Weber always insisted that the major legal institutions, on which modern capitalism rests, have their origin in medieval law and not in Roman law. More precisely, they had typically been developed by merchants living in independent cities with their own autonomous legal systems. The accomplishments of the medieval merchants in establishing commercial law were truly amazing, according to Weber. Summing up the contributions that medieval law has made to modern capitalism, he wrote:

> The characteristically amateurish notion of the littérateurs that "Roman law" promoted the development of capitalism belongs in the nursery. Every student is obliged to know that all the characteristic legal institutions of modern capitalism were completely unknown under Roman law and are medieval in origin, to a considerable degree even specifically Germanic, and that Roman law has never gained a foothold in England, the motherland of modern capitalism. These institutions include shares, bonds, the modern law on the use of land as a security, bills of exchange and all forms of commercial documents up to and including the capitalist forms of association in industry, mining and trade. [50]

Natural law is another type of law that is unique to the West and that has helped to develop the formal side of Western law.[51] From a sociological viewpoint, natural law can be characterized as a number of legal principles that do not have their origin in ordinary lawmaking and are seen as valid independently of positive law. Weber paid little attention to the early forms of natural law and concentrated instead on modern times, from the Renaissance onward. He was especially interested in the Rights of Man and claimed, together with his friend, the jurist Georg Jellinek, that the freedom of conscience was the most basic of these rights and perhaps also the oldest.[52] Several economic rights were later added to the freedom of conscience, such as the freedom of contract and the inviolability of individual property. The Rights of Man had made a unique contribution to Western freedom, in Weber's mind, but he was also quite clear that they had played a role in the rise of the bourgeoisie. "The basic Rights of Man made it possible to use things and men freely," he noted drily; "they facilitated the expansion of capitalism."[53]

Natural law was abstract; it was valid for all individuals; and it had helped to undermine local laws as well as laws that were valid only for certain groups of people. Weber made a distinction between formal natural law and substantive natural law. The contract was the prototype of formal natural law, and the emphasis here was on the way that something had originated. Property and money, for example, were legitimized through their origin in contracts. In contrast, substantive natural law focused on content rather than on form and can be exemplified by the notion that wealth can be created only through the individual's own labor. Three rights derived from this principle: the right to work, the right to a minimum standard of living, and the right to the full product of one's labor. Weber called these rights the "'socialist' rights of the individual."[54] The natural law type of thinking, however, soon disappeared from the socialist doctrine, and it also played little role around the turn of the century, according to Weber. There still existed a latent influence of natural law in the West, but that was all.

• • •

It is clear that Weber paid quite a bit of attention to law and economy in his sociology of law. In describing legal systems from ancient China to modern Europe, Weber covered enormous territory but still succeeded in making a number of penetrating observations on the relationship between legal and economic factors. Many of these observations could easily be expanded into major studies in law and economy—for example, what Weber says about the innovative commercial legislation of Islamic merchants, the role of economic factors in the Reception of Roman law, and the centrality of labor in socialist natural law. Weber also makes a number of additional observations that I have not mentioned but that are equally suggestive. One of these is Weber's observation that some of the legal institutions in Indian law could have fostered a capitalist take-off; and another is that the Protestant sects developed a legal-religious argument for prices being set through competition in the market, which went directly counter to the medieval notion of a just price.[55]

It is also clear from Weber's sociology of law that although Weber was sensitive to the individual profile of each legal system, he pursued certain themes in all of them. Some of these themes are of special interest to law and economy, such as the type of commercial legislation in each legal system, its level of formal rationality, and its potential contribution to the emergence of rational capitalism. Figure 4.4 summarizes Weber's observations on these three issues. From this figure we see, for example, that the sacred legal systems made very little contribution to the rise of rational capitalism, that their commercial laws were not well developed, and that their level of formal rationality was low (with the exception of canon law). This roughly agrees with Weber's opinion that sacred law tends to obstruct the emergence of economic rationality. There are several reasons for this: religious law typically prohibits certain economic activities, it rejects change, and it is unpredictable when it comes to issues that are not explicitly mentioned in the law.[56] A phenomenon that stands out very clearly in figure 4.4 is furthermore that sophisticated commercial legislation tends to be accompanied by a *low* level of formal rationality, and vice versa. The two examples that show this the most clearly are Roman law and medieval law. Although Roman

	LEVEL OF FORMAL LEGAL RATIONALITY	STATUS OF COMMERCIAL LEGISLATION	CONTRIBUTION TO THE RISE OF RATIONAL CAPITALISM
INDIAN LAW	low level due to the influence of sacred law and absence of specially trained legal experts	potentially important, but in actuality not well developed	no independent contribution
CHINESE LAW	low level due to the influence of magic, patrimonialism and the absence of specially trained legal experts	not well developed	no independent contribution
ISLAMIC LAW	low level due to the influence of sacred law, patrimonialism, and the *quadi*	innovative legislation by Islamic merchants	some institutions from commercial law were taken over by the West
JEWISH LAW	low level due to the influence of sacred law	not well developed; strongly dualistic economic ethic	no independent contribution
CANON LAW	high level due to the impact of Roman law and the Catholic Church	poorly developed; its law on usury was not effective	no independent contribution
ROMAN LAW	high level; the foundation for formal law in the West	no advanced commercial legislation	a few contributions, including the notion of dominium
MEDIEVAL LAW	low level; very pragmatic in nature	created all the characteristic legal institutions of modern capitalism	a great number of contributions to the legal foundation of rational capitalism
NATURAL LAW	several rational aspects	important philosophical-legal ideas on the contract, property, and the like	helped to pave the road for capitalism, e.g., through the Rights of Man

law laid the foundation for legal formalism in the West, it failed to develop some of the major legal institutions on which modern capitalism is based; and although medieval law created all of these institutions, it was rudimentary from a formal viewpoint. In the next section of this chapter, which is devoted to modern law and capitalism, the question whether there is indeed a contradiction in Weber's work between rational capitalism and legal formalism (the England Problem) is further discussed.

III. The Relationship between Law and Modern Capitalism (Including the England Problem)

Weber's analysis of the relationship between modern law and modern rational capitalism represents one of the most difficult aspects of his work on law and economy, as the discussion of the England Problem shows. Here I argue that one way of approaching Weber's analysis on this topic, which allows one to avoid certain pitfalls, is to begin with Weber's analysis of rational capitalism and its legal prerequisites in Part 1 of *Economy and Society,* rather than with the book-length chapter on the sociology of law. This approach allows one to take Weber's last formulations as the point of departure rather than his unrevised chapter in the sociology of law; and the focus is from the very beginning on the link between capitalism and law, not on the general evolution and rationalization of the law.

Weber, to recall, portrays the essence of modern rational capitalism in Part 1 of *Economy and Society* as a form of systematic buying and selling in the market by rational enterprises. A closer look reveals that Weber believed that rational or modern capitalism has three legal prerequisites: (1) there must be *advanced commercial contracts* through which systematic as well as rational buying and selling can take place; (2) there must be *a legal concept of the modern corporation;* and (3) there must be *a calculable legal order.*[57] In the rest of this chapter I present Weber's view on each of these three legal prerequisites for modern capitalism as a prelude to a discussion of the England Problem.

Fig. 4.4 *(left).* Legal Systems throughout History: Level of Formal Legal Rationality, Status of Commercial Legislation, and Contribution to the Rise of Rational Capitalism

Source: For exact references to the different legal systems, see the endnotes to the text in section II of this chapter.

Comment: In his sociology of law in *Economy and Society,* Weber analyzes some of the major legal systems throughout history, such as Chinese law, Indian law, Roman law, and canon law. Weber looks at their commercial legislation as well as their contribution to the rise of modern capitalism more generally. Sophisticated commercial legislation has tended to be accompanied by a low level of formal rationality and vice versa, to judge from Weber's argument.

Legal Prerequisite #1 for Modern Capitalism:
Advanced Commercial Contracts

The reader may recall that Weber basically saw law (from a sociological perspective) as a way of increasing the likelihood that a certain action will take place as intended; and that an economic action is primarily oriented to another economic actor, while the legal order is simultaneously taken into account (see figure 4.2). If this perspective is applied to Weber's analysis of the role of law in modern rational capitalism, we get the following picture. A rational economic action is typically driven by material interests; it is primarily oriented to another economic actor; and it usually takes the legal form of a contract. The legal order is simultaneously taken into account, and it operates in a perfectly predictable manner. The economic actors are as a rule rational enterprises; and the legal order is managed by legal experts (see figure 4.5).

Weber's discussion of the three legal prerequisites for modern capitalism occupies an important part of the chapter on sociology of law in *Economy and Society*. This is particularly true for the contract, to which a very extensive section is devoted.[58] The contract has its historical origin in disputes between different kinship groups within the same political community and is defined by Weber as "a voluntary agreement constituting the legal foundation of claims and obligations."[59] What is remarkable about the contract from a sociological viewpoint, Weber points out, is that it both increases the certainty that some social action will take place and—and this is what makes it unique— allows one to create new legal relationships through voluntary agreement. In relation to the economy, this means that a contract can create new economic relations, and that these relations are ultimately guaranteed by the state. More precisely, in an advanced capitalist economy, the law provides the legal actors with a kind of space, within which they are allowed to form new economic relations by shifting around economic power and control through contracts.[60]

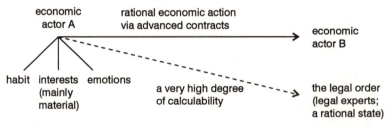

Fig. 4.5. The Role of Law in Modern Rational Capitalism
   Source: Max Weber, *Economy and Society* (Berkeley: University of California Press, 1978), pp. 33, 109–14, 161–66.
   Comment: The primary orientation of economic (social) actions is toward some other economic actor, although the legal order is taken into consideration as well. The economic actor is always an individual, but he or she may be acting on behalf of a corporation.

Weber distinguishes between two kinds of contracts: "the status contract," which is typical for primitive society, and "the purposive contract," which is typical for more advanced societies. A status contract addresses a person's total legal situation and entails a change from one status to another, say, to become someone's slave, wife, or vassal. Status contracts are common in economies that are self-sufficient and rarely touch on economic matters, apart from inheritance and other family issues. Purposive contracts are different from status contracts; they do not address a person's whole legal status, they are secular, and they "aim solely . . . at some specific (especially economic) performance or result."[61] Purposive contracts have close links to the market and have become more common as well as more complex with the expansion of the market. In this process, the purposive contract has been highly influenced by actors with strong market interests. We live today in a "contractual society," Weber says, where the purposive contract has more or less eliminated the status contract.[62] Inheritance is one of the few status contracts that still exists and is of economic importance.

Modern rational capitalism can only coexist with highly sophisticated purposive contracts, and it has taken many centuries for these to develop.[63] Barter was the first form of the purposive contract, and it was constructed primarily on the basis of possession. No obligations were involved, and possession was simply switched from one person to another. The money contract was a step forward in the sense that it is more precise and also more abstract. "The money contract," Weber says, "represents the archetype of the purposive contract."[64] The original money contract, however, contained no promissory elements and had a very simple legal structure. The notion of obligation, which is central to the very idea of the contract, comes originally from criminal law, Weber notes. *Wergilt* is an example: if you commit a certain wrong, you are obliged to pay a certain sum of money. The notions of obligation and efficient execution were slowly introduced into the contract. An individual was, for example, originally responsible for a contract with his physical person, not with his property. Weber cites several examples of how difficult it has been throughout history to get someone to pay back a debt, even when it was clear that the debtor did not lack assets. Originally, one's only resort was to seize the debtor in person, and then kill him, sell him, or keep him as a slave. "Where there were several creditors," Weber notes, "they could, as the Twelve Tables [in Roman law] show, cut him into pieces."[65]

But a commercial society needs contracts that are more sophisticated than simple enforceable money contracts, according to Weber. In particular, one must be able to transfer legal claims and to do so safely. Important steps in this direction were taken during the Middle Ages, when legal instruments payable to the bearer and to the order of the payee got their modern form through the influence of Roman, Germanic, and Arabic law. Weber also mentions that contractual relationships to third parties have gradually become regulated and that private contracts are nowadays viewed as a novel kind of special law, guaranteed by the modern state. But he says little more about the historical evolution of the contract than this, referring the reader instead to an article in the *Grundriss der Sozialökonomik,* "The Modern Private Legal Order and Capitalism."[66]

In describing the existing "contractual society," Weber emphasizes that the freedom to contract is primarily of a formal nature. What Weber has to say on this point is not very different from what Marx had said fifty years earlier in *Capital,* but deserves nonetheless to be mentioned.[67] To the worker, the freedom to enter into a contract with his or her employer is often illusory: "In the labor market, it is left to the 'free' discretion of the parties to accept the conditions imposed by those who are economically stronger by virtue of the legal guarantee of their property."[68] The property owners, on the other hand, benefit from the institution of contracts, which allow them to safeguard and increase their interests; "conditions of formal freedom are officially available to all; actually, however, they are accessible only to the owners of property and thus in effect support their very autonomy and power positions."[69] One difference between Weber and Marx is that Weber views this issue as one of formal versus substantive legal rationality, while for Marx it is exclusively a question of exploitation.

Legal Prerequisite #2 for Modern Capitalism: The Legal Concept of the Modern Corporation

If the first legal prerequisite for rational capitalism, according to Weber, is that there exist sophisticated contracts, the second is that the legal order can accommodate the rational corporation. According to Weber, the modern enterprise can be characterized as a legally autonomous organization that is part of a legal order dominated by the state. The modern enterprise can come into being only through permission by the state, but it nonetheless has its own distinct autonomy. From a legal point of view, the corporation belongs to the general category of contracts and constitutes, more precisely, a form of "associational contract." The modern enterprise can enter into contracts of its own and has a "legal personality."

The notion of legal personality is very interesting from a sociological perspective, and also very complex from a legal perspective. Its origin goes far back in Western legal history, and its evolution is much too difficult to summarize in a few sentences. Eventually, however, a rational form of legal personality appeared, and Weber describes it in the following manner:

> The most rational actualization of the idea of the legal personality of organizations consists in the complete separation of the legal spheres of the members from the separately constituted legal sphere of the organization; while certain persons designated according to rules are regarded from the legal point of view as alone authorized to assume obligations and acquire rights for the organization, the legal relations thus created do not at all affect the individual members and their property and are not regarded as their contracts, but all these relations are imputed to a separate and distinct body of assets.[70]

A modern economic enterprise constitutes a legal personality in this sense but in addition must fulfill the following two conditions: it must have capital, and its members must be able to share in its profits. In legal terms, this entails adher-

ing to a number of additional rules, especially about the members or sharehold-
ers of the corporation. In a profit-making enterprise, for example, the number
of members must be restricted, one should be able to transfer memberships, and
the members must have votes in direct proportion to their share of the capital.

From a legal viewpoint, today's enterprise represents the end product of a long
and complex historical development, which Weber traces in broad strokes. In
particular, he tries to show how two separate legal traditions have contributed to
the modern legal concept of the enterprise: one that has to do with the evolution of the notion of legally autonomous organizations, and another that deals
more specifically with the legal development of economic organizations.[71] In his
discussion of the notion of legally autonomous organizations, Weber looks especially at the German tradition of sodalities and how different kinds of autonomous organizations have been conceptualized in Roman law, English law,
and canon law. And in his account of the legal concept of economic organizations, Weber focuses in particular on the *commenda* and the joint-stock corporation as well as on a few separate legal features, such as joint liability and
limited liability.

With the corporation in mind, Weber briefly analyzes non-Western law too,
but largely with negative results. In India, for example, the law of separate organizations appeared late; it tended to involve religious organizations and was of
little legal consequence.[72] In China, the clan and the patrimonial state more or
less prevented any private organizations from appearing.[73] A kind of firm did develop in China, which had a special corporate name and where family resources
were pooled. Its purpose, however, was not to make a profit through trade or
production but to invest in the education of a bureaucrat and to purchase an office; and it is therefore not an example of rational capitalism but of political capitalism. In neither China, India, nor the Orient, Weber concludes, did private
economic organizations succeed in separating the enterprise from the family
unit; and no legal distinction was consequently drawn between the property of
family members and that of the economic enterprise.

A sophisticated legal theory of organizations was developed in Roman law, but
mainly in the political sphere. When it came to the economy, the situation was
quite different; and the only way for a Roman to invest a sum of money in an ordinary business venture was, as we know, through a slave (*peculium*). There did
exist autonomous economic organizations with their own legal structure in
Rome, Weber says, but their purpose was profit-making through tax farming,
and they did not fall under private law. This type of organization was closely
tied to the state and was a manifestation of political capitalism, not rational
capitalism.[74] Ordinary economic organizations were not legally recognized in
Roman law.

The great breakthrough for the legal concept of the private enterprise, Weber
says, came during the Middle Ages.[75] As the hold of the clan and the household
on the individual began to disintegrate, Italian jurists and merchants perfected
some old legal techniques and invented new ones that were essential for the
emergence of modern capitalism. It became possible to assign collective liabil-

ity through contract, to limit economic responsibility in a business enterprise to a specific amount, and to separate the property of an individual from the property of an enterprise. Weber points out:

> What is crucial [in these developments during the Middle Ages] is the separation of household and business for accounting and legal purposes, and the development of a suitable body of laws, such as the commercial register, elimination of dependence of the association and the firm upon the family, separate property of the private firm or limited partnership, and appropriate laws on bankruptcy.[76]

Many of the legal principles that had been devised during the Middle Ages did not become common practice until several centuries later. Limited liability, for example, was not accepted until the nineteenth century in England and on the Continent. But independent legal evolution of the firm also took place after the Middle Ages, especially in connection with the evolution of the joint-stock company. As the small trading units of the Mediterranean were replaced by ever larger industrial units in Northern Europe, their need for huge amounts of capital was eventually accommodated through the notion of the joint-stock company. Weber does not provide much detail about this development, but says that the technique of gathering together a large number of investors was first used by political organizations and by enterprises that had been granted monopolies by the state, such as the Dutch and British East India Companies.

Legal Prerequisite #3 for Modern Capitalism: A Calculable Legal Order

The third legal requirement for modern or rational capitalism consists of what Weber calls "calculable law."[77] The concept of "calculability" covers a host of phenomena in this context. For one thing, because rational capitalism is sensitive to disturbances of any sort, it is imperative that surprises be kept to a minimum. The state must not make arbitrary interventions in the economy through its legal system, but respect its autonomy. Property must be respected and contracts must not be broken (*pacta sunt servanda*). The law must also be clear and logical, and it should be administered in a professional and predictable manner. Calculability furthermore means that the legal system—in contrast to religious law—is predictable when it comes to matters that are not covered by the law. From early on, Weber says, bourgeois groups demanded

> an unambiguous and clear legal system, that would be free of irrational administrative arbitrariness as well as of irrational disturbance by concrete privileges, that would also offer firm guaranties of the legally binding nature of contract, and that, in consequence of all these features, would function in a *calculable* way.[78]

But even if bourgeois groups want a calculable law of this type, they have not created the current legal system, Weber points out. They have given some impetus in the direction of a calculable law, but two other forces have played a much more decisive role in the creation of the modern legal system: the patrimonial prince and the legal experts. Both of these have had their own "legal interests" throughout history, but they have also come to contribute to the emergence of a calculable law in the West, albeit often in an unintended manner.[79] The patrimonial prince, for example, wanted to replace the legal privileges of the estates with a more uniform type of law. He also had a financial interest in catering to bourgeois groups and their legal demands; and because he wanted a more efficient administration, he hired people with formal legal education who created a more rational legal procedure. Finally, in order to bring more order to his empire, the prince sometimes decided to codify its law. These codifications typically entailed an important unification and systematization of the existing laws.

Legal experts have primarily made Western law more calculable in two ways: by making legal administration more reliable, and by giving the law itself a more formal and logical structure. Weber does not say much about the first of these two contributions, except to emphasize the role that legal education has played in creating a dependable and professional group of administrators. Whether the law that is being taught is of a more formal nature, as on the Continent, or of a more empirical nature, as in England and the United States, matters little in this regard. Weber is also skeptical that common law necessarily results in a less calculable law than the formally rational law of the Continent. Jurists clearly have a predilection for the latter type of law, Weber notes (except when it conflicts with their professional and economic interests). The dominant economic groups in modern capitalism, however, have no particular interest in the law's being a gapless system of legal norms or the like; they just want a clear and calculable law. Weber sums up the last point in the following way:

> Practical needs, like those of the bourgeoisie, for a "calculable" law, which were decisive in the tendency towards a formal law as such, did not play any considerable role in [creating the idea of law as a gapless system]. As experience shows, these needs may be gratified quite as well, and often better, by a formal, empirical case law.[80]

The England Problem

It is now time to turn directly to the so-called England Problem. The notion that Weber's analysis of the relationship between law and capitalism contains a serious flaw, and that this comes out the most clearly in his analysis of England, was introduced into the debate of Weber's work in the early 1970s by a legal scholar, David Trubek.[81] Trubek's key argument is that according to Weber's scheme, capitalism demands a calculable law, and that Weber also equates calculability with formal legal rationality. This very "identification of calculability with logical formalism" in Weber's work, however, turns out to be problematic when it comes to England, Trubek says, where the law is characterized by a fairly low degree of formal legal rationality, even though it was in England that modern capitalism had its breakthrough.[82]

According to Trubek, Weber never gave up on his initial thesis that capitalism demands a high degree of formal legal rationality, but always tried to find ways to maintain it. England was consequently viewed as "the deviant case," and Weber cited a number of special historical circumstances as evidence of why it had been historically possible to unite capitalism with a low degree of formal legal rationality. Weber, for example, suggests that capitalists were favored in the English court system, while justice was denied to the lower classes. Trubek also cites Weber's statement that capitalism had been achieved in England "not because but rather in spite of its judicial system" (leaving out, it should be noted, Weber's qualifying remarks, including that this was only "to some extent" the case).[83]

The idea that an "England Problem" exists has come to dominate the debate during the past few decades, not only on capitalism and law in Weber's work but also on law and economy more generally.[84] Most scholars have, in one way or another, endorsed Trubek's thesis about the "identification of calculability with logical formalism" in Weber's analysis, and some have even added a few new arguments to the list that Weber supposedly produced to avoid changing his basic thesis. One of these novel arguments is that since there does not exist any direct link between law and economy, according to Weber, capitalism can take off under a number of different legal systems.[85] It has also been noted that Weber, from very early in his career, argued that businessmen want a law that is calculable and are uninterested in its level of formal rationality.[86]

My own position on the England Problem is that Trubek is mistaken in asserting that there is a necessary identity in Weber's work between calculability and a high degree of logical formalism or formal legal rationality. Weber makes clear that what bourgeois groups demand from the legal system is first and foremost that it is calculable, and that this demand is fully compatible with a low level of formal legal rationality. This is particularly the case with Weber's last works, in which he plainly states that English common law "while not rational . . . was *calculable*."[87] I also think that implicit in Trubek's formulation of the England Problem is a much too narrow view of the relationship between capitalism and law. For rational capitalism to exist, it is not enough that the law is calculable and that it has a high degree of formal rationality. In addition, there must be sophisticated legal rules about a variety of advanced economic institutions, especially contracts and economic enterprises. That Weber himself was of this opinion I have shown in the preceding discussion of legal prerequisites 1 and 2 (advanced commercial contracts and the legal concept of the modern corporation).

It is, finally, also surprising that Trubek and other participants in the debate over the England Problem treat the relationship between capitalism and law as if it were exclusively a theoretical problem, to be decided by a careful reading of Weber's work. Some of the issues involved are empirical rather than conceptual in nature, and these should be decided with the help of historical facts and not by referring to Weber's work. It can, for example, be noted that England is portrayed by most participants in the debate about the England Problem as if its legal system were a purely native one. In reality, however, England assimilated the law merchant very early into its legal system and thereby came to have many of the same legal rules for commerce as the Continent.[88] It has also been argued that Weber exaggerated the nonanalytical nature of English law, ignoring, for example, the treatises by Matthew Hale and William Blackstone.[89] Details need to be filled in to complete our understanding on these two points, and legal developments are notoriously complex. It nonetheless seems clear that the England Problem not only represents a polemical misreading of Weber's argument but also is based on a simplification of the legal history of England.

By way of concluding this chapter I would like to move beyond the England Problem and look at Weber's analysis of economy and law as a whole. In doing so, I am struck by its richness as well as by the enormous erudition that informs it. More research is naturally needed, on Weber's conceptual apparatus as well as on the historical dimension of his work. The comparative aspect of Weber's work on law has, for example, not been sufficiently appreciated; neither has the way that his sociology of law is informed by his notion of interest-driven social action. These tasks, however, should not detract from a realization even today that Weber's analysis represents a solid—and much needed—foundation for the analysis of law in contemporary economic sociology.

The Economy and Religion

WEBER was preoccupied with religious questions during much of his life, and according to his wife, his work testifies to "a permanent concern with religion."[1] A closer look at Weber's writings shows that he usually approached religion from the angle of its relationship to the economy. This is indeed true for *The Protestant Ethic and the Spirit of Capitalism*, which to many people has come to embody Weber's contribution to economic sociology. But it is also true for a number of his other writings, including the giant work entitled *The Economic Ethics of the World Religions* and the massive section on religion in *Economy and Society*. One of the main goals of this chapter is therefore to outline the *whole* analysis of economy and religion in Weber's work. I do this by discussing, besides *The Protestant Ethic* and the debates it has led to (in section II), Weber's general sociology of religion (in section I), and his analysis of the economic ethics of the world religions (in section III). I especially attempt to show that Weber's analysis contains—in addition to the spectacular thesis of *The Protestant Ethic*—a number of concepts and approaches that are very useful in analyzing the relationship between economy and religion from a sociological perspective. The general backdrop to this chapter, as to the preceding chapters, is Weber's conception of social action as a special form of interest-driven action. What Weber says about religion, it should be added, is also applicable to nonreligious forms of ideal interests, from humanism to more politically inspired ideologies.

I. AN INTRODUCTION TO WEBER'S ANALYSIS OF THE RELATIONSHIP BETWEEN THE ECONOMY AND RELIGION: CENTRAL THEMES AND CONCEPTS IN *ECONOMY AND SOCIETY*

Weber paints a magnificent panorama in the chapters on religion in *Economy and Society*, starting with the birth of religion and ending with the five great world religions, covering along the way such phenomena as priesthood, hierocracy, prophecy, and salvation.[2] Most of this material is not related to economic concerns and can perhaps best be characterized as an attempt, from Weber's side, to lay a foundation for the sociological study of religion. Quite a bit, however, does deal with the relationship between the economy and religion, and here too Weber's analysis is rich. In what follows I have selected what I consider to be the central themes in Weber's analysis of economy and religion, specifically:

the attitude toward riches in religion;

religious organizations and their relationship to economic affairs;

the religious propensity of certain socio-economic classes and strata; and

different ways to approach salvation and how these may affect the economy.

Weber also devotes quite a bit of space to two other, equally central themes, namely attitudes toward the economy in the great world religions and the relationship between economy and religion in the Reformation. Both of these topics are discussed later in this chapter, in connection with the analysis of *The Protestant Ethic* and *The Economic Ethics of the World Religions*.

Before presenting the first of these themes in Weber's analysis of economy and religion, something should be said about the general point of departure for his analysis of religious phenomena and how it is related to his concept of social action and interests. Since *Economy and Society* is a work in sociology, religious action is analyzed as a special form of social action or action oriented to the behavior of others. Religious social action, as well as religious action in general, is driven by a combination of ideal interests, habits, and emotions. Weber was furthermore concerned about eliminating value judgments from his analysis, and with this purpose in mind he looked for a term to express what attracted people to religion that was both fairly neutral and broad enough to encompass different types of religions. The term he chose for the final version of *Economy and Society* was "goods of salvation" or "*Heilsgüter*," which has deep roots in German theology and can be traced at least to the late sixteenth century.[3] Weber, however, used it to mean something closer to "*religious benefits*" (as it has been translated in *Economy and Society*) or "*religious goods*."[4] In economic theory the term "goods" covers any item for which there is a need or preference, and "religious benefits" similarly encompasses a variety of religious desirables, as Weber uses it. More precisely, Weber argues, religious benefits can be this-worldly or other-worldly as well as material or spiritual; and religious social action is defined as a form of action that is oriented simultaneously to some religious benefit and to other actors (see figures 5.1 and 5.2). The term "religious benefits" or "religious goods" also suited Weber's purposes well in that it gives associations to religious behavior as, to a certain extent, an interest-driven process, rather than one inspired by ideas.[5] This last point was very important to Weber and is also reflected in his use of such terms as "psychological premium [on certain religious behavior]" and "ideal interests," which are discussed later.

The first theme in Weber's sociology of religion in *Economy and Society*—the *attitude toward riches in religion*—is directly connected to his concept of religious benefits. In primitive religions, Weber points out, the benefits were typically material in nature and consisted of such things as a long life, health, and wealth.[6] This has also been true of more advanced religions, such as Hinduism, Buddhism, Islam, and Judaism. Except for ascetic movements and certain forms of Christianity, Weber says, religious benefits have tended to include material wealth. "Riches were the wages of piety," he notes in his discussion of early Judaism.[7]

RELIGIOUS BENEFITS

	THIS-WORLDLY	OTHER-WORLDLY
MATERIAL	primitive religions	
SPIRITUAL		advanced religions

Fig. 5.1. The Goal of Religious Action: "Religious Benefits" or "Religious Goods"

Source: Max Weber, *Economy and Society* (Berkeley: University of California Press, 1978), pp. 54–56.

Comment: Religious benefits (*Heilsgüter*) differ according to religion; they can be this-worldly or other-worldly as well as spiritual or material.

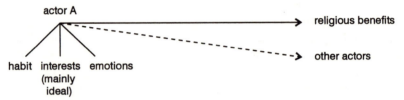

actor A

religious benefits

other actors

habit   interests   emotions
        (mainly
         ideal)

Fig. 5.2. The Structure of Religious Social Action, according to Weber

Source: Max Weber, *Economy and Society* (Berkeley: University of California Press, 1978), pp. 4, 22.

Comment: Religious social action takes place when an actor pursues religious benefits, driven mainly by ideal interests, while taking other actors into account.

Early forms of religion, Weber also says, tend to affect behavior, including economic behavior, in a "stereotyped" manner. "The first and fundamental effect of religious views upon the conduct of life and therefore upon economic activity was generally stereotyping."[8] By "stereotyping" Weber means that something gets "fixed or perpetuated in an unchanging form" (*Oxford English Dictionary*). Weber wrote around the turn of the century, before the modern concept of stereotype had come into being.[9] Using modern social science terminology, one could perhaps say that Weber's notion of stereotyping involves the labeling of a phenomenon, followed by a lock-in. A wide range of economic activities and goods can be stereotyped, according to Weber, including people's attitudes toward tools and products. The ways of stereotyping that mainly concern us here, however, are those that affect the attitude toward riches; and these include notions about acceptable types of trade and more generally, how individuals think wealth can be "honestly" acquired. When some economic activity is religiously stereotyped, Weber points out, the force of religion (that is, the incentive of religious benefits) is fused with the force of tradition (that is, the value of keeping things as they are), and the result is a formidable obstacle to economic innovation.

As history moves on, Weber says, religious stereotyping is eventually broken down, mainly through prophecy and religious rationalization. In more advanced religions, the religious benefits tend to be other-worldly and noneconomic, and religious activity itself is no longer seen exclusively in terms of ends and means, as it is in primitive religions. "The goal of religious behavior," Weber notes, "is successively 'irrationalized' until finally other-worldly non-economic goals come to represent what is distinctive about religious behavior."[10] As religious benefits become less economic and this-worldly in character, Weber adds, a general tension develops between religious values and the values of ordinary secular life. This tension can be resolved in a variety of ways; it usually also leads to a number of unintended consequences, which play a central role in Weber's analysis.

As religion becomes more advanced and rationalized, its attitude toward riches changes, Weber notes, especially toward riches that come from capitalist activities. At this point in his analysis Weber introduces the concept of "impersonality" ("*Unpersönlichkeit*") into his economic sociology.[11] All religions view personal relationships as central to life, he explains, and they try to regulate these relationships according to their vision of the need for *caritas* or charity toward the unfortunate. This vision draws on the old neighborhood ethic, according to which one should always try to help a brother in need.[12] But while it is possible to regulate certain economic relationships according to a religious vision of personal relationships and charity—such as the relationship between a master and his slave or between a patriarch and the members of his household—this is *not* the case, according to Weber, with most capitalist relationships. In a capitalist economy, people are typically related to one another less directly, such as a factory owner to the workers in the factory or a shareholder to the people who work for a corporation. There is also the crucial fact that if capitalist relationships were to be altered according to some notion of charity, economic difficulties would soon result. In a capitalist economy, Weber says, one must follow the rules of the market or go under—there is simply no place for *caritas*.

The second theme in *Economy and Society*—*religious organizations and their relationship to economic affairs*—is also directly connected to the notion of religious benefits or religious goods. "Hierocracy" is thus defined by Weber as the kind of organization "which enforces its order through psychic coercion by distributing or denying religious benefits."[13] A "church," according to *Economy and Society*, is similar to a hierocracy, but at a later and more rational stage of development. A sect uses religious benefits and psychic coercion as well, but is less universalistic than a church or a hierocracy. One cannot be born into a sect, as one can into a church or a hierocracy; and each person has to qualify on the basis of his or her individual merits.

The final type of religious organization Weber discusses in *Economy and Society* is the monastic order. He provides no formal definition of a monastic order, but one can perhaps characterize it as a sect in which the members devote the whole day to religious activities and often also live together.

Much of Weber's discussion of hierocracy is naturally devoted to its relationship to political power. Since the strength of a hierocracy is directly related to how much power the political authorities have, Weber says, this type of organization is typically opposed to an enlargement of the treasury of the prince and his troops. The religious power also often collides with the secular power over the issue of landholdings, which both of them like to accumulate. For that reason, the landholdings of the hierocracy are a source of tension in its relationship to the aristocracy. The relationship of the hierocracy to the bourgeoisie has been considerably better throughout history than to the aristocracy, because the hierocracy tends to introduce trust and stability into commercial life, which merchants appreciate. In antiquity, for example, temples were used as depositories for money and valuables, and during the Middle Ages religious authorities often lent money, relying on their reputation and control over religious benefits to ensure repayment. But there has also been some tension between the religious powers and the commercial classes, Weber says, in particular because the monasteries have had a much cheaper labor force at their disposal than their secular competitors.

Hierocracy has definitely affected economic development, Weber says, but less through its economic activities than through its general attitude to the secular world. A hierocracy is inherently traditionalistic and tends to stereotype its surroundings, including the economy, according to Weber. As a consequence, it is suspicious of all innovations and displays "a deep antipathy toward the nontraditional power of capitalism."[14] In other words, hierocracy often encourages economic traditionalism.

Typically, a church develops out of a hierocracy. Although a church is a later and more rational kind of organization, Weber says, its influence on economic development has nonetheless been fairly similar to that of hierocracy. Many churches all over the world have attempted to directly influence the economy through rules about usury and the notion of a just price, for example.[15] In the West, the prohibition against usury deeply influenced legislation and also created many problems for the merchants. But they found ways of circumventing it, and the prohibition against usury never succeeded in blocking capitalism. In the seventeenth century a Calvinist produced the first theoretical justification of usury, and in the following two centuries the Catholic Church reversed its position on lending money against a market-based rate of interest.

All in all, Weber says, the Western church did not have much of an economic program. In addition, "the church did not decisively influence economic institutions" and "it did not make or unmake [economic] institutions." The church did influence people's attitudes toward the economy—but mostly in a negative manner because the economic mentality it furthered was essentially traditionalistic. The church, like hierocracy more generally, has usually encouraged a "noncapitalistic and partly anti-capitalistic [mentality]," Weber concludes.[16]

Sects have influenced the economy somewhat differently from the church, largely owing to their unique sociological structure, according to Weber. By definition, a sect chooses its members, and it can control their behavior to an extent that is not possible for a church. A sect screens candidates for honesty, good character, and the like, and maintains a high ethical standard through a continuous and mutual scrutiny by its members. Membership in a sect has thus often been used as a sign of creditworthiness by secular economic institutions. Weber also points out that it was two sects—the Quakers and the Baptists—that introduced fixed prices in the West as an alternative to haggling.[17]

The fourth type of religious organization that Weber discusses in *Economy and Society* is the monastic order, and he distinguishes between two stages in its development. Early on, a monastic movement is typically charismatic in nature and anti-economic in spirit. Its members do not work for a living but live off donations and gifts; private property is also rejected. When routinization sets in, however, some agreement is often reached with the ruling church. The hostility to economic matters is weakened, and the order typically acquires property of its own.[18]

Routinization, however, does not mean that economic behavior in the monastic order becomes identical to that in the secular world. Weber points out that in the monasteries work was used as an ascetic tool for the first time. The monks often lived and worked in a methodical and self-controlled manner. Weber also describes how religious enthusiasm—especially in combination with a methodical approach to work, as existed in the monasteries—has resulted in a number of magnificent economic accomplishments that outstrip those that are possible through ordinary labor:

> The pyramids appear preposterous unless we realize that the subjects firmly believed in the king as god incarnate. The Mormon achievements in the salt desert of Utah violate all rules of rational settlement. This is all the more typical of the monastic achievements, which almost always accomplish that which appears economically not feasible. In the midst of the Tibetan snow and sand deserts Lamaist monasticism produced economic and architectural wonders that in magnitude, and apparently also in quality, measure up to the largest and most famous artifacts of men: witness the *Potala* [Palace in Lhasa].[19]

In his discussion of the third major theme in *Economy and Society*—*the religious propensity of certain socio-economic classes and strata*—Weber introduces two concepts that describe the different roles that religion plays for privileged and nonprivileged groups in society: "hope for compensation," which denotes what the nonprivileged strata want from religion; and "theodicy of good fortune," which explains why privileged groups are interested in religion.[20] Privileged groups, according to Weber, are fundamentally content with their position in society, and their sense of honor and self-esteem is closely connected to their *being*. The nonprivileged, in contrast, suffer from their current position in the world and focus their sense of honor or self-esteem on what they one day might *become*. As a consequence, nonprivileged groups have a need for a religion based on an ethic of compensation or what Weber calls "hope for compensation" and which he describes as fairly calculating in nature.

Privileged and successful groups need religion for a very different purpose, namely legitimation. Their members are convinced that they deserve their good fortune and that the poor deserve their misfortune. Weber calls this "the theodicy of good fortune" and explains it in the following manner:

> When a man who is happy compares his position with that of one who is unhappy, he is not content with the fact of his happiness, but desires something more, namely his right to this happiness, the consciousness that he has earned his good fortune, in contrast to the unfortunate one who must equally have earned his misfortune. Our everyday experience proves that there exists just such a need for psychic comfort about the legitimacy or deservedness of one's happiness, whether this involves political success, superior economic status, bodily health, success in the game of love, or anything else. What the privileged classes require of religion, if anything at all, is this legitimation.[21]

One of the most interesting aspects of Weber's discussion of the religious propensity of socio-economic classes and strata is that he also discusses the extent to which economic forces shape religion—the opposite causal direction, in other words, from the one in *The Protestant Ethic*. Weber was very critical of the Marxist argument that religion can be explained exclusively in terms of economic forces and he publicly said so.[22] His own position was more along the lines of his 1904 essay on objectivity: that religious phenomena at the most can constitute "economically conditioned phenomena," or "behavior in non-'economic' affairs [that] is partly influenced by economic motives." In other words, the religious behavior of various socio-economic strata and classes can never be completely explained through economic forces—only "partly" so.[23]

The nobility and warrior classes, according to Weber, have historically been prevented from developing a deep religiosity both by their strong sense of honor and by their frequent exposure to the unpredictable fortunes of war. At the most they would pray for military victory and for some protection against evil magic. The gods of the nobility were strong, passionate, and not very rational. As a consequence, the religion of the nobility tended to reinforce economic traditionalism. Something similar was also true for the peasants—but their economic traditionalism was enforced by their propensity for magic rather than for a pantheon of warring and jealous gods. Their attraction to magic, Weber explains, was a result of the peasants' being so close to the organic processes and unpredictable events of nature. For peasants to become truly religious, Weber says, something very powerful has to tear them away from their normal situation in life, such as enslavement or proletarianization. The idea that peasants are very religious people is a modern notion, as he points out (see figure 5.3 for the relationship between religion and economy among peasants and the aristocracy).

The work circumstances of the early artisans differed from those of the peasants, and so did their religious propensity. Artisans were much less exposed to the forces of nature: they typically worked indoors; they used different muscles

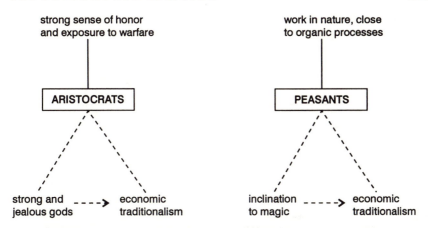

Fig. 5.3. Religious Propensity and Attitude toward Economic Life among Aristocrats and Peasants

Source: Max Weber, *Economy and Society* (Berkeley: University of California Press, 1978), pp. 468–76.

Comment: Through their religious propensities, peasants as well as aristocrats tend to encourage economic traditionalism.

to perform their work; and they had more opportunity to reflect on the nature of things. Furthermore, artisans often lived in the city, where blood bonds were many times replaced by new social relations. As a result, artisans tended to develop congregational and ethical types of religion, especially in the West, and these encouraged a rational lifestyle as well as a rational attitude in economic matters.

Though Weber makes clear that artisans and other petty bourgeois groups have embraced many religious experiences, from orgiasticism to mysticism, he also notes that it was from these strata that the Protestant ascetic sects would eventually emerge—and it was in these that a positive as well as a methodical religious attitude toward economic affairs would appear for the first time in history. The upper bourgeoisie, in contrast, had little interest in religion. Great merchants and early financiers had a worldly orientation to life and were skeptical toward or indifferent to religion. And while the ascetic elements in the middle classes often were positive about a rational type of capitalism, the upper strata tended to gravitate toward political capitalism, which lacked an ethical dimension (see figure 5.4).

Weber also discusses the religious propensity of two other groups in society: government officials and modern workers.[24] The former are sober rationalists and tend to be suspicious and distrustful of religious behavior. The Confucian official exemplified this type, Weber says; he had no need for transcendence himself, but thought that magic and religion were useful to control the masses. Government officials are also ambivalent about profit-making and tend to prefer economic traditionalism. Modern workers are equally uninterested in reli-

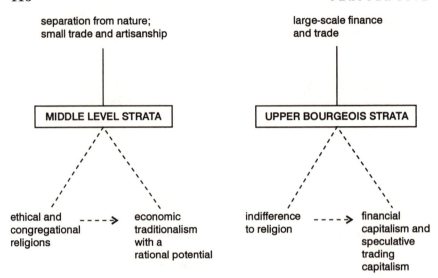

Fig. 5.4. Religious Propensity and Attitude toward Economic Life among Some Middle-Level and Upper-Bourgeois Strata

Source: Max Weber, *Economy and Society* (Berkeley: University of California Press, 1978), pp. 477–84, 1178–81.

Comment: While the ascetic elements in the middle classes often were receptive to a rational type of capitalism, the upper strata gravitated toward political capitalism, which lacked an ethical dimension.

gious questions, according to Weber, although their attitude has a different origin. The workers know from experience that they can trust their own efforts and that their fate is determined by social and economic forces, rather than natural forces of the type that govern the lives of peasants. Thus the workers reject or are indifferent to religion; and only the most desperate sections of the proletariat constitute an exception in this regard. What the workers want is "just compensation"—but of a political rather than of a religious kind. In their relationship to socialism, however, workers often display a quasi-religious attitude (see figure 5.5).

The fourth theme in Weber's general sociology of religion—*different ways to approach salvation and how these may affect the economy*—provides important background to his analyses in *The Protestant Ethic* and *The Economic Ethics of the World Religions.* Weber argues that the various roads to salvation may affect the economy in two different ways. First, they all entail some explicit attitudes toward economic life; and the more rational a religion is, the more systematic these attitudes tend to become. The mystic, for example, rejects the secular world—including work—while the Lutheran ignores the secular world and views work as a vocation. There are, however, "certain limits," Weber cautions, to the impact that this type of explicit religious attitude can have on the economy.[25]

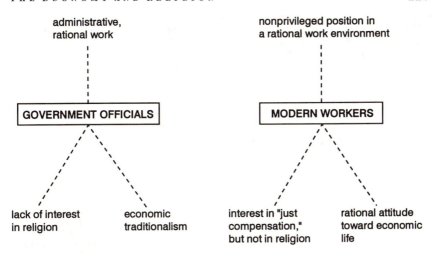

Fig. 5.5. Religious Propensity and Attitude toward Economic Life among Government Officials and Modern Workers

Source: Max Weber, *Economy and Society* (Berkeley: University of California Press, 1978), pp. 476–77, 484–86.

Comment: Workers are usually indifferent to religion and tend to have a rational attitude toward economic life. Government officials are also indifferent to religion but are ambivalent to profit-making and inclined to economic traditionalism.

But the different ways of seeking salvation also have a number of unintended consequences, which in certain circumstances can affect economic institutions in a profound manner. The mechanisms through which these unintended consequences influence the economy (typically in combination with intended ones) are the following. Different paths to salvation can either leave the personality of the believer intact or change it deeply and permanently. A permanent change typically entails a purification of the individual or being born again ("sanctification"). Believers whose personalities have been fundamentally changed will either withdraw from the world or attempt to change its institutions in accordance with some religious ideal. Weber says that only the efforts of the believers to change society may challenge economic traditionalism. In all other cases, the unintended consequences of salvation efforts will probably strengthen economic traditionalism (see figure 5.6).

Weber analyzes a number of different ways of seeking salvation in *Economy and Society,* some of which leave the personality of the believer more or less intact and do not aim at changing social and economic institutions very much either. These include ritualism, ecstasy, doing good deeds, institutional grace, and salvation through pure faith. The impact of ritualism on the believer, Weber says, is about as superficial as that of a moving theater performance. Certain ritualistic religions also impose so many rules on the believer that only rich people can afford to follow them. Using ecstasy as a way to reach salvation has ephemeral

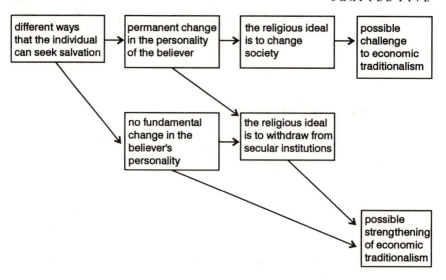

Fig. 5.6. Different Ways of Seeking Salvation and Their Potential Influence on Economic Traditionalism

Source: Max Weber, *Economy and Society* (Berkeley: University of California Press, 1978), pp. 518–76.

Comment: The various ways of reaching salvation may affect the economy in different ways. Ritualism and ecstasy, for example, do not change the believer's personality in a fundamental manner; and they tend to strengthen economic traditionalism. World-rejecting asceticism and mysticism do lead to profound personality changes but leave secular institutions intact and may inadvertently strengthen them. Only inner-worldly asceticism and fatalism have the potential to challenge economic traditionalism. The effects of the different roads to salvation are typically a combination of intended and unintended consequences.

effects and also leads in a nonrational direction. Doing good deeds has little effect on the believer's personality, especially if it is thought that bad deeds can be compensated for through good deeds.

The same is true for salvation through institutional grace and through faith alone. In the case of salvation through institutional grace, everything hinges on the institution that dispenses grace, and the individual is encouraged to obey rather than to change his or her behavior. Although the Catholic Church has a potentially powerful tool in the confession, Weber says, the way that the Church handles confessions blunts its power: sins are forgiven, and the believer is not forced to permanently change his or her behavior.[26] Salvation through faith alone—which Lutheranism offers, for example—has a similar weak effect on the behavior of the believer; it also encourages traditionalism in economic and social affairs. At the same time, Lutheranism challenges the notion of religious virtuosi in Catholicism, which restricts salvation to a minority; it furthermore proclaims ordinary secular labor to be a religious task for everyone in society (a "vocation").

There are also a few ways of seeking salvation that lead to a deep change of the believer's personality but nonetheless leave social and economic institutions intact or even strengthened. Mysticism is one of these, and here the believer sees himself or herself as a vessel to be filled by God. The mystic encourages economic traditionalism by leaving secular institutions as they are and by refusing to work. What Weber terms "world-rejecting asceticism" represents a second road to salvation that totally changes the believer's personality but again leaves the world as it is. This kind of ascetic does not want private property or a family, and he or she typically withdraws from society together with other religious virtuosi. Unlike the mystic, however, the world-rejecting ascetic works for his or her living. The fact that he or she rejects secular society in such a radical manner nonetheless tends to strengthen economic traditionalism. Since following God means withdrawing from society, economic and social institutions are automatically devalued.

According to Weber, there are only two ways of seeking salvation that change the believer's personality and may also challenge society's institutions: "inner-worldly asceticism" and predestination. The former is a very active and alert type of asceticism, which typically demands a change of society in accordance with some religious ideal. Some of the Protestant ascetics, for example, consciously introduced ethical-religious norms into economic life and extended their methodical approach in religious matters to money-making—two measures that would deeply affect the Western economy. That predestination may lead to changes in society, rather than to fatalism, may seem counterintuitive, Weber says. Nonetheless, predestination can make the believer feel that he or she is an instrument of God and that God's will must be carried out in a methodical manner. When the forces of inner-worldly asceticism and predestination are combined, their influence becomes particularly powerful, as I show in the next section.

II. HISTORICAL STUDIES OF ECONOMY AND RELIGION (PART I): *THE PROTESTANT ETHIC AND THE SPIRIT OF CAPITALISM*

The Protestant Ethic is Weber's most celebrated study and has led to a debate that is still going on today, nearly a century after its publication. Though the main thesis—that ascetic Protestantism helped form the mentality of modern, rational capitalism—was conceived in 1898, Weber wrote the work itself a few years later, in 1903–4.[27] At the time, Weber was much concerned with methodological issues as well as with religious questions. The first part of *The Protestant Ethic,* for example, appeared in 1904, or the same year as his essay on "'Objectivity' in Social Science and Social Policy." From the terminology of the latter essay, it is clear that *The Protestant Ethic* primarily deals with an "economically relevant phenomenon" or a phenomenon that is itself noneconomic (ascetic Protestantism) but has important economic consequences (it encouraged the emergence of new type of capitalist mentality). *The Protestant Ethic* also illustrates other methodological principles, which are discussed in the essay on ob-

jectivity, and contains an analysis of various religious phenomena, especially
Christian churches and sects. In this discussion of *The Protestant Ethic,* however, I highlight its contributions to economic sociology rather than to the sociology of religion or the methodology of the social sciences. With this purpose in
mind, I proceed to a presentation of the content of *The Protestant Ethic* that
follows its main argument closely, but also pays special attention to economic
phenomena. I then say something about the writings of Weber that complement
The Protestant Ethic and about the debate it has generated.

The Protestant Ethic appeared in two installments in 1904–5 in *Archiv für
Sozialwissenschaft und Sozialpolitik.* Part 1, or the first installment, is entitled
"The Problem" and consists of three short chapters in which Weber presents the
problem to be studied, how to study it, and in which direction a solution is to be
sought. In Part 2, which appeared about half a year later, Weber presents the solution to his problem. Its title is "The Ethics of Vocation in Ascetic Protestantism," and it is about twice as long as Part 1, although it consists of only two
chapters. Weber revised the whole text in 1919 for its inclusion in a multivolume
set entitled *Collected Essays in the Sociology of Religion.* He added a sentence
here and there and some footnotes, but changed nothing in the main argument.

Weber starts *The Protestant Ethic* with a general discussion of why Protestants
seems to be much more economically successful than Catholics (chap. 1, "Religious Affiliation and Social Stratification"). The purpose of this chapter is not so
much to analyze the stratification of Catholics in relation to Protestants in
Weber's day as to slowly guide the reader into a more precise understanding of
the problem and the terminology. In countries where there are both Catholics
and Protestants, Weber notes (reproducing a statistical error in the process),[28]
there are proportionally more Protestants than Catholics among managers and
capital owners as well as among technically and administratively skilled workers.
With this problem in mind, Weber proceeds to a discussion of several theories
that had been suggested at the time as possible solutions. He also touches on the
role of minorities in economic life and on the powerful effect that migration can
have on economic attitudes.[29] Weber rejects all of the suggested solutions, however, either because they are outright wrong or because they use such clumsy
concepts that they fail to get a handle on the problem. To produce a successful
solution, Weber notes in chapter 1, the problem must be formulated much more
precisely and better concepts introduced. In the next chapter Weber moves
away from his initial and rather general discussion of the relationship between
religious affiliation and stratification, and states what he intends to look at in his
study (chap. 2, "The Spirit of Capitalism"). What is central to modern capitalism, he says, is the tendency to view work (including money-making) as a vocation or an end in itself, and it is the origin of *this* attitude that needs to be established. It is not possible, Weber argues, that this specific approach to work is
somehow the invention of a single individual; it has to originate in the collective
lifestyle of a group of people. He also points out—and this is an important part
of the argument in *The Protestant Ethic*—that today, when the capitalist system
is safely established, there is less of a need that everybody accepts the notion of

a vocation with an explicitly ethical dimension because people have to work in a systematic and restless manner anyway if they are to survive economically. At one time, however, systematic money-making and work for its own sake were looked down on in religion and hence in society at large—and the original concept of vocation consequently had to have a strong ethical component if it were to successfully establish itself.

To illustrate what he calls "the spirit of (modern) capitalism"[30]—of which vocation constitutes the central part—Weber cites some of the writings of Benjamin Franklin (1706–90). According to Franklin, the individual should work constantly, not only when he needs money or feels like it: "He that idly loses five shillings' worth of time, loses five shillings, and might as prudently throw five shillings into the sea." To not use one's capital is equally wrong because money begets money: "He that kills a breeding-sow, destroys all her offspring to the thousandth generation. He that murders (!) a crown, destroys all that it might have produced, even scores of pounds." At one point in his autobiography Franklin also quotes a passage from the Bible that his Calvinist father had often repeated to him: "Seest thou a Man diligent in his Calling? He shall stand before Kings."[31] Weber summarizes the section on Franklin by saying that this type of attitude toward work and money-making is truly novel in human history: every person has an ethical duty to work and make money as methodically and diligently as possible.

This ethical component clearly differentiates the spirit of modern capitalism from "the instinct of acquisition," which according to Weber can be found in all ages since the dawn of history. Weber was suspicious of this concept, which he later would criticize sharply and which has since fallen into well-deserved oblivion.[32] Weber also points out that one can find examples of the instinct of acquisition in acts that are characterized by ruthless acquisition and bound by no ethical rules whatsoever. The unethical type of capitalism that results from this type of acquisitive activity Weber labels "adventurers' capitalism," and describes as follows:

> Capitalist acquisition as an adventure has been at home in all types of economic society which have known trade with the use of money and which have offered it opportunities, through *commenda*, farming of taxes, State loans, financing of wars, ducal courts and officeholders. Likewise the inner attitude of the adventurer, which laughs at all ethical limitations, has been universal. Absolute and conscious ruthlessness in acquisition has often stood in the closest connection with the strictest conformity to tradition.[33]

The concept of adventurers' capitalism cuts across two of the categories that Weber uses in his discussion of the different types of capitalism in *Economy and Society,* namely political capitalism and traditional commercial capitalism.[34] The term "adventurers' capitalism" is not used in the theoretical chapter on economic sociology in *Economy and Society;* and Weber presumably introduced it in *The Protestant Ethic* in order to get a good contrast to the moral type of capitalism that ascetic Protestantism helped to create.

Weber is also careful to distinguish the spirit of modern capitalism from what he calls "the traditionalist spirit" in capitalism.[35] Unlike adventurers' capitalism, the traditionalist spirit does have an ethical component. It is, for example, held to be wrong to work in any but a traditional manner, to invest in any but a traditional manner, and so on. Weber uses an example from the textile industry in the mid-nineteenth century to illustrate the difference between the modern capitalist spirit and the traditionalist spirit of capitalism, and also to make the important point that "the capitalist form" can remain the same even if the economic spirit that animates it changes. There is naturally a tendency for a certain "form" and a certain "spirit" to go together, Weber says, but this is by no means always the case.[36] Benjamin Franklin's printing business, for example, had a traditional "form" but was animated by a nontraditional "spirit."

Weber's example of the textile industry in the mid-nineteenth century fills in some important details in his argument. Around this time in continental Europe, Weber says, a textile manufacturer typically managed a putting-out system, with some local peasants producing the cloth. The manufacturer bought the cloth from the peasants at a traditional price and then sold it from his warehouses, making a moderate profit in the process. The working day lasted some five or six hours for the owner, so there was plenty of time for leisure and rest. Capital accounting was used in this type of business, Weber notes, but things nonetheless went on in a fairly tranquil and traditional manner. One day, however, an entrepreneur would appear, with a similar type ("form") of economic organization, but with a different idea about how things should be done ("spirit"). This newly arrived entrepreneur might choose his suppliers among the peasants more carefully; he might personally approach his customers; or he might introduce a higher volume of production in combination with a lower price. Similar to Schumpeter, Weber argues that this new and innovative entrepreneur would have had to be very strong overcome all the mistrust and indignation he was apt to encounter. In contrast to Schumpeter, however, Weber says that his strength would have had to be of a moral kind.[37]

Weber discusses both the new type of entrepreneur and the new type of worker. When offered a higher wage, traditional workers will accept it—but also reduce their hours of work because their traditional needs can now be more easily satisfied. In other words, the supply curve for this type of labor is backward-sloping. In addition, the traditional workers attach no special value to work itself. On both accounts, the new workers differ: even if their wages are raised, they will continue to work the same number of hours, and they will invest more of their own character in the work because they regard it as an end in itself.

In the last chapter of Part 1 of *The Protestant Ethic*, Weber moves from the nineteenth century to the sixteenth century to look at the concept of vocation (chap. 3, "Luther's Concept of the Calling: Task of the Investigation"). The idea that one has a religious duty to properly carry out one's worldly activity, Weber says, can be traced directly to Luther's translation of the Bible. This was the first time in the history of religion, he emphasizes, that ordinary labor was infused with a positive religious meaning—and not just the activities of a small religious elite, as in the monasteries and nunneries. And from Luther the notion of vocation (*Beruf*) spread to the everyday language of all the Protestant countries. To

Luther, however, work constitutes a lot to be accepted, unlike a task set by God in which one should strive to excel. As a consequence of this, Weber says, Luther's role in the development of the modern capitalist spirit was to be minor.

Calvinism and some of the Protestant sects took a more active approach to vocation than Lutheranism and were in many ways closer in spirit to modern capitalism than to the economic traditionalism of Luther. Weber notes that numerous Calvinists and members of ascetic Protestant sects had been extremely successful in their economic dealings. But exactly how to analyze the relationship between the non-Lutheran types of Protestantism and capitalism raises some difficult questions, according to Weber. One cannot find an explicit argument in favor of a new capitalist spirit in the statements of Calvin and other important Protestant leaders. The primary concern of these leaders was always with the salvation of the soul, Weber emphasizes, and not with money-making and capitalism. Some other way to investigate the relationship between religion and economy had therefore to be found. Only if this were done would it become possible to determine—and now Weber states the main task of his study—how the Protestant ethic has contributed to *"the qualitative formation and quantitative expansion"* of the modern capitalist spirit (see figure 5.7 for the diffusion of Protestantism).[38]

Weber provides the solution to this problem in two steps in Part 2 of *The Protestant Ethic*: he first explicates the general mechanism (chap. 4), and then applies it to the economy (chap. 5). In chapter 4 ("The Religious Foundations of Worldly Asceticism") Weber states that he is not interested in tracing the influence of either theological ideas on the individual or the teachings of the Church. Instead, he says, he will take the adoption of a certain religious faith by the individual as his point of departure in the analysis. The mechanism through which the adaption of a religious faith translates into practical behavior, he suggests, is the following one: religious benefits set "psychological premiums" on specific types of behavior, and in certain circumstances these may then lead to the formation of novel "psychological impulses."[39] Ascetic behavior, to use Weber's terminology, is the product of a religion that directs practical behavior in such a manner that impulses toward systematic and self-denying behavior are produced. Calvinism, Weber also points out, is the most consistent example of such an ascetic religion.

Calvinism had a very somber vision of humanity, in which predestination played a key role. No one but God knew who the elect were, and there was absolutely nothing that the individual could do to change his or her preordained fate. This, one might have thought, would have led to fatalism and resignation, but such was not the case. Instead, the starkness of the choice between damnation and salvation predisposed the individual to a methodical conduct in the service of God, as did the crucial fact that no forgiveness could be given for one's sins, even if they were minor. A strong hostility to the natural state of man (*status naturalis*) and the fact that religious benefits could only be had in the next world, not in this life, operated in the same direction. Calvinism also contained a vigorous element of activism—man should serve God by changing the world

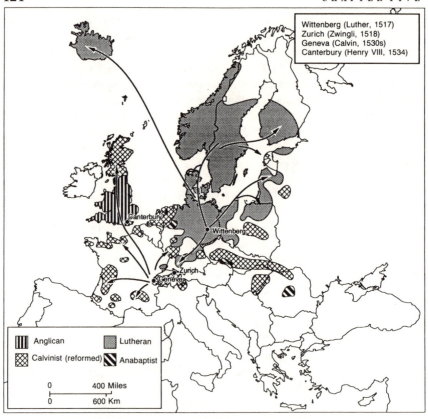

Fig. 5.7. The Diffusion of Protestantism in Europe, circa 1570
  Source: Chris Park, *Sacred Worlds* (London: Routledge, 1996), p. 113.
  Comment: According to Weber, the spirit of modern capitalism was formed
under the influence of ascetic Protestantism during the late sixteenth and the
seventeenth centuries. A map of the West at the end of the seventeenth century would also show that the ideas of Calvin and the English Puritans had
spread to the English colonies on the East Coast of North America. It should
also be noted that by 1685, through the revocation of the Edict of Nantes, the
French Protestants or Huguenots had begun their exodus to England, Holland,
Prussia, and America.

in his image—and this element directed the systematic and restless activities of
the believers outward, toward the existing social institutions.

Weber says that a similar ascetic and activist approach to life could also be
found in Pietism, Methodism, and the Baptist sects, even though all of these
started out from a somewhat different set of religious ideas than Calvinism. He
also contrasts Calvinism with Lutheranism and Catholicism in order to bring out
its special character. While Lutheranism emphasizes faith and a mystical union
with God, thereby weakening its ascetic and activist element, Catholicism ends

up doing more or less the same, Weber argues, through the sacrament of abso-
lution. Neither one sets a premium on the kind of behavior that can give "psychological impulses" to a consistently methodical lifestyle. Although Calvinism
and the ascetic Protestant sects, as well as Lutheranism and Catholicism, all are
based on the same body of thought—the Bible, which condemns the accumula-
tion of riches as a goal in life—some of them end up encouraging economic rationalism and others economic traditionalism (see figure 5.8).

An ascetic lifestyle of the type that Calvinism leads to, Weber argues, influences the economy primarily through "maxims for everyday economic conduct"
(chap. 5, "Asceticism and the Spirit of Capitalism").[40] According to one of these
maxims, one should work hard and systematically in one's vocation. If this restless activity leads to wealth, it was imperative not to use this wealth for leisure
or for the consumption of luxury items. Making a fortune was not wrong per se—
as long as the riches were not used for personal indulgence. "You may labour to
be rich for God, though not for the flesh and sin," as one of the authorities on
Puritan ethics put it. Making plenty of money was even encouraged in Calvinism, since it was a sign that God looked upon one's labor with favor: "It is true
that the usefulness of a calling, and thus its favour in the sight of God, is mea-

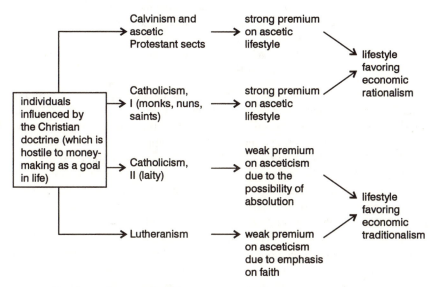

Fig. 5.8. The Influence of Different Types of Christianity on the Economy,
according to *The Protestant Ethic*

    Source: See especially Max Weber, *The Protestant Ethic and the Spirit of
Capitalism* (London: Allen and Unwin, 1930), pp. 197 n. 12, 259 n. 4.

    Comment: Religious benefits, according to Weber, set psychological premi-
ums on certain forms of behavior. Some of these behaviors produce impulses
toward an ascetic lifestyle and economic rationalism, while others encourage
economic traditionalism.

sured first in moral terms, and then in terms of the importance of the goods produced in it for the community. But a third criterion—which is naturally the most
important one in practice—is private profitableness."[41]

That this type of Puritan ethics was very close to the nonreligious "spirit of
(modern) capitalism" as propounded by Benjamin Franklin is clear. Even if the
Puritans did not equate time with money, it must nonetheless not be wasted;
there was also a general premium on restless activity in one's vocation (see figure 5.9 for Benjamin Franklin's moral bookkeeping). Because consumption of
luxuries was not allowed, additional funds were constantly made available for
new investments. Furthermore, the Puritans introduced a stern and honest
morality into economic life. They detested the aristocracy for its idleness and
luxuries, and they deeply disapproved of everything that came close to adventurers' capitalism. The hostility of the Puritans to monopolies and political capitalism undoubtedly helped a competitive and private kind of capitalism to
emerge. The viewpoint that money-making and religion could very well go together also helped to legitimize capitalism:

> A specifically bourgeois vocational ethic grew up. With the consciousness of standing
> in the fullness of God's grace and being visibly blessed by Him, the bourgeois business
> man could now follow his pecuniary interests as he would and feel that he was fulfill-
> ing a duty in doing so—as long as he remained within the bounds of formal correct-
> ness, as long as his moral conduct was spotless and the use to which he put his wealth
> was not objectionable. The power of religious asceticism provided him in addition with
> sober, conscientious, and unusually industrious workmen, who clung to their work as
> to a life and purpose willed by God.[42]

The ascetic form of the Protestant ethic, Weber says, helped to shape and to
spread the spirit of modern rational capitalism. It accomplished this by breaking down the ethical disapproval surrounding traditional capitalism and by actively creating and promoting a more methodical approach to economic affairs
(see Weber's whole argument in *The Protestant Ethic* as summarized in figure
5.10). Once this had been done, however, capitalism did not need any further
assistance from religion, and today's rational capitalism is a system that operates
largely according to its own dynamics.[43] In the famous ending of *The Protestant
Ethic* Weber says that economic life has hardened into an "iron cage" from the
viewpoint of the individual.[44] The original Puritans are long gone, and so is their
concept of vocation as a religious task. "The idea of duty in one's calling," Weber
says, "prowls about in our lives like the ghost of dead religious beliefs."[45]

For a complete picture of what Weber tried to accomplish with *The Protestant Ethic,* some additional material needs to be taken into account. There is,
first, his article "The Protestant Sects and the Spirit of Capitalism" (1st version
1906; 2d revised version 1920), which contains a wealth of interesting observations about the relationship between the ascetic sects and economic life. It is also
one of Weber's most inspired and beautifully written essays. Insofar as the general argument in *The Protestant Ethic* is concerned, the main contribution of this
article is that it indicates a new mechanism that played a role in the formation

TEMPERANCE.

Eat not to dulness: drink not to elevation.

	Sun.	M.	T.	W.	Th.	F.	S.
Tem.							
Sil.	•	•		•		•	
Ord.	•	•	•		•	•	•
Res.		•				•	
Fru.		•				•	
Ind.			•				
Sinc.							
Jus.							
Mod.							
Clea.							
Tran.							
Chas.							
Hum.							

Fig. 5.9. Moral Bookkeeping as an Example of a Methodical Attitude toward Life: Benjamin Franklin's Schedule for Developing His Character and Using Time Efficiently

Source: Benjamin Franklin, *Memoirs of the Life and Writings of Benjamin Franklin* (Philadelphia: T. S. Manning [1793] 1818), p. 91; cf. Max Weber, *The Protestant Ethic and the Spirit of Capitalism* (London: Allen and Unwin, 1930), pp. 124, 238 n. 100.

Explanation: The horizontal line lists the days of the week; the vertical line lists virtues (Tem. = temperance; Sil. = silence; Ord. = order; Res. = resolution; Fru. = frugality; Ind. = industry; Sinc. = sincerity; Jus. = justice; Mod. = moderation; Clea. = cleanliness; Tran. = tranquillity; Chas. = chastity; and Hum. = humility).

Comment: This figure reproduces one page in a booklet that Benjamin Franklin (1706–90) put together for himself in order to develop his character. Each week he focused on one virtue (in this case temperance), hoping in that manner to gradually become a better person. Weber calls Franklin's table of virtues "a classic example" of the type of methodical lifestyle that the ascetic Protestants developed, but he also points out that without sanctions, a scheme of this type would be less efficient. Weber himself received a copy of Franklin's autobiography as a Christmas gift when he was eleven years old.

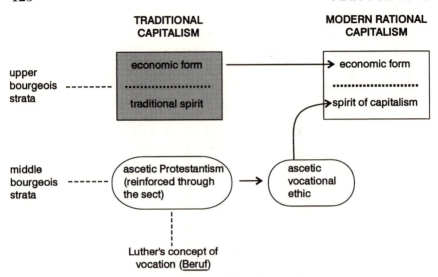

Fig. 5.10. The Contribution of Ascetic Protestantism to the Qualitative Formation of the Modern Capitalist Spirit in the Late Sixteenth and Seventeenth Centuries, according to *The Protestant Ethic*

Source: See especially Max Weber, *The Protestant Ethic and the Spirit of Capitalism* (London: Allen and Unwin, 1930), pp. 75, 91, 220, 159, 273.

Comment: Weber's goal in *The Protestant Ethic* was to outline and explain the contribution made by ascetic Protestantism to "the qualitative formation and the quantitative expansion" of the modern capitalist spirit. The formation of the spirit of modern capitalism started toward the end of the sixteenth century, continued during the seventeenth century, and was complete by the eighteenth century in some parts of the West. The organizational form of capitalism, however, did not undergo any changes due to religion. The shaded area in the figure represents economic activity that was considered "ethically unjustifiable or at best to be tolerated," according to the prevalent religious view. The argument about the sect's reinforcing the ideas of ascectic Protestantism was added in an article from 1906.

of the spirit of modern capitalism, namely the sect. According to Weber, the individual member of a sect feels compelled to always hold his or her own in the presence of other sect members. The sect, in other words, helps turn the "impulses" to engage in inner-worldly ascetic behavior into a character trait that is favorable to economic rationalism.

Weber's essay on the Protestant sects also supplies new information on the spread of the Protestant ethic. The main argument in *The Protestant Ethic,* to recall, deals not only with the formation of a new capitalist spirit but also with its diffusion. Weber's essay adds a very interesting analysis of the role played by the sects in the United States and their influence on the American social structure. Especially among the middle strata, Weber says, the sects helped to maintain and diffuse the business ethos during the nineteenth century. The reader also gets a distinct sense that the sects in the United States (as well as their secular offspring, the voluntary associations) have left an important imprint on the American national character and also contributed to the dynamism of its economic system.[46]

Another place where Weber supplies complementary information on the problem in *The Protestant Ethic* is in his lecture course known as *General Economic History*.[47] Toward the end, Weber lectured on the evolution of the modern capitalist spirit, and the main thrust of what he said is more or less identical to the argument in *The Protestant Ethic*. What emerges with more clarity in the lecture series, however, is how much the Puritan business ethics differed from what Weber calls "the double ethic."[48] Earlier in history, he explains, there had been one type of ethics for one's family, clan, or community of believers, and another moral code for strangers and outsiders, which was considerably more ruthless in character. The Puritans dramatically broke with this by introducing a new type of ethics into business, according to which every individual should be treated in the same way, regardless of creed or origin.

The *General Economic History* also makes another, very important contribution to the understanding of *The Protestant Ethic*. Just by reading through Weber's account in *General Economic History*, chapter by chapter, of how modern capitalism came into being, the reader comes to realize that this was a process that took many centuries and also involved other factors than the religious ones. Modern capitalism, in other words, was not the result of some new capitalist spirit that suddenly emerged in the sixteenth and seventeenth centuries and jump-started an already existing economic organization. Weber, of course, makes this point in *The Protestant Ethic*, but he does it in a more subtle manner; and this makes it harder to understand that he is only talking about one single phase—albeit a particularly important one—in the long and difficult evolution of the modern capitalist system, namely the creation of a new capitalist spirit. Modern rational capitalism, as Weber repeatedly states in *General Economic History*, is the result of a number of events that took place *before* as well as *after* the creation of a new capitalist spirit. Among the events that took place before this event is the birth of the Western city and modern (Roman) law; and among those that came after is the factory system and the systematic use of science in production. Weber's argument on this point is particularly important to keep in mind since the consensus seems to be that *The Protestant Ethic* advocates a religious or "cultural" explanation of the birth of capitalism.[49]

The Protestant Ethic caused quite a bit of controversy in Weber's day, and the debate endures today, nearly a century later. Typical for the ambivalence that many social scientists apparently still feel toward Weber's study is the following statement by Barrington Moore, Jr., from the late 1970s: "It is by no means clear whether Max Weber's famous contribution in *The Protestant Ethic and the Spirit of Capitalism* constituted an important breakthrough or a blind alley."[50] To properly present the major arguments and counterarguments in the debate on Weber's thesis during the nearly one hundred years it has been going on is not possible in this work, in which I attempt instead to present Weber's sociological analysis of the economy in general. I shall therefore say only a few words about Weber's own participation in the debate, and about two recent and particularly interesting contributions from the viewpoint of economic sociology. Economists, it may be added in passing, have not shown much of an interest in Weber's thesis.[51]

Weber published four comments during 1907–10 in response to his original critics—primarily German economists and economic historians—and these articles are still worth reading since many of the criticisms directed at *The Protestant Ethic* are often repeated and based on a few misunderstandings of what Weber actually said. In his answers to the critics, Weber, for example, points out that he by no means had said that one will find the modern capitalist spirit wherever one finds ascetic Protestantism or that one will find capitalism wherever one finds the modern capitalist spirit.[52] This is true because other factors may intervene in the particular historical case and sometimes have done so. Weber also points out that he had never said that religion or the Reformation had somehow "caused" capitalism to emerge; his argument in *The Protestant Ethic* was rather that ascetic Protestantism had played an important role during the late sixteenth and the seventeenth centuries in the creation of a new kind of economic mentality ("the [modern] capitalist spirit") but had left the economic organization ("the economic form") unchanged.[53]

Weber furthermore says he agrees with the criticism that Calvin's opinion should not be confused with the ideas of later Calvinism—and that he had said so in *The Protestant Ethic.* He responds to his critics that a financier like Jacob Fugger (1459–1525) did not display the modern capitalist spirit at all (as defined in *The Protestant Ethic*) because Fugger lacked a sober and systematic approach to life.[54] Similarly, Sombart had been wrong to argue that the concept of the modern capitalist spirit was more or less identical to economic rationalism, since this left out its ethical dimension, which was crucial to Weber's argument.[55]

Given the enormous size of the secondary literature on *The Protestant Ethic,* one might well think that by the mid-twentieth century most of what could be said, had indeed been said.[56] However, two recent contributions to the debate are of special interest to economic sociology. One of these is James Coleman's brief comment on *The Protestant Ethic* in his famous article "Social Theory, Social Research and a Theory of Action," and the other is Gordon Marshall's effort to empirically test the main thesis in Weber's work. Coleman uses *The Protestant Ethic* as an illustration of how a sociological analysis can be improved by being carried out in accordance with the principle of methodological individualism.[57] In an ingenious manner Coleman reconstructs the logic in Weber's argument according to what he calls the macro-micro-macro transition. Collective religious values influence the individual believer (Step 1: macro to micro); these religious attitudes will eventually change the believer's attitude to work and profit-making (Step 2: micro to micro); and when this happens simultaneously to many individual actors, the result is a new collective attitude to economic matters (Step 3: micro to macro). For Coleman's reconstruction of Weber's argument, see figure 5.11.

According to Coleman, Weber starts out the analysis well enough but fails at Step 3, the micro-to-macro transition. This part is difficult to handle in any so-

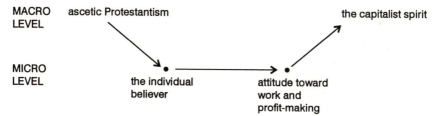

Fig. 5.11. James Coleman's Reconstruction of the Argument in *The Protestant Ethic*

Source: James Coleman, "Social Theory, Social Research, and a Theory of Action," *American Journal of Sociology* 91 (1986): 1322 (the figure has been amended).

Comment: Coleman emphasizes that the individual believer is influenced by religious beliefs (*Step 1*); how these beliefs affect his or her attitude about economic matters (*Step 2*); and how one individual's attitudes fuse with similar attitudes of other individuals into a collective lifestyle or mentality (*Step 3*).

ciological analysis, Coleman says, but also the most important one since it is here that the individual actors, by taking one another into account, create a new type of social phenomenon ("the problem of transformation" in Coleman's terminology). Weber, Coleman says, failed to specify the mechanism through which the individual actors in *The Protestant Ethic* created a new social phenomenon—more precisely, the spirit of modern capitalism.

In my opinion, Coleman exaggerates Weber's failure on this point. It is perhaps true that Weber does not specify the exact mechanism at Step 3 in his analysis, but he nonetheless makes very clear that the new spirit of capitalism is the result of social interaction. More precisely, Weber emphasizes that the capitalist spirit was not the invention of a single individual but of a whole group of people, and that it should be characterized as a kind of collective "lifestyle."[58] In the article on the sects, Weber also adds a mechanism that helped the new capitalist spirit to harden into a collective mentality, namely the social structure of the sect. Nonetheless, Coleman's argument about "the problem of transformation" represents an original and important attempt to show how methodological individualism is at the center of Weber's argument in *The Protestant Ethic,* something that had been forgotten in the debate of this work. Coleman's own interest-based form of analysis, it may furthermore be added, displays many similarities to that of Weber.

The second important contribution to the debate of *The Protestant Ethic* that I want to highlight is that of Gordon Marshall. In a number of articles and two books—*Presbyteries and Profits* (1981) and *In Search of the Spirit of Capitalism* (1982)—Marshall argues that "the capitalist side" of the argument in *The Protestant Ethic* has been left "virtually unexplored" in the secondary literature.[59] By this he means that practically no attention has been paid in the debate on *The Protestant Ethic* to the following three central questions: (1) What exactly were the economic consequences of the ascetic Protestant ethic? (2) What would count as empirical evidence for these consequences? and (3) Is it possible to find empirical evidence for these consequences? Marshall's discussion of these questions represents, in my opinion, a very substantial contribution to the debate of *The Protestant Ethic* as well as to economic sociology more generally.

Marshall proposes several ways of establishing whether the ascetic Protestant ethic had indeed had the economic consequences that Weber claimed it did. As to the new entrepreneurs (Marshall discusses the new type of workers as well), one would expect these to be unscrupulously honest, to reinvest rather than to consume, to systematically expand their businesses, and to feel impelled to use their time efficiently. Empirical evidence in matters of this type, Marshall continues, would include business records from the late sixteenth and seventeenth centuries. Weber had also in Marshall's opinion added another difficulty by not being consistent in his analysis of "economic form" and "economic spirit." While Weber sometimes argued as if a special form of enterprise implies a certain type of economic mentality, at other times in *The Protestant Ethic* he makes a sharp distinction between the two and insists that the spirit does not always follow the form.[60]

As to the question whether it is possible to produce empirical evidence for the main thesis in *The Protestant Ethic,* Marshall first notes that Weber himself presented no empirical evidence for the existence of a new capitalist spirit among businessmen other than some citations from Benjamin Franklin's writings. Empirically, Marshall says, the case that Weber puts forward is so thin that it can only be labeled *"not proven."*[61] He also points out that the kind of data needed to confirm or disprove the main thesis in Weber's study are rarely available for the period in question. Ideally, Marshall adds wistfully, one would have liked to interview the entrepreneurs and workers in question.

Some relevant empirical material does exist, however, and Marshall himself uses the case of Scotland to show this. His own major study, *Presbyteries and Profits,* analyzes the business records of a seventeenth-century business called the Newmills Cloth Manufactory; and according to the author this particular case largely confirms Weber's thesis.[62] Weber did not empirically prove his case in *The Protestant Ethic,* Marshall concludes, and certain parts of his argument will in all likelihood never be proven or disproven because the necessary data do not exist. But we must attempt to establish what these parts of his arguments are, he says, and locate the relevant material for the others. If this is done in a systematic manner for Holland, New England, Scotland, and so on, Marshall speculates, it might very well turn out that Weber's thesis in *The Protestant Ethic* is largely correct.[63]

III. HISTORICAL STUDIES OF ECONOMY AND RELIGION (PART II): *THE ECONOMIC ETHICS OF THE WORLD RELIGIONS*

Toward the end of *The Protestant Ethic* Weber says that his study is part of a larger research project focusing on ascetic rationalism in general. One of the subjects he wants to explore in the future, he says, is the role of ascetic rationalism in the history of modern science and technology; and another is the way that the formation of ascetic rationalism has been influenced by different factors, "especially economic ones."[64] But Weber decided not to proceed with these and similar questions in part because his colleague and friend Ernst Troeltsch was working along similar lines. After *The Protestant Ethic* and the essay on the sects had been completed, Weber therefore turned to other topics. He expanded his article from the late 1890s on the social and economic history of antiquity into a book-length study and also produced some work on "the psychophysics of industrial work."

Around 1911, however, he decided to resume his research project from *The Protestant Ethic,* but from a different angle. He had earlier primarily been interested in the emergence of capitalism in the West, under the influence of religious forces, but he now set out to investigate why a similar process—and again with special reference to religion—had *not* taken place anywhere else in the world. The central question became, Why had rational capitalism not emerged in China, India, Japan, and elsewhere, but only in the West? One commentator has observed that Weber "now tried to work the proof [from *The Protestant Ethic*] in reverse," and this is essentially correct.[65] As will soon be seen, however, Weber's new studies also differed in some important respects from *The Protestant Ethic.*

In his new research project, entitled *The Economic Ethics of the World Religions,* his aim was to cover all the major religions of the world.[66] Weber died before he had time to complete it, and only some of the projected studies were produced. Among those that are missing are, most important, analyses of Islam and Christianity, but Weber did complete three major studies—*The Religion of China* (1915, revised 1920), *The Religion of India* (1916–17), and *Ancient Judaism* (1917–20), plus a couple of theoretical articles. Like *The Protestant Ethic,* the three major studies address specific, historical situations, while the articles are primarily of interest for their introduction of new concepts and discussion of the theoretical implications of the empirical studies. Weber's project was primarily intended to result in a contribution to the section on the sociology of religion in *Economy and Society,* but also to "economic sociology."[67]

Of the new concepts that can be found in Weber's studies of religion during these years, three are especially important to economic sociology: "economic sphere," "ideal interests" versus "material interests," and "economic ethic." All have deep roots in Weber's work, but it was not until the 1910s—and primarily in these theoretical articles from *The Economic Ethics of the World Religions*— that Weber chose to discuss them more thoroughly and as part of his sociology.[68] The concept of "economic sphere" essentially denotes that economic activities, as history evolves, tend to become separate from other human activities and also to a certain extent to be governed by their own rules or laws ("limited autonomy" or *"Eigengesetzlichkeit,"* in Weber's terminology).[69] A certain tension is also typical for the relationship of the economic sphere to the other spheres in society. The economic sphere clashes, for example, with the religious sphere in capitalist society because it is very difficult to regulate rational economic actions through religious rules.

The concepts of "ideal" and "material interests" and "economic ethic" raise the issue of the role of norms in economic life. The concept of ideal interests complements the concept of material interests, which is central to the work of Marx and the Marxists. According to Weber, people are just as driven their desire for ideal interests—such as religious benefits, status honor, and so on—as they are by their desire for material interests. Indeed, to cite one of Weber's well-known formulations, it is "not ideas but material and ideal interests [that] directly govern men's conduct."[70] But even though interests propel the actions of people, Weber continues, these interests do not necessarily determine the exact direction of people's actions. In *The Protestant Ethic,* for example, Weber attempted to show how people who were driven by more or less identical interests in salvation ended up with very different attitudes toward economic life (see figure 5.8). In the second half of the famous formulation, just cited, about its being ideal and material interests, not ideas, that govern people's actions, Weber adds the following important qualification: "Very frequently the 'world images' that have been created by 'ideas' have, like switchmen, determined the tracks along which action has been pushed by the dynamics of interest."[71] In *The Economic Ethics of the World Religions,* Weber supplies several examples of such "world-images," including Hinduism, Buddhism and Confucianism, and shows how these have set similar ideal interests on very different "tracks."

A central concept in Weber's new studies of religion is that of "economic ethic," which is reminiscent of but not identical to what has later been called "moral economy."[72] Quite a bit of confusion, however, surrounds this concept, and there is little consensus on what Weber meant by it. One author, for example, equates economic ethic with Weber's notion of "practical ethics," while another argues that it is only applicable to a situation like the Middle Ages in Europe, when religion dominated everything in society, including its economy.[73] The most common interpretation, however, is the following one, which may first have been formulated by Marianne Weber: "By economic ethic he [Weber] meant, as he did in his first study [*The Protestant Ethic*], not ethical and theological theories but the practical impulses toward action that derive from religion."[74] Weber's wife, and several commentators after her, base their interpretation primarily on the following statement by Weber in one of the theoretical essays in *The Economic Ethics of the World Religions*: "The term 'economic ethic' points to the practical impulses for [economic] action which are founded in the psychological and pragmatic contexts of religions."[75] This interpretation, however, is difficult to reconcile with some other statements about economic ethic, which Weber makes in the same article from which this definition comes. Weber writes, for example, that "an economic ethic is not a simple 'function' of a form of economic organization," and that religion is "one—note this—only one of the determinants of the economic ethic."[76] These two statements make no sense if economic ethic is defined as practical impulses toward economic behavior, produced in a religious context.

Some of the difficulties surrounding Weber's notion of economic ethic disappear, however, when it is realized that when Weber speaks of "practical impulses for [economic] action which are founded in the psychological and pragmatic contexts of religions," he is not defining economic ethics in general, but is talking exclusively about one of its subcategories, namely "the economic ethic *of a religion.*"[77] In *The Protestant Ethic*, Weber similarly spoke of the "impulses" generated by ascetic Protestantism and how these under certain circumstances can turn into rational attitudes toward the economy (see figure 5.8). He now also says that the religious type of economic ethic comes to its fullest and most characteristic expression in one specific social stratum, which is "[the] characteristic bearer of a religion."[78]

But it should be noted that in the article from *The Economic Ethics of the World Religions*, where Weber speaks about the economic ethic of a religion, he also speaks of an economic ethic of a more general type. This latter type of economic ethic is that of a whole society, and *this* type of economic ethic is not "a simple 'function' of a form of economic organization"—a statement that reminds us of a similar argument about the capitalist spirit versus the economic form in *The Protestant Ethic.*[79] Weber also points out that an economic ethic of this second type has "a high measure of autonomy" in relation to religion, and that it is shaped just as much by "economic geography" and "history" as by religious forces.[80]

Once it is realized that Weber is using the concept of economic ethic in a few different ways in *The Economic Ethics of the World Religions*, it becomes easier to follow the complex argument in his three case studies. For China, India, and Palestine, Weber is first of all trying to track down the specific economic ethics of Confucianism, Hinduism, and Judaism and to determine in which social stratum these have come to their fullest and most characteristic expression. In the process of doing this, he also touches on the general economic ethic of these societies, as these have been formed by historical and economic-geographical conditions as well as by their religions. Weber's overarching purpose in carrying out the analysis in *The Economic Ethics of the World Religions* was to find out why rational capitalism did not emerge in non-Western societies; and just as in *The Protestant Ethic*, his answer has more to do with the spirit or mentality of the economic actors than with the concrete organization of the economy. But Weber's answer in *The Economic Ethics of the World Religions* is not limited to the economic ethics of different religions and what their characteristic bearers can tell you; he also looks at the economic ethic of the economy or society at large—and this is very different from what he does in *The Protestant Ethic.*

The characteristic features of the two types of economic ethics that Weber is referring to are summarized in figures 5.12 and 5.13, where I have also indicated what kind of practical and evaluative attitudes make up an economic ethic. Another way of expressing the whole thing is to use the term "norms" rather than "attitudes," even if it should be noted that Weber avoids this term and instead talks of actors' being oriented to a "legitimate order" in the form of a "convention" (for Weber's discussion of "legitimate order," see chapter 2). The norms that make up an economic ethic have been divided into a number of different categories, to make it easier to follow what Weber was looking for when he was writ-

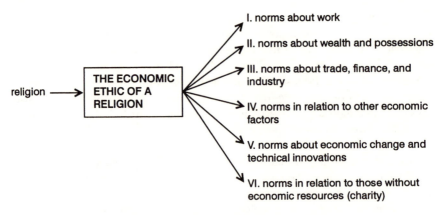

Fig. 5.12. The Economic Ethic of a Religion, according to Weber

Source: See especially Max Weber, "The Social Psychology of World Religions," pp. 267–68 in Hans Gerth and C. Wright Mills, eds., *From Max Weber* (New York: Oxford University Press, 1946).

Comment: An individual's adoption of a religious faith produces impulses to action in a variety of spheres, including the economic sphere. A number of individuals produce in this manner what Weber calls the economic ethic of a religion. Like all types of economic ethic, the economic ethic of a religion implies specific evaluative attitudes (or norms) toward work, wealth, trade, and so on. A certain stratum in society is typically central in shaping and expressing the characteristic features of a religion, and hence also its economic ethic.

ing *The Economic Ethics of the World Religions*: norms about work; norms about wealth and possessions; norms about trade, industry, and finance; norms about economic change and technical innovation; norms about giving to those without economic resources (charity); and norms about other economic actors.

Work, for example, can be viewed with contempt; it can also be viewed with indifference; and it can be viewed as a vocation. Religions often forbid certain types of work. Possessions and wealth can similarly be approved or disapproved of; and their owners may be encouraged to indulge in luxuries or told that doing so would be wrong. Usually, wealth is acceptable to other members of one's stratum only if it has been acquired in a certain way, such as through war, inheritance, or work. Most religions have disapproved of lending money for profit, and aristocrats have usually viewed trade as a form of trickery ("qui trompe-t-on?"— "who is being cheated?"—as Bismarck allegedly characterized trade).

There is also an ethical dimension to the way that people behave toward other people in economic affairs more generally. For most of history, the individual has been restrained in his or her economic dealings with people from the same tribe or family, while it has been permissible to be ruthless toward strangers and outsiders. This "double ethic," as Weber calls it, does not exist in modern society, and it is today considered "wrong" not to treat everybody the same way. Those with no economic resources have sometimes been treated with hostility,

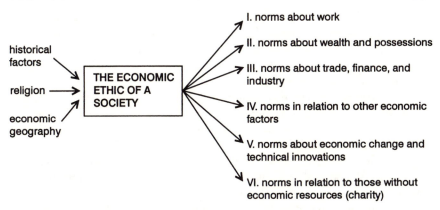

Fig. 5.13. The Economic Ethic of a Society, according to Weber

Source: See especially Max Weber, "The Social Psychology of World Religions," pp. 267–68 in Hans Gerth and C. Wright Mills, eds., *From Max Weber* (New York: Oxford University Press, 1946).

Comment: An economic ethic can be characterized as a number of evaluative attitudes (or norms) toward the different activities that make up an economy (such as work, trade, finance, and the like). The economic ethic of a society has a certain autonomy; and it is influenced by historical, religious, and economic-geographic factors.

and at other times with a certain benevolence. The Puritans, for example, were against begging, while most other religions have encouraged charitable behavior toward those who are poor and who beg. Finally, an economic ethic also entails specific attitudes toward economic change and technical innovations. Economic novelties and technical changes can be seen as something positive or as something to be feared. In China and India, for example, technical innovations were deeply feared for magical and religious reasons; there was also, as we know, a tendency to stereotype existing tools and technology.

In *The Religion of China,* which is the first study in *The Economic Ethics of the World Religions,* Weber addresses two related questions: Why did rational capitalism not emerge in China, and what impact did the economic ethic of its various religions—primarily Confucianism—have on the failure of modern capitalism to develop?[81] Weber's answer reads like one of the many lists that can be found in *General Economic History* that enumerate the factors that account for the rise of rational capitalism in the West (see figure 1.2). No bourgeoisie of the Western type emerged in China or in any independent cities. Its legal system as well as the state were patrimonial and therefore not conducive to industrial capitalism, which demands a high level of predictability and calculability from the political system. There was little rational technology, science, or accounting in China; and its economic organizations were poorly developed in comparison with the ones that could be found in the city states around the Mediterranean in the late Middle Ages. The Chinese economic mentality was thoroughly traditionalistic, and so were its various forms of religion. Weber does not single out one specific reason why rational capitalism failed to develop in China, but he notes that in more recent times there were many reasons for this failure, and that "nearly all [were] related to the structure of the state."[82] Religion, in any case, was not the decisive factor.

As in his other studies of economic ethics, Weber begins *The Religion of China* by presenting the social and political structure; next comes a detailed analysis of religion. China, Weber says, was dominated by traditionalism in all spheres of life. The clan controlled most of what was going on at the local level, including social life and the cult of the ancestors. It also owned the land. Magic was prevalent among the peasants, and all innovations were seen as a potential threat to the spirits. Geomancy and similar types of popular magic dominated the thinking of the population and blocked any attempt to rationalize the economy. Mining, for example, was believed to disturb the spirits, and so did railways and smoke from the factories.

The literati, who were in charge of the local administration and important parts of the tax system, were firm believers in Confucianism; and the Confucian worldview was thoroughly traditionalistic in economic, social, and political matters. The Chinese state was patrimonial in nature, which meant that it was positive to substantive justice but suspicious of market forces. The state failed to rationalize the economy, to develop an economic policy, and even to control the money. The local economy was in the hands of the clans, which were bastions of economic traditionalism. The population was very hardworking and exceedingly thrifty. Individuals who were not members of one's clan were met with suspicion; and distrust permeated the economy. Economic organizations either imitated the structure of the clan or did not extend beyond the clan.

As already mentioned, Weber does not argue that a modern type of capitalism failed to emerge in China simply because Confucianism did not develop a capitalist mentality similar to the one produced in the West with the help of ascetic Protestantism. Nonetheless, Weber was particularly interested in the economic ethic of Confucianism, and the last chapter of *The Religion of China* is devoted to a comparison between Puritanism and Confucianism. These two religions differed on crucial points, Weber says, even though they were both rationalistic in spirit. Puritanism, however, wanted to radically change society, while Confucianism was reconciled to the existing order. Also their economic ethics were completely different. Puritanism viewed wealth with suspicion, whereas Confucianism valued wealth because one needed money to live like a gentleman. The Puritan regarded work as a vocation, and the Confucian shunned all types of professional specialization as contrary to the ethos of the gentleman. Successful and systematic profit-making was viewed positively in Puritanism; in Confucianism profiteering and deals in the market were viewed with disdain. In general, Weber concludes, the economic ethic of Confucianism constituted an obstacle to the emergence of a rational capitalism in China. *The Religion of China* ends with the statement that "the mentality" of Chinese society has had an autonomous influence on the economic development of the country, and that this influence has been "sharply counteractive to [modern] capitalist development."[83] Translated into the terminology of our two types of economic ethics, this means that the economic ethic of Chinese society at large helped to block the emergence of a rational type of capitalism.

Weber's second study in *The Economic Ethics of the World Religions—The Religion of India*—has a goal similar to that of *The Religion of China*, namely to determine why rational capitalism did not emerge in India and the possible role of religion—or more precisely, its economic ethic—in preventing it.[84] "Here we shall inquire," Weber says, "as to the manner in which Indian religiosity, as one factor among many other, may have prevented capitalistic development (in the occidental sense)."[85] Most of Weber's study of India is devoted to an analysis of Hinduism and the caste system, which he viewed as the most important feature of India's social structure. The Indian state varied in size: it was split into petty kingdoms at certain times and was a great empire at others. It was usually patrimonial in nature and relied heavily on the administrative skills of the Brahmans as well as on Brahmanic ideology to tame the population. The cities in India contained strong merchant groups but nonetheless failed to develop into independent sources of power. The notion of citizenship, for example, could not develop in the kind of atmosphere produced by the caste system. Pacifist sentiments of a religious origin also prevented the city merchants from developing a military power of their own; and the political rulers did not need the financial resources of the bourgeois strata as much as their counterparts in the West did. In India, Weber notes, the village was far more important than the city.

Weber defines caste as a closed status group, and he points out that it can be found in many places throughout the world, not only in India. What made the caste system in India so tremendously strong, however, was first and foremost that it had the support of a religion that advocated a very similar type of social organization, namely Hinduism; it was also supported by the kinship system. To the Hindu, in other words, it was a religious duty to uphold the caste system. The main goal in life, according to Hinduism, was to follow religious rituals strictly, thereby qualifying for a better position in the next life. An individual who did this over many lifetimes would eventually be released from "the wheel of rebirth" and enter into an eternal and dreamless sleep. Marrying the wrong kind of person, eating with the wrong kind of person, or even touching or glancing at the wrong kind of person could be ritually defiling and have fatal consequences for one's position in the next life. Different types of work were typically associated with different castes, and ritual restrictions surrounded these as well.

Historically, there have existed a bewildering number of castes, Weber notes, and it is not possible to rank them with any precision. Nonetheless, the four main castes are the Brahmans (priests), the Kshatriyas (knights), the Vaishyas (free commoners), and the Shudras (serfs). The Brahmans were originally magicians and worked as religious counselors to princes, administrators, and the like. They were paid with gifts of land; they were very greedy; and they looked down on agricultural work, money-lending, and trade. The Kshatriyas (later replaced by the Rajputs) worked as knights and soldiers for political rulers and typically got

paid through prebends. Like the Brahmans, they were allowed to own land and
were a privileged caste. The Vaishyas (free commoners) were mostly peasants
and traders; like the Shudras (serfs), they were among the lower castes. For a
variety of religious reasons the peasants were even more looked down upon in
India than in the West; and to their rulers they were little but a source of taxation. The Shudras could not own land and were often craftsmen. Some Shudras
worked at the royal courts; others did simple handicrafts in the villages or cities.
Weber also mentions certain kinds of ritually defiling jobs, such as tanning and
the handling of dead animals.

After presenting the social and political structure in the first part of *The Religion of India,* Weber attempts to show how the economic ethic of Hinduism has
created obstacles to the emergence of a rational type of capitalism in India. Many
ritual rules in Hinduism conflicted directly with measures that would have led
to a rationalization of the economy, but Weber emphasizes that it was first and
foremost the very "spirit" of the Hindu system that created problems in this regard. Since it was the religious duty of every Hindu to follow a series of ritualistic rules very closely, work tools and economic practices typically remained the
same. Technical innovations were deeply feared for magical reasons; and
changes from one type of work to another as well as social mobility were in-
stinctively disapproved of. Weber notes: "A ritual law in which every change of
occupation, every change in work technique, may result in ritual degradation is
certainly not capable of giving birth to economic and technical revolutions from
within itself, or even of facilitating the first germination of capitalism in its
midst."[86]

It is true that Hinduism, according to Weber, contained some rational elements. Unlike ascetic Protestantism, however, Hinduism advocated a radical
withdrawal from the world—and no "practical impulses" toward economic rationalism could consequently be created. Hinduism also had its magical elements, which were especially strong outside the religious and social elite. Just as
in China, in India the great mass of peasants lived deeply immersed in magical
thinking. All in all, rational capitalism was blocked by a number of factors in
India. On the one hand, the economic ethic of Hinduism, which was most fully
developed among the Brahmans, kept the rest of society in an iron grip through
the caste system. And on the other hand, the patrimonial state, the kinship system, and the absence of independent cities and a powerful bourgeoisie all made
it more difficult for a rational economic ethic to emerge.

Weber's third installment in *The Economic Ethics of the World Religions* is entitled *Ancient Judaism,* and it differs quite a bit from *The Religion of China* and
The Religion of India.[87] As in the other two studies, Weber attempts to lay bare
the economic ethic of Jewish religion and to establish why the Jews had failed to
establish a rational type of capitalism. In addition, however, he pursues another
theme, namely how Judaism made a decisive break with magic. This latter contribution of Judaism, Weber says, constitutes a true turning point in world history and was to have enormous consequences for Western society, including its
economy.

141

Ancient Judaism opens with a magnificent sociological picture of early Palestine, which includes its economic geography, its major social groups, and its political and economic structure. There was little unity in Palestine at this stage, Weber says, but in times of war the different social groups came together in a confederation under the protection of Yahweh, a war god from the mountains. Yahweh was in fierce competition with Baal, a god of Phoenician and Canaanite origin with strong orgiastic and magical elements. The supporters of Yahweh fought a hard battle to eliminate Baal and rituals like "the dance around the golden calf." Yahwism was later helped in its campaign against magic by the strong emphasis in Judaism on the study of law. The prophets also helped to combat the power of magic by demanding that people follow Yahweh's commands strictly and methodically in their everyday lives. The end result of all these different forces was that Judaism, as the first religion in world history, was able to break with magic. Weber further notes that, unlike many non-Western religions, which advocated a withdrawal from the world, Judaism remained oriented to this world.

Weber's analysis of Judaism, including its economic ethic, is dominated by his portrayal of the Jews as a "pariah people," or a people ritually segregated from other peoples and in a position of political and social inferiority.[88] Many factors were involved in turning the Jews into a pariah people, Weber says, and he devotes quite a bit of attention in *Ancient Judaism* to this process. One factor that early on began to set the Jews apart from other peoples was their exclusive worship of Yahweh. Another was the notion that the Israelite peoples were unique in the sense that they—and only they—had entered into a special contract or *berith* with God. Religious rituals and rules also separated the Jews from the non-Jews, such as circumcision, the prohibition of work on the sabbath, and the rule that usury must not be practiced against other members of the Jewish faith. Under the threat of assimilation, the Jewish priesthood strengthened these rules, with full ritual segregation as a result. Political and social inferiority were later added by the Gentiles, completing the process of turning the Jewish people into a pariah people.

One important reason the Jews have been willing to put up with so much adversity and suffering throughout history, Weber says, was that their religion contained a strong messianic element. One day, far off in time, the Jewish people believed they would reap a reward for being God's chosen people. In the meantime, however, wealth was fully appreciated by the faithful in Palestine, and so was luxury. From early on, Judaism also contained numerous rules requiring charitable behavior of the faithful toward other Jews, such as widows, the poor, and those in debt. This strong emphasis on charity was remarkable, according to Weber, because it was not so much the result of a patrimonial state (which for its own reasons often displayed an interest in the welfare of its subjects), but grew out of religious concerns. Another important feature of Jewish economic ethic was its double ethic and how it affected the issue of usury. According to Deuteronomy 23:20, "You may exact interest on a loan to a foreigner but not on a loan to a fellow-countryman." This double ethic naturally increased in strength when Judaism became the religion of a fully segregated people—and also when the Jews were met by hostility of other peoples.

According to Weber, early Judaism had strong rational elements, such as an emphasis on vigilant self-observation and self-control. But there were also decisive differences between the Jewish economic ethic and the ethic of ascetic Protestantism. While the Jewish businessman got blessed with riches for his behavior in areas other than the economy, especially the diligent study of religious law, the ascetic Protestant got rich because he worked so hard in his vocation. The double ethic also precluded the equal treatment of all economic actors, along the lines of the Baptists and the Quakers; and it allowed for a certain ethical laxity, since non-Jews could be treated in dubious ways. Whereas the Puritans despised such economic activities as usury and political capitalism, these were common among Jewish businessmen. For a variety of reasons, in other words, the Jews never developed a rational capitalist spirit; and neither did they contribute to the growth of industrial capitalism. Weber's term for the type of economic activities that the Jewish merchants excelled in was "pariah capitalism," which can be described as a form of traditional commercial capitalism.[89]

That Judaism broke so decisively with magic made it possible for rational capitalism to emerge many centuries later in Europe. As to the situation in Palestine itself, Weber's account in *Ancient Judaism* makes it clear that many factors besides the economic ethic of the Jews prevented the emergence of rational capitalism. One can perhaps describe Weber's two types of economic ethic—the economic ethic of a religion and the economic ethic of a whole society—in the following way. While Weber believed that for each world religion there was one particular stratum that had been "decisive in stamping the characteristic features of [its] economic ethic," this was in his opinion somewhat less the case with Judaism.[90] The reason for this is that the Jews were a pariah people in the eyes of other people and typically in exile. In brief, the two economic ethics had a tendency to merge in the case of Judaism.

As mentioned earlier, Weber never had the time to carry out his studies of the economic ethic of Islam and Christianity. However, he did include a short section on the economic ethic of Islam in *Economy and Society*.[91] A full study of Islam would probably have provided a detailed sociological profile of Islamic society (including its general economic ethic) as well as an analysis of the doctrine of Islam and of the emergence of the Islamic ministry. There would, no doubt, also have been a discussion of the factors that Weber saw as important to the emergence of rational capitalism: the cities and their middle strata, the political and legal machinery, and so on.[92] Weber's picture of the economic ethic of Islam, however, would probably not have been very different from the one that can be found in the section in *Economy and Society*.

Originally, Islam had a pietistic character, Weber says, and a tendency to withdraw from the world. Soon, however, Islam developed into the national religion of Arabic warriors with a strong feudal ethic. The goal of the holy war was to expand the political power of Islam and to supply tributes. There would be plenty of war booty, and Islam's vision of paradise, Weber notes, was one that any soldier would love. Islam also had rules against usury and gambling, and the faithful were supposed to support the poor. Weber briefly compares the Islamic economic ethic with that of the Puritans, and it is clear that the two differed on several fundamental points. The Puritan businessman, for example, rejected the notion of becoming rich through war-related activities, especially through the acquisition of booty. He also disapproved of the sensual dimension of the feudal ethic as well as its concept of sin. According to Weber, the Islamic concept of sin was ritualistic in nature and did not reach very deeply into the soul of the believer. Also the Islamic concept of predestination failed to produce the "practical impulses" toward economic rationalism that Weber was looking for, primarily because it did not make the individual assume full and methodical control over his or her everyday life.[93] There did exist some ascetic elements in Islam— for example, fasting and a certain tendency among its warriors to live simply— but these were not very systematic, especially in comparison with the lifestyle of the Puritan middle strata. In brief, no modern capitalistic spirit was ever produced in Islam.

When Weber died, his friend and colleague Emil Lederer wrote that the studies in *The Economic Ethics of the World Religions* "mark a totally new epoch, especially in sociological research."[94] But the discussion of Weber's work has been meager, especially in comparison with the amount of writing devoted to *The Protestant Ethic*. For a long time there existed only a few scattered comments on Weber's work on economic ethics, most of which singled out one of his three studies and ignored the fact that they were part of a larger work. Some comments were also influenced by the modernization debate in the 1950s and 1960s, which was often simplistic in character.[95] In the 1980s, however, Wolfgang Schluchter edited a series of volumes about *The Economic Ethics of the World Religions*. And more recently, *The Religion of China* and *The Religion of India* have also appeared in first-rate scholarly editions as part of Weber's collected works.

Although these newer works are of high quality, most of the secondary literature on *The Economic Ethics of the World Religions* is still marred by misunderstandings of Weber's argument, just like the debate on *The Protestant Ethic*. One common error, for example, is to claim that Weber viewed countries like India and China as ill-suited for capitalist development. In fact, what Weber tried to explain was something quite different, namely why rational capitalism did not spontaneously emerge anywhere outside the West.[96] A further common error is to state that capitalism did not develop in India, China, and other places, according to Weber, because these countries, like ascetic Protestantism, lacked a religion that could create a capitalist spirit.[97] In *The Economic Ethics of the World Religions*, however, Weber argued that a number of factors other than religion also had prevented rational capitalism from emerging. These other factors, as we know from the preceding pages, include the structure of the state, the nature of the cities, the absence of a powerful bourgeoisie, and so on. In none of his three case studies did Weber attempt to establish—in the spirit of, say,

John Stuart Mill's method of difference and agreement—that everything hinged on the absence of a certain type of economic religion.

Most of the high-quality contributions to the debate on *The Economic Ethics of the World Religions* have dealt with the religious side of Weber's argument. And even though Weber explicitly stated that his studies were intended as a contribution to "economic sociology," there are no attempts to establish exactly what this contribution is.[98] It seems to me, however, that three tasks are of special importance when it comes to economic sociology and *The Economic Ethics of the World Religions,* and I shall say a few words about each of them.

The first task for economic sociology would be to confront Weber's analysis in *The Economic Ethics of the World Religions* with current findings in economic history. Not much of this has been done, except on China, where the current verdict is that Weber was wrong on several historical points.[99] Unfortunately, the secondary literature on Weber's analysis of India, Islamic society, and Jewish "pariah capitalism" is mostly polemical and ideological rather than factual in nature.[100]

A second task would be to submit Weber's analysis in *The Economic Ethics of the World Religions* to the same rigor Gordon Marshall applies to *The Protestant Ethic.* There are naturally some important differences between *The Protestant Ethic* and the later studies of the world religions, but one should still be able to make some progress by addressing Marshall's three key questions: What were the economic consequences of the religion in question? What would count as empirical proof of these consequences? And can we get access to historical material on these consequences? It is true that the single studies in Weber's series on the world religions contain more references to historical material than *The Protestant Ethic* does, but one is nonetheless tempted to extend Gordon Marshall's verdict on this latter study to *The Economic Ethics of the World Religions* as well: "not proven."

The third task that deserves to be carried out has to do with the way that Weber's main argument in the individual studies in *The Economic Ethics of the World Religions* is constructed. While the general thrust of these studies is clear—to study why rational capitalism has emerged only in the West—their analytical logic is nonetheless elusive and has not been fully established. Although the reader of *The Protestant Ethic* can follow Weber's argument step by step, the the same is not true for *The Economic Ethics of the World Religions.* Wolfgang Schluchter uses the term "constellational *description*" to characterize Weber's approach in *The Economic Ethics of the World Religions,* which may well describe the current state of the art.[101] Schluchter, however, does not state why Weber would have wanted to replace a causal historical analysis with a description of this type. Even though Weber was not interested in simply imposing his series of preconditions for rational capitalism in the West onto the development in other parts of the world, these preconditions nonetheless play a significant role in the analysis in *The Economic Ethics of the World Religions.* In Weber's individual studies we also find an attempt to get some leverage by using the concept of economic ethic in two different meanings. How all of these parts fit together, however, is by no means clear.

But even if *The Economic Ethics of the World Religions* still represents something of a challenge to modern scholarship, the analysis of economy and religion that can be found in Weber's work from *The Protestant Ethic* onward is tremendously rich and filled with suggestive ideas and concepts. Weber's analysis of economy and religion is, in my mind, by far the most imaginative part of his economic sociology—even if it is obvious that Weber knew considerably less about religion than, say, about law. It was, however, far more difficult and counterintuitive to show that religion had played an important role in the creation of the modern economic order than that law or politics had played such a role. Weber's linking of ascetic Protestantism with rational capitalism is particularly ingenious and represents the foremost achievement in his early work on economy and religion. Weber's second great discovery in this area, which took place some years later, has to do with his concept of economic ethic. Religion and the economy, he suggested, are always related to to each other through the moral evaluation of economic activities. Again, the concrete way in which Weber worked out the link between the economy and religion in *The Economic Ethics of the World Religions* represents a magnificent achievement in economic sociology.

CHAPTER SIX

Epilogue: Weber's Vision of Economic Sociology

WEBER had a powerful and original vision of what the science of economics should look like. Economics—or social economics, to use Weber's preferred term—should be a broad science and cover a number of different and well-defined fields, especially economic theory, economic history, and economic sociology.[1] Weber's own work was mainly in the field of economic sociology, although he also wrote and lectured in economic history as well as in economic theory. His work in economic sociology was, however, by far the most innovative. In translating his vision of economic sociology into innovative scholarship, Weber proceeded in a very systematic manner and looked at the economy itself and at its relationship to politics, law, and religion.

But Weber's vision of social economics was even broader, as I shall try to show in this epilogue. First, scattered throughout Weber's work are remarks about the relationship of the economy to topics besides politics, law, and religion. For example, in his economic sociology he touches on the relationship of the economy to art, science, technology, race, and geographic conditions; and each of these merits some attention (see section I). I will also say something about how Weber attempted to realize his vision of economics in his capacity as editor for the *Grundriss der Sozialökonomik*. This giant handbook in economics has quite a bit to tell us about Weber's vision of economics, especially about the topics that he thought economists should work on (see section II). Finally, I comment on what is still useful about Weber's work from the viewpoint of today's economic sociology. In brief, what is still alive and what is dead in Weber's economic sociology (see section III)?

I. ON THE RELATIONSHIP OF THE ECONOMY TO ART, SCIENCE, TECHNOLOGY, RACE, AND GEOGRAPHIC CONDITIONS

Weber was primarily concerned with politics, law, and religion in his economic sociology, but he also discusses its relationship to other topics, including art, science, technology, race, geographic conditions, and others.[2] Weber had originally planned to analyze art and science in a special pamphlet on "the economic and material dimension of cultural sociology," according to the *Grundriss*.[3] He never got around to writing this pamphlet, however, even though cultural sociology was of much interest to him.

Nonetheless, Weber's other writings provide a sense of how Weber viewed the relationship between the economy and art, especially his 1904 essay on objectivity. Artistic phenomena, he here notes, are typically not "economic phenomena," but are often influenced by the economy and hence constitute "economically conditioned phenomena." As an example of this, Weber mentions that the artistic taste in a society is often influenced by the social stratification of those who are interested in art. He also notes that material interests and other economic forces influence all types of art, and that they even penetrate "into the finest nuances of aesthetic feeling."[4] The idea that economic factors can totally "explain" a piece of art, however, Weber firmly rejects.

Weber also gives a few indications how he viewed the role of art in the emergence (or hindrance) of rational capitalism. In discussing the role that luxury has played in history, he often points out that the consumption of luxury items indicates a nonmethodical and nonrational approach to the economy. He describes, for example, how one family of artisans in China worked on the same vase for several generations. But art may also provide a stimulus for rational capitalism, Weber says. The notion of the scientific experiment, for example, which is so central to rational science (and consequently also to modern capitalism) emerged originally in Renaissance art, through the efforts of Leonardo da Vinci and others. The negative attitude toward art that can be found in ascetic Protestantism also helped to eliminate spontaneity and sensuality, and so encouraged rational economic behavior. Through its negative attitude toward art, Weber notes, ascetic Protestantism furthermore made behavior more uniform and thereby helped to standardize production.[5]

A few other hints of what Weber's pamphlet on "the economic and material dimension of cultural sociology" might have contained can be found in *The Rational and Social Foundations of Music*. The main theme in this work is how a rational approach to music has emerged only in the West; and from Weber's analysis it is clear that economic factors played a very small role in this process. He does say that a relationship between music and the economy exists, however, noting, for example, that there was a social ranking of instruments at the royal courts during the Middle Ages. Those who played the lute at Queen Elizabeth's court in England, for example, were paid several times more than those who played the violin or the bagpipe. In modern times certain instruments have also gained prominence through the ease with which they can be mass produced. This is especially true of the piano, which Weber discusses at some length, and which he labels "a middle-class home instrument."[6]

Although art has had only a minor influence on the economy, the same is not true for science—and this makes what Weber has to say on this topic of special interest. Rational science, Weber argues, has emerged only in the West and plays a very important role in modern capitalism. By "rational science" Weber means natural science with a mathematical foundation, which is developed through experimentation by a specially trained staff in laboratories. Western science united with capitalism in the eighteenth century, according to Weber, and this meant that the production of goods could be liberated from economic traditionalism. "The freely roving intelligence [of the scientist]" was now set free; and ever since this time, "modern science [has constituted] the technical basis of capitalism."[7]

Weber's statements on science have attracted quite a bit of attention in the secondary literature, including his alleged thesis that only ascetic Protestantism, not Catholicism, helped modern science to emerge. Weber's position on this last issue is, however, somewhat different from what is usually believed. For example, he does *not* suggest that only ascetic Protestantism helped modern science to emerge, but argues that both Catholicism and ascetic Protestantism have been active in this regard, albeit in different ways. Ascetic Protestantism has in particular made two contributions to modern science. First, even though the ascetic Protestants strongly disapproved of idle speculations, including scientific ones, they very much encouraged the practical use of science. Second, ascetic Protestantism fostered the economic use of science. In Weber's formulation, ascetic Protestantism played an important role in "the practical and . . . methodical inclusion of natural science in the service of the economy."[8]

Weber's statements on science and economy are so fragmentary that they are better characterized as interesting suggestions rather than as systematic propositions, but his views on the relationship between technology and the economy are more well developed. There is, for example, a section on what characterizes technology in the chapter on economic sociology in *Economy and Society* (§1), and the historical evolution of technology is also discussed in a few places in *General Economic History*. In *Economy and Society*, Weber explains that both economic action and technical action are oriented to the *means* of action, but in very different ways. In economic action, the primary orientation is to the scarcity of means, and there is also a choice between different ends. A consumer may, for example, choose between buying item A or item B, and an entrepreneur may decide between producing item A or item B. A technical action, in contrast, is oriented exclusively to the means; and the only interesting question is in principle the following one: Given a particular goal, what means should be used? Weber illustrates the difference between economic action and technical action with an example from mining. How to bring minerals to the surface is a technical problem; whether doing so is also profitable is an economic problem.

In principle, technical action is not concerned with prices or costs, only with how something can be done. If a technical problem demands the use of platinum rather than iron, Weber says, platinum will be used. In most cases, however, economic concerns are also present in technical problems; and this means that technical action, in addition to being oriented to technical problems, is usually oriented to the scarcity of means as well. "In reality," as Weber once put it at a meeting of the Verein für Sozialpolitik, "technology is nothing but a form of applied economics, which is determined by a certain problem, since in the last instance each technician asks, What does it cost?"[9]

Weber furthermore notes that economic concerns have been the most important factor in the evolution of technology throughout history, and that especially in modern capitalism, the development of technology is determined by the profit motive. This does not mean, however, that no other forces have influenced the development of technology throughout history. As usual, the situation is more complex: "In addition, a part has been played by the games and cogitations of impractical ideologists, a part by other-worldly interests and all sorts of fantasies, a part by preoccupation with artistic problems, and by various other non-economic motives."[10]

Weber explains that there is no room for a history of technology in the chapter on economic sociology in *Economy and Society,* but he does discuss aspects of such a history in *General Economic History.* In the chapter on transportation, for example, he looks at technological advances in commerce that have helped to expand the market. These innovations include everything from the inflated goat bags that once were used to cross rivers in Assyria and Babylonia to the invention of modern nautical instruments many centuries later. The most substantial discussion of the history of technology in *General Economic History* is in a chapter called "The Development of Industrial Technique," in which Weber covers a host of interesting issues, including the emergence of the modern factory, the technological advances of the eighteenth century, and why no rational technology has appeared outside of the West. Weber notes, as most economic historians do, that the cotton industry led the way, thanks to several important mechanical innovations, but he attributes a much more strategic role to the iron industry than most others do. By the seventeenth century the forests of England had been used up, Weber says, and industrial development had practically come to a standstill. A substitute for wood and charcoal had to be found, and this problem was not solved until the coking of coal was discovered in the early 1700s. If this discovery had not been made, Weber says, Western capitalism might well have been stopped. "What would have happened to the development of capitalism or to Europe in the absence of this development, we do not know."[11]

A central theme in Weber's writings on technology is his critique of technological determinism. He sharply criticizes the idea that technology constitutes the final or ultimate cause in the evolution of mankind; and he argues that technology may influence the economy or politics—but also the reverse.[12] A given state of technology, he adds, does not necessarily entail a special organization of the economy, and neither does one type of economy entail a specific technology. Weber furthermore warns against the tendency to overemphasize the technical dimension of socio-economic phenomena. It may, for example, be tempting to define the modern factory purely in terms of machinery, he says, but what really distinguishes the factory from the workshop of antiquity is something else—namely, the social status of the labor force (free labor) and the way that profit-making is organized (capital accounting).[13]

Much of today's debate about the relationship between the economy and technology focuses on the role of the Industrial Revolution, and it may therefore be of some interest to see how Weber viewed this event. It is clear that Weber believed that the technological innovations of the Industrial Revolution were not the most important factor in the development of capitalism. Weber also chose not to use the term Industrial Revolution, which was becoming popular in his day.[14] In Weber's view, political as well as religious and economic factors had played very important roles in the economic developments during 1760–1830; and there was no reason to focus exclusively on the contribution of technology. Indeed, Weber criticizes "the common error of thinking that particular *techni-*

cal achievements were the sole cause of the development of capitalism."[15] In addition, Weber believed that the role of technology in the Industrial Revolution had been exaggerated. In his judgment, the reason technology could develop so forcefully in the first place during this period was that a mass market already existed—a fact that in its turn had much to do with the changing distribution of wealth and income. The idea that technological discoveries could somehow by themselves set off an industrial revolution was utterly alien to Weber.

But Weber did not only consider how social phenomena—such as art, science, and technology—interacted with the economy. He also addressed the role played by nonsocial phenomena in the methodological chapter of *Economy and Society* (§1), saying they are phenomena that are in principle devoid of meaning. Typical examples are race, biological constitution, and the geographic environment. Because these phenomena are not meaningful, according to Weber, they cannot in themselves be analyzed with the help of sociology. They do, however, affect social actions, and it is in this respect that they enter the domain of sociology.

Phenomena devoid of meaning primarily affect social actions in the following ways, according to Weber: as "stimuli," as "results," as "favoring circumstances," and as "hindering circumstances." Nonsocial phenomena can, for example, stimulate different types of economic behavior, and their results may also affect action. They can further constitute favorable or negative circumstances for economic action. Some examples of how nonsocial phenomena may influence economic behavior help clarify Weber's argument: hunger, for example, typically produces a stimulus to look for food; and physical exertion results in fatigue. Or a climate with poor soil and extreme cold makes it hard for human beings to survive, while a better soil and a moderate temperature constitute favorable circumstances in this respect.

One of the nonmeaningful phenomena that interested Weber was race, and in his outline for the *Grundriss* from 1910 he had put himself down as the author of a section on "economy and race" (it was later assigned to Robert Michels).[16] The early version of the *Grundriss* was also to have contained a section on capitalism and "modern degeneration problems" in the population.[17] In his writings from the 1890s Weber used the concept of race in a rather loose sense, to mean something similar to *Volk*, and he argued that it played an important role in the economy.[18] "The Slav race" and "the German race," Weber said in his inaugural lecture in Freiburg, have, for example, very different attitudes about what constitutes a minimum standard of living, and these attitudes help to explain their economic behavior.[19]

A few years later, Weber became critical of the loose way the concept of race was used in academic circles and began referring to race more cautiously. In his 1904 article on objectivity, which contains Weber's program for social economics, he emphasizes that race is often used nonscientifically, but should be accepted as an argument only when the argument is based on serious empirical research.[20] From then until his death, Weber sharply criticized the way that some of his colleagues used race to explain practically everything in society. Even though race may be an important phenomenon, he argued, there is practically no adequate research on the topic. As a rule, he said, one should always try to explain a social phenomenon with the help of the social sciences and resort to race only when everything else has failed. Many economic phenomena, for example, which at first may seem to be caused by race, are in reality the result of tradition.[21]

Weber's work after the turn of the century does not directly link race and economic behavior.[22] Nevertheless, he often mentions instances in which people's *perception* of race (whether accurate or not) has influenced economic phenomena. When a group of people think that they belong to the same race, Weber says, this will typically make them view their relationships to other groups in terms of attraction or repulsion—something that will affect their economic relationship to these groups. Furthermore, when a group feels economically threatened, it will typically react by closing itself off to prospective new members and use any pretext for this, including race.[23]

Weber was interested in the relationship between the economy and race, as well as in the relationship between the economy and people's biological constitution in general. In *Economy and Society,* for example, he touches on this issue when he discusses "selection." According to Weber, there are two different types of selection: "social selection," which takes place during the lifetime of the actors and means success for some actors in some particular area or activity, and "biological selection," which involves "the survival of hereditary characteristics."[24] At the heart of Weber's distinction between these two types of selection is an attempt to distinguish between the social and the biological in order to make the analysis more sophisticated. Social Darwinism, he adds, is far too undifferentiated and crude as an explanation to be helpful in sociology. [25]

Especially at one point in his life Weber devoted himself to the study of the relationship between people's biological constitution and the economy. This was in the years 1908 and 1909, in connection with a research project sponsored by the Verein, in which his brother Alfred and economist Heinrich Herkner also participated. The main goal of the study was to analyze the effects of modern industrial enterprises on the work force, and especially to study what kinds of workers were selected for work in the factories and how they adapted to their work tasks. In connection with this project, Weber conducted an empirical study of his own at a textile factory in Oerlinghausen, which was owned by his relatives. He studied wage records and constructed a number of charts in order to understand the fluctuations in productivity of the workers, on an hourly as well as on a daily and weekly basis. Chapter 2 of *Economy and Society* alludes to some of the more general findings from this research. Weber says, for example, that not only biology ("aptitude") but also 'inclination' and "practice" play a part in explaining the productivity of workers.[26]

Weber was favorably disposed to the Verein's desire to analyze problems that involved social as well as biological factors but believed this type of research raised difficult methodological issues. To point out some of the dangers involved, Weber wrote a methodological guide for the Verein as well as a book-length essay entitled "On the Psychophysics of Industrial Work" (1908–9). He says in this work that there exists a sizable scientific literature on the biological aspects of work, primarily by anthropologists, psychologists, and psychiatrists. In particular, Emil Kraepelin (1856–1926)—one of the most famous psychiatrists of Weber's day—had analyzed the productivity of workers with the help of "psychophysics," defined as the science that attempts to quantify the relationship between psychological and physiological events. Weber reviews Kraepelin's work in painstaking detail but concludes that most of Kraepelin's discoveries were of little or no use to empirical research because his research had been conducted under stringent laboratory conditions. Furthermore, although Kraepelin looked at such factors as fatigue, habituation, and recuperation, he did not, for example, discuss the impact of alcoholism or eating habits on productivity. Neither did he take into account the fact that workers have a financial interest in their work (!), or that they sometimes work less hard because they feel solidarity with other workers.[27]

In all his writings in connection with the Verein project Weber kept coming back to what he saw as the main issue—namely, the relationship between people's biological constitution and their work behavior. Weber's conclusions on this topic can be summarized in the following way. First, he thought that in principle it should be possible to integrate biological and social scientific data on work but that this integration was still "far away" in time.[28] Weber's second conclusion has already been mentioned but deserves to be repeated.

> It appears methodologically advisable, when analyzing [topics of this kind] not to take as one's starting point hypotheses of heredity, but ever conscious that the 'ancestral estate' may play a part at any point, always to examine *first* the influences of social and cultural background, upbringing and tradition, and *to proceed as far as humanly possible with this principle of explanation.*[29]

According to the methodological chapter in *Economy and Society*, the geographical environment is a further example of a phenomenon that is devoid of subjective meaning. From the beginning of his academic career, Weber had been fascinated by the influence of geographical factors on society and on the economy. For example, when he lectured on economics in the 1890s, he recommended that his students consult works in *"Handelsgeographie"* and *"Wirtschaftsgeographie."* And in his first major work in economics—the study of the rural workers east of Elbe—he paid careful attention to geographical factors. Polish workers, his data showed, were not only in the majority in the areas with poor soil; they also had the lowest standard of living in the areas with rich soil. Nonetheless, it was the better-off rural workers—the German workers, not the Polish workers—who wanted to leave the countryside and move to the cities. The reason for this, Weber said, was that the German workers required a higher minimum standard of living and had a more developed sense of freedom.

As this example from the study of the rural workers makes clear, Weber was no proponent of geographical determinism. In his writings he tried as a rule to examine the interaction of geographical and socio-economic factors, without any predetermined notion about which factor was the most important. He notes, for example, in his discussion of the different forms in which agricultural land has been appropriated in *Economy and Society* that these forms have often been "partially" determined by geographical conditions—but that "a large role" has also been played by political, military, and economic conditions.[30] Weber argues that Europe has been favored by its many useful rivers, unlike, say, large parts of Asia. The fact that residents need more consumer items in a cold climate, such as that of Northern Europe, than in Southern Europe or Asia has also affected the emergence of industrial capitalism.[31] That the economic geography of the West should somehow have been the decisive factor in the rise of the West, Weber firmly rejects, however.[32] Similarly, Weber notes that capitalism in antiquity tended to develop along the coast—but, again, ascribes no determinacy. Coastal capitalism was often some kind of political capitalism, he points out, and when industrial capitalism developed, it took place inland.

The most controversial part of Weber's analysis of the interaction between geographic and economic factors is his theory of "'hydraulic' bureaucracy," or the impact of water control on society.[33] In several studies Weber argues that the watering of land through irrigation, rather than through rainfall, typically sets in motion a process that leads to despotism and creates obstacles to rational capitalism. Among the examples that Weber cites are ancient Egypt and Mesopotamia, and to some extent China. Controlling water in these parts of the world entailed collective efforts and organization, and this led to centralization and bureaucratization. Bureaucratization, in its turn, meant that the ruler got control over the means of warfare—something that prevented the emergence of a Western-style feudalism as well as independent cities. Though Weber's thesis of a close relationship between the control of irrigation and despotism may sound logical enough when presented in this summary fashion, recent historical and archaeological research indicates that it is probably wrong.[34]

II. WEBER'S VISION OF ECONOMICS AND THE *GRUNDRISS DER SOZIALÖKONOMIK*

It is commonly recognized today that the structure and content of *Economy and Society* was deeply influenced by the fact that this work was produced as part of a huge work in economics, the *Grundriss der Sozialökonomik*. It is also understood that the various transformations that *Economy and Society* went through had much to do with what happened to the *Grundriss* itself, and that Weber made changes in his manuscript in response to what he believed were deficiencies in the contribution by Karl Bücher (for the history of *Economy and Society* as well as Bücher's contribution, see the appendix). What is much less known, however, is what Weber tried to accomplish with this handbook in economics, and what it can tell us about Weber's vision of economics as a science; what he viewed as useful in contemporary economics and what he felt was missing. Just as it stands to reason that the basic identity of *Economy and Society* has to be sought in the fact that it was part of a huge work in economics, it is also clear that if we want to get a good picture of how the mature Weber viewed economics, the *Grundriss* is a good place to look.

The *Grundriss* was a major publishing event in German social science. It appeared during the years 1914–30 in more than a dozen volumes, several of which were published in a second edition in the 1920s.[35] Approximately fifty economists contributed to the first edition and produced some five thousand pages of text. According to Hayek, the *Grundriss* was "a huge project . . . in which the most outstanding scholars of the time participated"; and according to Schumpeter, it was "an important landmark in the world of German economics."[36] Despite this praise from two economists who were experts on the history of economics as well as contributors to the *Grundriss*, there is no secondary literature on the *Grundriss*.[37] No articles on its history or on its contribution to economics are to be found; and conventional histories of German economics mention the *Grundriss* only in passing, if at all. Part of the reason for this lack of attention is probably that the publication of the *Grundriss* took place over such an extended period—nearly two decades. In addition, the two first volumes appeared a few weeks before World War I broke out and were quickly forgotten in the ensuing turmoil; and during the war itself Weber more or less stopped working on the *Grundriss*. A few years after the war ended, Weber died, and the editorship passed on to Emil Lederer, a less competent and exciting scholar than Weber.[38] Interest in the *Grundriss* probably also faded because the idea of "social economics" never really caught on.

In order to write the full history of the *Grundriss* one would need access to parts of Weber's correspondence that are still unpublished as well as to the records of the publishing house, J.C.B. Mohr (Siebeck) in Tübingen. Weber's unpublished correspondence—such as his letters to von Wieser and Schumpeter—probably contains some new information that is not yet available. It should be noted, however, that his correspondence during the years when the *Grundriss* was conceived is available but contains little material on the structure of the *Grundriss* or on Weber's goal with this work more generally. What it does tell us is that Weber's publisher wanted to replace Gustav Schönberg's successful *Handbuch der Politischen Oekonomie* with something more modern, and that he eventually persuaded Weber to be the editor of the new handbook. Weber's published correspondence from 1906–10 also allows us to follow his troubles with certain authors and discusses problems that any editor of a huge project like the *Grundriss* has to face. Yet there is surprisingly little information in these letters about why Weber decided to structure the *Grundriss* as he did. To find out something more substantial on this issue, we must draw on two other sources: Weber's brief preface to the first volume of the *Grundriss*, which appeared in 1914, and his two plans for the handbook, from 1909–10 and 1914.

Weber had originally wanted to publish all the volumes of the *Grundriss* at the same time; this would have made it easier for him to convey his conception of *Sozialökonomik* and his ideas about the topics modern economics should deal with. As things turned out, however, the first installment of the *Grundriss* consisted of two rather disparate volumes: *The Economy and the Science of Economics* and *The Relation of Nature and Technology to the Economy.*[39] Several famous economists had contributed to the first of these two volumes, such as Karl Bücher and Friedrich von Wieser, but also the young Joseph Schumpeter. It was an oddly structured work, beginning with a short article by Bücher on the stages in economic history; then there is a history of economics by Schumpeter, the size of a small book; and the whole thing ends with a giant treatise in Austrian economic theory by von Wieser, entitled *The Theory of the Social Economy.*[40] The accompanying volume makes a peculiar impression as well, with a number of brief articles on the relationship of the economy to geography, population, and consumption, followed by a huge treatise on technology by Friedrich Gottl-Ottlilienfeld.[41]

There was, of course, a logic to all of this, which Weber spelled out in his preface to the first volume of the *Grundriss*. In particular, he tries to distinguish the view of economics that had infused the *Grundriss* from the one in Schönberg's handbook of political economy. It is often pointed out that Weber drew such a sharp line between the handbook of political economy and the *Grundriss* because Schönberg's heirs were threatening to sue (they thought they were being cheated out of their rights). But Weber wanted to distance himself from Schönberg for intellectual reasons as well, and these are more important in this context. Schönberg's handbook was divided into three parts, and it is clear from this division that Schönberg was still very much under the spell of cameralism. The first part of the handbook was on economics, the second on finance, and the third on administration (including poor-law administration).[42] In his preface Weber explicitly states that finance and poor-law administration are not discussed as independent topics in the *Grundriss*, but are referred to when they are of interest to social economics. In other words, Weber did not want to reproduce Schönberg's approach in the *Grundriss*, but he was willing to include topics from the cameralist tradition as long as they fit with his own vision of social economics.

It is also clear from Weber's preface that he did not want the *Grundriss* to be dominated either by historical economics or by theoretical economics. If Schmoller rather than Weber had been the main editor of the new handbook, the *Grundriss* would no doubt have been centered on some version of economics that was close to economic history, and it would not have contained a long section on theoretical economics. But the *Grundriss*—and Weber points this out in the preface—contains no general work in economic history. He also states that the *Grundriss* will not contain more economic theory than is necessary to understand the social economy. Economic theory, in other words, has a place to fill within the framework of social economics—but Weber was no more willing to let theoretical economics dominate the structure of the *Grundriss* than historical economics.

It would no doubt have been to Weber's advantage to include a forceful statement about the nature of social economics in his preface or at the beginning of each volume in the *Grundriss*. For some reason, however, he chose not to do so, perhaps because he did not want to impose his own ideas on the other authors. Instead of having a programmatic statement about social economics in the preface—for example, along the lines of the 1904 essay on objectivity—Weber emphasized that the contributors to the *Grundriss* belonged to different camps in economics and that no attempt had been made to coordinate their works. "In the long run," he writes, "all the different roads [in economic methodology] will come together"; and in a sense all of them *did* come together in Weber's vision of social economics.[43] Still, Weber did not make it easy for the readers of the *Grundriss* to follow his ideas about social economics, and many readers were in all likelihood unaware of the vision embodied in the work as a whole.

The very structure of the handbook also tells us something about what Weber wanted to accomplish with the *Grundriss*. According to the four-page chart that accompanied some of the original volumes, the *Grundriss* was to be divided into five "books," and these in their turn were to be divided into "volumes," which were to be divided into "parts," and so on. The final structure of the work is too complicated to be reproduced here, but a simplified version gives the gist of it (see figure 6.1). The *Grundriss* focuses on three topics: how to analyze economic phenomena; the nature of modern capitalism; and the different branches of the modern capitalist economy. The first of its five books is entitled *Foundations of the Economy*, and it is subdivided into three parts: "The Economy and the Science of Economics," "The Relations of the Economy to Nature and Technology," and "Economy and Society."[44] The last of these topics, as we know, was the one that Weber had reserved for himself. "The Relations of the Economy to Nature and Technology" has articles on the relationship of the economy to geography, population, and race. "The Economy and the Science of Economics" was to contain three works: one on the different stages of economic history (by Karl Bücher); a history of economics (by Joseph Schumpeter); and a treatise on "the theory of the social economy"(by Friedrich von Wieser).

Weber's outline of the *Grundriss* makes it clear that the reader was supposed to consult Book I for the basics of economics and then get concrete information from the other books: the two books on the nature of modern capitalism and the two books on the different branches of the modern capitalist economy. The principles of economic analysis presented and discussed in Book I were also applied in Books II–V, which consequently draw on economic history as well as on economic theory and sociology. The two books on the nature of modern capitalism deal with the economic and the social aspects of capitalism (*Specific Elements of the Modern Capitalist Economy* [Book II] and *Social Relations of Capitalism and Domestic Social Policy in the Modern State* [Book V]). The lead essay in the book on the economic dimension of capitalism is entitled "What is Distinctive about Modern Capitalism" (written by Sombart) and contains essays on "The Modern Legal Order and Capitalism" and "The Modern State and Capitalism."[45] Another essay in this book is devoted to the problem of price formation in the capitalist economy. Somewhat surprisingly, there is no essay on entrepreneurship. The book on the social dimension of capitalism has several essays on different strata and classes, including the workers, the middle classes, and the

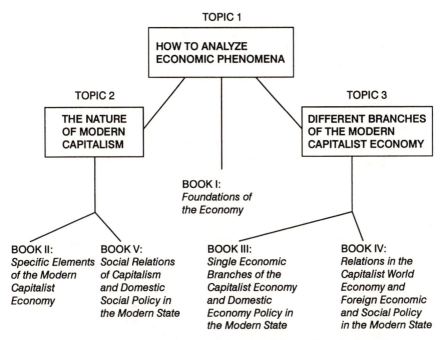

Fig. 6.1. The Structure of *Grundriss der Sozialökonomik,* Which Weber Planned and Worked on during 1908–20

Source: "Grundriss der Sozialökonomik. Einteilung des Gesamtwerkes," pp. x–xiii in *Wirtschaft und Wirtschaftswissenschaft. Grundriss der Sozialökonomik I. Abteilung* (Tübingen: J.C.B. Mohr, 1914).

Comment: Grundriss der Sozialökonomik was published during 1914–30 in more than a dozen physical volumes. This figure provides a simplified picture of its quite complicated structure. The *Grundriss* focuses on three major topics, which are analyzed in five major "books." These books are divided into further subdivisions.

peasants.[46] Other articles analyze income distribution, social policy, and opposition to capitalism. The two books on capitalism were published several years after Weber's death but nonetheless follow Weber's initial outlines.

The next two books of the *Grundriss* have long and awkward titles: *Single Economic Branches of the Capitalist Economy and Domestic Economic Policy in the Modern State* (Book III) and *Relations in the Capitalist World Economy and Foreign Economic and Social Policy in the Modern State* (Book IV). The former consists of about thirty articles devoted to different aspects of commerce, production, and insurance.[47] Most of these cover conventional topics, such as mining, banking, and agriculture, and are not very different from what can be found in any economic encyclopedia, including Schönberg's *Handbuch.* One article by Friedrich Leitner is innovative in its emphasis on the role of accounting in industry; and an interesting article by Alfred Weber on industrial location theory complements his famous monograph on the subject.[48] Book IV was one of the last works to be published, and it consists of a single volume on foreign trade and foreign economic policy.[49] Books III and IV, like Books II and V, were also faithful to Weber's original plan.

Three features of Weber's approach in the *Grundriss* make it unique and provide us with some additional insight into his vision of economics. First, the *Grundriss* brings an unusually broad perspective to the study of economics, especially in Book I. Economic phenomena are to be studied, but also their connection to and interaction with noneconomic phenomena, such as the state, the geographic surroundings, social institutions, and so on. Furthermore, economic phenomena are to be studied with the help of several different methods, including those used in economic history, theoretical economics, economic geography, and population theory. Members of different schools of economics had been invited to participate; Karl Bücher, for example, was a member of the German Historical School, von Wieser a member of the Austrian School, and Schumpeter an independent theorist (albeit with more sympathy for Menger than for Schmoller). Weber, as is clear from his choice of contributors, was open to the different perspectives in his day's economics and believed that they all had something to contribute.

Second, for the first time in the history of economics a sustained effort was made in the *Grundriss* to introduce a *sociological* perspective on the economy. This was done mainly through Weber's own contribution in *Economy and Society*, but also through the contributions of other sociologists and economists interested in sociology such as Robert Michels, Alfred Weber, and Werner Sombart.

Third, the *Grundriss* broke new ground by devoting so much attention to capitalism as a distinct economic and social system. Schönberg's *Handbuch* did not even have the word "capitalism" in its index, and theoretical economists, then as now, rarely speak of "capitalism."[50] Four of the *Grundriss*'s five major books are, however, devoted to this topic. In short, the *Grundriss* was unique because (1) it drew on the combined strength of several different perspectives in the science of economics; (2) it added sociology to these perspectives; and (3) it attempted to apply all of them to capitalism as well as to more traditional topics in economics.

Was the *Grundriss* a success—and did Weber get across his message about social economics? One can answer these questions in a number of ways, and looking at the reviews of the *Grundriss* is one of them. In general, the reviews were positive, even if not laudatory. It was recognized that the *Grundriss* represented a massive collective effort from the side of German economists, and that each contribution had been carefully crafted. The well-known historian Georg von Below, for example, wrote a review of the three first volumes of the *Grundriss* in this spirit.[51] But criticisms were also voiced. A few reviewers thought that the *Grundriss* would not be useful as a textbook, contrary to Weber's intentions, because it was well beyond the average student. This was the view of Eugen von Philippovich, himself the author of a popular textbook in economics.[52] Most of the reviews also pointed out that the individual contributions gave the impression of not having been sufficiently coordinated, and that there was no real unity to the *Grundriss*.

Weber furthermore failed to convey his message about social economics, to judge from the reviews. None of the reviews discussed the term *Sozialökonomik* or the ideas associated with it. A few reviewers, including Robert Liefmann, commented on the large role that sociology had been assigned. Like von Below, Liefmann reviewed some of the volumes of the *Grundriss* that had appeared in 1914 and which Weber himself had supervised. Liefmann said that the *Grundriss* should have contained a thorough discussion of the price mechanism early on and was also critical of how little von Wieser had to say on this topic. Liefmann was in general dubious about Weber's attempt to introduce sociology into economics. German economics, he said, did not need to expand its scope, but to delimit it. Weber's ambition in the *Grundriss*, he realized, was different: "A polymath like Schmoller, Weber attempts to encompass as much as possible [in this work] and to understand the connection between the economy and all other phenomena, including social, political, religious, and several natural scientific and technical phenomena."[53] The result, however, was "more breadth than depth," in Liefmann's judgment.

From the point of view of German economics we can say a bit more about the *Grundriss*. Several of the individual articles were important contributions to various branches of German economics, while others only summarized what was already known. Karl Bücher's short article on the stages in economic history is an example of the latter, while Gottl-Ottlilienfeld's long analysis of technology was an original work that was to dominate the German debate on this topic for several decades.[54] It should also be mentioned that three contributions to the *Grundriss* were to be singled out for international fame. The most important is no doubt Weber's *Economy and Society*, which has been translated into several languages and is still sold and discussed more than half a century after its original publication. According to Georg Siebeck, "[the *Grundriss*] was not a big success at its time—except the part by Max Weber."[55] The two other contributions that have become internationally known are Schumpeter's history of economics and von Wieser's treatise on theoretical economics. Most of the reviews of the *Grundriss* praised Schumpeter's work, which has also been translated into many languages. Von Wieser's contribution was singled out early for special attention in German-speaking Europe, and after World War I it was translated into English and published with a preface by Wesley Mitchell.[56] Unlike Weber's work, however, neither von Wieser's work nor that of Schumpeter is part of today's discussion, and they are rarely read, except by historians of economic thought.

Von Wieser's *Social Economics* and Schumpeter's *Economic Doctrine and Method* are usually discussed as independent works; the fact that they were originally part of the *Grundriss* is mentioned only in passing. Both works, however, show the influence of Weber's ideas on social economics. In other words, Weber's thoughts on this topic were taken seriously by some of the most outstanding economists of his day. That von Wieser found Weber's ideas of great importance is clear not only from the title that he gave to his treatise, *Theory of the Social Economy (Theorie der gesellschaftlichen Wirtschaft)*,[57] but also from the way that he structured his argument. In part 1 ("theory of the simple economy") there is only one individual, who behaves in accordance with a number of simplifying assumptions. In part 2 ("theory of the social economy") von Wieser introduces a number of other individuals as well as exchange; and he also discusses the role played by power in the economy. Part 3 ("theory of the state-economy") adds the state to the analysis, and part 4 ("theory of the world economy") assumes the existence of many social economies and state-economies. Von Wieser summarizes the thrust of his analysis in the *Grundriss* by stating that "modern economic theory needs to be completed by a sophisticated theory of society in order to be convincing."[58]

Weber was upset when he received von Wieser's contribution to the *Grundriss* and felt compelled to compensate for its deficiencies by making additions to his own manuscript. Weber's response may seem odd today, especially given the way many other economists have reacted to von Wieser's work: "the greatest synthesis achieved in economic theory in our time" (Hayek), "the first systematic treatise upon economic theory at large produced by the Austrian School" (Mitchell), "the greatest treatment by an Austrian in which the principle of marginal utility is analyzed in all its ramifications" (Morgenstern), and "his last and ripest message on pure theory" (Schumpeter).[59]

Exactly what caused Weber's displeasure with von Wieser's contribution is not presently known, except that it had to do with von Wieser's failure to discuss certain "sociological problems."[60] If we take this last statement as a clue, however, a likely candidate for Weber's reaction is the section in *Social Economics* that deals with sociology, where von Wieser was supposed to make the transition from pure economic theory to empirical reality.[61] This section is found at the point where von Wieser goes from "the simple economy," with one actor, to "the social economy," with a multitude of actors. In about twenty pages of text von Wieser presents his views on "social action," "social institutions," the dynamic between "the leaders" and "the mass," and so on. The whole thing, however, is of low quality and makes a poor impression. Von Wieser uses no other sources than his own thinking, and he failed to assimilate the far more sophisticated works in sociology by people like Simmel and Tönnies.[62] Belonging to the Austrian School, von Wieser naturally knew of and referred to Menger's ideas about institutions, but these also got bungled in his "sociology." In brief, while Weber and von Wieser may have agreed in principle that economic theory needed to be "completed" by sociology, the way they proposed to construct this sociology was very different.

Schumpeter was much younger and impressionable than von Wieser when the *Grundriss* came into being (he was in his twenties), and his contribution represents more of an attempt to follow Weber's ideas on social economics. Schumpeter's history of economics, it should be noted, is usually presented as a history of economic theory, but it is more correctly characterized as an attempt to write a history of *Sozialökonomik*—a somewhat different enterprise. To cover both what has been said about the economy and what has been said about the relationship of the economy to society, nature, and so on, was, of course, an extremely demanding task, and Schumpeter was not ready to take it on in its totality. He solved the problem by presenting and commenting on the contribution of each economist to economic theory and by noting what each had said about social institutions ("sociology") and about economic institutions ("economic sociology").[63] That Schumpeter more or less agreed with Weber's position in the *Methodenstreit*—that the historical-empirical approach of Schmoller was as necessary as the theoretical-analytical approach of Menger—is clear in his assessment of the Battle of Methods. Indeed, Schumpeter's whole theory about the birth of economics seems to have been conceived in an attempt to do justice to the different branches of economics. The science of economics, he says, came into being when the analytical approach of philosophy was united with the empirical approach of those who were interested in practical economic questions; and the first time in history that this happened was in the work of the physiocrats.

That Schumpeter continued to think about the project of social economics during the rest of his career is clear from his output after 1914 (when his contribution to the *Grundriss* was published).[64] Interestingly, Schumpeter brought up *Sozialökonomik* most insistently in the *History of Economic Analysis,* which is a much expanded version of his work for the *Grundriss.* In the beginning of *History of Economic Analysis,* which was written in the 1940s, Schumpeter explains in great detail how he views "the science of economics" and what it takes to be an "all-round economist." Economics, he emphasizes, is not a discipline that has been constructed according to some blueprint; it is rather a science with several different roots and a complex history. "The science of economics" or "*Sozialökonomik,*" Schumpeter then says, can best be conceptualized as consisting of a number of "fundamental fields": "economic history," "[economic] statistics," "[economic] theory," and "economic sociology."[65]

Schumpeter discusses each field at some length in *History of Economic Analysis,* where he also makes the famous statement that if he were to relive his life as an economist and could pick only one field to study, he would definitely choose economic history. This statement is usually interpreted as an example of Schumpeter's desire to go against the grain or otherwise "épater le bourgeois." If it is taken together with a statement that he made in his history of economics from 1914, however, a different explanation seems more plausible. In this work Schumpeter had criticized the suppression of economic theory in Germany during the second half of the nineteenth century. He also noted that this was all in the past, and what was much more worrisome was the hostility directed at the historical-empirical approach in economics. "We have every prospect," he said, "of seeing the unpleasant spectacle that the historical school suffers the same injustice which in its time it had inflicted on the theorists."[66] In brief, what Schumpeter wanted—and why he defended economic history so fiercely in the 1940s—was a proper balance between the different approaches in economics as a whole.

Like Weber, he felt that social economics could only prosper if no single approach were allowed to unduly dominate the others.

III. Weber's Vision and Economic Sociology Today

In the preceding detailed account of Weber's economic sociology I have said little about its relevance for current scholarship. The reason for this is that since Weber's death little attention has been paid to his economic sociology, and no attempt has been made to explore its systematic nature and the fact that it covers not only economic phenomena but also the interaction between these and other phenomena. Nonetheless, the ultimate value of any ideas in social science resides in their use for current empirical research, and in the remaining pages I therefore discuss Weber's ideas on economic sociology from this perspective. I first outline what is distinctive about the Weberian approach to economic sociology, and then contrast this approach with the one that is predominant in today's economic sociology. I then discuss a few areas in economic sociology where Weber, to my mind, was ahead of contemporary research.

Although my emphasis in this concluding section is on the relevance of Weber's ideas on economic sociology for empirical research today, I do not say much about their potential use in economic history and economic theory. That economic historians have not exhausted Weber's work seems clear enough. This goes not only for *General Economic History* but also for *Economy and Society* and *The Agrarian Sociology of Ancient Civilizations.* Some parts of Weber's work should also be of considerable interest to economic theorists, especially today, when many economic theorists are interested in understanding the role that social institutions play in economic life. Exactly what economic theorists will use in their quest for a more analytical and stringent approach to social institutions is not easy to predict. In general, however, it would seem that Weber's attempt to introduce social structure into economic analysis by starting with individual action, which is primarily driven by interests, would fit very well with the basic approach in today's microeconomic theory.

The emphasis in Weber's work on social action as action that is oriented to the behavior of others is, for example, also to be found in such classic analyses as Leibenstein's theory of bandwagon effects and Thomas Schelling's tipping models. A bandwagon effect is defined by Leibenstein as what happens when the demand for a commodity increases because others are interested in the same item; and in Schelling's tipping models, when a specified number of individuals decide to do something, other individuals change their behavior as well.[67] While both Leibenstein and Schelling have constructed formal models based on action that is oriented to the behavior of others, Weber does not. But Weber did make an interesting attempt to develop a set of categories in sociology from the perspective of other-oriented behavior: struggle, convention, exchange, organization, and so on. Weber also tried to use this perspective to account for some of the

I. *The unit of analysis is economic social action, defined as interest-driven action that is oriented to utility and also to the behavior of others.*

> Just as in economic theory, the analysis starts with individual action oriented to utility and driven by mainly material interests. Unlike economic theory, however, economic sociology views economic action as oriented to the behavior of others. Habit and emotions may furthermore influence economic social action.

II. *Economic action is presumed to be rational until otherwise proven.*

> In sociology the action that is analyzed is initially assumed to be rational. If empirical reality does not fit the rational model, another type of explanation is sought, based on traditional or affectual action.

III. *Struggle and domination are endemic to economic life.*

> Struggle pervades economic life, in part because actors are driven by interests in a situation of scarcity. Domination characterizes most economic organizations and also the political system within which the capitalist economy exists.

IV. *Economic sociology should analyze economic behavior as well as behavior that is economically relevant and economically conditioned.*

> Economic sociology looks not only at economic phenomena alone, but also at economic phenomena that are influenced by noneconomic phenomena ("economically relevant phenomena") and at noneconomic phenomena that are influenced by economic phenomena ("economically conditioned phenomena").

V. *Economic sociology should cooperate with economic theory, economic history, and other approaches within the framework of a broad type of economics (social economics).*

> Economic phenomena need to be analyzed using several different approaches, each of which has its place to fill within economics (primarily economic theory, economic history, and economic sociology).

Fig. 6.2. The Weberian Approach to Economic Sociology: Basic Principles

Sources: See especially Max Weber, *Economy and Society* (Berkeley: University of California Press, 1978), pp. 63–211; Max Weber, "'Objectivity' in Social Science and Social Policy," p. 63 ff. in *The Methodology of the Social Sciences* (New York: Free Press, 1949).

Comment: Principles I–III can best be studied in chapters 1 and 2 of *Economy and Society*, IV and V in the 1904 essay on objectivity.

interaction between economic and noneconomic phenomena, including law and religion.

In order to better understand what is distinctive about Weber's economic sociology, and how it differs from the perspective that is predominant in today's economic sociology, it may be useful to summarize its basic principles (see figure 6.2). The fundamental principle of this approach is, to repeat, that economic social action is conceptualized as action that is primarily driven by interests and also oriented to the behavior of others. Behavior becomes action through the meaning that the individual attaches to his or her behavior; through this meaning, action is also oriented to the behavior of others. Weber furthermore advocates a kind of methodological individualism in that he always starts with the individual. However, this methodological individualism is of a social rather than an atomistic nature, as in economic theory. In other words, individuals do not just happen to interact when it suits their interests, but consciously orient their behavior to one another in such a way that it affects their behavior. Different types of social structure are in principle to be understood as combinations of individual behavior, oriented to the behavior of others (even though the individual may think that the state or some other collective unit really exists). A central task for the researcher, in general sociology as well as in economic sociology, is consequently to establish the mechanisms through which a number of individual actions turn into collective social actions of a new type.[68]

Another important principle of the Weberian approach is rationality; and here the basic rule is as follows: action is assumed to be rational until proven otherwise. Rational action can be roughly defined as action that is consciously undertaken to realize what the actor views as an interest; this interest can be material as well as ideal. Ideal interests are typically related to values whose worth is inherent (value rationality). Material interests, in contrast, usually involve achieving a result (instrumental rationality). That all actors are presumed to act in a rational manner also helps explain another fundamental phenomenon in economic life, namely struggle. Struggle may be a consequence of scarcity, which makes actors go after the same resources in their attempts to realize their interests;likewise, when individuals feel that their resources are being threatened, they tend to monopolize or appropriate them. Domination characterizes most economic organizations and also the political system within which the economy, including the capitalist economy, exists.

Weberian economic sociology attempts to explain an exceedingly wide range of phenomena: "economic phenomena," such as pure economic institutions like the market and the firm, as well as noneconomic phenomena that influence economic phenomena ("economically relevant phenomena") and noneconomic phenomena that are influenced by economic phenomena ("economically conditioned phenomena"). *The Protestant Ethic,* with its thesis of how ascetic Protestantism has helped to shape modern capitalist mentality, is an example of the former; an example of an "economically conditioned phenomenon" would be the location of actors in different economic classes and strata, which influences religious beliefs. Finally, the Weberian approach to economic sociology is characterized by a cooperative attitude toward economic theory and economic history, in accordance with the principles of social economics. Weber leaves quite a few questions about social economics unanswered, but it is nonetheless clear from his writings that economic phenomena cannot be adequately analyzed by a single discipline.

Now, in order to get a sense of where Weberian economic sociology stands in relation to current research in economic sociology, some idea is needed about the evolution of economic sociology after Weber's death. Briefly, economic sociology did not take off and flourish with the publication of *Economy and Soci-*

ety in the early 1920s, either in Germany or elsewhere.[69] Influenced by people like Weber, Sombart, and Schumpeter, a few good studies in economic sociology were produced in Europe, but that is about all. The situation was more or less the same in American sociology. American sociologists showed some interest in economic topics during the interwar period, but not much. After World War II a couple of attempts were made to revive economic sociology—the most famous being *Economy and Society* (1956) by Parsons and Smelser—but little came of these efforts. To the extent that economic topics were analyzed at all from a sociological perspective, it was done within the framework of such fields as consumer studies, industrial sociology, stratification studies, and the like. In other words, most of the central economic problems were left to the economists.

The situation began to change in the early 1980s when a few major sociologists in the United States—especially Harrison White, James Coleman, and Arthur Stinchcombe—became interested in analyzing economic phenomena.[70] These sociologists had a number of talented students—such as Mark Granovetter and Ronald Burt—who quickly began making contributions of their own, especially by using network theory. The movement spread, perhaps fueled by other factors as well, and by the early 1990s one could for the first time in the history of sociology speak of a critical mass in the area of economic sociology. A number of high-quality monographs had been published as well as several collections of essays, including the *Handbook of Economic Sociology* (1994).[71]

In order to facilitate a comparison between Weberian economic sociology and the contemporary approach, I have summarized the basic principles of the latter in figure 6.3). Whereas Weberian economic sociology, for example, starts from a carefully constructed notion of economic (social) action, the equivalent notion in contemporary economic sociology is the more nebulous concept of "embeddedness." Sociologists' belief that economists have emptied the analysis of economic phenomena of all social content and that economic behavior consequently needs to be reinserted or "embedded" into society probably accounts for the popularity of this concept. In his programmatic and inspiring 1985 article, "Economic Action and Social Structure: The Problem of Embeddedness," Mark Granovetter says that the concept of embeddedness is carefully tied to network analysis. Economic behavior, Granovetter says, "is closely embedded in networks of interpersonal relations."[72]

In many works in current economic sociology that refer to embeddedness, however, this concept is used rather vaguely. Especially when embeddedness is used imprecisely, Weber's notion of economic action is to my mind preferable because it has a solid conceptual foundation. Weber's approach may also be preferable because it emphasizes the interest-driven aspect of economic (social) action, a feature that tends to get lost in much of sociology, including economic sociology.[73] The concept of embeddedness can lead one astray in this context by drawing more attention to the embedding than to what is being embedded. But Weber ties his economic sociology directly to interests; he also incorporates "embedding" elements through his notion of "orientation to others." Weber's

I. *Economic behavior is always embedded in social structure.*

It is essential to embed or reinsert economic behavior into its social context in order to explain it. The concept of embeddedness comes from the work of Karl Polanyi and was popularized by Mark Granovetter in a programmatic article in *The American Journal of Sociology* from 1985.

II. *The economy and its institutions can be conceptualized as a form of social construction.*

The notion of social construction comes from a notable and well-known work in the sociology of knowledge by Peter Berger and Thomas Luckmann, *The Social Construction of Reality* (1966), and it has become popular in many branches of contemporary sociology, including economic sociology. The economy can be socially constructed through networks (Granovetter), but also through other social structures as well.

III. *Rationality is not suitable as a point of departure in economic sociology because it makes unrealistic assumptions.*

Rational choice analysis is built on unrealistic assumptions; the actors are, for example, isolated from one another and have perfect information. Social structure needs to be introduced into economic analysis.

IV. *The main thrust of economic sociology should be to analyze economic phenomena, with less emphasis on phenomena at the intersection of the economy and other parts of society.*

In deliberate opposition to yesterday's economic sociology, it is argued that economic sociology and economics should address the same problems, namely those problems situated at the center of the economy, such as prices and different types of markets.

V. *Little cooperation is envisioned with mainstream economists; economic history is largely ignored.*

A few developments in mainstream economics are followed with interest, especially New Institutional Economics; more sympathy is probably felt for traditional economic history, which, however, is not followed very closely.

Fig. 6.3. The Approach of Contemporary Economic Sociology: Basic Principles

Comment: Since the early 1980s there has been a revival of economic sociology among sociologists, especially in the United States. This figure represents an attempt to formulate its basic principles, and it can be compared with figure 6.2 on the Weberian approach to economic sociology.

distinction between ideal and material interests is furthermore absent in contemporary sociology, which tends to view the former as belonging to sociology and the latter to economics.

The notion in current economic sociology that economic phenomena can be seen as "socially constructed" has a similar history as the notion of "embeddedness": it was launched by Granovetter, in whose works it is given a precise and useful definition, but it has often been used as a slogan, with little content of its own. According to Granovetter, the idea of social construction has its origin in Peter Berger and Thomas Luckmann's *The Social Construction of Reality*

(1966), where it is used to explain the emergence of social institutions. The way things are done in everyday life acquires under certain circumstances a specific "facticity" and is seen by the social actors as having an independent existence. How this process takes place in more concrete terms, Granovetter suggests (using economic institutions as his example), is through networks.[74] People interact through networks, and these can under certain circumstances "congeal" into stable structures, such as new economic institutions. Once an institution has come into being, Granovetter continues, further action is often "locked in" and follows a different logic than one that is driven by efficiency concerns.

In many of the works that speak of social construction, however, the term is used imprecisely and simply indicates that economic behavior and economic institutions come into being through some kind of social interaction. Just as people who interact may produce or "socially construct" a religion, they may also produce the economy. This approach, however, tends to neglect the role of interests and to result in a disembodied concept of the economy.

A further difference between the Weberian approach and current economic sociology has to do with the concept of rationality. Weber wanted rationality to be used as a heuristic tool in sociology, but many of today's economic sociologists believe that rationality per se is such an unrealistic assumption that it seriously distorts empirical research. To some extent, no doubt, the difference in attitude is due to the changes that have taken place in economics since Weber's time. Still, it seems to me that Weber's position is the more congenial one, since it is hard *not* to assume that most actors will indeed try to realize their interests or, more precisely, what they perceive to be their interests. It should also be emphasized that Weber has his own version of rationality, which sets him apart from the mainstream economics of today. Rational action, to repeat, is either instrumentally rational or value-rational, and interests are either ideal or material. Furthermore, not all actions are assumed to be rational in Weber's scheme; there is traditional behavior and affectual behavior as well. Finally, rationality can be a variable as well as an assumption in Weber's scheme, a fact I shall return to later in this chapter.

One of the really important points on which I think that the Weberian approach and contemporary sociology largely agree is that social structure needs to be introduced into economic analysis in order to improve certain parts of it. Weber's whole economic sociology can be read as a plea in this direction, and this issue is also central to contemporary economic sociology. James Coleman, for example, argued at the annual meeting of the American Economic Association in 1983 that economics would not be able to progress much further unless some of its underlying assumptions about isolated actors were changed. "The social assumptions on which economic analysis depends," Coleman said, "have allowed economics to make important strides in social theory, but [I would also like] to suggest that further progress lies in modifying or discarding those assumptions."[75] Granovetter has made a similar point, arguing that economics has gone wrong, not so much through its assumptions about rationality as through the assumption that actors are isolated from one another:

Critics who have attempted to reform the foundations of economics have mainly been economists themselves. Their attack has typically been on the usual *conception of rational action.* It is my argument here that there is another fundamental feature of neoclassical economic theory that provides more fertile ground for attack: the assumption that economic actors make decisions in isolation from one another—independent of their social connections: what I call *the assumption of 'atomized' decision-making.*[76]

One of the most exciting parts of contemporary economic sociology is that it attempts to analyze central economic topics in order to produce new insights using a sociological rather than an economic approach. On this point, today's economic sociology differs significantly from the economic sociology of the 1950s and 1960s, which shied away from the topics that were popular among the economists, thereby turning economic sociology into some kind of leftover science. Indeed, looking at exactly the same phenomena as the economists do has become an important theme in what is sometimes called New Economic Sociology, in contrast to Old Economic Sociology.[77] One result of this development, however, has been that many phenomena at the intersection of the economy and other sectors of society, such as politics, religion, and law, have sometimes been viewed as less exciting and important for progress in the field. Weber, though, believed that *all* types of economic behavior belong to economic sociology. As the reader is well aware by now, he also supplied a useful set of categories to handle this broad concept of economic behavior (economic phenomena, economically relevant phenomena, and economically conditioned phenomena).

A final point on which it is possible to compare the Weberian approach and contemporary economic sociology is their attitude toward the relationship of economic sociology to economic theory and economic history. As has been repeatedly pointed out, Weber hoped for a close and creative cooperation among these three sciences, under the umbrella of social economics. Contemporary economic sociologists, however, have much less knowledge of economic history than their German colleagues did a century ago. One reason for this is that economic history is today an independent field with a powerful tradition of its own; but there is also the fact that today's economic sociologists do not feel compelled to keep up with developments in economic history. Many of today's economic sociologists feel a mixture of alienation and hostility toward economists—a feeling that is usually reciprocated. The attempts by economists to introduce a more social or institutional approach into economics are, however, followed by sociologists with much interest and sympathy. The great attention that economic sociologists have devoted to the works of such people as Oliver Williamson and Douglass North testifies to this.

A comparison like the one I have just made between the basic principles of Weberian and contemporary economic sociology easily becomes abstract, and I shall therefore comment on some recent studies in economic sociology to make it more concrete. The ones I have chosen come from three central areas in contemporary economic sociology: networks in the economy, economic organizations, and cultural aspects of the economy. *Network research* developed long after Weber was around and has become one of the most interesting branches of today's economic sociology. Studies such as *Getting a Job* (1974) by Mark Granovetter and *Structural Holes* (1992) by Ronald Burt combine theoretical ingenuity with a creative use of network methods. There are also a number of important network studies of industrial districts and corporate interlocks. I believe the Weberian approach is a good fit with structural sociology (as network theory is also known), since both of them conceive of social structure as consisting of clearly specified and concrete interactions between actors. A problem with network theory, however, is that it is often better at structure than at dynamics, and here Weberian sociology could be a corrective. What drives economic action, Weber says, are primarily ideal and material interests, as these are perceived by the actors. Further dynamics can be introduced into network analysis by drawing on Weber's ideas of open and closed economic relationships, especially the idea that competition tends to be curtailed as the number of competitors increases while the profit potential remains the same.

Organization theory often overlaps with economic sociology to the extent that the organizations being studied are economic organizations. Weber's analysis of bureaucracy belongs to the classics in organization theory and has influenced many studies of economic organizations. But his theory of bureaucracy has been severely criticized over the years, and many of today's most interesting studies of economic organizations draw on sources other than Weber. For example, Ronald Burt's study *Corporate Profits and Cooperation* (1983) draws on a perspective in organization theory known as resource dependency. Burt's thesis is that the structure of competition affects the level of profit, and that the more structural autonomy a corporate actor has, the higher the profits will be. Other important sociological studies of economic organizations, which are mainly inspired by non-Weberian theories, include Neil Fligstein's *The Transformation of Corporate Control* (1990) and Frank Dobbin's *Forging Industrial Policy* (1994). In the former work, Fligstein traces the history of the big corporation in the United States; and in the latter, Dobbin makes a comparative analysis of nineteenth-century industrial policy toward railroads in the United States, France, and England.

But even if Weber's influence in organization studies is currently not very strong, it should be noted that contemporary organization theory and economic sociology have a restricted picture of Weber's theory of organizations.[78] Weber, it should be noted, discusses organizations not only in the famous passages on bureaucracy in *Economy and Society*, but also in many other places in his work.[79] Most important, Weber analyzes economic organizations as part of his economic sociology in chapter 2 of *Economy and Society* and in the chapter on the sociology of law. One interesting—and ignored—contribution of Weber in this respect is his attempt to construct the notion of economic organization, using economic action as his basic unit (see figure 2.7 in chapter 2). Another contribution is his attempt to analyze the birth of the notion of an economic organization per se; a development that took place especially in the Mediterranean city-states during the Middle Ages.[80] All in all then, only a small part of Weber's analysis of organizations (including economic organizations) is known today.

A few of the leading scholars in today's economic sociology, such as Viviana

Zelizer and Paul DiMaggio, argue that many or perhaps most economic sociologists fail to do justice to *the cultural dimension of economic phenomena.* By culture, Zelizer and DiMaggio roughly mean values, ideas, and cognitive maps and guides used by people in their everyday lives. Viviana Zelizer's study of people's resistance to life insurance in nineteenth-century America can be characterized as a type of economic sociology that pays particular attention to culture, as can her work on the changes in popular attitudes toward the economic value of children.[81] Zelizer and DiMaggio have also criticized structural sociology for reducing everything to networks and for being hostile to the idea that culture can be explained through means other than networks.

Many of Weber's studies in the sociology of religion are similar in approach to what is today being called cultural sociology. This goes for *The Protestant Ethic* as well as the individual studies in *The Economic Ethics of the World Religions* with their analyses of how ethical values infuse economic phenomena. In addition, Weber was interested in the relationship of the economy to art—a topic that contemporary economic sociology has more or less ignored. Today's economic sociologists have also paid little attention to the relationship between the economy and science, a field that Weber opened up for study.

Is one then to conclude from this comparison between Weber's economic sociology and contemporary economic sociology that Weber's work is sufficient to guide us today? I do not think so. Both historical research and sociology have advanced rapidly since Weber's day. Many economic topics considered important today are naturally not much discussed or even mentioned in Weber's economic sociology. The role of gender in the economy is one example; environmental problems are another. Today's economy also differs in many ways from the economy in Weber's time and presents new problems for the researcher. The role of huge economic organizations, for example, has increased dramatically, and Weber had very little to say about the internal structure of this type of organization, apart from his theory of bureaucracy. Also, today we have much better information about the structure of the German corporation around the turn of the century than Weber himself had, thanks to the work of people such as Alfred Chandler, Jürgen Kocka, and many others.

But even with all these reservations in mind—and one could easily add others—it is hard not to feel that Weber's economic sociology still holds up quite well. The idea that one must unite an interest-driven analysis with a social one is as important today as it was at the beginning of the twentieth century. Weber's suggestion that social action is action that is oriented to the actions of others is also ingenious—and to a large extent unexplored. The emphasis on struggle and power that can be found in Weber's work is furthermore a strength. And to this can be added—as I try to show in the next few sections—that on several important issues Weber is *ahead* of today's economic sociology. I use four topics to illustrate this last statement, but there are others as well. The ones I have chosen are law and economy, rationality, capitalism, and economic ethic.

Apart from a few suggestive hints in contemporary economic sociology, there exists very little work on the topic of *law and economy.* In Weber's writings, however, one can find a systematic analysis of law and economy, which has never been much discussed and even less used by economic sociologists. Among the many important questions that Weber addresses are the following: What kinds of legal systems facilitate or obstruct market capitalism? What is the relationship between economic development and democratic rights? Under what circumstances does law influence the economy, and vice versa? What is the relationship of the legal profession to economic issues? Through his knowledge of sociology, economics, and comparative legal history Weber was in an excellent position to tackle questions of this type.

A second area in which I believe that Weber is far ahead of contemporary economic sociology is in his analysis of *rationality*. As noted earlier, he argues that the assumption of rationality in sociological research is a useful heuristic tool. To this statement, however, should immediately be added that Weber's concept of rationality is unique, not only among sociologists but also among economists. One of Weber's most fascinating ideas about rationality is that a society, or some part of a society, can be more or less rational, depending on its past. That Weber viewed rationality from a historical perspective is well known in the sociological profession, but very little research has been done on this topic. Studies of the construction (or destruction) of economic rationality in different groups or in whole societies can, however, easily be imagined, and would constitute a real contribution to the field.

Weber also had the interesting idea that the modern form of rationality is to some extent a product of ascetic Protestantism. Weber's argument in *The Protestant Ethic*, to recall, is that the ascetic Protestants, through their belief in predestination and similar religious notions, changed their approach to everyday life in a most dramatic manner. A profound shift in personality took place, with methodical and repressive behavior of a certain type replacing traditional spontaneity and emotive behavior. Weber describes this process as the creation of new "psychological impulses" that develop into a kind of program for individual behavior in all spheres of life. That the very idea of modern economic rationality—just like the political party, human rights, and the modern capitalist mentality—has been deeply influenced by ascetic Protestantism is an idea that deserves to be further explored. Here as elsewhere, what Weber has to say about the influence of ascetic Protestantism needs to be assimilated and followed up.

Finally, there is the topic of *capitalism,* which always interested Weber. As we know, Weber came from a tradition started by Marx according to which capitalism was seen as "the most fateful force in modern society."[82] Weber contributed to this tradition, especially through *Economy and Society,* as did Sombart. After Weber's death it was continued, first and foremost, by Schumpeter in *Capitalism, Socialism and Democracy* (1942). Some sociologists, like Immanuel Wallerstein and his followers, analyze what they call the capitalist world system, but they play a marginal role in economic sociology and have also failed to incorporate many earlier insights in sociology and economics. On the whole, most of today's economic sociologists seem to shy away from capitalism as a macrophenomenon and seem more comfortable with a middle-range approach to economic topics.

This is a pity in my opinion because contemporary capitalism still represents a formidable social force and deserves to be closely studied from a sociological perspective. I also think that Weber's concepts of rational capitalism and political capitalism are evocative and have been far too little used. Contemporary examples of political capitalism would, for example, include industries that are economically dependent on the state, from modern farming to arms manufacturers and national airlines. Quite a bit of what is called privatization in the former Soviet Union and in East Central Europe also exemplifies what Weber called political capitalism, in that political contacts are used to acquire control over assets. It also deserves to be pointed out that although the concept of political capitalism is close to the idea of rent-seeking, there is no real equivalent in modern economics to the notion of rational capitalism.[83] In fact, today's economists still avoid using the concept of capitalism, just as they did in Weber's day. Nonetheless, Weber's idea that what characterizes modern capitalism is its methodical and rational nature deserves to be taken seriously. What kinds of institutions help to produce the contemporary version of economic rationality? What role in this process is, for example, played by accounting, education, rating techniques, and modern computers? Does global capitalism represent a novel version of rational capitalism?

Finally there is Weber's concept of an *economic ethic*, which is not to be found in today's economic sociology. This concept raises a host of interesting research questions, all having to do with the values and norms that inform economic activities and how ideal and material interests are intertwined. Certain types of work, for example, are looked down upon in modern society, as in all societies, and so are certain ways of making a profit. Wealth, possessions, and economic change are similarly viewed in negative or in positive terms. All of these attitudes, Weber tried to show, have important consequences on the macro level, more precisely for the type of capitalism that is possible.

Implicit in the notion of economic ethic is also a conception of what kind of human being should be valued in society. Weber himself, as will be discussed in the appendix, raised this issue in his inaugural lecture from 1895 in Freiburg and came to the following conclusion. The economic approach to things, he said, has suddenly become popular in all the social sciences, and people have begun to view economics as a guide to action. This position was unacceptable to Weber, who argued that it is impossible to derive value judgments from science. People should instead be encouraged to make their own value judgments, he said—and they can then use economics to realize those values. For his own part, he added, he preferred a society whose main goal is to produce individuals characterized by "*human greatness and nobility*," to one where "*well-being*" was the supreme good.[84] If the Nietzschean overtones of this statement are ignored, I would agree with Weber's viewpoint. These comments, however, take us into the realm of value judgments and also raise so many new questions that this may be a good place for the book to end.

A P P E N D I X

THE EVOLUTION OF WEBER'S THOUGHT ON ECONOMICS

ANYONE who is interested in Weber's work in economics will quickly encounter the somewhat paradoxical fact that although Weber saw himself as an economist with broad-ranging interests (as did his contemporaries), posterity insists that he is a Sociologist with a capital "S." Talcott Parsons, for example, early cast Weber primarily as a sociologist, and this is also the opinion of most sociologists today. Similarly, according to a number of economists, including Mark Blaug, Weber was not an economist but "one of the major figures in sociology."[1] Mainstream sociology and mainstream economics, in other words, agree at least on this point.

Weber's main academic appointments, however, were all in economics; most of the teaching he did was in economics; and throughout his life he presented himself professionally as an economist. In one of his last writings before his death, "Science as a Vocation" (1919), Weber speaks of "us economists"—just as he had done at the beginning of his career, as well as during the middle of it.[2] Add to this that during his last years Weber worked very hard as chief editor for a work that was to replace Schönberg's famous handbook in political economy, namely *Grundriss der Sozialökonomik*. Why, one wonders, would a "sociologist" be given the assignment to produce a handbook in economics? Why, in addition, would a sociologist refuse the establishment of chairs in sociology, as Weber did? And why should someone who was first and foremost a committed sociologist publicly state that "most of what goes under the name of sociology is fraud" and soon withdraw from the newly started German Sociological Society, while muttering how disgusted he was with this "Salon des Refusés"?[3]

The answer is *not* that Weber was an economist and not a sociologist—that would simply be to replace one misconception with another. Part of the paradox of Weber's being seen as an economist by his contemporaries and as a sociologist today is resolved when one realizes that economics was a much broader science in Weber's day than it is today. Around the turn of the century it was possible to advocate a social type of economic analysis as well as lecture on general sociology within the economics profession in Germany. There were several reasons for this. For one thing, because the professionalization of economics had just begun, the boundaries between economics and its closest neighbors in the social sciences were not as sharp as they are today. In addition, sociology did not yet exist as an independent topic, with chairs of its own and departments bearing its name. The most important reason, however, is that German economics from early on had developed in its own unique direction.

I. The German Tradition in Economics

Historians of economic thought in Germany usually start with cameralism, which emerged in Germany in the eighteenth century. The term cameralism comes from *Kammer,* or the place in the prince's palace from which his domain was administered, and as a doctrine it can be described as a mixture of state administration, state finance, and economic policy.[4] A similar emphasis on the role of the state rather than the individual (as in British economics), can, incidentally, also be found in two other early forms of German economics: the work of Friedrich List (1789–1846) and that of the Romantics. For List, economic individualism had to be subordinated to the task of constructing a viable national economy out of the German states. The Romantics were more radical: they celebrated the organic unity of the German people, strongly opposed individualism, and advocated economic autarchy. List, it can be added, was to become an important influence on German economics, while the Romantics were always marginal.

The Historical School of Economics, which dominated German economics from the mid-nineteenth century to the 1920s, clearly has some links to cameralism, List, and Romanticism, such as a positive attitude toward the state and to the German nation. Still, the Historical School was not only an outgrowth of these early forms of German economics; it was also part of an intellectual movement that was to have an enormous influence on German culture as a whole, namely historicism. A small work that Wilhelm Roscher published in 1843 is generally regarded as the charter of the Historical School in economics. Roscher here argues that one also has to use "the historical method" in economics, and that "this method aims at much the same results for economy as the method of Savigny and Eichhorn has attained in jurisprudence."[5] What Roscher meant by this statement is that just as jurisprudence had entered a new and progressive phase of its development, through the sustained use of a historical perspective, so should economics.

What was so useful about the historical method, according to Roscher, was that it allowed one to portray economic life as it exists in reality. "Our aim," he asserted, "is purely to describe man's economic nature and economic wants."[6] Economics should not only look at man's self-interest and be a guide in "chrematistics" ("the art of becoming rich"); it must also take into account man's "sense of community" and help to improve the human community. Roscher advocated the historical method for comparative purposes, and he was convinced that laws of development could be established with its help. Economics, he said, was "the doctrine of the laws of development of a nation's economy."[7]

The founding fathers of the Historical School of Economics include, besides Roscher (1817–94), Karl Knies (1821–98) and Bruno Hildebrand (1812–78); and all three strongly agreed that the use of "the historical method" was imperative in economics. Roscher and Knies only used the historical method for illustrative purposes, but Hildebrand applied it with full vigor in his own scholarship.

Knies, whose lectures Weber followed in Heidelberg in 1883, is usually regarded as the systematizer among the three founders and was a prolific writer. A central theme of the Historical School, to which Knies made an especially fine contribution, was the notion that the subject area of economics went far beyond the economy proper. In order to fully understand the economy, Knies argued, one must investigate its core as well as its links to the rest of society: to the state, to law, and to religion.[8] Weber was later to argue along very similar lines.

By the time Weber began studying at the university in the early 1880s, a new generation of historical economists had emerged—the so-called Younger Historical School. This group was led by Gustav von Schmoller (1838–1917) and included such prominent scholars as G. F. Knapp, Karl Bücher, and Lujo Brentano. The younger generation devoted itself to professional economic-historical research, often of a very detailed nature. According to Schmoller, theoretical economics only resulted in useless "Robinson Crusoe stories" and should not be taught in Germany.[9] Since Schmoller had excellent contacts with the Prussian Ministry of Education, he succeeded for several decades in barring economic theorists from professorships in Germany.

Schmoller also controlled an important journal and was one of the founders of the powerful Verein für Sozialpolitik. Ethics, according to Schmoller, was an integral part of economics, and this attitude was dominant in the Verein as well. Economics, he argued, must not be reduced to "a mere theory of market and exchange" but should be "a great moral and political science."[10] In their efforts to institute social reforms, Schmoller and many other of the leading economists in the Verein consciously blurred the line between science and politics. Lectures were characterized by a mixture of value judgments and facts, and Schumpeter describes the lecturing style of the so-called *Kathedersozialisten* in the following way: "Lujo Brentano addressed his classes as he would have political meetings, and they responded with cheers and countercheers. Adolph Wagner shouted and stamped and shook his fist at imaginary opponents, at least before the lethargy of old age quieted him down. Others were less spirited and effective but not less hortatory in intent."[11]

According to the influential Schmoller, economic theorists made the mistake of trying to isolate the economy from the rest of society, while historical economists had as their task to carefully study and describe the living economy of the people.[12] The proper way to proceed was to put together as many specialized studies as possible, and one day there would be enough knowledge to start constructing general theories. This goal, however, was still far in the future, and Schmoller warned against premature generalizations. During seminars Schmoller would often end his comments with the statement, "But then again, gentlemen, it is all so very complicated."[13]

But even if Schmoller had the power to ensure that only the "right" kind of economist got appointed to professorships in Germany and that economic theorists were blocked, there were several challenges to his intellectual authority. The two most important of these were the *Methodenstreit*, or the Battle of Methods, and the *Werturteilsstreit* or the Battle of Value Judgments. The Battle of the Methods erupted in 1883–84 through some exchanges between Schmoller and Carl Menger, a brilliant theoretical economist in Austria. The two main protagonists soon stopped communicating with each other, but the fight continued for many years between their followers and divided the economists in Germany and Austria into two sharply opposed camps. In the initial exchange between Schmoller and Menger, the former accused the latter of exaggerating the role of economic theory and of unduly glorifying one little room in the big house of economics. Menger responded in kind: Schmoller, he said, was like someone who came to a building site, dumped some building material on the ground, and called himself an architect.[14]

Many more insults were exchanged, and the lack of civility that came to characterize the debate testifies to the passions involved. As a result, the real issues tended to be lost or at least caricatured in such a way that little of their original meaning remained. Historical economists just put together facts without analyzing them, those on the side of Menger charged; and economic theorists just play around with abstractions without knowing the facts, Schmoller's supporters replied. Schmoller and his followers also made sure that the Austrian version of economics was not taught in Germany.

The issue in the Battle of Methods, however, was not only whether one should rely mainly on theory or on history in analyzing economic phenomena, but also what roles the different social sciences should play in economic analysis in general and what constituted the subject area of economics. Schmoller argued that the subject area of economics should be broad because the economy is an integral part of society. Economics as a science, as Schmoller saw it, consisted of a mixture of individual psychology, economic history, and economic theory. The economist starts with the concrete individual (*psychology*), gathers facts for a very long time (*economic history*), and after an even longer time tries to make generalizations using all of the facts (*economic theory*). Menger took a very different position. According to Menger, economics should concentrate on a much more restricted area. Although the economist should use a number of social sciences in analyzing the economy, these sciences must be kept absolutely distinct from one another because they address different issues and analyze them in different ways. Economic theory, for example, is sharply separated from economic history as well as from economic policy in Menger's scheme, but not in that of Schmoller, who believed that because they all deal with the same phenomena it would be artificial to keep them apart (see figure A.1).

On the division of labor between the social sciences, Weber's position would parallel that of Menger; but on the scope of the subject area of economics, it would be closer to that of Schmoller. Weber would also be much closer to Menger than to Schmoller on the issue of using rationality as a method in economic research; and he especially liked Menger's suggestion that economic institutions are often "the unintended result" of individual actions.[15] According to Friedrich von Hayek, Weber was "considerably influenced" by Menger's sharp separation between economic theory and economic history.[16]

The second big dispute that the Historical School of Economics got embroiled in was the so-called Battle of Value Judgments. This debate erupted in 1909 at a meeting of the Verein für Sozialpolitik, and this time it was Weber who led the attack on Schmoller's position. "I cannot bear it," he stated emphatically, "when problems of world-shaking importance and of the greatest ideal consequence— in some respect those ultimate questions which are capable of stirring the human soul—are transformed into technical economic questions . . . and thereby made into objects of discussion for an *academic* discipline, which is what economics is."[17] The second big clash over values versus facts took place in 1914, again at a meeting of the Verein and again with Weber leading the attack. On a series of issues Weber sharply criticized Schmoller and those who did not accept that facts and values must be sharply separated in a scientific analysis. No clear winner emerged in the debate, which was to continue after World War I and beyond Weber's death until the Nazis put an end to it.

II. The Emergence of *Sozialökonomik* and *Wirtschaftssoziologie* in Germany

There are two further developments in German economics that must be mentioned but which are usually passed over by historians of economic thought. These have to do with the emergence of social economics (*Sozialökonomik*) and economic sociology (*Wirtschaftssoziologie*)—two ways of doing economics that attracted quite a bit of attention around the turn of the century but that subsequently have been more or less forgotten. Weber made a great effort to further develop both approaches for his own uses. To cite Schumpeter: "the man who did more than any other to assure some currency to [the word 'Social Economics' or '*Sozialökonomie*'] was Max Weber." Schumpeter also notes that "[Weber's] work and teaching had much to do with the emergence of Economic Sociology."[18]

The term "social economics" is commonly thought to have originated in a work by Jean-Baptiste Say from 1828, which was immediately translated into German.[19] To Say, the term *économie sociale* was identical to *économie politique* and in principle more appropriate because it clearly indicates the social nature of the economy. It was sporadically used in England, France, and Italy in the decades following the publication of Say's work. John Stuart Mill, for example, commented in the 1830s on Say's use of the term, which he translated into English as "social economy."[20] In Germany *Sozialökonomik* (in various spellings) made an occasional appearance in the works of such people as Bruno Hildebrand (1848), Wilhelm Roscher (1854 and later), Albert Schäffle (1867), Eugen Dühring (1873, 1876), Heinrich Dietzel (1883), Karl Knies (1883)—Weber's teacher in economics—Carl Menger (1883), Werner Sombart (1888), and Adolf Wagner (1892).[21] Two important works in Germany that flagged the concept by having it in the main title were published in 1895 and 1907, and had been

I. SCHMOLLER'S CONCEPT OF ECONOMICS

A. The Subject Area of Economics:

   the economy is part of a larger whole, namely society; and it includes such phenomena as law, moral values, and the state.

B. The Division of Labor between the Social Sciences in Analyzing the Economy:

   you start from knowledge about the individual's psychology, gather together huge amounts of data, and then theorize – and the result should be used for economic reforms.

ECONOMICS
(Volkswirtschaftslehre)

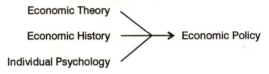

II. MENGER'S CONCEPT OF ECONOMICS

A. The Subject Area of Economics:

   the economy is a restricted area which must be analyzed separate from society as a whole

B. The Division of Labor between the Social Sciences in Analyzing the Economy:

   there are sharp divisions between the different branches of economics; priority should be given to theoretical economics; and the issue of reforms is separate from that of science

ECONOMICS
(Wirtschaftswissenschaft)

1.	2.	3.
The Historical Sciences of Economics (economic history, statistics)	Theoretical Economics	The Practical Sciences of Economics (economic policy, finance)

Fig. A.1. Gustav von Schmoller and Carl Menger on the Nature of Economics
   Sources: Carl Menger, *Investigations into the Method of the Social Sciences with Special Reference to Economics* (New York: New York University Press [1883] 1985); Carl Menger, "Toward a Systematic Classification of the Economic Sciences (1889)," pp. 1– 38 in Louise Sommer, ed., *Essays in European Economic Thought* (New York: D. Van Nostrand, 1960); and Gustav von Schmoller, "Volkswirtschaft, Volkswirtschaftslehre- und Methode" (1894), pp. 527–63 in Vol. 8 of J. Conrad et al., eds., *Handwörterbuch der Staatswissenschaften* (Jena: Gustav Fischer, 1911)

written by Heinrich Dietzel and Adolph Wagner respectively. Though variations appear, the main meaning of the term was that the economy is a *social phenomenon*.[22]

By 1910 the concept of social economics had become enough of a competitor to *Volkswirtschaftslehre*, which is the term that Schmoller preferred, that the doyen of German economics found it necessary to state why this term, rather than social economics, should be used.[23] In 1914 the first volumes of Weber's *Grundriss der Sozialökonomik* started to appear and a few years later Gustav Cassel published his popular textbook *Theoretische Sozialökonomie* (1918). The situation in the 1910s, however, may well have represented the peak of the effort to introduce the term *Sozialökonomie* in Germany; and many years later Schumpeter would note in his *History of Economic Analysis* (1954) that "[the term] *Sozialökonomie* or *Sozialökonomik* never caught on."[24] Something similar also happened in England, though on a smaller scale since social economics was less often referred to there. In any case, Alfred Marshall used "social economics" as synonymous with "economics" in the third and fourth editions of *Principles of Economics* (1895, 1898), but dropped it from the fifth edition (1907) and thereafter.[25]

Economic sociology in Germany came about mainly as the result of native developments. There was no awareness of similar attempts abroad—for example, W. Stanley Jevons's attempt to introduce the term as well as the idea of "economic sociology" in 1879.[26] One can distinguish between two stages in the emergence of economic sociology in Germany. During the first stage, which began during the latter half of the nineteenth century, economists began to discuss sociology, and sociological articles began to appear in economics journals. The type of sociology that existed during this period, it should be mentioned, was in many ways different from today's very specialized academic sociology. Nonetheless, a few economists—especially Schäffle and Schmoller—argued that since the economy is part of society, economic theory is also part of sociology.[27] In an important work from 1894, Schmoller stated: "Today general economics [is] of a philosophical-sociological character. It starts from the nature of society."[28] Several observers have indeed noted that there was a sociological quality to

---

Comment (to fig. A.1): Schmoller and Menger had very different views of the nature of economics and how to study economics. Schmoller said that one should start by assembling psychological and historical data and then gradually construct economic theory through generalizations; Menger argued, as did Weber, that even though economics draws on several different sciences, these must be kept distinct from one another because they analyze their subject matter in different ways. Menger, unlike Schmoller, also wanted to draw a sharp line between economics as a science and its use for economic policy purposes. While Schmoller's ideas remained largely the same, Menger in 1889 revised his scheme and added a further category, "the morphology of economic phenomena," which is an attempt to classify real economic phenomena according to type and species.

Schmoller's work, even though it should be observed that Schmoller's notion of sociology was vague and lacked precision.[29] Nonetheless, Schmoller had established a tentative link between economics and sociology—and through it, to the Historical School of Economics.

Some time later—during the second stage—economic sociology proper began to appear, as did the idea that one can apply the theoretical insights of sociology as a distinct social science to economic phenomena, and thereby elucidate some novel aspects of those phenomena. This movement got some wind in its sails when the German Sociological Society was founded in 1909, and when a chair in sociology and two chairs in "economics and sociology" were created a decade later.[30] Sociological articles became common in economics journals after the turn of the century.[31] A small number of works, more or less explicitly in economic sociology, also began to appear, starting with Georg Simmel's work on money (1900) and soon followed by the more straightforward studies in this field by Rudolf Goldscheid, Werner Sombart, and Joseph Schumpeter.[32] Weber's major work in economic sociology—*Economy and Society*—was produced during the 1910s as well.

From what has just been said it is clear that it was not Weber who in a strict sense "invented" either social economics or economic sociology; both of these emerged, rather tentatively, in Germany and elsewhere in Europe during the nineteenth century, well before Weber was in any position to pay attention to them. Once Weber had decided to do work in social economics and economic sociology, however, he did so with determination and creativity, transforming them in the process into solid and exciting projects. The story of how Weber gradually came to realize that social economics and economic sociology represented worthwhile enterprises is told in the next three sections.

III. WEBER'S EARLY WORKS IN ECONOMICS (1882–1898)

Weber's work in economics occurred can be divided into two fairly distinct periods in his life. The earlier period began with Weber's university studies in 1882 (he was born in 1864) and ends with his falling ill in 1898. During those years Weber was introduced to economics and worked several years as a professor of economics, first at Freiburg University and later at the University of Heidelberg. The second period began in 1903, when Weber had recovered enough to start writing again, and ends with his death in June 1920. Here I outline Weber's view of social economics in both periods as well as the contributions he made to its three major parts: economic theory, economic history, and economic sociology.

When Weber entered the University of Heidelberg in 1882, at the age of eighteen, he probably knew little or no economics. As a student of law, however, he had to study some economics, and he therefore took a course taught by Karl Knies. Weber found the first lecture "boring," but once he started attending regularly he began to appreciate his teacher's "extremely intelligent and creative disquisitions."[33] One reason for this change of mind was that Weber had now begun to study economics and to understand how economists think. As he wrote in a letter of May 5, 1883, to his father, "Now that I know a few basic economic concepts through studying Adam Smith and others, Knies makes a quite different impression on me."[34]

According to an interesting essay by Wilhelm Hennis, Knies made a profound impression on the young Weber through his insistence on the need to view economics as a science of man and to analyze the links between the economy and the noneconomic parts of society.[35] Though there is some opposition to Hennis's view—it has, for example, been argued that Schmoller was a more potent influence on Weber than Knies—it seems reasonable to assume that Weber's first (and only) professor in economics, whom he also admired, had an important influence on his thinking.[36] Many decades before Hennis's article appeared, Alexander von Schelting similarly emphasized that it was from the Historical School—"especially from Knies"—that Weber learned to view the economy as an integral part of a larger whole.[37]

Even though Weber was attracted to economics as a student and at one point even declared that he had "become approximately one-third economist," he never saw himself as an economist during these years.[38] He also chose not to take any courses in economics while in Berlin, even though Schmoller and other well-known economists were there.[39] All in all, Weber only took one course in economics as a student. His main identity was always as a student of law, and he was also extremely interested in history. His first doctoral dissertation was "in the border area between legal and economic history," according to his future wife and biographer, and the same can be said about his second thesis.[40] Both of these works, it should be added, also testify to a deep interest from Weber's side in the origin of capitalism. The first thesis was part of a larger work entitled *On the History of Trading Companies in the Middle Ages, according to Southern-European Sources* (1889) and looked at early forms of the business firm, drawing mainly on legal sources.[41] Special attention was paid to the role that the family played in these early corporations and to the concept of corporate liability. Weber's second thesis was called *Roman Agrarian History and Its Importance to Public and Civil Law* (1891); it dealt with another problem that was central to the birth of capitalism, namely how individual property in land had emerged in Rome.[42]

In 1888, Weber had joined the Verein für Sozialpolitik, of which many prominent economists were members, and during his years as a young barrister in Berlin he often associated with economists.[43] When Weber had just presented his second thesis in early 1892, the Verein appointed him and a few others to study the situation of the agricultural workers in Germany, assigning to each of them a special geographic region. Weber's allotted area was Germany east of the river Elbe, which was of special political interest because of the fierce competition between Polish immigrants and the native German population. Weber quickly produced a huge book on his assigned topic, *The Conditions of the Agricultural Workers in the Areas East of Elbe* (1892), which became a great success and was publicly praised by the foremost expert on the topic, G. F. Knapp.[44] According to Knapp, Weber had initiated a whole new approach to the topic:

"our expertise has been surpassed—we have to start learning from scratch."[45]

Weber's main thesis in the Verein study was that if things were left alone, the Polish agricultural workers would gradually push out the German workers, since they were willing to work for lower salaries than the native population; and his implicit conclusion was that some political measures should be taken to put an end to this development. Another difficult problem was that the Junkers, the powerful land-owning class in Prussia and Eastern Germany, had a direct economic interest in using the Polish workers—and hence, as Weber saw it, in weakening the German state.

According to Marianne Weber, her husband's interest in the Verein study was primarily political, but Weber's work also contains much material that is of a social scientific nature, indicating his interest in a social analysis of the economy. There is, for example, his important observation that what drove the German agricultural workers to move to the cities were not only material reasons but also "the *magic* of freedom."[46] This insight would later reemerge in his work as "ideal interests" versus "material interests." Another example is Weber's interesting and frequent use of the concept of "constitution of work" ("*Arbeitsverfassung*"), which he uses more or less synonymously with "the social and economic organization of work."[47] Also, Weber insists at several points in his study that it is not possible to rely exclusively on a narrowly economic approach when analyzing a problem such as the situation of the agricultural workers in Germany. "A purely economic standpoint," he states, becomes "unrealistic" and has therefore to be complemented with other approaches.[48] And finally, he argues that the causal relationship between the economy and society is not one-way, with the economy always affecting society in a certain manner; it can also go the other way, with "the causal relationship reversed."[49]

The success of Weber's Verein study led to an offer in 1893 from Freiburg University to become professor of economics and finance (*Nationalökonomie und Finanzwissenschaft*). The position had earlier been held by Eugen von Philippovich (who had moved on to Vienna, after recommending Weber), and it was believed in Freiburg that a very good replacement was needed.[50] Schmoller, who wanted Weber to stay in Berlin and remain in law, at first succeeded in blocking the appointment through his political contacts at the Prussian Ministry of Education. When the offer was repeated in 1894, however, Weber accepted.

Saying yes had not been easy for Weber, who had an excellent career in law ahead of him and who had wanted to remain in Berlin for a variety of reasons. He accepted the offer, however, because economics was such a broad and intellectually exciting science at that particular time in Germany, and because it was easier to be politically effective as an economist than as a legal scholar. In her biography of Weber, his wife explains Weber's decision to go to Freiburg:

> As a science, economics was still elastic and "young" in comparison with law. Besides, it was on the borderline of a number of scholarly fields; it led directly to the history of

culture and the history of ideas as well as to philosophical problems. Finally, it was more fruitful for a political and a sociopolitical orientation than the more formal problems of legal thought.[51]

Once in Freiburg, Weber took his task as a professor very seriously. He succeeded, for example, in upgrading economics by moving it from the Faculty of Philosophy to the Faculty of Law. He also spent a huge amount of time on his lectures because he had received so little training in the field as a student. Weber taught, as was customary, "General Theoretical Economics" and "Practical Economics," plus a few special courses (such as "Finance" and "The History of Economic Thought").[52] According to some students, Weber's lectures gave a "rather unsystematic" and "unfinished" impression; and his wife says that it was not until the spring of 1896 that Weber felt he had mastered his new subject.[53]

Weber gave his inaugural lecture, as was customary, at the beginning of his second term in Freiburg. The topic he had chosen was "Nationality in Economic Life" (in the printed version the title was changed to "The Nation State and Economic Policy"). Weber sent out a huge number of copies to various people, hoping his address would have a political impact. He probably miscalculated its potential effect, however, and soon came to realize that the "brutality" of his views had upset quite a few people.[54] What was brutal about Weber's views was, among other things, the aggressive manner in which he wanted economics to be a used as a weapon by the German state in its struggle with other states. Weber proudly announced himself as an "economic nationalist" and spelled out the national implications of his 1892 study for the Verein, arguing that the immigration of Poles into Germany had to be stopped: There must be a "stemming [of] the tide of Slavs."[55]

But in addition to its political message, Weber's speech contained a number of interesting ideas, most of which dealt with the role of economics in modern society. Weber noted, for example, that there was a general tendency in the public debate in Germany to let economics or "the economic way of looking at things" become the accepted norm, something which meant that the value judgments implicit in much of economics were accepted without any reflection. Weber saw this tendency as part of "the modern over-estimation of the 'economic,'" and he was deeply critical of it. To believe that one could extract values directly from a scientific analysis, Weber said, is just an "optical illusion."[56] Instead of hiding behind the authority of science, economists should be honest enough to step forward and say what they think should be done in their capacity as citizens. This is what Weber himself did, and what he wanted, to repeat, was a strong Germany that would stem the tide of the Slavs.

Weber gave another celebrated lecture while in Freiburg entitled "The Social Causes of the Decay of Ancient Civilizations" (1895/96).[57] In this lecture, which is still considered an excellent piece of scholarship, Weber presented his own theory of why the Roman Empire had declined. Once the conquests of new land ended, he argued, there were no more cheap slaves who could feed the Roman economy—and this led eventually to a return to a self-sufficient economy, centered on the *oikos*. As it became harder for the public authorities to collect taxes, the Roman state soon started to lose its hold on society.

While in Freiburg, Weber also wrote a number of articles on the stock exchange, mainly because he wanted to participate in the public debate. Many people believed that a stock exchange only led to swindles and speculation, and to counter this opinion Weber wrote a little educational pamphlet for workers entitled *The Stock Exchange* (1894–96). It became very popular for its clear description of the workings of the stock exchange and its role in the modern economy. That Weber's work on the stock exchange was inspired by his political interest is obvious from the final passage in the pamphlet, which says a stock exchange constitutes a "means of power in the economic struggle." Just as "rifles and cannons" are needed in war, Weber says, "a strong stock exchange" is needed in peace—"as long as nations carry on their inexorable and inevitable struggle for national existence and economic power."[58]

In 1896 Weber was appointed professor in economics and finance (*Nationalökonomie und Finanzwissenschaft*) in Heidelberg, to replace his former teacher Karl Knies. The reason why Weber was picked, to cite the people who decided to hire him at the University of Heidelberg, was that the young Weber "even today . . . promises to be one of the leading men in his field."[59] The aged Knies had let economics deteriorate, and one of Weber's first acts was to start a seminar in economics, something which was considered a necessity at the time in German universities.[60] Weber was also one of the founding members in an association called the Socialökonomische Vereinigung, possibly even the one who had taken the initiative to establish it. Little is known about this association, apart from the fact that its main function was to further knowledge in economics through contacts between economists and students from the other social sciences.[61]

As in Freiburg, in Heidelberg Weber taught "General Theoretical Economics," "Practical Economics," and a few special courses (such as "Agrarian Policy" and "The Social Question and the Labor Movement").[62] Marianne Weber describes her husband's lectures in economics at Heidelberg in the following way:

> He had now mastered his discipline and enjoyed the lucid, tight organization of his important lectures . . . His courses were always carefully planned, but for the rest he surrendered to the inspiration of the moment and spoke without notes. The severe conceptual structure was clothed with a wealth of historical knowledge; his uncommon mental acuity was supplemented by an equally uncommon descriptive power. Thus he made even the most abstract ideas comprehensible by a profusion of examples and the directness of his lecturing style. Each course of lectures seemed to have been freshly produced in the workshop of his mind.[63]

Even though Weber's oratory skill and encyclopedic knowledge must have made his lectures memorable, everyone was not happy with them. It was, for example, noted in one issue of *Der Sozialistische Student* from 1898 that those who had brought Weber to Heidelberg in the hope of strengthening the Historical

School were deeply disappointed when they realized that he was in fact a "champion of the Austrian School."[64]

While at Heidelberg, Weber produced two early versions of what was later to become a book on the social and economic history of antiquity, *Agrarverhältnisse im Altertum*, or *The Agrarian Sociology of Ancient Civilizations*, as it is known in English.[65] His attempt to master practically the whole economic history of humanity is also evident from his course on general economic theory and a celebrated series of public lectures that Weber gave in Mannheim in 1897 entitled "The Course of Economic Development." No manuscript has survived from the latter lecture series, but its general content is known from some newspaper articles.[66] We know quite a bit about Weber's course "General Economic Theory," however, because an outline and notes for the first part were printed for the students. In the late 1890s Weber also had plans to write a textbook in economics, and, as part of this, to rewrite his course notes on general economic theory.[67]

The course outline and the notes were published in 1990 as *Outline of Lectures in General ("Theoretical") Economics (1898)*, and they provide a unique insight into Weber's view of economics during the 1890s.[68] The course outline is twenty-five pages long and divided into six major sections, starting with "The Conceptual Foundations of Economics" and ending with "The Development and Analysis of Economic and Social Ideals." The four other sections are entitled: "The Natural Foundations of the Economy" (#2), "The Historical Foundations of the Economy" (#3), "Stages in the Development of Economic Theory" (#4), and "Theoretical Analysis of the Modern Market Economy" (#5). For each section Weber suggests works that the students may consult, close to six hundred in all. The notes for the first part of the course are of about the same length, thirty-four pages. Their title is "Book Number One: The Conceptual Foundations of Economics," and they follow the reading guide closely. Through the notes the student is introduced to key concepts in economics such as "the economy," "goods," and "needs"; they also discuss such topics as price formation, money, and production.

From the reading guide it is clear that Weber was knowledgeable in economics; among the works that he recommended to his students were not only the standard items in historical economics by Roscher, Knies, and Schmoller, but also works by the Austrian economists and by Marshall, Walras, and Jevons. He referred often to the works of Marx, whose ideas Weber obviously knew well.[69] From the notes for the first part of the course it is also clear that Weber approved of using the fiction of *homo economicus* in economic analysis. "Abstract theory," he points out, "takes its point of departure in modern Western man and his economic actions." He then adds that economic theory:

> a. *ignores*, treats as if *not present* all those motives which have an influence on real men which are specifically *non-economic*, i.e. all those motives not arising from the satisfaction of material means;
>
> b. *imputes* as actually present in men particular qualities which are either not present or only incompletely, namely

a) complete insight into the given *situation*—perfect economic knowledge;

b) exclusive selection of the *most appropriate means* for a given end—absolute 'economic rationality';

c) exclusive devotion of one's own powers to the attainment of economic goods—tireless economic endeavour. It therefore argues on the basis of *unrealistic* men, analogous to a mathematical ideal.

It thus postulates an *unrealistic* person, analogous to a mathematical model.[70]

This passage from the *Outline* may give the impression that Weber was indeed a "champion of the Austrian School," as the socialists students had accused him of being. But the reading guide shows that it is more accurate to say that Weber advocated different approaches in economics, depending on the problem at hand. When Weber discussed price formation on a theoretical level, for example, he drew exclusively on the Austrian version of marginal utility theory; and when he discussed "the historical foundations of the economy," he referred to works by historians and historically oriented economists, such as Karl Bücher, Eduard Meyer, and August Meitzen. Finally, in a section entitled "the relationship of the economy to other cultural phenomena, especially law and the state," Weber suggested that the students consult works in sociology by people like Comte, Spencer, and Tönnies.

Is it correct to say that Weber had developed his own distinct brand of economics by the end of the 1890s? In my opinion, there are two aspects to Weber's approach to economics at this stage that set it apart from those of other economists and that allow us to say that Weber had developed his own profile in economics. First, Weber recommended that his students study *both* historical economics *and* analytical economics; and he advised them to use whatever method was best for the problem at hand. Weber was also attempting to incorporate the insights of both of these perspectives into his own economics.

Second, it is clear from the *Outline*—the notes for the first part in the course on general economics provide the main evidence—that Weber was to some extent attempting to go beyond both analytical economics and historical economics in what he taught. In the end, this effort would allow him to develop economic sociology through a combination of an interest-driven analysis and a social perspective. Several of the concepts that were to play major roles in his economic sociology two decades later are already present in the *Outline*, albeit in an embryonic form: "economic action," "power of control and disposal," "opportunity," and "struggle" ("price struggle," "struggle between competitors," and so on). All of these concepts Weber would later develop in a sociological direction and bring together into a coherent whole in his economic sociology in chapter 2 of *Economy and Society*.[71] In the *Outline* Weber also speaks of "material needs" and "ideal needs," terminology that foreshadows what he would later call "material interests" and "ideal interests."

Another sign of Weber's desire to go beyond historical and analytical economics can be found in his attempt to develop a theory of price formation that drew on the Austrians as well as on the Historical School. When "the theoretical price" was decided, Weber argued, what mattered were the needs of the buyers, ranked according to the principle of marginal utility. But when "the empirical price" was decided, several additional factors had to be taken into consideration, such as the struggle between economic actors ("economic struggle"), imperfections in the market, and the historical formation of the needs.[72] All in all, one gets the distinct impression from the *Outline* that Weber wanted to mediate between analytical economics and historical economics, and sometimes also to go beyond both of them.

To what extent did Weber develop a theory of *Sozialökonomik* during his first period during the years 1882–98? Insofar as the term itself is concerned, it is clear that Weber had encountered it in his reading of, for example, Menger (1881), Knies (1883), and Dietzel (1895). He had also helped to found the Socialökonomische Vereinigung in 1897. Nonetheless, it is clear that if Weber had wanted to use the term "social economics," it would have appeared in his lectures on economics, and it does not. The terms that Weber used in his *Outline* are instead the more common *Volkswirtschaftslehre* and *Nationalökonomie*.

A more important question is whether Weber used *the idea* of *Sozialökonomik* in his early works. The concept of economics in the *Outline* is very broad, which is characteristic of social economics. Weber, for example, speaks of the historical evolution of the economy, of the relationship between the economy and nature, and of the relationship between the economy and society. The second half of the idea of *Sozialökonomik*—that there has to be a division of labor within economics itself—was, however, not well developed at this stage. Weber speaks of "abstract theory," and one can no doubt find an implicit distinction between economic theory and economic history in the *Outline*. But—and this is the point—it remains implicit. It is also obvious that Weber did not have much inkling in the mid-1890s that "economic sociology" could be a useful approach to the study of the economy. The only references to sociology in the course outline from the 1890s are to general works on "society," such as those by Comte, Spencer, and Tönnies. None of the works in sociology that Weber cites, and nothing of what he himself says in the *Outline* or anywhere else during these years, indicates that Weber was particularly interested in applying sociology directly to economic phenomena.

What concrete contributions, then, can we say that Weber made to the fields of economic theory, economic history, and economic sociology during his first period? As to economic theory, Weber did not produce a single article in this field during the 1890s. In other words, he taught economic theory as part of his duties as a professor in economics, but he made no attempt to further develop it. One fine accomplishment from these years was nonetheless the clarity with which Weber presented the nature of *homo economicus* in his lectures, to judge from the *Outline*. Frank Knight has produced the classic statement on this topic in *Risk, Uncertainty and Profit* (1921), and it is strikingly similar to Weber's version.[73] Both Weber and Knight were aware that economic man was an analytical construct and did not exist in reality. As to the rest of Weber's work in economic theory from these years—in particular the thirty-odd pages of notes for the beginning of his theory course in economics—one can find some interesting ideas here, especially the attempt to mediate between and go beyond analytical economics and historical economics. But these ideas were not well developed, and their importance is clear only in retrospect.

Weber's work in economic history during 1882–98 was substantial. It includes his two dissertations (or more precisely, the parts of those two works that did not constitute legal history), the two articles entitled "The Social Causes of the Decay of Ancient Civilizations" and "Agrarian Conditions in Antiquity," plus a few other items, including the lectures in Mannheim entitled "The Course of Economic Development." A common theme in all of these writings is Weber's fascination with the nature and origin of capitalism. In his first dissertation, for example, there is a discussion of the *commenda,* which Weber throughout his life would single out as an early form of rational enterprise. He also attempts to determine to what extent "capitalism" could be found in antiquity and whether it was related to the kind of capitalism that exists in the modern world. Finally, the sweep of Weber's knowledge was enormous, and his interest included the whole economic evolution of humanity.

Though Weber did not explicitly identify any of his own works from these years as sociology or economic sociology, his writings on economic topics contain a number of observations that today can be seen as more or less sociological. This is true for much of what Weber wrote on German agriculture and on the stock exchange, and together these writings make up the bulk of what we rather loosely can call Weber's economic sociology during this period. A few of the observations have already been mentioned, such as the struggle between German and Polish workers and Weber's analysis of the ideological role that economic analysis had come to play in Germany around the turn of the century. But there is quite a bit more that is of interest in Weber's early work, from the viewpoint of economic sociology. There is, for example, his suggestive idea that interest payments, in certain circumstances, can be seen as a modern kind of *tribute;* and his discussion of the different ways in which a stock exchange can be regulated, depending on the economic strength and commercial experience of its members. There also exists a kind of sociology of knowledge of economic theory scattered throughout Weber's early work—and quite a bit more.

If Weber had died at the end of the 1890s, when he was in his mid-thirties, he would not have been remembered as a young genius who had made seminal contributions to social science. He had already proved that he had an excellent talent as a researcher, as the reception of his work for the Verein clearly shows, but there was perhaps more promise than accomplishment to Weber's work in the 1890s. A few years after the turn of the century, however, Weber began pouring out the works with which his name today is associated: *The Protestant Ethic and the Spirit of Capitalism, The Methodology of the Social Sciences, Economy and Society,* and many more. How these are related to Weber's social economics, his economic sociology, and his attempt to combine an interest-driven analysis with a social one is told in the rest of this appendix.

IV. WEBER'S WORK IN ECONOMICS AFTER HIS RECOVERY (1903–1909)

Weber's most important works in economics were produced during the years from 1903, when he had recovered enough to start doing work in economics again, to 1920, when he died while still working on his contribution to *Economy and Society*. It was during this period that Weber succeeded in developing an economic sociology and that his vision of a social economics, or *Sozialökonomik*, took shape. Two phases in Weber's work during 1903–20 can be distinguished: one that starts in 1903 and ends around 1910, and a second that begins around 1910 and ends in 1920. During the first of these Weber was primarily interested in the relationship of the economy to other parts of society, such as politics, law, and religion. Even though his approach was social in many ways, he had not yet decided to try to develop a distinct sociology. It was also during this period that he found a way to unite an interest-driven analysis with a social one.

During his last decade, he developed a general foundation for sociology as well as a number of basic sociological concepts. Two versions exist of this general sociology, and the most authoritative is to be found in chapter 1 of *Economy and Society* ("Basic Sociological Terms"). During these years Weber also—very importantly—decided to apply his new sociological approach not only to the links between economy and other social phenomena, such as politics, law, and religion, but also to economic phenomena themselves. It was through this last application that his economic sociology, in the more strict sense of the word, was born.

Once Weber had fallen ill in 1898, he went through a cycle of crises followed by periods of temporary recovery. At times, he was totally incapacitated and could neither read nor write; but there were also periods when he felt better and even thought that he could resume his full academic duties. Sometimes Weber read voraciously, but not in economics ("anything but literature in my own field"). To some extent Weber's illness allowed him to explore writings that he earlier had wanted to read but had not found time to. His wife noted in her diary during one of the recovery periods that, "We are now living with all sorts of books that one never gets a chance to read otherwise." "Max is absorbing a marvellous mixture [of books]," she continued, including literature about "the organization and economy of convents."[74]

But Weber's illness, of course, first and foremost, caused him terrible grief and created many problems. One of these had to do with his sense of responsibility for the teaching of economics at the University of Heidelberg. From the beginning, Weber had realized that Heidelberg was understaffed and needed a second professor of economics, and when he fell ill the administration decided to appoint such a second professor. As in Freiburg, Weber wanted his friend and colleague Werner Sombart to replace him, but the one who was chosen was Karl Rathgen, an expert on the economy of Japan.[75] Rathgen began teaching in Heidelberg in 1900, and not until three years later did the faculty decide to replace Weber himself and appoint a new professor to his chair. This time an economist named Eberhard Gothein was chosen.[76] Gothein later became Weber's friend but accomplished little.

The faculty made its decision to find a replacement for Weber himself after a decision in 1903 to finally accept his request for an early retirement. Until then, Weber had been on paid leave, with no academic responsibilities. That he was paid even though he did not work tormented Weber, and by 1903 he had had enough. From then on, he and Marianne lived off private money, mainly from his mother, until Marianne received an inheritance in 1907 that made them financially independent. For someone with Weber's personality, however, it was not unproblematic even to live on inherited money. As he later noted:

> Anyone who has even a penny of investment income which others have to pay directly or indirectly, anyone who owns any durable goods or consumes any commodity produced not by his own sweat but by that of others, lives off the operation of that loveless and unpitying economic struggle for existence . . . in which not millions but hundreds of millions of people, year after year, waste away in body and soul.[77]

During the years 1903–9 Weber continued to define himself primarily as an economist, but he also began working in new fields, such as the methodology of the social sciences and religion. Being a private scholar also made it easier for Weber to follow political events and do some writing in this field. In connection with the Russian Revolution of 1905, for example, Weber wrote a few articles that made even Lenin take notice of him ("this piece of professorial wisdom of the cowardly bourgeoisie").[78]

During the years 1903–9, Weber continued to associate with economists, although most of his close friends were in such fields as philosophy, law, and theology. Weber gradually began to renew his interest in the Verein, which was still dominated by the economists, and he also worked closely with some economic colleagues at the *Archiv für Sozialwissenchaft und Sozialpolitik*. This journal had been purchased by Edgar Jaffé, a close friend and an economist, and one of his motives was to give Weber something to do. The three first editors were Jaffé, Weber, and Sombart; Schumpeter was brought in at a later stage. Apart from Schumpeter, with whom Weber had superficial but friendly relations in the 1910s, Weber does not seem to have had any friends among the Austrian economists. Most of his economist colleagues belonged to the Historical School, and Weber had a polite but distant relationship with its powerful leader, Gustav von Schmoller. Weber's own sympathies, it seems, lay somewhere in between the Historical School and Austrian economics; and he usually defended the historical economists against the Austrians and vice versa. When Schmoller, for example, celebrated his seventieth birthday, Weber complimented him for not being exclusively interested in analytical economics: "At the time of the most barren economic rationalism you have created a home for *historical* thought in our science in a way . . . that cannot be found in any other nation."[79] And when Lujo Brentano, around the same time, impatiently brushed aside Austrian economics, Weber immediately reminded him of Menger's "excellent views."[80]

The position that Weber took at the 1909 meeting of the Verein in Vienna was also closer to the Austrian position than to that of the historical economists. He firmly rejected the idea of Schmoller et al. that economics should be an ethical science. The historical economists, he argued, had understandably reacted against the attempt of some earlier economists to portray the seeking of profit as something morally positive—but only to commit a similar error, when they constructed their own type of moralistic economic theory. The introduction of values into economic science, Weber charged, trivialized the very idea of taking an ethical stance. To again cite what he said at a meeting in Vienna in 1909:

> The reason why I take every opportunity . . . to attack in such extremely emphatic terms the confusion of *what ought to be* with *what is*, does not mean that I underestimate the question of what ought to be. On the contrary, it is because I cannot bear it when problems of world-shaking importance and of the greatest ideal consequence—in some respect those ultimate questions which are capable of stirring the human soul—are transformed into technical economic questions of "production" and thereby made into objects of discussion for an *academic* discipline.[81]

Weber's arguments on the issue of objectivity were supported by some participants at the meeting but opposed by others, including Othmar Spann, Rudolf Goldscheid, and Eugen von Philippovich (whose presentation on productivity had triggered Weber's statement). The debate about the role of value judgments in economics could not be terminated at the Vienna meeting but continued for several years at the meetings of the Verein (it came to be known as the Battle of Value Judgments).

Most of what Weber wrote during the years 1903–9 is relevant to an understanding of his general view of economics. In one of his many methodological essays, several of which dealt mainly with economics, he severely criticized Roscher and Knies; in another he presented a whole program for *Sozialökonomik;* and in a third he discussed marginal utility theory. There is also his brilliant study *The Protestant Ethic and the Spirit of Capitalism* (1904–5), to which should be added a complementary essay on sects as well as Weber's answers to his critics. Weber also wrote on industrial workers, primarily in some essays on "the psychophysics of industrial work" (1908–9) and in a methodological essay that he put together for the Verein around the same time. Weber capped off his scholarly activities during this period by producing—in a few months in the winter of 1907–8—a book-length study of the social and economic history of antiquity, *The Agrarian Sociology of Ancient Civilizations.*

The key to Weber's view of *Sozialökonomik* during this period of his scholarship can be found in his contribution to the first issue of *Archiv für Sozialwissenschaft und Sozialpolitik*, the famous essay called "'Objectivity' in Social Science and Social Policy" (1904). The "Objectivity" essay contains a full program for *Sozialökonomik*, and it constitutes, next to the *Grundriss der Sozialökonomik*, Weber's most important statement on this topic. The centrality of Weber's essay for his view of economics makes it necessary to take a closer look at it.

The "Objectivity" essay consists of two parts: a general one, for which all three editors were responsible (Jaffé, Sombart, and Weber; fourteen pages), and a special one, for which Weber alone was responsible (fifty pages). The general part was meant to be read and discussed together with an announcement, signed collectively, in the first issue of the *Archiv*. In the announcement the editors say that the main focus of the new journal will be on *"the general cultural signifi- cance of the capitalist development"* and that the *Archiv* will draw on a number of "neighbouring" sciences in this enterprise.[82] To study what the editors call "the economic struggle of being" means that one must not only look at the econ- omy itself, but also at its links to noneconomic phenomena. The following is added in the first part of the "Objectivity" essay to these general points: facts and values must under no circumstances be mixed in an economic analysis, and it is imperative with an "analytical ordering of empirical social reality."[83] They express regret that contemporary economics has split into *"two* sciences" as a result of the Battle of Methods: one that is "historical" and another that is "theoretical."[84]

The term *Sozialökonomik* does not appear until the second part of the "Ob- jectivity" essay, for which Weber was alone responsible, and here it is used about a dozen times. Weber says that he wants to give an informal definition of "the science of social economics" (*"die sozialökonomische Wissenschaft"*) but pro- vides a rather complicated one, which can be summarized in the following way: *social economics deals with those phenomena that are scarce, that are necessary to satisfy ideal and material interests, and that can only be provided through planning, struggle, and in cooperation with other people.*[85] Weber says that scarcity of means is "the fundamental social-economic phenomenon" and that social economics is a *"science of reality."* But he also adds the following impor- tant qualification:

> The quality of an event as a "social-economic" event is not something which it pos- sesses "objectively." It is rather conditioned by the orientation of our cognitive inter- est, as it arises from the specific cultural significance which we attribute to the partic- ular event in a given case.[86]

In the rest of the "Objectivity" essay Weber gives some more information about social economics and says that it draws on elements from both historical economics and theoretical economics. The scope of social economics, Weber says, is "almost overwhelming," and he refers on this point approvingly to Roscher and Marx.[87] He suggests a way to conceptualize the different categories that make up the subject area of economics and tries to theorize about them. So- cial economics, he suggests, covers the following three phenomena: (1) "eco- nomic phenomena" (2) "economically relevant phenomena," and (3) "economi- cally conditioned phenomena."[88] The first category includes economic events or institutions—that is, social phenomena "the economic aspects of which consti- tute their primary cultural significance for us." The second category, economi- cally relevant phenomena, denotes phenomena "which do not primarily interest us with respect to their economic significance" but that "have consequences which are of interest from the economic point of view."[89] Religion can be an ex- ample of this, as Weber was to show in *The Protestant Ethic.*

The third category—economically conditioned phenomena—is somewhat problematical to my mind, at least the way that Weber defines it in the essay on objectivity. Economically conditioned phenomena, he says, are phenomena that are not economic and have no significant economic effects, but involve "behavior in non-'economic' affairs [that] is partly influenced by economic motives."[90] The only example that Weber gives is that the artistic taste of a certain period is partly dependent on the social stratification of those who are interested in art. In my mind, this is a fairly trivial example, and Weber gives a much too restricted interpretation of what constitutes economically conditioned phenomena. This may well have been in reaction to Marx's sweeping claims in this regard and to his insistence that most phenomena in society, if not all, are determined exclusively by economic factors. In any case, Weber later expands the category of economically conditioned phenomena, and in his later work it means roughly noneconomic phenomena that are directly influenced by economic phenomena (see figure A.2).[91]

But even though Weber expresses his approval of what Roscher and Marx have to say about the wide scope of social economics, he is critical of other aspects of historical economics as well as of Marxism. Historical economics, he notes in the essay on objectivity, takes a naive approach to concept formation in economics and constantly confuses facts and values. As to Marxism, it attaches "supreme significance [to] the economic factor" but fails to realize that society can just as well influence the economy.[92] What Weber finds useful about historical economics and Marxism is, in brief, their broad concept of the economy; most of the rest he is critical of.

That Weber wants the "the science of social economics" to include an analytical approach comes out with great clarity in his discussion of theoretical economics. In economic theory one always starts from an abstraction, Weber says: "[economic theory] offers us an ideal picture of events on the commodity market under conditions of society organized on the principles of an exchange economy, free competition and rigorously rational conduct."[93] Weber knows that this amounts to "a cosmos without contradictions," but he nonetheless applauds "abstract economic theory" for having realized what the Historical School had failed to understand, namely that no analysis in economics can do without scientific concepts—and that these always entail abstraction from certain aspects of reality as well as a selection among them.

These scientific concepts Weber calls "ideal types," and they are characterized by an "analytical accentuation of certain elements of reality."[94] Weber emphasizes that all the different kinds of "cultural sciences"—history, economic theory, and so on—use these ideal types, whether they are aware of it or not. To phrase it differently: the ideal type, as Weber sees it, is something that all the cultural sciences have in common and that also unites them. In Weber's hands, the ideal type practically becomes a tool to overcome the split between the social sciences.

Abstract economic theory, which might seem unrealistic at first, consequently consists of ideal types and represents a legitimate approach in social science. Weber, however, also cautions against a misunderstanding of the use of ideal

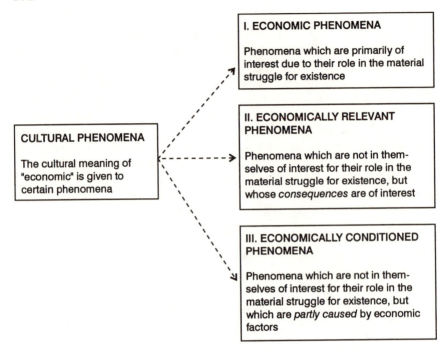

I. ECONOMIC PHENOMENA

Phenomena which are primarily of interest due to their role in the material struggle for existence

CULTURAL PHENOMENA

The cultural meaning of "economic" is given to certain phenomena

II. ECONOMICALLY RELEVANT PHENOMENA

Phenomena which are not in themselves of interest for their role in the material struggle for existence, but whose *consequences* are of interest

III. ECONOMICALLY CONDITIONED PHENOMENA

Phenomena which are not in themselves of interest for their role in the material struggle for existence, but which are *partly caused* by economic factors

Fig. A.2. The Constitution and Scope of Social-Economic Phenomena, according to Weber in the Essay on "Objectivity" (1904)

Source: Max Weber, "'Objectivity' in Social Science and Social Policy," pp. 64–65 in *The Methodology of the Social Sciences* (New York: Free Press, 1949).

Comment: According to Weber, people attach the cultural meaning of "economic" to phenomena that they view as central in the material struggle for existence and that are characterized by scarcity. The analyst must also take this cultural constitution of economic phenomena as the point of departure for the analysis. In his essay "Objectivity," Weber suggests a broad definition of economics; it includes not only what he calls "economic phenomena," but also "economically relevant phenomena" and "economically conditioned phenomena."

types in economic theory. The analytical precision of economic theory does not mean that one can predict exactly what will happen in empirical reality, Weber points out, and adds that claims to the contrary are simply "fantastic." Weber also says that all energy in economics should not be directed at elaborating abstract economic theory; social economics consists of several disciplines, all of which need to be developed. There is also the fact, as he puts it, that "the 'theory of marginal utility' is not exempt from the 'law of marginal utility' itself."[95]

The only work in economic theory that Weber produced during these years was a short but important review of a book by Lujo Brentano on the evolution of the theory of value. Brentano had argued, among other things, that the theory of marginal utility is based on psychology, a position that Weber thought was utterly wrong. Like the other social sciences, Weber says in his review, economic theory starts from everyday experience—in this case from the following three common experiences: (1) people are motivated by needs that can be satisfied through scarce material means; (2) the more that is consumed, the more a need is usually satisfied; and (3) people allocate scarce goods according to the importance they attach to different needs. But these elements of everyday experience, Weber points out, are *not* used by the economist in the same way that a psychologist would use them. For a psychologist, they would all constitute valid topics of research, while the economist simply uses them as stepping stones in order to construct theories of economic behavior. These theories are useful devices when one wants to conceptualize how the economy operates; and even though they may seem unreal from a psychological point of view, they are nonetheless firmly grounded in everyday reality.[96] The economist makes the economic logic of a situation appear with perfect clarity and consistency, Weber says, precisely by eliminating those parts of the picture that a psychologist would see as central to his or her research.

Weber adds another interesting twist to his argument about the nonpsychological foundation of marginal utility theory. Some economists claim that rational behavior has always existed, Weber says, but the fact is that as economic reality itself becomes more rational, the notion of rational economic action becomes increasingly useful in analyzing this reality. It is no coincidence, he says, that Böhm-Bawerk's theory of price formation fits so nicely the behavior at the Berlin stock exchange. In general, one "historical peculiarity of the capitalist epoch" is precisely that there exists an increasing "approximation of reality to the theoretical propositions of economics. . . . The heuristic significance of marginal utility theory rests on this *cultural-historical* fact, not on its supposed foundation in [psychology]."[97]

During the years after his recovery Weber continued to do work in economic history and produced his important study *The Agrarian Sociology of Ancient Civilizations* (1909), which is still regarded as a standard work in its genre. The word "sociology" in the title was added by the translator; a literal translation would be *Agrarian Conditions in Antiquity* (*Agrarverhältnisse im Altertum*). Several themes that had earlier only been hinted at in Weber's writings are fully developed here, such as the coastal location of civilization in antiquity, the political importance of controlling the water supply in certain parts of the world, and the special character of capitalism in antiquity. Weber cast his analytical net very wide in *The Agrarian Sociology of Ancient Civilizations* and looked in particular at the relationship between the economy on the one hand, and geography, nature, and politics on the other. The key to capitalism in antiquity, Weber says, is to be sought in the close relationship between the economy and politics:

> Capitalism in antiquity was shaped by political forces. It was, one might say, only indirectly economic in character, for the critical factors were the political fortunes of the *polis* and the opportunities it provided for profit through contracts for tax farming and wars for human and (especially in Rome) territorial booty.[98]

The Agrarian Sociology of Ancient Civilizations opens with a famous discussion of whether economic theory can be used to analyze the economy of antiquity, and where Weber sharply rejects the idea that one can use such concepts as "factory" and "factory worker" in analyzing pre-industrial societies. "Nothing could be more misleading," he says, "than to describe the economic institutions of antiquity in modern [economic] terms."[99] At one point Weber also says that a certain phenomenon cannot be explained through "demand and supply" but only through the "social constitution" ("*Sozialverfassung*") of the Roman Empire.[100] How to interpret these two statements by Weber is open to discussion: some commentators argue that Weber meant to say that economic theory cannot be used in explaining pre-capitalist societies, and others say that he was critical of economic theory in general. The latter opinion is definitely wrong, in my opinion, while the former is a bit closer to the truth. There is no place in *The Agrarian Sociology of Ancient Civilizations* (or anywhere else in Weber's work), where he says explicitly that economic theory cannot be used in analyzing the economy of pre-capitalist societies. This may nonetheless have been his opinion, at least insofar as *modern* economic theory is concerned. In his private notes (more precisely, in his marginal notes to a work by Menger), Weber suggests that it should in principle be possible to construct different kinds of economic theories for different stages in history.[101]

There are two groups of writings from the 1903–9 period, which are usually seen as being of a sociological rather than an economic-historical or economic-theoretical character: *The Protestant Ethic and the Spirit of Capitalism* (1904–5) (as well as Weber's interventions in the ensuing debate), and his writings on industrial workers from 1908–9. The latter include a long article on the "psychophysics" of labor plus a methodological article, produced for a project on the labor force and modern industry that had been initiated by the Verein and on which Weber worked together with his brother Alfred and economist Heinrich Herkner. In these writings Weber asked whether studies of heredity and laboratory experiments with fatigue, productivity, and the like could be of help in analyzing industrial work. He answered this question affirmatively in principle, but also emphasized that next to nothing had yet been produced that was of interest to empirically oriented social scientists. Another issue Weber discussed was one that the Verein was very interested in, namely the selection and adaptation of the workers at major industrial enterprises. The heart of this *problematique*, Weber noted, had to do with the relationship between the type of workers produced by modern industry and how modern industry had to adapt to the existing workers. Weber was pessimistic on both scores. The modern factory, he said, constituted a kind of "monstrous cage" for the individual, and large-scale industry threatened to change "the spiritual face of mankind almost to the point of unrecognizability."[102]

The Protestant Ethic is discussed in more detail in chapter 5, and here I make only a few comments about the place of this study in Weber's general conception of economics. Conceived and executed at about the same time as the "Objectivity" essay of 1904, *The Protestant Ethic* makes many similar points: economic phenomena must be analyzed not only in terms of scarcity but also in terms of their cultural significance; this significance is socially produced; and rational economic action (as in modern capitalism) is consequently a social as well as a historical product. To illustrate the link between economic rationality and social reality, Weber notes, for example, how "the Quaker [in his or her attitudes to economic affairs] was, so to speak, a living law of marginal utility."[103]

Economic theory plays no role in *The Protestant Ethic,* where the problem was rather to evaluate the influence of a certain religious mentality on people's attitudes toward economic affairs. Using the terminology of the "Objectivity" essay, Weber had in other words chosen to look at an "economically relevant phenomenon." A certain critique of Marxism is no doubt implicit in Weber's study, since he chose to look at the reverse causality from the one that fascinated Marx. Another important point that Weber wanted to make in this study was to show— in accordance with the program in social economics—that what went on in the economy could at certain times only be understood if noneconomic forces were also taken into account.

In conclusion, one can say that Weber's work on social economics occupied a considerable part of his activities during the 1903–9 period. The term *Sozialökonomik* appeared for the first time in his writings, and Weber devoted a full programmatic article to this type of economics, namely the "Objectivity" essay from 1904. One important aspect of this essay is Weber's anchoring of social economics in a full philosophy of social science: economic phenomena have to be understood in terms of the meanings held by the actors; all concepts that are used to analyze the economy entail analytical abstractions, regardless of what social science they come from; and economic theory represents a legitimate way of analyzing rational economic action.

Social economics, Weber furthermore argues in the "Objectivity" essay, is primarily to be concerned with modern capitalism, and it studies economic phenomena as well as phenomena that are related in some way to the economy. As he said in the 1890s, Weber states that economics is a broad subject area, but he now also attempts to conceptualize its structure and theorize about its different parts (economic phenomena, economically relevant phenomena, and economically conditioned phenomena). Finally, at this stage of his thinking, Weber was clear about the need to use different social sciences to study economic phenomena including especially economic theory, economic history, and a sociological approach.[104] The reason for using the expression "a sociological approach" rather than "sociology" or "economic sociology" in the preceding sentence is that Weber had not yet decided to turn his full attention to sociology and apply it directly to economic phenomena (creating an economic sociology in a more strict sense). This, however, is exactly what he would do during the last period of his life.

V. WEBER'S WORKS IN ECONOMICS DURING HIS LAST DECADE (1910–1920)

During the last ten years of his life Weber continued to present himself as an economist, but he had developed many other professional interests as well. For example, he helped to organize the German Sociological Society and for the first time produced works that he himself labeled "sociology." After a while, Weber's relationship with the Sociological Society turned sour, and in 1912 he decided to leave it, among other reasons because his call for value-neutrality had not been heeded. Separating values from facts in scientific analysis continued to be of crucial importance to Weber, and he participated fully in the so-called Battle of Value Judgments. This debate had erupted in 1909, peaked in the 1910s, and then slowly petered out. Weber's main contribution was a famous article called "The Meaning of 'Ethical Neutrality' in Sociology and Economics."[105]

Weber worked on two giant projects during his last years: the *Grundriss der Sozialökonomik* and *The Economic Ethics of the World Religions.* He had started as editor of the *Grundriss* in 1908, and apart from the duration of World War I, when he did next to nothing on the *Grundriss,* he continued to be occupied with it until his death. A first version of his famous *Economy and Society* was produced during the years 1910–14, and a second version (of some of its parts) in 1918–20. The complicated story of the writing of *Economy and Society* is discussed later in this appendix.

Weber was the sole author of *The Economic Ethics of the World Religions.* His ambition was to produce a work that would appear simultaneously with *Economy and Society* and in particular complement its section on the sociology of religion. The key idea was to expand the research on the relationship between religion and the economy, which Weber had initiated with *The Protestant Ethic* (1904–5). This time, however, Weber also wanted to look at religions other than Christianity, such as Islam, Hinduism, Buddhism, and Judaism. He wanted to analyze both the way that religion had influenced the economy and the reverse relationship. In *The Protestant Ethic,* Weber said, he had only looked at "one side of the causal chain," while in the new studies of economic ethic he wanted to "follow out both causal relationships."[106] The contributions to economic sociology in *The Economic Ethics of the World Religions* have mainly to do with the relationship between religion and the economy and are discussed in chapter 5.

Toward the end of World War I, Weber felt healthy enough to start teaching again, and when the University of Vienna invited him to replace Philippovich (who had died in 1917), he finally said yes.[107] Though Weber occupied a chair in economics in Vienna, he preferred to teach his own version of social economics. His course during the summer term of 1918 was thus entitled "Economy and Society (A Positive Critique of the Materialistic Conception of History)" and was mostly about the economy, religion, and the state.[108] Weber enjoyed being back in an academic milieu and became friendly with, among others, Ludwig von Mises.[109] His lectures were a huge success, and Friedrich von Hayek would later recall that "Max Weber had taught in Vienna the year I was fighting in Italy, and when I returned the following year the university was full of talk about that great man."[110]

Despite the positive reception in Vienna, Weber soon decided that he wanted to be in Germany rather than Austria. This was not difficult to arrange, since

Weber immediately got a number of offers when it became known that he was able to lecture again. One came from the Berlin Business School, another from the Institute of Public Welfare in Frankfurt, and a third from the University of Bonn. For personal reasons, however, Weber wanted to be in Munich, and after a few problems had been ironed out, he assumed the prestigious chair of Lujo Brentano (who had just retired) at the University of Munich in 1919. Weber had been the Munich faculty's second choice (together with Schulze-Gaevernitz, and after Moritz Julius Bonn), but the Bavarian authorities ignored the faculty rec-ommendations and appointed Weber.[111] The local revolutionaries declared that they wanted a professor in economics who was less hostile to socialism than Weber, but they were also ignored.[112] Finally, Weber did not want to teach the standard courses that professors of economics were supposed to teach. Accord-ing to his wife, "Weber [especially] did not want to commit himself again to teaching political economy and finance, two subjects he had outgrown."[113] The university authorities were willing to comply with Weber's wishes, and he was al-lowed to teach more or less whatever he wanted. Although Brentano had been professor in "economics, finance, and economic history," Weber's chair was changed to "social science, economic history, and economics" (*Gesellschaftswis-senschaft, Wirtschaftsgeschichte und Nationalökonomie*).[114] Before his death on June 14, 1920, Weber had time to teach only a couple of courses, including one in general economic history.[115] This last course became famous when his lec-tures were published as a book under the title *Wirtschaftsgeschichte*, or *General Economic History* (1923).

Economy and Society has a long and complicated history, which starts with the decision of Weber in late 1908 to accept his publisher's offer to be the main editor for a work that was to replace Gustav Schönberg's famous *Handbuch der Politischen Oekonomie* (1st ed. 1882; 4th ed. 1896–98).[116] The publisher be-lieved Schönberg's work had become outmoded, and Weber accepted the offer to become the new editor, despite some misgivings. He quickly enlisted a large number of collaborators and drew up a master plan for the new handbook, which was to be centered on the nature of contemporary capitalism, in contrast to Schönberg's conventional division of the work into sections on economics, fi-nance, and public administration. The first of the five projected "books" was in Weber's opinion especially important because it would introduce the rest of the work and explain how to approach and analyze social-economic phenomena. Weber got Karl Bücher to write on economic history and Joseph Schumpeter on the history of economic thought for Book I. He also needed someone to present economic theory and especially to show how it was related to empirical reality. "The *key* question is how *theory* is introduced," Weber noted, "and once this is properly done, everything else will fall into place."[117] One of the leading Aus-trian economists, Friedrich von Wieser, was asked to write the section on eco-nomic theory, and to Weber's great relief he accepted (for a detailed account of the structure and content of *Grundriss der Sozialökonomik*, see chapter 6 in this volume).

Weber's own contribution to the new handbook went through many stages over the years. From the beginning, it was clear that Weber wanted to be included in the first and central book, "Foundations of the Economy"; and according to Marianne Weber, "he assigned the most important parts to himself."[118] According to the version of the table of contents prepared in 1909–10, Weber was to be the sole author of a section in Book I called *Economy and Society* (*Wirtschaft und Gesellschaft*). Weber, it can be noted, was not to write on the economy itself, but on the relationship between the economy on the one hand, and law, social groups, and culture, on the other. The exact titles of these sections were: "Economy and Law (1. Fundamental Relationship, 2. Epochs in the Development of Present Conditions)," "Economy and Social Groups (Family and Community Associations, Status Groups and Classes, State)," and "Economy and Culture (Critique of Historical Materialism)." Weber had also assigned a number of other articles to himself, often to fill in various gaps.[119] Two of these articles were intended for Book I: "Economy and Race" and "The Object and the Logical Nature of the Central Questions [in Economics]."

Weber began working on his contributions to the new handbook in 1910, and a few years later he had more or less finished his assignment for the section called *Economy and Society*. Other contributors to Book I, however, were late with their assignments, and when their manuscripts finally arrived, some were in less-than-satisfactory condition. Weber was especially disappointed with the contributions of Bücher and von Wieser, and he was clearly annoyed that he had to change his own manuscript in order to make up for their deficiencies. On December 8, 1913, Weber wrote to the other contributors that he had felt compelled to "provide a rather comprehensive sociological discussion for the section on economy and society."[120] What Weber was referring to were changes in response to Bücher's article. A few weeks later he explained his proposed changes in more detail to his publisher:

> Since Bücher's treatment of the "developmental stages" is totally inadequate, I have worked out a complete theory and exposition that relates the major social groups to the economy: from the family and household to the enterprise, the kin group, ethnic community, religion (comprising all religions of the world: a sociology of salvation doctrines and of religious ethics—what Troeltsch did, but now for all religions, if much briefer). I can claim that nothing of the kind has ever been written, not even as a precursor.[121]

The delays, in combination with other editorial difficulties, made it impossible to publish the whole handbook at once, as Weber had originally hoped, so the decision was made to publish it in installments. The first of these appeared in 1914, and the title for the whole series had by then been changed to *Grundriss der Sozialökonomik*. The reason for the change in the title from *"politische Oekonomie"* to *"Sozialökonomik"* had primarily to do with the publisher's desire to avoid a lawsuit from Schönberg's heirs. As to the replacement for the term "political economy," Weber wrote to his publisher in August 1909 that he preferred the term *Sozialökonomik* and that it was "the best name for the discipline [of economics]," while making clear that he did not attach much importance to what term was used.[122] It was also noted in the first installment from 1914 that the handbook should be didactic and that it would not include sections either on "finance" or "welfare provisions for the poor" since these constituted independent fields in Germany.

By 1914, Weber's own contribution to the *Grundriss* had changed quite a bit from the original plan of a few years earlier. Weber had chosen a slightly different overall title for his own key articles, "The Economy and the Social Orders and Powers" (Die Wirtschaft und die gesellschaftlichen Ordnungen und Mächte), although they were still to be part of a larger section entitled *Economy and Society*.[123] His contribution had also grown approximately four times larger than its original projected size. The three original sections—"Economy and Law," "Economy and Social Groups," and "Economy and Culture"—had become eight.[124] There was still a section on economy and law, but it had been changed, and the section on economy and culture had been eliminated. The section called "Economy and Social Groups" had swelled considerably, and Weber had added sections with such titles as "Domination," "The Political Association," and "Market Relationships."

After all these rewritings Weber was almost finished with his own contribution to *Economy and Society* when World War I broke out in August 1914. The war imposed new duties on Weber, and he more or less stopped working on the *Grundriss,* to the chagrin of his publisher. It was probably not until 1918 that Weber began to work on his own manuscript again, and by then he had a different conception of what needed to be done. For one thing, he wanted the handbook to be "*shorter*" and "more *textbook*-like," he wrote to his publisher.[125] He also wanted to include a section in which he analyzed the economy itself from a sociological viewpoint. Whereas he earlier had focused on the influence of the economy on society and vice versa, he proposed adding a sociological analysis of key economic institutions—in brief, an economic sociology—to his contribution.

By the time of Weber's death in June 1920 he had finished rewriting the first installment of his contribution to *Economy and Society* and sent it off to the publisher. This installment consists of four chapters on the following topics: general sociology (chap. 1), economic sociology (chap. 2), domination (chap. 3), and status groups and classes (chap. 4). The full title of chapter 2 is "Sociological Categories of Economic Action" ("Soziologische Grundkategorien des Wirtschaftens"). That Weber was working under pressure, and was trying to rush his work, is clear from the fact that the last of the four chapters is only a few pages long. What the rest of Weber's contribution to *Economy and Society* would have looked like if he had had time to finish it is not at all clear, even though most commentators agree that it probably would have contained sections on law, religion, and the state, all in relation to the economy. To add confusion to the whole thing, Marianne Weber and a coeditor later published the first part of Weber's contribution to *Economy and Society*—more precisely, the first part of *The Economy and the Social Orders and Powers*—in the same volume as Weber's manuscript from 1914 (plus a few other assorted writings) and reverted to the pre-1914 title. What is today known as *Economy and Society* is consequently not so much a coherent work as a collection of manuscripts—some of which were revised by Weber, while others were not. The title itself may also be wrong.[126]

During Weber's last decade, the term *Sozialökonomik* appears only sporadically in his writings, even though it is highly visible during this period as part of the title of *Grundriss der Sozialökonomik.*[127] As we now know, Weber thought that *Sozialökonomik* was the most modern and "the best" term for the science of economics, but he also emphasized that what term to use was not of much interest to him. As to the considerably more important issue of the content of social economics, it is clear from the *Grundriss* that it encompassed a very wide area: this work contains a full discussion of the relationship between the economy and society as well as of its relationship to nature, technology, population, and race. Weber repeats during these years what he had earlier said in the "Objectivity" essay (1904), namely that the science of economics has to encompass not only the economy but also the impact of the economy on society and the impact of society on the economy. Weber, however, was more explicit than earlier about which different sciences should be involved in the enterprise of analyzing economic phenomena. He mentions "economic theory" and "economic history," but most important, he adds a novel approach: that of "economic sociology."[128]

The greatest innovation during this period is definitely Weber's conception and development of a distinct *Wirtschaftssoziologie.* That Weber decided to work on this topic is naturally connected to his decision to develop a full-blown sociology. Weber originally had doubts whether it was appropriate to include a section on general sociology in the *Grundriss,* and the first version he produced on this topic was published separately in 1913 in a philosophical journal; the second version was included as chapter 1 of *Economy and Society.*[129] It is also clear that the main focus of Weber's contribution to the *Grundriss* as it existed in its 1914 version was on the links between economy and society, while later it was also on the economy itself. An economic sociology in the narrow sense of the word—meaning a sociological analysis of core economic institutions and behavior—consequently did not appear in Weber's work until 1919–20, when he wrote the chapter entitled "Sociological Categories of Economic Action" for *Economy and Society.*[130] It was also first during the latter part of the 1910s that terms such as "economic sociology" and "sociology of the economy" began to appear in Weber's writings.[131]

The chapter on economic sociology in *Economy and Society* is the size of a small book. The text is dense and often difficult to penetrate, and its contents are discussed in chapter 2 of this work. Also, Weber's thinking from these years on the links between the economy and society is extremely rich and is analyzed elsewhere in this book (in chapter 3, on the relationship between the economy and politics; chapter 4, on the economy and law; and chapter 5, on the economy and religion).

Economic history also continued to be of central interest to Weber during his last decade. The precise role of economic history in analyzing certain aspects of the economy is, for example, clarified in *Economy and Society,* where Weber argues that sociology deals mostly with types and uniformities, whereas history looks at individual events and persons. Nonetheless, in Weber's view economic sociology and economic history are closely related and often use the same concepts. This last tendency can be exemplified by the course on general economic history that Weber taught in 1919–20 and during which students took such careful notes that it could be published posthumously. Throughout *General Economic History* Weber uses concepts that also play a key role in his economic sociology and can be found in chapter 2 of *Economy and Society*.

Though Weber did not make any distinct contribution to economic theory during his last decade, he retained a very positive attitude toward it. When he was involved in the German Sociological Association, for example, he suggested the creation of a section for theoretical economics, to establish a closer link between sociology and economics.[132] And when Edgar Jaffé in 1917 published an article criticizing Weber and Sombart for neglecting economic theory and for having a low opinion of its potential for further development, he was immediately answered that this was totally wrong and that both Weber and Sombart attributed "the greatest significance" to economic theory.[133]

Weber was aware that he had made no real contribution to economic theory during his career, and he expressed regret about this fact to Robert Liefmann.[134] Besides Ludwig von Mises, Liefmann seems to have been one of the few people during Weber's last years with whom he discussed economic theory. In a letter written just a few months before his death, Weber sums up his attitude toward economic theory in the following way:

> I am supposed to claim that the epistemological value of theory is "slight." *Where* might that be? Theory constructs ideal types and and for me that is a most indispensable contribution. One of my fundamental convictions is that sociology and history can *never* replace theory. I am [supposedly] more interested in the "special" relationships [between the economy and parts of society?]? *Yes*—if you call the question "*Why* has a rational capitalism based upon calculability developed *solely* in the Occident?" a "special" relationship! But somebody has to explore this question![135]

VI. WEBER'S WORK IN ECONOMICS AS SEEN BY ECONOMISTS, ECONOMIC HISTORIANS, AND SOCIOLOGISTS

What first strikes anyone considering how Weber's work in economics has been viewed in the secondary literature is that no one—be it an economist or a sociologist—has been interested in Weber's work in this field; analysts have instead singled out some particular aspect and ignored the rest. There are several reasons for this, including the fact that Weber's overall conception of economics—the idea of social economics—has been ignored. The small number of contemporary social scientists who have stumbled across the term *Sozialökonomik* have usually not known what to make of it; they have confused it with economic sociology, suggested that it represented a transitional phase in Weber's work from economics to sociology, and the like.[136] Some of Weber's contemporaries were of course familiar with his ideas on *Sozialökonomik*, but with one noticeable exception, none of them was interested enough to take a closer look.[137]

The exception was Joseph Schumpeter, Weber's coeditor at the *Archiv* (1916–20) and also a contributor to the *Grundriss*. Schumpeter and Weber saw economics in very similar terms and also used the same term—*Sozialökonomik*. Schumpeter's view of social economics, including its roots in Weber's work, is discussed in more detail in chapter 6. After Schumpeter's death in 1950, however, Weber's idea of social economics fell again into oblivion.

Economic theorists, economic historians, and sociologists have instead selected pieces of Weber's work in economics that for some reason have appealed to them. In histories of economic thought Weber is rarely mentioned and, if so, usually in connection with the Historical School.[138] Even then, much more space is devoted to figures such as Schmoller and Roscher, who today seem considerably less creative than Weber. Usually singled out in Weber's work are his ideas on objectivity, the concept of ideal types, *The Protestant Ethic*, and sometimes his ideas on the difficulties of a socialist economy. The general point is typically that Weber was a sociologist or an institutionalist—but not a true economist.

German economists have not shown much interest in Weber's economic writings, and this includes those who were active in the 1920s. Already by 1925, for example, a well-known German economist noted Weber's "remarkably small impact on German economics," but did not try to explain why this was the case or to rectify it.[139] Anyone who has read the self-centered works of German economists in the 1920s can, however, easily guess why: these economists were much more interested in developing their own theories than in further developing what someone else had accomplished, be it Menger, Schmoller, or Weber. In a small survey from the late 1920s that Schumpeter carried out, the conclusion was similar: German economics was in a "chronic crisis" because all economists were trying to lay a new foundation for economics, disregarding what had already been accomplished by better minds than themselves.[140]

When speaking of German economics and its low quality during the years after World War I, an exception must be made for the branch that is usually referred to as Austrian economics. Several of the younger members of Austrian economics were fascinated by Weber's work, while the old guard—Menger, Böhm-Bawerk, and von Wieser—showed little, if any interest.[141] Ludwig von Mises, as already mentioned, took a strong liking to Weber personally and was also impressed by certain aspects of his work. Through the famous Mises Seminar (1920–34)—where Weber's ideas on methodology constituted one of the "favorite topics"—Weber's work was transmitted to a new generation of talented economists, such as Fritz Machlup, Friedrich von Hayek, Oskar Morgenstern, Gottfried Haberler, and Paul Rosenstein-Rodan.[142] Hayek would later initiate the translation of *Wirtschaft und Gesellschaft* into English; and Machlup, who ended up as a well-known expert on international economics at Princeton, was preoccupied with Weber's concept of ideal types into the 1970s.[143] Alfred Schutz was also a member of the Mises Seminar, and in 1930 he gave a lecture on some of the ideas that were going to be part of his important, Weber-inspired work *The Phenomenology of the Social World* (1932).[144] One of the topics that Schutz addresses in this work is the extent to which Weber's notion of the ideal type is truly compatible with the idea of marginal utility. This might sound like an obscure topic, but it raises some important problems in economic theory.[145] In summarizing Weber and Austrian economics, one can say that the younger generation of Austrian economists were extremely interested in what Weber had to say on social science methodology (especially the ideal type)—but that they showed no interest in his ideas on *Sozialökonomik* and economic sociology.[146]

When it comes to Weber's work on economic theory, the following can be reported. According to Mises, "economics was alien to [Weber]" and according to Schumpeter, "Weber was not really an economist at all."[147] Other economists, commenting on Weber, have said the same thing.[148] This opinion would presumably also explain why a number of economists, such as Alfred Marshall, Knut Wicksell, Vilfredo Pareto, and John Maynard Keynes, did not know about or ignored Weber's work.[149] On at least one point, however, it is sometimes argued by well-known economists that Weber has made a fine contribution to economic theory, namely his article on marginal utility theory from 1908. Weber's argument in this article, to recall, is that economic theory does not rest on a foundation of psychology, but rather constructs its own foundation. George Stigler refers approvingly to "Max Weber's famous essay," and also other economists have expressed positive opinions, including Lionel Robbins, Friedrich von Hayek, and Paul Rosenstein-Rodan.[150] That Weber made a similar argument why law may be disregarded in economic theory (but not in sociology) has not been noticed, however.[151] Finally, Lionel Robbins and others have pointed out that Weber helped to transform modern economics in an analytical direction, by drawing attention to the abstract quality of economic reasoning.[152]

Finally, how have economists perceived Weber's historical and sociological writings? The impression one gets is that many economists have taken a quick look at *The Protestant Ethic,* but few seem to have studied *Economy and Society* or *General Economic History.*[153] Interestingly, *General Economic History* was translated into English by one of the most brilliant economic theorists of the early twentieth century, Frank Knight. That Knight had a very high opinion of Weber is clear from the following anecdote, which has been told by one of his students. One year after Knight had retired from the University of Chicago, he was asked what he would do differently as an economist if he could relive his life. Knight did not hesitate: "There has been the work of one man whom I have greatly admired. If I were to start out again, I would build upon his ideas. I am referring, of course, to Max Weber."[154]

Economic historians have usually been interested in the following three works by Weber: *The Protestant Ethic, The Agrarian Sociology of Ancient Civilizations,* and *General Economic History.*[155] The debate about *The Protestant Ethic* is discussed elsewhere in this book; and here it suffices to note that the scholarly discussion of the origins of industrialism nowadays tends to totally overshadow the discussion of the birth of capitalism. Weber's work, which uses such old-fashioned terms as "the spirit of capitalism" and also presupposes a sophistication in the history of religion and the philosophy of social science that rarely exists among today's economic historians, has as a consequence come to be seen as somewhat passé. As an example of this one can mention Rondo Cameron's recent textbook in economic history, in which Weber's work is not even mentioned, or Fernand Braudel's dismissive comment that "all historians have opposed [Weber's] tenuous theory" that capitalism is "a creation of . . . Puritanism. . . . It is clearly false."[156]

The Agrarian Sociology of Ancient Civilizations is less often referred to than *The Protestant Ethic,* but seems to have better retained its reputation as a minor classic among economic historians. In the 1930s, Raymond Aron said that "every historian knows his *Agrarverhältnisse im Altertum*," and this work has also more recently been praised by such eminent historians as Arnaldo Momigliano and M. I. Finley.[157] *General Economic History* has a less secure status among historians, but when one comes across an occasional mention it is usually praise of the highest order. On this last point, one can refer to the already cited verdicts of such first-rate economic historians as Eli Heckscher and A. P. Usher: "*General Economic History* [is] invaluable through its richness of ideas" (Heckscher) and "[it is] the most important single contribution that has been made in economic history for more than fifty years" (Usher).[158]

Finally, sociologists, like economists and economic historians, have picked out only those parts of Weber's work in economics that have suited their purposes. Sociologists have in particular been fascinated by *The Protestant Ethic,* by Weber's methodological writings, and by the noneconomic parts of *Economy and Society.* As a rule, sociologists have ignored Weber's economic sociology, especially as it can be found in *Economy and Society* and *The Economic Ethics of the World Religions.*[159] Although numerous studies have been devoted to Weber's general sociology, his political sociology, and his sociology of religion, there are practically no studies of his economic sociology. As mentioned in chapter 2, there exist a few articles, but that is all.

N O T E S

INTRODUCTION

1. Amartya Sen, "Rational Fools: A Critique of the Behavioral Foundations of Economic Theory," p. 84 in *Choice, Welfare and Measurement* (Cambridge, Mass.: MIT Press, 1982).

2. Ralf Dahrendorf, "Homo Sociologicus (1958)," pp. 19–87 in *Essays in the Theory of Society* (Stanford, Calif.: Stanford University Press, 1968); Peter Berger and Thomas Luckmann, *The Social Construction of Reality: A Treatise in the Sociology of Knowledge* (New York: Penguin Books, [1966] 1991). Although the work of Berger and Luckmann contains a sophisticated analysis of the emergence of institutions, it largely avoids the issue of interests or what drives the individual.

3. See Thráinn Eggertsson, *Economic Behavior and Institutions* (Cambridge: Cambridge University Press, 1990); Eirik Furubotn and Rudolf Richter, eds., *The New Institutional Economics* (Tübingen: J.C.B. Mohr, 1991); and Steven N. S. Cheung, "On the New Institutional Economics (Comments by Gary Becker and R. H. Coase)," pp. 48–75 in Lars Werin and Hans Wijkander, eds., *Contract Economics* (Cambridge: Blackwell, 1992). For North, see Gary Libecap, "Douglass North," pp. 227–64 in Warren J. Samuels, ed., *New Horizons in Economic Thought* (Aldershot, Eng.: Edward Elgar, 1992). See also the interviews with Becker, Hirschman, Schelling, Williamson, and others in Richard Swedberg, *Economics and Sociology: Redefining Their Boundaries* (Princeton, N.J.: Princeton University Press, 1990). For a sociological perspective on new institutional economics, see Mark Granovetter, "Economic Action and Social Structure: The Problem of Embeddedness," *American Journal of Sociology* 91 (1985): 481–510; Anthony Oberschall and Eric Leifer, "Efficiency and Social Institutions," *Annual Review of Sociology* 12 (1986): 233–55; and Paul DiMaggio and Walter W. Powell, "Introduction," pp. 1–40 in Paul DiMaggio and Walter W. Powell, eds., *New Institutionalism in Organizational Analysis* (Chicago: University of Chicago Press, 1991).

4. For a discussion of contemporary economic sociology, see section III in chapter 6. In the meantime, the following works should be mentioned: Neil Fligstein, *The Transformation of Corporate Control* (Cambridge, Mass.: Harvard University Press, 1990); Mark Granovetter, *Getting a Job: A Study of Contacts and Careers* (Chicago: University of Chicago Press, 1995); Arthur Stinchcombe, *Economic Sociology* (New York: Academic Press, 1983); Arthur Stinchcombe, *Stratification and Organization* (Cambridge: Cambridge University Press, 1986); Harrison White, "Where Do Markets Come From?," *American Journal of Sociology* 87 (1981): 514–47; Viviana Zelizer, *Morals and Markets: The Development of Life Insurance in the United States* (New Brunswick, N.J.: Transaction Books, 1983); and Viviana Zelizer, *The Social Meaning of Money* (New York: Basic Books, 1994).

5. There does not exist any standard work on the history of interest-oriented analysis in Western thought. In the meantime, see Stephen Holmes, "The Secret History of Self-Interest," pp. 267–82 in Jane Mansbridge, ed., *Beyond Self-Interest* (Chicago: University of Chicago Press, 1990); see also Albert O. Hirschman, *The Passions and the Interests* (Princeton, N.J.: Princeton University Press, 1977); and Albert O. Hirschman, "The Concept of Interests," pp. 35–55 in *Rival Views of Market Society and Other Essays* (New York: Viking, 1988). For strong versions of interest theory in sociology, see Gudmund

Hernes, *Makt og Avmakt* (Oslo: Universitetsforlaget, 1977) and James S. Coleman, *Foundations of Social Theory* (Cambridge, Mass.: Harvard University Press, 1990); for a more flexible (and skeptical) approach, see Paul DiMaggio, "Interest and Agency in Institutional Theory," pp. 3–21 in Lynne Zucker, ed., *Institutional Patterns and Organizations* (Cambridge, Mass.: Ballinger, 1988).

6. Guenther Roth, "'Value-Neutrality' in Germany and the United States," p. 37 in Reinhard Bendix and Guenther Roth, *Scholarship and Partisanship: Essays on Max Weber* (Berkeley: University of California Press, 1971).

7. Max Weber, *Economy and Society: An Outline of Interpretive Sociology* (Berkeley: University of California Press, 1978), p. 4, or *Wirtschaft und Gesellschaft. Grundriss der verstehenden Soziologie* (Tübingen: J.C.B. Mohr, 1972), p. 1; emphasis added.

CHAPTER ONE
THE RISE OF WESTERN CAPITALISM

1. The title in English was chosen by its translator—economist Frank Knight. The original German title, picked by the two editors (Melchior Palyi and Siegmund Hellmann) and presumably also approved by Weber's widow, is *Wirtschaftsgeschichte*. For a bibliographical list of works on Weber's economic sociology, see Richard Swedberg, "Max Weber's Economic Sociology: A Bibliography," *Working Papers Work-Organization-Economy*, Department of Sociology, Stockholm University, 1998.

2. In *Economy and Society,* Weber states that while sociology aims at developing "type concepts" and "generalized uniformities" with which to explain social reality, history has a different goal, namely to explain "individual" structures, actions, and personalities. Sociology is a generalizing science, unlike history, which is an individualizing one; and it will therefore develop more abstract but also more exact concepts. See Max Weber, *Economy and Society: An Outline of Interpretive Sociology* (Berkeley: University of California Press, 1978), p. 19, or *Wirtschaft und Gesellschaft. Grundriss der verstehenden Soziologie* (Tübingen: J.C.B. Mohr, 1972), p. 9. In a famous letter to Georg von Below, written a few years earlier, Weber says that sociology performs "very modest preparatory work" in relation to history. See Weber, letter to von Below, dated June 21, 1914, and reproduced on pp. xxiv—xxv in Georg von Below, *Der deutsche Staat des Mittelalters* (Leipzig: Quelle und Meyer, 1925). It may be added that in the conceptual introduction to *General Economic History* (which Frank Knight omitted from the English translation), Weber addresses the question of similarities and differences between economic history and economic theory.

3. For the coming into being of *Economy and Society* as well as the handbook of economics (*Grundriss der Sozialökonomik*), see the appendix on the evolution of Weber's thought on economics. The content of the handbook and its reception are discussed in chapter 6.

4. Talcott Parsons said that "by the term 'Weber's economic sociology', we refer to Chapter II of [*Economy and Society*]"; and according to Otto von Hintze, "the second chapter [of Part 1] of *Economy and Society* can in all brevity be characterized as 'economic sociology.'" Alan Sica speaks of the "almost unreadable accretion of definition piled upon definition" in chapter 2; Herbert Marcuse, in commenting on the early chapters in *Economy and Society,* has spoken of their "veritable orgies of formal definitions, classifications [and] typologies"; and according to Guenther Roth, chapter 2 has "proved a waste of effort" and "economists and sociologists [with minor exceptions] have ignored it." See Talcott Parsons, "Occupation and Economy," p. 407 in Vol. 1 of *Theories of Society* (Glencoe, Ill.: Free Press, 1961); Otto von Hintze, "Max Webers Religionssoziologie (1922),"

p. 126 in *Soziologie und Geschichte* (Göttingen: Vandenhoeck und Ruprecht, 1982); Alan Sica, *Weber, Irrationality and Social Order* (Berkeley: University of California Press, 1988), pp. 146, 208; Herbert Marcuse, "Industrialism and Capitalism," p. 134 in Otto Stammer, ed., *Max Weber and Sociology Today* (New York: Harper Torchbacks, 1971); and Guenther Roth, "Weber's Political Failure," *Telos* 78 (Winter 1988–89): 149.

5. The term used in the introduction to chapter 2 is *"Wirtschaft,"* translated as "the economic sphere"; Weber, *Economy and Society,* p. 63, or *Wirtschaft und Gesellschaft,* p. 31.

6. Max Weber, *Wirtschaftsgeschichte. Abriss der universalen Sozial- und Wirtschafts-geschichte* (Berlin: Duncker und Humblot, 1991), p. 16. Note that Weber is speaking of economy in the sense of a profit-oriented economy (*Erwerbswirtschaft*). Note also that there exist organic links between the economic and the political spheres in modern society, according to Weber (for a discussion of this, see the next chapter). Weber uses "sphere" in several different meanings and in many different parts of his work, the most famous of which are in the "Politics as a Vocation" and "Religious Rejections of the World and Their Directions"; see, e.g., Hans Gerth and C. Wright Mills, eds., *From Max Weber* (New York: Oxford University Press, 1946), pp. 123, 323 ff.; or Max Weber, "Politik als Beruf," pp. 554–55 in *Gesammelte Politische Schriften* (Tübingen: J.C.B. Mohr, 1988); and Max Weber, "Zwischenbetrachtung," p. 536 ff. in Vol. 1 of *Gesammelte Aufsätze zur Religionssoziologie* (Tübingen: J.C.B. Mohr, 1988). As examples of spheres, Weber here mentions "the economic sphere" (*die ökonomische Sphäre*), "the political sphere," "the erotic sphere," and "the esthetic sphere," and he says that all of these have a certain autonomy and inner logic (*Eigengesetzlichkeit*). Note that the concept of sphere (*Lebensordnungen, Wertsphären*) is not the same as an institutional arena, but rather some kind of existential arena, perhaps a distinct and meaningful department of life. Weber, however, also uses "sphere" to mean "institutional sphere" now and then (*Gebiet, Sphäre, Ordnung*), although it is not one of the concepts that he highlights in *Economy and Society*. What I refer to in the text as "sphere in the institutional meaning" was clarified in an exemplary manner by Robert K. Merton in his 1970 introduction to *Science, Technology and Society in Seventeenth-Century England* (New York: Harper and Row, [1938] 1970), pp. ix–x. Merton here talks about "sphere" as an "institutional sphere" or "institutional domain" and says that there exist "various kinds of . . . interdependence" between these "seemingly autonomous departments of life." He also says that these are in truth "only partially autonomous" and are linked through the fact that an individual has "multiple statuses and roles" as well as through the fact that there exist "social, intellectual, and value consequences" of what is done in one sphere for the other spheres. For evocative yet somewhat different concepts of social sphere, see finally also Fredrik Barth, "Economic Spheres in Darfur," pp. 149–74 in Raymond Firth, ed., *Themes in Economic Anthropology* (London: Tavistock Publications, 1967); and Michael Waltzer, *Spheres of Justice: A Defense of Pluralism and Equality* (New York: Basic Books, 1983).

7. Weber in a letter to Mina Tobler, postmarked January 15, 1920, in Wolfgang J. Mommsen and Wolfgang Schluchter, "Einleitung," p. 21 n. 82 in Max Weber, *Wissenschaft als Beruf. 1917/1919. Politik als Beruf. 1919. Max Weber Gesamtausgabe I/17* (Tübingen: J.C.B. Mohr, 1992).

8. That Weber had not had enough time to prepare for his course was pointed out by the noted historian Georg von Below in his review of the book based on Weber's lectures. Von Below said that Weber's other research projects during recent years had prevented him from pursuing this type of study; see Georg von Below, "Review of Max Weber, *Wirtschaftsgeschichte,*" *Weltwirtschaftliches Archiv* 20 (1924): 487.

9. Siegmund Hellmann and Melchior Palyi, "Vorbemerkung der Herausgeber," p. xviii

in Weber, *Wirtschaftsgeschichte*. Only one of the notebooks on which *General Economic History* is based still remains, although it is likely that the original editors of this work had five to eight sets at their disposal. See Johannes Winkelmann, "Vorwort zur dritten Auflage," p. [xiii] ff. in *Wirtschaftsgeschichte*. Details about the contents of the notes do not exist; it is also not known what the editors decided to add to them. Because Weber's own notes for the course consisted of extremely concentrated notations, they were apparently of little help in the editing process. One hopes that some light will be shed on the production of *General Economic History* when it is published in the *Gesamtausgabe*.

10. Among the factual errors, one can mention Weber's statements that coking of coal was discovered in 1735 (p. 305) and that it was Simon Stevin who in 1698 was the first to insist on the device of the balance in accounting (p. 275). The coking of coal is today generally thought to have been invented a few decades earlier, even though there is some question about the exact year. See e.g., David Landes, *The Unbound Prometheus* (New York: Cambridge University Press, 1969), p. 89. As to the issue of who was the first to insist on the device of the balance in accounting, the current view is that this happened much earlier than Weber thought. According to several sources, Lucas Pacioli did this in the fifteenth century; see, e.g., Bruce Carruthers and Wendy Nelson Espeland, "Accounting for Rationality: Double-Entry Bookkeeping and the Rhetoric of Economic Rationality," *American Journal of Sociology* 97 (1991): 36 ff.; Alfred Plummer, "Review of Max Weber, *General Economic History*," *Economic Journal* 38 (1928): 465. For an even earlier date, see Raymond de Roover, *Business, Banking, and Economic Thought* (Chicago: University of Chicago Press, 1974), p. 120. A more difficult but equally relevant issue in this context is whether Weber's view of certain historical phenomena was in general correct or not. Raymond De Roover claims, for example, that Weber is guilty of displaying an "idyllic view" of the guilds in *General Economic History*. By this he means that Weber "presented [the guilds] as welfare agencies which prevented unfair competition, protected consumers against deceit and exploitation, created equal opportunities for their members, and secured for them a modest but decent living in keeping with traditional standards." See Raymond De Roover, "The Concept of the Just Price: Theory and Economic Policy," *Journal of Economic History* 18 (1958): 418–19. It should be noted that none of the great historians who have reviewed *General Economic History*—such as Heckscher, Usher and Below—have pointed out or mentioned errors in the text. That they disagreed with the emphasis Weber placed on certain phenomena and thought he had neglected certain issues is another matter. I am aware of only two errors of transcription. According to Robert K. Merton, there exists a probable error of transcription in *General Economic History* having to do with the relationship between Protestantism and science; and according to Ernst Moritz Manesse, there is one about race. See Robert K. Merton, "Puritanism, Pietism and Science (1936)," p. 634 in *Social Theory and Social Structure* (New York: Free Press, 1968); Ernst Moritz Manasse, "Max Weber on Race," *Social Research* 14 (1947): 210 n. 41. In general, as Merton notes elsewhere, texts that have been reconstructed in the manner of *General Economic History* are "vulnerable to criticism on various counts." See Robert K. Merton, "On the Oral Transmission of Knowledge," p. 24 in Robert K. Merton and Matilde White Riley, eds., *Sociological Traditions from Generation to Generation* (Norwood, N.J.: Ablex Publishing Corporation, 1980). Talcott Parsons calls *General Economic History* "a mere sketch" and says that it "cannot be considered an adequate statement of the results of [Weber's] researches in economic or institutional history, to say nothing of sociological theory and the methodology of the social sciences." See Talcott Parsons, "Introduction," p. 3 in Max Weber, *The Theory of Social and Economic Organization* (New York: Oxford University Press, 1947). Parsons's

critical stance may be due to the fact that many of Weber's definitions were garbled in the reconstruction of Weber's course. Eli Heckscher, who was less sensitive than Parsons to conceptual definitions—but more knowledgeable in economic history—says that "the students were able to capture his [Weber's] ideas in their notes without, as it seems, any serious errors"; see Eli Heckscher, "Den ekonomiska historiens aspekter," *Historisk tidskrift* 15 (1930): 20.

11. For more information on this course, see the appendix on the evolution of Weber's thought on economics.

12. Eli Heckscher, *Industrialismen. Den ekonomiska utvecklingen sedan 1750* (Stockholm: Kooperative förbundets bokförlag, 1938), p. 346; A. P. Usher, "Review of Max Weber, *General Economic History*," *American Economic Review* 18 (1928): 105.

13. According to Usher, *General Economic History* was primarily to be seen as an example of "the sociological interpretation of economic history"; see Usher, "Review of Max Weber, *General Economic History*," pp. 104–5. According to Eli Heckscher in 1930, Weber's *Wirtschaftsgeschichte* was "very close" to "economic sociology (*ekonomisk sociologi*)"; see Heckscher, "Den ekonomiska historiens aspekter," p. 28. A few years later, when Heckscher prepared a shortened version of the same article for an English audience, he said that since Weber disregarded chronological order "*General Economic History* . . . is properly speaking not economic history at all, but economic sociology"; see Eli F. Heckscher, "The Aspects of Economic Development," p. 706 in (no editor), *Economic Essays in Honour of Gustav Cassel* (London: George Allen and Unwin, 1933). According to Torsten Gårdlund, Heckscher himself showed no interest in Weber's sociology or in economic sociology per se (Torsten Gårdlund, telephone conversation with the author, December 5, 1995). Finally, according to Georg Brodnitz, "A scheme of definitions arising from Weber's sociology forms the foundation [of *General Economic History*]"; and according to Edgar Salin, *General Economic History* was little but "an introduction to his [Weber's] sociology." See Georg Brodnitz, "Recent Work in German Economic History," *Economic History Review* 1 (1928): 345; Edgar Salin, "Der 'Sozialismus' in Hellas," p. 26 in Georg Karo et al., eds., *Bilder und Studien aus drei Jahrtausenden. Eberhard Gothein zum siebzigsten Geburtstag als Festgabe* (Munich: Duncker und Humblot, 1923), p. 171.

14. See the appendix on the evolution of Weber's thought on economics.

15. Max Weber, *General Economic History* (New Brunswick, N.J.: Transaction Books, 1981), p. 24, or *Wirtschaftsgeschichte*, p. 39. We clearly know more on this topic today than was known in Weber's day. See, e.g., the literature cited in "Annotated Bibliography: Economic Development in Ancient Times," p. 410 in Rondo Cameron, *A Concise Economic History of the World* (New York: Oxford University Press, 1993).

16. Weber, *General Economic History*, pp. 7, 14, or *Wirtschaftsgeschichte*, pp. 23, 29. The translation has been slightly altered.

17. Throughout this book I translate the German word *Sippe* simply as "clan," although Weber was explicitly critical of the word "clan." In *The Religion of India* (written before *General Economic History*), Weber says that "the Irish term 'clan' is ambiguous"— and this made the translators of this work use the term "sib." See Weber, *The Religion of India* (New York: Free Press, 1958), p. 53, or "Hinduismus und Buddhismus," p. 56 n. 1 in Vol. 2 of *Gesammelte Aufsätze zur Religionssoziologie* (Tübingen: J.C.B. Mohr, 1988). Weber also briefly discusses the term *Sippe* in *General Economic History*, p. 43, or *Wirtschaftsgeschichte*, p. 54.

18. Weber, *General Economic History*, p. 116, or *Wirtschaftsgeschichte*, p. 111.

19. The German term is *Herreigentum;* see Weber, *General Economic History*, p. 51 ff., or *Wirtschaftsgeschichte*, p. 59 ff.

20. Weber, *General Economic History*, p. 95, or *Wirtschaftgeschichte*, pp. 95–96.

21. Weber, *General Economic History*, p. 115, or *Wirtschaftsgeschichte*, p. 110.

22. Georg von Below, "Review of Max Weber, *Wirtschaftsgeschichte*," *Weltwirtschaftliches Archiv* 20 (1924): 488; and Usher, "Review of Max Weber, *General Economic History*," p. 104. See, however, also Raymond De Roover's critique, as cited in note 10.

23. Weber, *General Economic History*, p. 122, or *Wirtschaftsgeschichte*, p. 116.

24. Weber, *General Economic History*, p. 174, or *Wirtschaftsgeschichte*, p. 158.

25. Ibid. This is surely wrong, in my opinion.

26. Usher, "Review of Max Weber, *General Economic History*," p. 104.

27. Weber, *General Economic History*, pp. 195, 202–20, or *Wirtschaftsgeschichte*, pp. 174, 180–95.

28. Weber, *General Economic History*, pp. 206–7, or *Wirtschaftsgeschichte*, p. 184. The translation has been slightly changed, to better fit the terminology of the current English translation of *Wirtschaft und Gesellschaft*.

29. Weber, *General Economic History*, p. 228, or *Wirtschaftsgeschichte*, p. 202.

30. Weber, *General Economic History*, p. 248, or *Wirtschaftsgeschichte*, p. 219.

31. Weber, *General Economic History*, p. 239, or *Wirtschaftsgeschichte*, p. 211.

32. For a discussion of what Weber called "internal" and "external ethics," see Weber, *General Economic History*, p. 268, or *Wirtschaftsgeschichte*, p. 234.

33. Heckscher, "Den ekonomiska historiens aspekter," p. 20; Usher, "Review of Max Weber, *General Economic History*," p. 104; and von Below, "Review of Max Weber, *General Economic History*," pp. 487–88.

34. Randall Collins, "Weber's Last Theory of Capitalism: A Systematization," *American Sociological Review* 45 (1980): 925.

35. For one thing, Collins argues that Weber summarized much of his recent research on the history of capitalism in *General Economic History*, while von Below is probably more on the mark when he says that Weber was not as fully prepared to give a course of this type as he would have been if he had not devoted himself to other research projects during his last years. See von Below, "Review of Max Weber, *Wirtschaftsgeschichte*," p. 487. I would also argue that Weber did have an "institutional" analysis already in *The Protestant Ethic*. I furthermore feel that Weber's notion of causality gets too simplified in Collins's "causal chain" (Collins, "Weber's Last Theory of Capitalism," p. 931).

36. For Weber's use of the term "rational capitalism" ("*rationaler Kapitalismus*", "*moderner rationaler Kapitalismus*") and 'Western capitalism" ("*okzidentaler Kapitalismus*"), see *General Economic History*, pp. 335, 350, 360, 312, or *Wirtschaftsgeschichte*, pp. 286, 307, 299, 269.

37. Weber, *General Economic History*, p. 360, or *Wirtschaftsgeschichte*, p. 307.

38. See Werner Sombart, *The Jews and Capitalism* (New Brunswick, N.J.: Transaction Books, [1913] 1982).

39. Weber, *General Economic History*, pp. 312–13, 356, 366, or *Wirtschaftsgeschichte*, pp. 269, 304, 312.

CHAPTER TWO
BASIC CONCEPTS IN WEBER'S ECONOMIC SOCIOLOGY

1. Max Weber, "Some Categories of Interpretive Sociology," *Sociological Quarterly* 22 (Spring 1981): 151–80, or "Ueber einige Kategorien der verstehenden Soziologie," pp. 427–74 in *Gesammelte Aufsätze zur Wissenschaftslehre* (Tübingen: J.C.B. Mohr, 1988).

More precisely, according to a note appended to the article, only the second half of the text is from material that Weber had produced in connection with his work for *Economy and Society*. Weber also says that the second half represents only a fragment of this earlier material. In referring to his article for *Economy and Society*, Weber means either a section described in the first version (1910) of *Grundriss der Sozialökonomik* as "The Object and Logical Nature of the Inquiry [in Economics]" or an early version of chapter 1. The whereabouts of the original manuscript is not known.

2. Max Weber, *Economy and Society: An Outline of Interpretive Sociology* (Berkeley: University of California Press, 1978), p. 4, or *Wirtschaft und Gesellschaft. Grundriss der verstehenden Sociologie* (Tübingen: J.C.B. Mohr, 1972), p. 1.

3. According to Weber, both economic theory and sociology make use of understanding (*Verstehen*) in their analyses or, more precisely, both make use of ideal types of meaning (see Weber, *Economy and Society*, p. 4, or *Wirtschaft und Gesellschaft*, pp. 1–2). As Shira Lewin suggests, the idea of revealed preferences is a behavioristic notion and therefore not compatible with the Weberian notion of understanding. Whether this disqualifies the use of revealed preferences in economics is, however, a different—and still open—question. See Shira Lewin, "Economics and Psychology: Lessons for Our Own Day from the Early Twentieth Century," *Journal of Economic Literature* 34 (1996): 1293–1323.

4. To illustrate the role of meaning in economic affairs on a more general level, the following example (from an essay by Weber from 1907) can be cited:

> Let us suppose that two men who otherwise engage in no "social relation"—for example, two savages of different tribes, or a European who encounters a savage in darkest Africa—meet and "exchange" two objects. We are inclined to think that a mere description of what can be observed during this exchange—muscular movements and, if some words were "spoken," the sounds which, so to say, constitute the "matter" or "material" of the behavior—would in no sense comprehend the "essence" of what happens. This is quite correct. The "essence" of what happens is constituted by the "meaning" which the two parties ascribe to their observable behavior, a "meaning" which "regulates" the course of their future conduct. Without this "meaning," we are inclined to say, an "'exchange' is neither empirically possible nor conceptually imaginable." (Weber, *Critique of Stammler* [New York: Free Press, 1977], p. 109, or "R. Stammlers 'Überwindung' der materialistischen Geschichtsauffassung," pp. 331–32, in *Gesammelte Aufsätze zur Wissenschaftslehre*.

The translation has been changed. A more concrete example of the decisive role that meaning plays is the following (from chapter 2 in *Economy and Society*):

> The administration of budgetary "wealth" and profit-making enterprises may be outwardly so similar as to appear identical. They are in fact in the analysis only distinguishable in terms of the difference in *meaningful* orientation of the corresponding economic activities. In the one case, it is oriented to maintaining and improving profitability and the market position of the enterprise; in the other, to the security and increase of wealth and income. (Weber, *Economy and Society*, p. 98, or *Wirtschaft und Gesellschaft*, p. 52)

5. The idea of methodological individualism came to an early expression in the works of John Stuart Mill and Carl Menger; Joseph Schumpeter coined the term in 1908; see Joseph A. Schumpeter, *Das Wesen und der Hauptinhalt der theoretischen Nationalökonomie* (Leipzig: Duncker und Humblot, 1908), pp. 88–98; and Lars Udehn,

Methodological Individualism: A Critical Appraisal (Uppsala: Ph.D. diss., Department of Sociology, 1987). Weber refers to the individual and his or her action as his "atom" in his 1913 article on interpretive sociology, and he explains why he felt that methodological individualism was so important to sociology in a famous passage in a letter to Robert Liefmann: "If I have become a sociologist (according to my letter of accreditation [in Munich]), it is mainly in order to exorcise the spectre of collective conceptions which still linger among us. In other words, sociology itself can only proceed from the actions of one or more separate individuals and must therefore adopt strictly individualistic methods"; see Weber, "Some Categories of Interpretive Sociology," p. 158, or "Ueber einige Kategorien der verstehenden Soziologie," p. 439 in *Gesammelte Aufsätze zur Wissenschaftslehre;* and letter to Robert Liefmann, dated March 9, 1920, as cited in Wolfgang Mommsen, "Max Weber's Political Sociology and His Philosophy of World History," *International Social Science Journal* 17 (1965): 44.

6. Weber, *Economy and Society,* p. 4, or *Wirtschaft und Gesellschaft,* p. 1; emphasis added. In an early version of chapter 1 in *Economy and Society* from 1913, Weber expressed the same idea in the following manner: "Action specifically significant for interpretive sociology is, in particular, behavior that: (1) in terms of the subjectively intended meaning of the actor, is related to the *behavior of others,* (2) is *codetermined* in its course through this relatedness, and thus (3) can be intelligibly *explained* in terms of this (subjectively) intended meaning." See Weber, "Some Categories of Interpretive Sociology," p. 152, or "Ueber einige Kategorien der verstehenden Soziologie," pp. 429–30 in *Gesammelte Aufsätze zur Wissenschaftslehre*. It can also be noted that there is a certain similarity between Weber's idea of social (economic) action and the concept of "transaction" in the work of John R. Commons. According to the latter, "While the economists start with a commodity or an individual's feelings towards it, the court starts with a transaction. Its ultimate unit of investigation is not an individual but two or more individuals—plaintiff and defendant—at two ends of one or more transactions." See John R. Commons, *Legal Foundations of Capitalism* (New Brunswick, N.J.: Transaction Publishers, [1924] 1995), p. 7.

7. Two excellent works on Weber's basic sociological concepts, including his typology of social action, are Raymond Aron, "Max Weber," pp. 219–317 in Vol. 2 of *Main Currents in Sociology* (New York: Doubleday, 1970); and Alexander von Schelting, *Max Webers Wissenschaftslehre* (Tübingen: J.C.B. Mohr, 1934). Other fine works include: Martin Albrow, *Max Weber's Construction of Social Theory* (London: Macmillan, 1992); Reinhard Bendix, *Max Weber: An Intellectual Portrait* (New York: Doubleday, 1960); Julien Freund, *The Sociology of Max Weber* (Harmondsworth, Eng.: Penguin Books [1966] 1972); and Dirk Käsler, *Max Weber: An Introduction to His Life and Work* (Cambridge: Polity Press, 1988).

8. Weber, *Economy and Society,* p. 31, or *Wirtschaft und Gesellschaft,* p. 16.

9. Among those who argue that Weber tried to "supplement" economic theory is, first and foremost, Talcott Parsons, but also Arthur Stinchcombe; see Talcott Parsons, "Introduction," p. 31 in Max Weber, *The Theory of Social and Economic Organization* (New York: Oxford University Press, 1947); and Arthur Stinchcombe, "Review of Max Weber's *Economy and Society,*" p. 286 in *Stratification and Organization* (Cambridge: Cambridge University Press, 1986). For those who feel that Weber constructed his sociology on the basis of marginalist economics, see especially Simon Clarke, *Marx, Marginalism and Modern Sociology: From Adam Smith to Max Weber* (London: Macmillan, 1982), pp. 204–12; see also Göran Therborn, *Science, Class and Society: On the Formation of Sociology and Historical Materialism* (London: NLB, 1976), p. 293. In criticizing Parsons for arguing that Weber was trying to supplement economic theory, Ludwig Lachmann has

pointed out that Parsons in all likelihood had other economists in mind than Weber did when he thought of economic theory (especially Marshall and Pareto), and that Parsons and Weber consequently meant different things when they said that there was a need to supplement economic theory; Lachmann adds that "to ascribe to [Weber's] economic sociology any intended relationship to the neoclassical orthodoxy of our own days would of course be grotesque"; see Ludwig Lachmann, "Socialism and the Market: A Theme of Economic Sociology from a Weberian Perspective," *South African Journal of Economics* 60 (1992): 43 n. 12). This, however, is what Robert Holton and Bryan Turner do when they assert that "Weber accepts the basic neo-classical conception of the economy"; see Robert J. Holton and Bryan S. Turner, *Max Weber on Economy and Society* (London: Routledge, 1989), p. 47. Similarly, Stephen Kalberg says that "Weber outlines a neoclassical world of economically-oriented action under capitalism"; see Stephen Kalberg, "Max Weber's Universal-Historical Architectonic of Economically-Oriented Action: A Preliminary Reconstruction," *Current Perspectives in Social Theory* 4 (1983): 265. Stinchcombe, who is more knowledgeable about economics, specifies that what Weber wanted to complete was "the classical model of the economy." This is clearly a plus, though it should be noted that Stinchcombe avoids the tricky question of where Austrian economics fits into all of this. Weber's view of economic theory was hardly the standard one, even in his own days, and it cannot be labeled "classical." Finally, Karl Polanyi calls Weber a "marketist" because his attempt to synthesize "the societal approach" to the economy (Marx) with that of "the economistic approach" (Menger) leads him to ignore production. See Karl Polanyi, "Appendix," pp. 123, 136 in *Primitive, Archaic and Modern Economies* (Boston: Beacon Press, 1971).

10. Therborn, *Science, Class and Society*, p. 293.

11. Weber simply says that one example of instrumentally rational action would be an actor's arrangement of his or her needs according to a scale of urgency so that they can be satisfied according to the principle of marginal utility. As Weber explains in his essay on marginal utility theory from 1908, the idea of marginal utility is not something that economic theorists make up but something that grows out of everybody's "common experience." See Weber, *Economy and Society*, p. 26, or *Wirtschaft und Gesellschaft*, p. 13; Max Weber, "Marginal Utility Theory and 'The Fundamental Law of Psycho-Physics,'" *Social Science Quarterly* 56 (1975): 28–9, or "Die Grenznutzlehre und das 'psychophysische Grundgesetz,'" p. 390 in *Gesammelte Aufsätze zur Wissenschaftslehre*. Even though one can find a smattering of references to "marginal utility" throughout the parts devoted to economic sociology in *Economy and Society*, the key idea of marginal utility theory—which is that the notion of declining utility can be used to solve a series of difficult problems in economic theory—plays no role whatsoever in Weber's economic sociology. Of the two most detailed references to marginal utility theory in chapter 2, both question its usefulness in certain situations for economic sociology. In one of these Weber suggests that power relations better account for the rate of interest than marginal utility theory; and in the second Weber says that it is often the producers, not the consumers (as in marginal utility theory) who determine what is to be produced. See Weber, *Economy and Society*, pp. 92, 97, or *Wirtschaft und Gesellschaft*, pp. 49, 52.

12. Weber, *Economy and Society*, p. 9, or *Wirtschaft und Gesellschaft*, p. 4. See also, for a similar statement, *Economy and Society*, p. 21, or *Wirtschaft und Gesellschaft*, p. 10. Weber adds that this type of strictly rational economic action can be found in contemporary reality only in "unusual cases," for example, at the stock exchange. It should be noted that Weber does not introduce the distinction between value-rational action and instrumentally rational action in this statement.

13. Weber, *Economy and Society*, p. 63, or *Wirtschaft und Gesellschaft*, p. 31.

14. Weber, *Economy and Society*, p. 22, or *Wirtschaft und Gesellschaft*, p. 11. That "others will respect his actual control" includes "legal rules" is clear from *Economy and Society*, p. 33, or *Wirtschaft und Gesellschaft*, p. 17. In commenting on this argument, Emil Lederer states that Weber's concept of economic (social) action applies only to market economies and that it excludes consumption. In this categorical form, Lederer's statement is wrong in my opinion. Consumption—say, everyday shopping—includes important elements of other-directedness. Status in general, as Weber points out, is connected to consumption. To the extent that people work together in nonmarket economies, their actions are similarly oriented toward the actions of others. See Emil Lederer's comments on chapter 2 in *Economy and Society* on pp. 11–13 in *Aufriss der ökonomischen Theorie* (Tübingen: J.C.B. Mohr, 1931).

15. Weber, *Economy and Society*, p. 6, or *Wirtschaft und Gesellschaft*, p. 2. For a similar statement, see *Economy and Society*, p. 21, or *Wirtschaft und Gesellschaft*, p. 10. Immediately after using the stock exchange as his example, Weber notes that one can equally well use the example of a political or military campaign. Weber makes perfectly clear that using a rationalistic method does not mean that one assumes that reality is predominantly rational; see *Economy and Society*, pp. 6–7, or *Wirtschaft und Gesellschaft*, p. 3. He also makes clear that sociology can use rational ideal types only when these correspond to something in empirical reality *"with a significant degree of approximation"* (emphasis added; the exact formulation is: "formulations of a rational course of subjectively understandable action constitute sociological types of empirical process only when they can be empirically observed with a significant degree of approximation"). See Weber, *Economy and Society*, p. 12, or *Wirtschaft und Gesellschaft*, p. 6.

16. See in particular Veit Michael Bader, Johannes Berger, Heiner Ganssmann, and Jost v.d. Knesebeck, "Max Weber: Soziologische Grundbegriffe des Wirtschaftens," pp. 193–320 in *Einführung in die Gesellschaftstheorie. Gesellschaft, Wirtschaft und Staat bei Marx und Weber* (Frankfurt: Campus Verlag, [1976] 1987); Julien Freund,"The Sociology of Economics," pp. 149–75 in *The Sociology of Max Weber* (Harmondsworth, Eng.: Penguin Books, [1966] 1972); Bryn Jones, "Economic Action and Rational Organization in the Sociology of Weber," pp. 28–65 in Barry Hindess, ed., *Sociological Theories of the Economy* (London: Macmillan, 1977); Kalberg, "Max Weber's Universal-Historical Architectonic," pp. 253–88; Talcott Parsons, "Weber's 'Economic Sociology,'" pp. 30–55 in the "Introduction" to Weber, *The Theory of Social and Economic Organization;* Gianfranco Poggi, "The Conceptual Context," pp. 13–26 in *Calvinism and the Capitalist Spirit: Max Weber's Protestant Ethic* (Amherst: University of Massachusetts Press, 1983); and Johannes Winkelmann, *Wirtschaft und Gesellschaft. Erläuterungsband* (Tübingen: J.C.B. Mohr, 1976), pp. 35–43. Many of these interpretations, however, do not look at chapter 2 from the viewpoint of economic sociology in a conscious manner: Kalberg is mainly interested in chapter 2 so that he can develop a universal-historical typology for civilizational analysis; Poggi argues that chapter 2 supplements the analysis in *The Protestant Ethic* through its focus on the way that capitalism operates rather than on its origin; and so on. To what extent chapter 2 in *Economy and Society* has been used in lectures and taught at various universities is, of course, impossible to say. As to the United States, however, the following three cases are of a certain interest. According to Edward Shils, "In the middle of the 1930s Frank Knight conducted a seminar [at the University of Chicago] on the first chapters of *Wirtschaft und Gesellschaft,* where we studied the text line by line." According to Daniel Bell, Alexander von Schelting taught a course in 1939 at Columbia University that was devoted exclusively to the two first chapters in *Economy and Society* ("we spent the entire term . . . mostly on definitions of economic and ratio-

nal actions"). Finally, Karl Polanyi (who taught at Columbia University between 1947 and 1953) discusses chapter 2 of *Economy and Society* in the mimeographed notes he distributed to his students in 1947 and which are reprinted as "Appendix," pp. 120–38 in Polanyi, *Primitive, Archaic and Modern Economies*. See also Edward Shils, "Tradition, Ecology, and Institution in the History of Sociology," *Daedalus* 99 (Fall 1970): 823 n. 21; and (for Bell) Richard Swedberg, *Economics and Sociology* (Princeton, N.J.: Princeton University Press, 1990), p. 217.

17. Talcott Parsons, "Introduction," pp. 1–86 in Weber, *The Theory of Social and Economic Organization*. This work is a translation of Part 1 of *Economy and Society,* which was published in 1921. The analysis of chapter 2 ("Weber's Economic Sociology") can be found on pages 30–55 and is correctly treated as the most important commentary on this chapter. See on this last point, e.g., Eduard Baumgarten, *Max Weber: Werk und Person* (Tübingen: J.C.B. Mohr, 1964), pp. 563–65; and Arnold Zingerle, *Max Webers historische Soziologie* (Darmstadt: Wissenschaftliche Buchgesellschaft, 1981), p. 94.—One can also get an impression of Parsons's study of Weber's chapter 2 by looking at his personal copy of *Wirtschaft und Gesellschaft* (inscribed "Heidelberg 1925"), which can be inspected at the Pusey Archives at Harvard University (HUG[FP] 42.55, box 2). From Parsons's underlinings it is clear that he studied chapter 1 (on general sociology) and chapter 3 (on domination) more thoroughly than he studied chapter 2 (on economic sociology). Parsons usually underlined important passages when he studied Weber, and his reading of chapter 2 seems to have been spotty at times, since there are only occasional or no underlinings in §12–30 and §32–38.

18. Weber uses the term *Wirtschaften,* which the editors of *Economy and Society,* following Parsons, translate as "economic action." Poggi suggests "economizing," which is perhaps less successful since it has a quite different meaning in everyday life than the one that Weber had in mind; see Poggi, *Calvinism and the Capitalist Spirit,* p. 15. Raymond Aron notes, "*Wirtschaft* means economy; and thanks to the flexibility of the German language, it is not difficult to create a verb signifying economic action: the exercise of a capacity oriented toward the economic"; see Aron, *Main Currents in Sociological Thought,* Vol. 2, p. 283. As noted in chapter 1, Weber used the concept of *Wirtschaften* in his lectures on economics in the 1890s. In the notes for his classes in general theoretical economics, according to the *Outline* from the 1890s:

Under 'economic action' we understand a specific kind of *external and purposive aspiration*—i.e., conscious, well-planned behavior with respect to nature and humans—that is *compelled* by those needs, which require *external means* for their satisfaction, regardless of whether they are 'material' or 'ideal' in kind, and which serve the purpose of providing for the future.

See Weber, *Grundriss zu den Vorlesungen über Allgemeine ("theoretische") Nationalökonomie (1898)* (Tübingen: J.C.B. Mohr, [1898] 1990), p. 29, as translated in Lawrence Scaff, *Fleeing the Iron Cage* (Berkeley: University of California Press, 1989), p. 32.

19. Weber, *Economy and Society,* p. 63, or *Wirtschaft und Gesellschaft,* p. 31. In saying that this definition of utility (*Nutzleistung*) is fairly conventional, I am referring to the part on utility ("satisfaction of a desire for 'utilities'"). It is, however, also clear that Weber has formulated his definition so that it will also fit sociology by highlighting the element of "subjective meaning." The distinction between "economic action" and "economically oriented action"—Weber is talking about the latter in the definition cited here—is discussed later in this chapter; here it suffices to say that economic action is a subcategory of economically oriented action. (The formal definition of economic action comes in the

sentence after the definition of economically oriented action, and goes like this:"'Economic action' [*Wirtschaften*] is any peaceful exercise of an actor's control over resources which is in its main impulse oriented towards economic ends"). Weber's definition of economic action in *Economy and Society* can be compared to the one provided in his lectures on economics in the 1890s, which is cited in the preceding note.

20. Weber uses *"Nutzleistung"* rather than the conventional *"Nutzen"* or *"Nützlichkeit."* For Weber on utility, see *Economy and Society,* pp. 68–69, or *Wirtschaft und Gesellschaft,* pp. 34–35. The term *Nutzleistung* is rarely found in German economic dictionaries; when it is found, its definition differs from that of Weber; see, e.g., Erwin Dichtl and Otmar Issing, eds., *Vahlens Grosses Wirtschaftslexikon,* Vol. 2 (Munich: Verlag C. H. Beck, 1993), in which the term is not mentioned; Rengasamy Tharmalingam Murugiah, ed, *Wirtschaftswörterbuch Deutsch-Englisch* (Munich: Verlag die Wirtschaft, 1993), in which it is translated as "effective capacity [output]" (p. 355); Andreas Schüler, ed., *Wörterbuch Wirtschaft Englisch-Deutsch* (Frankfurt: Verlag Harri Deutsch, 1980), in which it is not among the terms for "utility" (p. 727); Artur Woll, ed., *Wirtschafts Lexikon* (Munich: R. Oldenbourg Verlag, 1988), which does not mention it. Raymond Aron translates *Nutzleistung* into French as *prestation d'utilité* (translated into English as "enactment of utility") and adds that *Leistung* comes from the verb *leisten,* which means to accomplish or to produce, and *Nutz* is the root of the word "utility"; see Aron, *Main Currents in Sociological Thought,* Vol. 2, p. 282. Karl Polanyi is very critical of Weber's concept of utility because he says that Weber implicitly equates human beings with things (since utility includes goods as well as services), and also because Weber does not grasp that one cannot divide an object (such as a horse) into a bundle of utilities. See Polanyi, "Appendix," pp. 136–37 in *Primitive, Archaic and Modern Economies.*

21. In the present editions of *Economy and Society* and *Wirtschaft und Gesellschaft,* one can find two definitions of economic action: one in chapter 2 of Part 1, which Weber oversaw himself, and another in the manuscripts that Weber left behind and which were later incorporated into *Wirtschaft und Gesellschaft.* In the latter definition, Weber stresses that economic action encompasses the satisfaction of wants as well as profit-making; cf. Weber, *Economy and Society,* p. 339–40, or *Wirtschaft und Gesellschaft,* p. 199. For a discussion of economic action, see also Weber, *Wirtschaftsgeschichte* (Berlin: Duncker und Humblot, 1991), pp. 1–2.

22. Ever since Frank Knight's famous dissertation on risk and uncertainty, it is usual to make a distinction between risk (or "measurable uncertainty") and uncertainity (or "unmeasurable uncertainty"); see Frank H. Knight, *Risk, Uncertainty, and Profit* (Chicago: University of Chicago Press, [1921] 1985), p. 19 ff. This distinction is not to be found in Weber, who uses the term *"Chance"* in a number of different meanings throughout *Economy and Society* (including "probability"). Parsons—and following him, the editors of *Economy and Society*—often translate *Chance* as "advantage" when it really means "opportunity." One example of this is in §2, where "economic opportunities" (*"ökonomische Chancen"*) is translated as "economic advantages"; see Weber, *Economy and Society,* pp. 68–69, or *Wirtschaft und Gesellschaft,* p. 34. A work that attempts to systematically draw attention to Weber's concept of *ökonomische Chance* is that of Birger Priddat; see especially section II.2 in Birger Priddat, *Zufall, Schicksal, Irrtum. Über Unsicherheit und Risiko in der deutschen ökonomischen Theorie vom 18. bis ins frühe 20. Jahrhundert* (Marburg: Metropolis-Verlag, 1993). A more general and very interesting discussion of this term can be found in the work of Ralf Dahrendorf. The notion of "life chances" is of particular interest to Dahrendorf, but he also comments on how *Chance* is used in Weber's economic sociology. At one point he notes, "Weber clearly implies that

economic chances are themselves scarce so that one has to compete for them. Weber is imaginative in finding names for such chances, and we have mentioned some of them already: market chances, chances of acquisition, exchange chances, price chances, interest chances, work utilization chances, capital formation chances." Ralf Dahrendorf, "Max Weber's Concept of 'Chance,'" pp. 67–68 in *Life Chances* (Chicago: University of Chicago Press, 1979). For a comment on how close the relationship is between life chances and "opportunity structure," see Robert K. Merton, "Opportunity Structure," pp. 28–29, 33, in F. Adler and W. S. Laufer, eds., *The Legacy of Anomie Theory* (New Brunswick, N.J.: Transaction Books, 1995). Finally, see also Johannes Winkelmann, "Chance," p. 980 in Vol. 1 of Joachim Ritter, ed., *Historisches Wörterbuch der Philosophie* (Basel: Schwabe und Co. Verlag, 1971).

23. A similar position has been taken by Felix Kaufmann, who was deeply influenced by Weber and who was a friend of Alfred Schutz. In a 1933 article Kaufman wrote: "The question . . . arises what it really is that the economic subject acquires when he gains possession of a thing. Clearly, what he acquires are opportunities of utilising the thing in question, and, therefore, a good must be defined as a totality of such opportunities, which can be realized partly together, partly as alternatives to each other. I *have* such an opportunity if there is a probability that some event, desired by me, will happen; I *acquire* the opportunity in so far as I create such a probability—i.e. if I behave in such a way that arises; and I *surrender* it if I so behave that the probability is removed before I avail myself of it"; Felix Kaufmann, "On the Subject-Matter and Method of Economic Science," *Economica* 42 (1933): 384.

24. Weber uses the term *Chance* more than fifty times in chapter 2 of *Wirtschaft und Gesellschaft*. The two most common uses are, in order of priority, opportunities for profit-making (*Erwerbschancen*) and market opportunities (*Marktchancen*).

25. Parsons is of course aware that Weber starts from the same basis that economic theory does—see, e.g., his statement to this effect on pp. 53–54 in his introduction to Max Weber, *The Theory of Social and Economic Organization*—but he fails to spell out the implications of this for what goes on at the macro level. It can be added that Weber's colleague Schumpeter argued in a similar manner as Parsons when he programmatically announced that economic theory, not economic sociology, "deals with behavior [that takes place] *within* the social framework." For a critique of the tendency to view economic theory and economic sociology as complementary, see Richard Swedberg, "Joseph A. Schumpeter and the Tradition of Economic Sociology," *Journal of Institutional and Theoretical Economics* 145 (1989): 513 ff.

26. Weber, *Economy and Society*, p. 116, or *Wirtschaft und Gesellschaft*, p. 63.

27. "Householding" is "*Haushalt*" in the original; and "profit-making" is "*Erwerben*." *Haushalt* is translated as "budgetary management" by Parsons as well as by the current editors of *Economy and Society* (who basically follow Parsons in chapter 2). Stephen Kalberg suggests "provision of needs," which is perhaps preferable to "budgetary management"; see Stephen Kalberg, "Max Weber's Universal-Historical Architectonic," pp. 283–84.

28. According to Finley, "The word 'economics,' Greek in origin, is compounded from *oikos*, a household, and the semantically complex root, *nem-*, here in its sense of 'regulate, administer, organize'"; see M. I. Finley, *The Ancient Economy* (London: Hogarth Press, [1973] 1985), p. 17. For Aristotle on economics, see especially M. I. Finley, "Aristotle and Economic Analysis," *Past and Present* 47 (1970): 3–25. The distinction between householding and profit-making is reproduced in such concepts as the distinction between use value and exchange value (e.g., Marx, following Aristotle) and between sub-

stantive and formal economy (Polanyi, transferring the distinction to the level of theory). That the distinction between householding and profit-making was very much alive in German economics in Weber's day is clear, for example, from its discussion in the works of Friedrich Gottl-Ottlilienfeld and Karl Bücher; see Johannes Winkelmann, *Wirtschaft und Gesellschaft. Erläuterungsband,* pp. 37–38. In modern anthropology the distinction has received renewed attention through the discussion of the distinction between "house" and "corporation" in Stephen Gudeman and Alberto Rivera, *Conversations in Colombia* (Cambridge: Cambridge University Press, 1990).

29. For the *oikos,* see, e.g., Weber, *Economy and Society,* pp. 100, 381, or *Wirtschaft und Gesellschaft,* pp. 54, 381 ff. The term *oikos* was originally introduced in 1865 by Karl Rodbertus, whose use of the term Weber challenged. Weber expresses his own view of the *oikos* in the fullest manner in his 1909 study of antiquity; see *The Agrarian Sociology of Ancient Civilizations* (London: NLB, 1976), pp. 42–43; or "Agrarverhältnisse im Altertum," p. 7 in *Gesammelte Aufsätze zur Sozial- und Wirtschaftsgeschichte* (Tübingen: J.C.B. Mohr, 1988). For the debate in historiography around this concept, see, e.g., John Love, "On the Economic Character of the Ancient Agricultural Estate: *Oikos* or Enterprise?," pp. 59–109 in *Antiquity and Capitalism: Max Weber and the Sociological Foundations of Roman Civilization* (London: Routledge, 1991).

30. For the profit-making enterprise (*Unternehmen*), see Weber, *Economy and Society,* p. 91, or *Wirtschaft und Gesellschaft,* p. 48.

31. For definitions of "wealth" (*Vermögen*), "capital" (*Kapital*), "income" (*Einkommen*), and "profit" (*Gewinn*), see Weber, *Economy and Society,* pp. 87, 91, 87, or *Wirtschaft und Gesellschaft,* pp. 46,48, 46, 48.

32. "Traditional" is *"traditional"* and "rational" is *"zweckrational"*; see Weber, *Economy and Society,* p. 69 ff., or *Wirtschaft und Gesellschaft,* p. 35 ff. Weber mentions a third form of economic action, "affectual economic action," which is clearly of less importance, though a few relevant examples exist. Loyalty may, for example, inspire a certain type of economic action. Why rational economic action is typically *zweckrational* rather than *wertrational* will soon be discussed.

33. See Weber, *The Agrarian Sociology of Ancient Civilizations,* p. 210, or "Agrarverhältnisse im Altertum," p. 146 in *Gesammelte Aufsätze zur Sozial- und Wirtschaftsgeschichte.*

34. Weber occasionally uses the term "economic traditionalism" (*ökonomischer Traditionalismus*); see Max Weber, *The Protestant Ethic and the Spirit of Capitalism* (London: Allen and Unwin, 1930), pp. 36, 64, or "Die protestantische Ethik und der Geist des Kapitalismus," pp. 48, 76 in Vol. 1 of *Gesammelte Aufsätze zur Religionssoziologie* (Tübingen: J.C.B. Mohr, 1988).

35. "Economic action" is *"Wirtschaften"* and "economically oriented action" is *"wirtschaftlich orientiertes Handeln"*; see Weber, *Economy and Society,* p. 63 ff., or *Wirtschaft und Gesellschaft,* p. 31 ff.

36. Weber, *Economy and Society,* p. 64, or *Wirtschaft und Gesellschaft,* p. 32. The translation has been slightly changed.

37. Max Weber, "Between Two Laws," p. 78 in *Political Writings* (Cambridge: Cambridge University Press, 1994), or "Zwischen zwei Gesetzen (1916)," p. 144 in *Gesammelte Politische Schriften* (Tübingen: J.C.B. Mohr, 1988).

38. "Power of control and disposal" or *"Verfügungsgewalt"* is introduced and discussed in Weber, *Economy and Society,* pp. 63, 67–68, or *Wirtschaft und Gesellschaft,* pp. 31, 33–34. Weber occasionally uses the term "economic power" (*"ökonomische Macht"*) and defines it in the early version of *Economy and Society* as "control (*Verfügung*) over eco-

nomic economic goods"; see Weber, *Economy and Society*, p. 942, or *Wirtschaft und Gesellschaft*, p. 541. The term can also be found in Weber's lectures on economic theory from the 1890s; see Weber, *Grundriss zu den Vorlesungen über Allgemeine ("theoretische") Nationalökonomie (1898)*, p. 58; see also pp. 33, 41, 43.

39. Weber, *Economy and Society*, p. 67, or *Wirtschaft und Gesellschaft*, p. 33.

40. While Weber clearly says that law is not essential to the concept of power of control and disposal, Parsons asserts that "the term *Verfügungsgewalt* [implies] legally sanctioned powers of control and disposal." See Weber, *Economy and Society*, pp. 67–68, 206 (note by Parsons), or *Wirtschaft und Gesellschaft*, pp. 33–34.

41. The German phrase is "*Brauch . . . bedingt durch Interessenlage ('interessenbedingt')*," and the translation used by Parsons plus Roth and Wittich in *Economy and Society* is "uniformity . . . 'determined by self-interest'"; see Weber, *Economy and Society*, pp. 29–31, or *Wirtschaft und Gesellschaft*, pp. 15–16. In his 1913 essay on interpretive sociology Weber called this type of action "consensus" or "*Einverständnis.*" See Weber, "Some Categories of Interpretive Sociology," pp. 167–73, or "Ueber einige Kategorien der verstehenden Soziologie," pp. 452–64 in *Gesammelte Aufsätze zur Wissenschaftslehre*.

42. Weber, *Economy and Society*, pp. 40–43, or *Wirtschaft und Gesellschaft*, pp. 21–23. Weber here follows Tönnies.

43. Weber, *Economy and Society*, p. 41, or *Wirtschaft und Gesellschaft*, p. 22.

44. Mark Granovetter, "Economic Action and Social Structure: The Problem of Embeddedness," *American Journal of Sociology* 91 (1985): 481–510. In this article, as well as in conversations with the author, Granovetter affirms the affinity between Weber's economic sociology and his own analysis of embeddedness. Karl Polanyi, it may be added, saw "embeddedness" in a different way; pre-capitalist economies, he argued, are embedded in religion and tradition, while capitalist economies are not embedded in this manner; see Karl Polanyi, Conrad M. Arensberg, and Harry W. Pearson, eds., *Trade and Market in the Early Empires* (Chicago: Henry Regnery [1957] 1971).

45. Parsons and the editors of *Economy and Society* prefer to translate "*Kampf*" as "conflict." See Weber, *Economy and Society*, p. 38, or *Wirtschaft und Gesellschaft*, p. 20.

46. "*Preiskampf*" and "*Konkurrenzkampf.*" Together these two types of struggle make up what Weber calls "exchange struggle" ("*Tauschkampf*"). See Weber, *Economy and Society*, pp. 72, 82, 93, or *Wirtschaft und Gesellschaft*, pp. 36, 43, 49.

47. "*Kampf des Menschen mit dem Menschen.*" This expression is used three times in chapter 2 of *Economy and Society*, each time referring to the market and to exchange. See Weber, *Economy and Society*, pp. 92 (twice), 108, or *Wirtschaft und Gesellschaft*, pp. 49 (twice), 58.

48. *Economy and Society*, p. 38, or *Wirtschaft und Gesellschaft*, p. 20. The translation has been slightly changed. The German term for "competition" is "*Konkurrenz.*"

49. "Selection" or "*Auslese*" is defined and discussed in Weber, *Economy and Society*, pp. 38–40, or *Wirtschaft und Gesellschaft*, pp. 20–21.

50. Weber, *Economy and Society*, p. 53, or *Wirtschaft und Gesellschaft*, p. 28. The term *Herrschaft* has been translated in a number of different ways besides domination, including rulership, leadership, and authority. For two authoritative discussions of the various translations, see Guenther Roth and Claus Wittich, pp. 61–62 n. 31 in *Economy and Society;* and Wolfgang Mommsen, *The Age of Bureaucracy* (Oxford: Basil Blackwell, 1974), p. 72 n. 1.

51. Weber only uses the concept of *Herrschaft* in connection with capital accounting in chapter 2—for example, when he says that "the maximum of *formal* rationality in cap-

ital accounting is possible only where the workers are subjected to domination (*Herrschaft*) by entrepreneurs." See Weber, *Economy and Society*, p. 138 (see also p. 108), or *Wirtschaft und Gesellschaft*, p. 78 (see also p. 58).

52. See Weber's discussion of "substantive conditions of formal rationality in a money economy," p. 108 in *Economy and Society*, or p. 58 in *Wirtschaft und Gesellschaft*. It might be argued that Weber is referring only to factory workers in this passage, not to white-collar workers. Regardless of one's interpretation on this score, Weber elsewhere comments on the domination among the latter groups (and this is discussed in the next chapter). It should furthermore be noted that all economic organizations are *not* characterized by domination over their members. For a discussion of an organization without domination (a "voluntary organization" in Weber's terminology)—namely a voluntary association of metal trades in Solingen—see Weber, *Economy and Society*, p. 123 (with a reference to a discussion of "voluntary organizations" on pages 52–53), or *Wirtschaft und Gesellschaft*, pp. 68–69 (with a reference to p. 28).

53. Weber, *Economy and Society*, pp. 943–44, or *Wirtschaft und Gesellschaft*, pp. 542–43.

54. Weber, *Economy and Society*, p. 214, or *Wirtschaft und Gesellschaft*, p. 123.

55. Weber, *Economy and Society*, pp. 341–43, or *Wirtschaft und Gesellschaft*, pp. 201–3.

56. Weber, *Economy and Society*, pp. 341–42, or *Wirtschaft und Gesellschaft*, p. 201.

57. This formulation is very similar to Weber's; see *Economy and Society*, p. 43, or *Wirtschaft und Gesellschaft*, p. 23.

58. For critical overviews, see Raymond Murphy, "Weberian Closure Theory: A Contribution to the Ongoing Assessment," *British Journal of Sociology* 37 (1986): 21–41; and Raymond Murphy, *Social Closure: The Theory of Monopolization and Exclusion* (Oxford: Clarendon Press, 1988).

59. See Frank Parkin, "Strategies of Social Closure in Class Formation," pp. 1–18 in Frank Parkin, ed., *The Social Analysis of Class Structure* (London: Tavistock Publications, 1974); and Frank Parkin, *Marxism and Class Theory: A Bourgeois Critique* (New York: Columbia University Press, 1979). See also Aage Sørensen, "Processes of Allocation to Open and Closed Positions in Social Structure," *Zeitschrift für Soziologie* 12 (1983): 203–24.

60. Weber, *Economy and Society*, p. 342, or *Wirtschaft und Gesellschaft*, p. 201.

61. Weber, "Vorwort," p. vii in K. Bücher et al., *Wirtschaft und Wirtschaftswissenschaft. Grundriss der Sozialökonomik. I. Abteilung* (Tübingen: J.C.B. Mohr, 1914). It is doubtful that all the other contributors to the *Grundriss* agreed with this statement.

62. Weber occasionally uses the term "economic rationality" or "*ökonomischer Rationalismus*"/"*Wirtschaftsrationalismus*"; see, e.g., Weber, *Economy and Society*, pp. 435, 436, 480, or *Wirtschaft und Gesellschaft*, pp. 266 (2), 293; *The Protestant Ethic*, p. 75, or "Die protestantische Ethik," p. 60 in vol. 1 of *Gesammelte Aufsätze zur Religionssoziologie*.

63. I owe this formulation to Stinchcombe's statement that "the central trouble with discussions of rationality is that we are taught by economists and decision theorists to treat rationality as an *assumption* . . . but in the real world rationality is a variable to be explained" see p. 5 in "Rationality and Social Structure" in *Stratification and Organization;* see also Arthur Stinchcombe, *Creating Efficient Industrial Administrations* (New York: Academic Press, 1974), p. 33.

64. "Formal rationality" is "*formale Rationalität*"; "substantive rationality" is "*materiale Rationalität*." See Weber, *Economy and Society*, pp. 85–86, or *Wirtschaft und Gesellschaft*, pp. 44–45.

65. The terms are easier to remember in German: *Naturalrechnung, Geldrechnung,* and *Kapitalrechnung.* See Weber, *Economy and Society,* pp. 86 ff., 90 ff., or *Wirtschaft und Gesellschaft,* pp. 45 ff., 48 ff.

66. Weber, *Economy and Society,* p. 85, or *Wirtschaft und Gesellschaft,* p. 45. The translation has been slightly altered.

67. Weber, *Economy and Society,* pp. 108–9, or *Wirtschaft und Gesellschaft,* p. 59.

68. Weber uses the term *Technik,* and Parsons makes the following comment: "The German word *Technik* which Weber uses here covers both the meanings of the English word 'technique' and of 'technology.'" Parsons adds that "since the distinction is not explicitly made in Weber's terminology, it will have to be introduced according to the context in the translation." See Weber, *Economy and Society,* p. 206 n. 4.

69. According to Adolph Löwe, "Attempts have been made—going back to Weber— to establish a basic distinction between technical activity and the Man-Matter core of the economy"; Löwe also refers to the writings of Lionel Robbins and Oscar Lange in this context. See Adolph Löwe, *On Economic Knowledge: Toward a Science of Political Economics* (New York: Harper and Row, 1965), p. 18. For more on this issue, see the discussion in chapter 6.

70. Weber, *Economy and Society,* p. 65, or *Wirtschaft und Gesellschaft,* p. 32. Emphasis in the original. Weber says that the scarcity has to be perceived, in order to make clear that scarcity can only exist in relation to the economic actor(s); see Weber, *Economy and Society,* p. 339, or *Wirtschaft und Gesellschaft,* p. 199.

71. Weber, *Economy and Society,* p. 65, or *Wirtschaft und Gesellschaft,* p. 32; emphasis added.

72. Weber, "Debattereden auf der Tagung des Vereins für Sozialpolitik in Wien 1909 zu den Verhandlungen über die Produktivität der Volkswirtschaft," pp. 422–23 in *Gesammelte Aufsätze zur Soziologie und Sozialpolitik* (Tübingen: J.C.B. Mohr, 1988).

73. Niklas Luhmann argues similarly that the postponement of consumption constitutes the very essence of the economy; or, as he phrases it, "economic life does not seem to depend upon specific delimitable needs. Instead it has to do with *the possibility of deferring a decision about the satisfaction of needs while providing a guarantee that they will be satisfied and so utilizing the time thus acquired"*; see Niklas Luhmann, "The Economy as a Social System," p. 194 in *The Differentiation of Society* (New York: Columbia University Press, 1982); emphasis in the original.

74. Weber, *Economy and Society,* p. 73, or *Wirtschaft und Gesellschaft,* p. 37.

75. Weber, *Economy and Society,* p. 86, or *Wirtschaft und Gesellschaft,* p. 45.

76. Weber, *Economy and Society,* pp. 86–90, or *Wirtschaft und Gesellschaft,* pp. 45–48.

77. Weber, *Economy and Society,* p. 91, or *Wirtschaft und Gesellschaft,* p. 48. The first historical use of capital accounting, according to Weber, was that of early professional traveling merchants; see Weber, *Economy and Society,* p. 155 or, *Wirtschaft und Gesellschaft,* p. 89. For more on early capital accounting as well as the argument that it can be more or less rational, see Weber, *The Protestant Ethic,* pp. 17–19, or pp. 4–5 in Vol. 1 of *Gesammelte Aufsätze zur Religionssoziologie*

78. Weber, *Economy and Society,* pp. 107–9, 161–64, or *Wirtschaft und Gesellschaft,* pp. 58–59, 94–95.

79. Weber defended capitalism in his political writings, but that is a different matter. The shrewdest attack on Weber for allegedly smuggling a defense of capitalism into his scientific writings can be found in an article by Herbert Marcuse, who argues that "in his sociology, Weber turns formal rationality into *capitalist* rationality." One problem with Marcuse's argument is that Weber does not attach any positive value to formal rational-

ity in the economy. See Herbert Marcuse, "Industrialism and Capitalism in the Work of Max Weber," p. 204 in *Negations: Essays in Critical Theory* (Boston: Beacon Press, [1965] 1974).

80. Weber, *Economy and Society*, pp. 93, 73, or *Wirtschaft und Gesellschaft*, pp. 49, 37.

81. Weber, *General Economic History* (New Brunswick, N.J.: Transaction Books, 1981), p. 277, or *Wirtschaftsgeschichte*, p. 240.

82. Weber, *Economy and Society*, p. 108, or *Wirtschaft und Gesellschaft*, p. 59. Adam Smith speaks of "effectual demand" and "absolute demand" in *The Wealth of Nations;* see Adam Smith, *An Inquiry into the Nature and Causes of the Wealth of Nations* (Oxford: Oxford University Press, 1979), Vol. 1, p. 73.

83. See, e.g., *Economy and Society*, pp. 108–9, 188–89, or *Wirtschaft und Gesellschaft*, pp. 59, 111; and *Wirtschaftsgeschichte*, p. 10 (note 2). Weber also makes some references to the role of income distribution in his lectures on economics from the 1890s; see Weber, *Grundriss zu den Vorlesungen über Allgemeine ("theoretische") Nationalökonomie (1898)*, pp. 49–50, 53.

84. Weber occasionally uses the term "institution" and "economic institution" in his work. For Weber's use of "economic institution," see Max Weber, "'Objectivity' in Social Science and Social Policy," p. 64 in *The Methodology of the Social Sciences* (New York: Free Press, 1949); and Max Weber, *Roscher and Knies: The Logical Problems of Historical Economics* (New York: Free Press, [1903–06] 1975), p. 79, or pp. 28, 162 in Weber, *Gesammelte Aufsätze zur Wissenschaftslehre*. Ludwig Lachmann regards it as a minus that "no general theory of institutions is to be found anywhere in Weber's work," while it is more likely that Weber simply did not find such a theory useful; see Ludwig Lachmann, *The Legacy of Max Weber* (London: Heinemann, 1970), pp. 49–91, esp. p. 52.

85. The exact definition of property in *Economy and Society* is the following: "Appropriated rights which are enjoyed by individuals through inheritance or by hereditary groups, whether communal or asssociative, will be called the 'property' of the individual or of groups in question; and, insofar as they are alienable, 'free property'"; see Weber, *Economy and Society*, p. 44, or *Wirtschaft und Gesellschaft*, p. 23.

86. Ibid. What is evocative about the concept of appropriation in the economy is that it makes possible an analysis that highlights the fact that while some actors are excluded in very special ways from having access to certain objects or human beings, others have this access. Appropriation is similar but not identical to the idea of property rights, to which it adds an interactive or social dimension. One of the few sociologists who has shown any interest in the idea of appropriation is Arthur Stinchcombe. See Arthur Stinchcombe, "Monopolistic Competition as a Mechanism: Corporations, Universities, and Nation States in Competitive Fields," in Peter Hedström and Richard Swedberg, eds., *Social Mechanisms* (Cambridge: Cambridge University Press, 1998).

87. Parsons, "Industry and Occupation," p. 408 in Vol. 1 of Talcott Parsons et al., eds., *Theories of Society* (Glencoe, Ill.: Free Press, 1961). For some post-Parsonian sociological discussions of property, see, e.g., Alvin Gouldner, "Towards a Sociology of Property," pp. 304–13 in *The Coming Crisis of Western Sociology* (New York: Avon Books, 1971); Parkin, *Marxism and Class Theory*, pp. 47–54; and John Campbell and Leon Lindberg, "Property Rights and the Organization of Economic Activity by the State," *American Sociological Review* 55 (1990): 634–47. In recent economic sociology several authors take a property rights approach, but I do not know of any major article exclusively or mainly about property.

88. See Weber, *Economy and Society*, pp. 125–50, or *Wirtschaft und Gesellschaft*, pp. 69–86. In *General Economic History* this type of material is spread throughout the

work (but see, e.g., the discussion of "property systems and social groups," pp. 26–50 in *General Economic History,* or pp. 40–59 in *Wirtschaftsgeschichte*).

89. For the formal definitions of an organization (*Verband*) and an economic organization (*wirtschaftlich orientierter Verband*), see Weber, *Economy and Society,* pp. 48–50, 74–75, or *Wirtschaft und Gesellschaft,* pp. 26–27, 37–38. Parsons preferred to translate *Verband* as "corporate group," to which Martin Albrow has responded that "this sounds too legalistic. *Verband* is as common a term in German as organization is in English." See Martin Albrow, *Bureaucracy* (London: Macmillan, 1970), p. 130 n. 25. It may be added that Weber actually makes a distinction between *Verband* and *Organisation* in part 1 of *Economy and Society* on the ground that in the former the regulations may be enforced by the head alone, not necessarily by a staff; see Weber, *Economy and Society,* p. 264, or *Wirtschaft und Gesellschaft,* p. 154. According to Parsons, however, "almost always" when Weber uses the term *Verband* he means that a staff is involved; see Weber, *Economy and Society,* p. 301 n. 12. To the confusion caused by the fact that Weber's concept of organization and the one that is current today do not totally overlap, should be added that Weber used a different terminology in the early versions of *Economy and Society.* In these for example, Weber speaks of "economic groups" ("*Wirtschaftsgemeinschaften*") or groups with primary economic interests, "groups with secondary economic interests" ("*wirtschaftende Gemeinschaften*"), and "regulatory groups" ("*wirtschaftsregulierende Gemeinschaften*"); see Weber, *Economy and Society,* pp. 340–41, or *Wirtschaft und Gesellschaft,* p. 200). See also the comment by the editors of *Economy and Society* on page 61 n. 27, where it is pointed out that there also exist older definitions of *Verband* and *Verbandshandeln.*

90. Weber speaks of the "division and combination of human services" ("*Verteilung und Verbindung menschlicher Leistungen*"); see Weber, *Economy and Society,* p. 114, or *Wirtschaft und Gesellschaft,* p. 62. The translation has been slightly changed. It was originally Friedrich List who in the 1840s had suggested that work was not only divided but also combined ("*Teilung der Arbeit*" and "*Vereinigung der Arbeit*"). See Friedrich List, *The National System of Political Economy* (New York: Longmans, Green, 1916), p. 121. List's idea was later popularized through Bücher's influential *Die Entstehung der Volkswirtschaft* (1893). See Karl Bücher, *Industrial Evolution* (New York: Augustus M. Kelley, [1901] 1968), pp. 244–81.

91. Weber, *Economy and Society,* pp. 114–40, or *Wirtschaft und Gesellschaft,* pp. 62–78.

92. Weber, *Economy and Society,* pp. 49–50, or *Wirtschaft und Gesellschaft,* pp. 26–27.

93. Weber, *Economy and Society,* p. 202, or *Wirtschaft und Gesellschaft,* p. 119; emphasis in the original.

94. In Weber's terminology, the capitalist firm (*Unternehmung*) is a form of enterprise in general (*Betrieb*); the latter term also means the technical units that make up a firm. See Weber, *Economy and Society,* pp. 52, 91, 116–17 (as well as Parsons's comment in note 27 on page 208), or *Wirtschaft und Gesellschaft,* pp. 28, 48, 63–64.

95. Weber, *Economy and Society,* p. 202, or *Wirtschaft und Gesellschaft,* p. 119.

96. Weber, *Economy and Society,* pp. 69, 110, 217–26, or *Wirtschaft und Gesellschaft,* pp. 35, 60, 124–30.

97. Ibid. Weber also mentions, as a possible source of motivation for the workers, that they see productive work as "a mode of life." For a reference to this fact, as well as to the factory discipline that exists in capitalist enterprises, see Weber, *Economy and Society,* pp. 53, 110, 114, 1155–56, or *Wirtschaft und Gesellschaft,* pp. 28, 60, 62, 686.

98. Stinchcombe argues that while individuals are not particularly rational in their be-

havior, they are forced to act rationally when they act on behalf of a business organization. See the interview with Stinchcombe on pp. 288–89 in Swedberg, *Economics and Sociology*. For James Coleman, see *Foundations of Social Theory* (Cambridge: Harvard University Press, 1990), pp. 422–25. Coleman argues that Weber's theory of bureaucracy is marred by his failure to realize that the workers also have interests to pursue in the corporation. Coleman calls this "the Weberian flaw." Coleman's point seems valid to me, though it should be noted that Weber says at one point in chapter 2 that *all* actors in a market economy are motivated by their "ideal or material interests"; see Weber, *Economy and Society*, p. 202, or *Wirtschaft und Gesellschaft*, p. 119.

99. Karl Polanyi writes, "The only economic activity of the worker [to follow Weber's analysis] is that of selling his labor power, and maybe, activities in his own domestic sphere.... The factory worker in the factory [is not] engaged in 'economic activity' (though he may be 'economically active' in his own household!)"; Karl Polanyi, "Appendix," pp. 137–38 in *Primitive, Archaic and Modern Economies* (Boston: Beacon Press, 1971). Lars Udehn has similarly argued that workers only obey orders but do not engage in rational social actions of their own because they are dominated and disciplined. See Lars Udehn, "The Conflict between Methodology and Rationalization in the Work of Max Weber," *Acta Sociologica* 24 (1981): 131–47. In my opinion, both Polanyi and Udehn are correct up to a point—but it should immediately be added that much of what goes on in the economy, according to Weber, is *not* economic action, rational social action, or domination.

100. There is also, for example, Weber's tendency to deemphasize the role of the individual in the organization and to exaggerate the growth of bureaucracy in the future, as well as his assertion that all the components in the ideal type of bureaucracy go together. Many of the criticisms that have been directed at Weber's analysis of bureaucracy are valuable, but most critics fail to note that a typical capitalist organization, according to Weber, consists of a *mixture* of traditional, charismatic, and bureaucratic elements. For the first wave of criticisms by sociologists (by such people as Peter Blau, Robert K. Merton, Philip Selznick, Reinhard Bendix, and Alvin Gouldner), see especially the fine work by Martin Albrow, *Bureaucracy* (London: Macmillan, 1970), pp. 50–66. For more recent critiques, see, e.g., Paul DiMaggio and Walter Powell, "The Iron Cage Revisited: Institutional Isomorphism and Collective Rationality in Organizational Fields," pp. 63–82 in Walter Powell and Paul DiMaggio, eds., *The New Institutionalism in Organizational Analysis* (Chicago: University of Chicago Press, 1991); W. Richard Scott, *Organizations: Rational, Natural, and Open Systems* (Englewood Cliffs, N.J.: Prentice Hall, 1992), pp. 38–45; and Stewart Clegg, "Max Weber and Contemporary Sociology of Organizations," pp. 46–80 in Larry J. Ray and Michael Reed, eds., *Organizing Modernity* (London: Routledge, 1994). The critique that has been directed at Weber during the last few years, one commentator says, has been so strong that one can speak of "the near disappearance of Weber from organization studies." See Marshall Meyer, "The Weberian Tradition in Organization Research," p. 191 in Craig Calhoun et al., eds., *Structures of Power and Constraint* (Cambridge: Cambridge University Press, 1990).

101. Weber, "Some Categories of Interpretive Sociology," p. 166, or "Ueber einige Kategorien der verstehenden Soziologie," p. 452 in *Gesammelte Aufsätze zur Wissenschaftslehre*.

102. There is no definition of the market in chapter 2 of *Economy and Society*, even though a full paragraph is devoted to the topic. However, the following definition can be found in a text later incorporated by the editors into *Economy and Society*: "A market may be said to exist wherever there is competition, even if only unilateral, for opportu-

nities of exchange among a plurality of potential parties. Their physical assemblage in one place, as in the local market square, the fair (the 'long distance market'), or the exchange (the merchants' market), only constitutes the most consistent kind of market formation. It is, however, only this physical assemblage which allows the full emergence of the market's most distinctive feature, viz. dickering"; Weber, *Economy and Society,* p. 635, or *Wirtschaft und Gesellschaft,* p. 382. See also "§8. The Market," pp. 82–85 in *Economy and Society,* or *Wirtschaft und Gesellschaft,* pp. 43–44.

103. Weber, *Economy and Society,* p. 638, or *Wirtschaft und Gesellschaft,* p. 384.

104. Weber, *Economy and Society,* pp. 638–39, or *Wirtschaft und Gesellschaft,* p. 384.

105. Weber, *Economy and Society,* p. 936, or *Wirtschaft und Gesellschaft,* p. 538. The translation has been slightly changed. Weber describes money in similar terms: "Money is the most abstract and 'impersonal' (*'unpersönlichste'*) that exists in human life"; see Weber, "Religious Rejections of the World and Their Directions," p. 331, or "Zwischenbetrachtung," p. 554 in Vol. 1 of *Gesammelte Aufsätze zur Religionssoziologie.*

106. Weber, *Economy and Society,* p. 637, or *Wirtschaft und Gesellschaft,* p. 383.

107. Weber uses primarily the term "*Versachlichung*" but also "*Unpersönlichkeit*" to denote this phenomenon. His idea is that this "impersonality" makes it hard to "transform" and "penetrate" capitalist relations "along ethical lines." See, e.g., Hans Gerth and C. Wright Mills, eds., *From Max Weber* (New York: Oxford University Press, 1946), p. 371; Weber, *General Economic History,* p. 357, or *Wirtschaftsgeschichte,* p. 305. The concept of impersonality is more fully discussed in chapter 5

108. Weber, *Economy and Society,* p. 108, or *Wirtschaft und Gesellschaft,* p. 58.

109. Weber to Robert Liefmann, dated March 9, 1920. Weber does not supply the full argument in this letter but only indicates the direction of his thoughts.

110. The reader is also referred on this point to Weber's argument about jurisprudence and "following a rule" in *Critique of Stammler* (1907). While jurisprudence—similar to marginal utility theory—deals exclusively with the logic of the rules themselves (for example, theft is forbidden), it is also legitimate for the researcher to ask what actually happens (some people steal, but most do not). See Max Weber, *Critique of Stammler* (New York: Free Press, 1977), pp. 98–143, or Weber, "R. Stammlers 'Überwindung' der materialistischen Geschichtsauffassung," pp. 322–59.

111. Weber, *Economy and Society,* p. 68, or *Wirtschaft und Gesellschaft,* p. 34. The translation has been changed. It is otherwise true, as Amonn has said, that the "purpose" of the concept of economics, as developed in *Economy and Society,* is very different from that of theoretical economics. Nonetheless, it is frequently hard, as noted by Lederer, to distinguish between economic theory and economic sociology in chapter 2 in *Economy and Society.* See Alfred Amonn, *Objekt und Grundbegriffe der Theoretischen Nationalökonomie* (Leipzig: Franz Deuticke, 1911), p. 161 n. 9; Lederer, *Aufriss der ökonomischen Theorie,* pp. 12–13.

112. Weber, *Economy and Society,* p. 79–82, or *Wirtschaft und Gesellschaft,* pp. 41–43.

113. For Weber's definitions of "money economy" ("*Geldwirtschaft*") and "natural economy" (*Naturalwirtschaft*"), see *Economy and Society,* p. 100, or *Wirtschaft und Gesellschaft,* p. 53.

114. Weber, *Economy and Society,* p. 108, or *Wirtschaft und Gesellschaft,* p. 58. The translation has been slightly changed.

115. "The formulation of monetary theory which has been most acceptable to the author is that of von Mises"; see Weber, *Economy and Society,* p. 78, or *Wirtschaft und Gesellschaft,* p. 40.

116. Weber writes that "we shall apply the term *economic order (Wirtschaftsordnung)* to the distribution of the actual control *(Verfügungsgewalt)* over goods and services, the distribution arising in each case from the particular mode of balancing interests consensually; moreover, the term shall apply to the manner in which goods and services are indeed used by virtue of these powers of disposition, which are based on *de facto* recognition." See Weber, *Economy and Society,* p. 312, or *Wirtschaft und Gesellschaft,* p. 181.

117. Weber, *Economy and Society,* p. 67, or *Wirtschaft und Gesellschaft,* pp. 33–34.

118. Weber, *Economy and Society,* p. 312, or *Wirtschaft und Gesellschaft,* p. 181.

119. Weber, *Economy and Society,* p. 100, or *Wirtschaft und Gesellschaft,* pp. 53–54.

120. Bruno Hildebrand, "Naturalwirthschaft, Geldwirthschaft und Creditwirthschaft," *Jahrbücher für Nationalökonomie und Statistik* 2 (1864): 1–24. For a positive assessment of Hildebrand's contribution on this point for economic history, see Eli Heckscher, "Natural and Money Economy as Illustrated from Swedish History in the Sixteenth Century," pp. 206, 219–20 in Frederic Lane and Jelle Riemersma, eds., *Enterprise and Secular Change* (London: George Allen and Unwin, 1953).

121. Weber, *Economy and Society,* p. 109, or *Wirtschaft und Gesellschaft,* p. 59.

122. For Weber's view of socialism and the socialist economy, see the next chapter.

123. See Bert Hoselitz, "Theories of Stages of Economic Growth," pp. 211, 222 in Bert Hoselitz et al., *Theories of Economic Growth* (Glencoe, Ill.: Free Press, 1960). Weber was more receptive to Bücher, according to whom the economy went through the following three stages: household economy, town economy, and national economy. In *Economy and Society* Weber has very little to say about economic stages, except that economic policy and economic stages should not be confused with each other in the manner of Schönberg and Schmoller. See Weber, *Economy and Society,* pp. 117–18, 208–9 n. 30, 1218–19, or *Wirtschaft und Gesellschaft,* pp. 64–65, 731.

124. For Weber's general position on this issue, see, e.g., Weber, *The Methodology of the Social Sciences,* pp. 101 ff., 130 ff., or *Gesammelte Aufsätze zur Wissenschaftslehre,* pp. 203 ff., 232 ff.; Weber, *The Agrarian Sociology of Ancient Civilizations,* p. 385, or "Agrarverhältnisse im Altertum," p. 288 in *Gesammelte Aufsätze zur Wirtschafts- und Sozialgeschichte;* and Weber, *Economy and Society,* p. 201, or *Wirtschaft und Gesellschaft,* p. 118. The first volume of *Grundriss der Sozialökonomik* was from the beginning scheduled to include an essay by Bücher on the different economic stages in history, an indication that Weber found the approach useful after all. The way that Bücher ended up treating his assigned topic was, however, deeply disappointing to Weber ("totally inadequate"). See Karl Bücher, "Volkswirtschaftliche Entwicklungsstufen," pp. 1–18 in *Grundriss der Sozialökonomik. I. Abteilung. Wirtschaft und Wirtschaftswissenschaft.* For the use of theories of stages in German economics, see, e.g., Winkelmann, *Wirtschaft und Gesellschaft. Erläuterungsband,* pp. 39–40. See finally also Otto Hintze's brilliant critique of Sombart's evolutionary scheme in *Der moderne Kapitalismus,* in which Hintze argues that Sombart is wrong in viewing each economic stage as caused exclusively by economic forces. Sombart's error, Hinze shows, comes from excluding the role of political forces from the analysis—for example, how the state in Europe helped to unify national markets. Otto Hintze, "Economics and Politics in the Age of Modern Capitalism (1929)," pp. 422–52 in *The Historical Essays of Otto Hintze* (New York: Oxford University Press, 1975).

125. Guenther Roth, "Rationalization in Max Weber's Developmental History," pp. 75–91 in Sam Whimster and Scott Lash, eds., *Max Weber, Rationality and Modernity* (London: Allen and Unwin, 1987).

126. Weber, *General Economic History,* p. 286, or *Wirtschaftsgeschichte,* p. 250;

Weber, "Socialism," p. 291 in *Political Writings,* or "Der Sozialismus," p. 507 in *Gesammelte Aufsätze zur Soziologie und Sozialpolitik.* Weber does not discuss business cycles in chapter 2 of *Economy and Society.* It may be added that Weber was presumably inspired by Juglar in his asumption that the average business cycle was ten years.

127. Weber, *Economy and Society,* pp. 164–66, or *Wirtschaft und Gesellschaft,* pp. 95–97. In the introduction to his sociology of religion, Weber also summarized, in a more popular form, how he saw capitalism toward the end of his life. See "Introduction," pp. 17–27 in *The Protestant Ethic and the Spirit of Capitalism,* or "Vorbemerkung," pp. 4–9 in Vol. 1 of *Gesammelte Aufsätze zur Religionssoziologie.*

128. *"Typische Richtungen 'kapitalistischer' Orientierung des Erwerbs."* See Weber, *Economy and Society,* pp. ix, 164–66, or *Wirtschaft und Gesellschaft,* pp. vi, 95–97.

129. No formal definition of capitalism can be found in chapter 2 of *Economy and Society* or elsewhere in *Economy and Society.* However, in a few places Weber discusses capitalism in general. See, e.g., Weber, *The Agrarian Sociology of Ancient Civilizations,* p. 51, or "Agrarverhältnisse im Altertum," pp. 50–51 in *Gesammelte Aufsätze zur Sozial- und Wirtschaftsgeschichte;* Weber, *General Economic History,* p. 275 (with error in the translation; should be "profit-oriented," not "industrial"), or *Wirtschaftsgeschichte,* p. 238. The fullest discussion of capitalism in general is perhaps to be found in the introduction to volume 1 of Weber's collected essays in the sociology of religion, where it is said that "capitalism is identical with the pursuit of profit, and forever *renewed* profit, by means of continuous, rational capitalistic enterprise." Weber also emphasizes the role of calculation: "The important fact [about capitalism in general] is always that calculation of capital in terms of money is made, whether by modern book-keeping methods or in any other way, however primitive and crude. . . . That a really accurate calculation or estimate may not exist, that the procedure is pure guess-work, or simply traditional and conventional, happens even to-day in every form of capitalistic enterprise where the circumstances do not demand strict accuracy. But these are points affecting only the *degree* of rationality of capitalistic acquisition." See Weber, *The Protestant Ethic and the Spirit of Capitalism,* pp. 17–19 (as well as pp. 19–27), or pp. 4–5 (as well as pp. 5–12) in Vol. 1 of *Gesammelte Aufsätze zur Religionssoziologie.* When capitalism is rational, Weber specifies elsewhere, capital accounting is used.

130. Capitalism as a category in social thought originates with the work of Marx. Unlike Weber, however, Marx identified capitalism with a specific mode of production centered on workers and capitalists. There exist some parallels between Marx's notion of "merchant capital" and Weber's item #2 in §31 (which I call "traditional commercial capitalism"). There is, however, no equivalent in Marx's work to what Weber calls "politically oriented capitalism" and which was strongly developed in antiquity. Indeed, according to Marx, it was "nonsense" to say that there had been capitalism in antiquity. (See Karl Marx, *Das Kapital* [Berlin: Dietz Verlag, 1977], Vol. 1, p. 182 n. 39). For a discussion of the concept of capitalism, see, e.g., Fernand Braudel, "Capital, Capitalist, Capitalism," pp. 232–49 in *The Wheels of Commerce* (London: Fontana Press, 1985); R. H. Hilton, "Capitalism—What's in a Name?," *Past and Present* 1 (1952): 32–43; and Henri Pirenne, "Stages in the Social History of Capitalism," *American Historical Review* 19 (1914): 494–514. In his entry on "Capitalism" in *Encyclopaedia of the Social Sciences,* Sombart points out that one cannot find the concept of capitalism in many important works in economic theory, including those of Marshall, Cassel, and Philippovich. See Werner Sombart, "Capitalism," p. 195 in Vol. 3 of Edwin R. A. Seligman and Alvin Johnson, eds., *Encyclopaedia of the Social Sciences* (New York: Macmillan).

131. Weber does not use the terms "Western rational capitalism" or "rational capital-

ism" in §31 but says twice that this type of capitalism has only existed in "the Western world." Elsewhere in chapter 2 of *Economy and Society,* however, he speaks of "rational market-oriented capitalism" (*"rationaler marktorientierter Kapitalismus"*). See Weber, *Economy and Society,* pp. 165, 199, 200, or *Wirtschaft und Gesellschaft,* pp. 96, 117, 118.

132. The most thorough analysis of the concept of political capitalism in Weber's work is to date to be found in Love, *Antiquity and Capitalism.* What Weber says in §41 in chapter 2 of *Economy and Society* on the kind of incomes and gains that are derived from political capitalism complements the information in §31. For Weber's view of antiquity, see also "Die Kulturbedeutung der Antike. Marginalien zu Weber," pp. 112–18 in Jürgen Kocka, ed., *Max Weber, der Historiker* (Göttingen: Vandenhoeck und Ruprecht, 1986).

133. Political capitalism is not formally defined by Weber, who however refers in one sentence to "the politically oriented events and processes which open up profit opportunities exploited by political capitalism." See Weber, *Economy and Society,* p. 166, or *Wirtschaft und Gesellschaft,* p. 96.

134. Weber, *Economy and Society,* p. 165, or *Wirtschaft und Gesellschaft,* p. 96. Weber nearly spells it out in the form of a distinct mechanism: "Capitalist financing of political activities was everywhere the product of competition of states with one another for power, and of the corresponding competition for capital which moved freely between them. All this ended only with the establishment of the unified empires."

135. See, e.g., Weber, *The Protestant Ethic,* p. 186 n. 6, or "Vorbemerkung," p. 8 n. 1 in Vol. 1 of *Gesammelte Aufsätze zur Religionssoziologie.*

136. It has also often been noted that in modern capitalist societies it might be as important for a firm to know how to handle the state authorities as to understand the workings of the market. See, e.g., Gudmund Hernes, ed., *Forhandlingsøkonomi og blandingsadministrasjon* (Oslo: Universitetsforlaget, 1978).

137. "Adventurers' capitalism" (*"Abenteuerkapitalismus"*) is a term that is used, for example, in the revised version of *The Protestant Ethic,* where Weber describes it as the kind of capitalism that "is oriented to the exploitation of political opportunities and irrational speculation"; see Weber, *The Protestant Ethic,* p. 76 (as well as pp. 20–21), or "Die protestantische Ethik," p. 61 (as well as p. 7) in Vol. 1 of *Gesammelte Aufsätze zur Religionssoziologie.* In the introduction to Weber's collected essays in the sociology of religion Weber also speaks of "politically oriented adventurers' capitalism." See Weber, *The Protestant Ethic,* p. 186 n. 6, or "Vorbemerkung," p. 8 n. 1 in Vol. 1 of *Gesammelte Aufsätze zur Religionssoziologie.* This type of capitalism contrasts sharply with the moral type of systematic capitalism that developed among the members of the ascetic Protestant sects and which constitutes the focus of *The Protestant Ethic.*

138. The Nietzschean term "economic superman" (*"ökonomischer 'Übermensch'"*) is close to Weber's category "adventurers' capitalism." Economic supermen have existed in all times, Weber says, and consider themselves "beyond good and evil." See, e.g., Weber, *The Protestant Ethic,* p. 258, or "Die protestantische Ethik," p. 160 in Vol. 1 of *Gesammelte Aufsätze zur Religionssoziologie.*

139. The term Weber uses is *"antiker Kapitalismus."* For the debate whether capitalism existed in antiquity (and, if so, what type), see part 2 in Love, *Antiquity and Capitalism.*

140. Weber, *The Agrarian Sociology of Ancient Civilizations,* p. 358, or "Agrarverhältnisse im Altertum," p. 271 in *Gesammelte Aufsätze zur Sozial- und Wirtschaftsgeschichte.*

141. See Weber, *Economy and Society,* pp. 165–66, or *Wirtschaft und Gesellschaft,*

pp. 96–97. Note, however, that there is no formal definition of rational capitalism in §31. As Durtschi notes, "Weber gives nowhere in his work an exact definition of 'modern capitalism'"; see Georges Durtschi, *Der Begriff des Kapitalismus bei Max Weber* (Zürich: University of Zürich, 1966), p. 28. For Weber's lists in *General Economic History* of what characterizes rational capitalism, what its preconditions are, and what caused it, see page 18 in this volume.

142. There is some ambiguity in the wording of mode #2 in §31, and "trade" ("*Handel*") might at first seem to refer to trade in money rather than to trade in goods, as I have assumed here. Since this, however, would mean that Weber somehow "forgot" about trade in commodities in §31—which I consider unlikely—I have chosen to interpret trade to mean trade in goods. For the record, it should also be noted that at one point in chapter 2 in *Economy and Society* Weber speaks explicitly of "speculative trade capitalism" and is obviously referring to trade in commodities ("*spekulativer Handelskapitalismus*"; see Weber, *Economy and Society*, p. 200, or *Wirtschaft und Gesellschaft*, p. 118. See also Weber, *General Economic History*, p. 334, or *Wirtschaftsgeschichte*, p. 286, with its discussion of "speculative trade capitalism" or "*händlerischer spekulativer Kapitalismus*"). In other parts of *Economy and Society* Weber comes back to the same theme and speaks of "trading capitalism" in general—and again is referring to trade in commodities ("*Händler-Kapitalismus*"; see *Economy and Society*, pp. 240, 1095, or *Wirtschaft und Gesellschaft*, pp. 139, 643). See also chap. 5, pp. 141–42.

143. Weber uses the term "pariah capitalism" to characterize the kind of capitalism that was created by the Jewish people. Money-lending and commerce were typical activities, but capitalist agriculture and industrial enterprises were not. "Pariah" refers to the ritual segregation of the Jews as well as to their negative status in the eyes of their surroundings. See, e.g., Weber, *General Economic History*, pp. 196, 358–60, or *Wirtschaftsgeschichte*, pp. 305–8.

144. Elsewhere Weber also notes that there is no sharp break between "rational calculation" and "speculative calculation" because the former will always contain an element of incalculability. In other words, there is always an element of incalculability in modern Western capitalism for this very reason. For Weber's view of speculation, see *Economy and Society*, p. 159, or *Wirtschaft und Gesellschaft*, p. 92. See in this context also some aspects of the argument in Mommsen, "The Alternative to Marx: Dynamic Capitalism instead of Bureaucratic Socialism," pp. 47–71 in *The Age of Bureaucracy*.

145. Weber, *The Protestant Ethic*, p. 186 n. 6, or "Vorbemerkung," p. 8 n. 1 in Vol. 1 of *Gesammelte Aufsätze zur Religionssoziologie*.

146. Weber, *Economy and Society*, p. 1118, or *Wirtschaft und Gesellschaft*, p. 659; emphasis added. Weber says, "The double nature of what may be called the 'capitalist spirit,' and the specific character of modern routinized capitalism with its professional bureaucracy, can be understood only if these two structural elements [that is, charismatic and rational elements], which are ultimately different but everywhere intertwined, are conceptually distinguished." Guenther Roth is one of the few who have paid attention to this passage; see Guenther Roth, "Max Weber as Scion of the Cosmopolitan Bourgeoisie," unpublished paper, London conference on Weber, 1995. Weber also refers to the two sides of contemporary capitalism in the introduction to his collected essays in the sociology of religion; see Weber, *The Protestant Ethic and the Spirit of Capitalism*, p. 21, or p. 7 in Vol. 1 of *Gesammelte Aufsätze zur Religionssoziologie*. See, finally, Weber's statement (discussed in note 144) that rational calculation also contains an element of incalculability.

147. Henry Villard (1835–1900) was born in Germany and became a major actor in

the railroad and electrical utility industries in the United States toward the end of the nineteenth century. Guenther Roth provides some fascinating information about Henry Villard, including the fact that he belonged to the circles of the father of Max Weber; see Roth, "Max Weber as Scion of the Cosmopolitan Bourgeoisie." In a later paper Roth also argues that Weber did not see modern capitalism as developing in a more rational direction, but rather "in the direction of more political, adventure, and robber capitalism"; see Guenther Roth, "Global Capitalism and Multiethnicity: Max Weber Now and Then" (1996, unpublished paper), p. 6.

148. For the hope of the entrepreneur, see Weber, *Economy and Society,* p. 97, or *Wirtschaft und Gesellschaft,* p. 52; and for "business imagination" (*"kaufmännische Phantasie"*), see Weber, "Science as a Vocation," p. 136 in Gerth and Mills, eds., *From Max Weber,* or "Wissenschaft als Beruf," p. 590 in *Gesammelte Aufsätze zur Wissenschaftslehre.* Weber's emphasis on the element of hope is interesting and has been little explored in studies of entrepreneurship. One exception is the work of Albert O. Hirschman, especially his discussion of "the principle of the hiding hand" or the fact that many entrepreneurs would never have started their enterprises if they had known how difficult it would be. See Albert O. Hirschman, "The Principle of the Hiding Hand," pp. 9–34 in *Development Projects Observed* (Washington: Brookings Institution, 1967).

149. A study needs to be made of how Weber viewed capitalism during World War I. For political capitalism during World War I, see, e.g., Weber, "Suffrage and Democracy in Germany," pp. 89–91 in *Political Writings,* or "Wahlrecht und Demokratie in Deutschland," pp. 253–55 in *Gesammelte Politische Schriften;* and Weber, *Economy and Society,* pp. 918–21, or *Wirtschaft und Gesellschaft,* pp. 525–27. See also Weber's comment on war economy in *Economy and Society,* p. 106, or *Wirtschaft und Gesellschaft,* p. 57.

150. For a general introduction to rent-seeking, see Gordon Tullock, *Rent Seeking* (Aldershot, Eng.: Edward Elgar, 1993). Rent-seeking is described in the following manner in the article where this concept was launched: "Government restrictions upon economic activity . . . give rise to rents of a variety of forms, and people often compete for the rents." See Anne Kreuger, "The Political Economy of the Rent-Seeking Society," *American Economic Review* 64 (1974): 291. Jagdish Bhagwati's concept of DUP (directly unproductive profit-seeking activities; pronounced "dupe") is similar. See Jagdish Bhagwati, "Directly Unproductive Profit-seeking (DUP) Activities," *Journal of Political Economy* 13 (1982): 988–1002. The concept of rent-seeking has been little used in sociology; for an exception see Aage Sørensen, "The Structural Basis of Social Inequality," *American Journal of Sociology* 101 (1996): 1333–65.

151. It is generally agreed that the German word *Stand* is difficult to translate and that it means something along the scale from "estate" to "status group." According to Parsons, "the term *Stand* . . . is perhaps the most troublesome single term in Weber's text [that is, in Part 1 of *Economy and Society*]"; see Weber, *Economy and Society,* p. 300 n. 4. For an introduction to the debate around *Stand,* see, e.g., Morton Wenger, "The Transmutation of Weber's *Stand* in American Sociology and Its Social Roots," *Current Perspectives in Social Theory* 1 (1987): 357–78.

152. All kinds of rents and similar kinds of predetermined forms of income are "economically conservative" (*"wirtschaftskonservativ"*), while profit (as well as piece rates and the like) is "economically revolutionary" (*"wirtschaftsrevolutionierend"*). See especially Weber, *Economy and Society,* pp. 204–05, 303–04, or *Wirtschaft und Gesellschaft,* pp. 120–21, 178–79; see also Weber, p. 369 in Gerth and Mills, eds., *From Max Weber.* In his plan for the *Grundriss* from 1909–10, Weber had included a section, to be written by his brother Alfred "possibly" together with himself, called "The Tendencies towards Inter-

nal Reorganization in Capitalism (Monopolistic, Collectivistic and Bureaucratic Developmental Tendencies in the Context of Their Social Effects; Rents (das Rentnertum); Tendencies towards Social Regrouping)." Pareto's distinction between "entrepreneurs" and "savers" (or, more generally, between "speculators" and "rentiers"), is similar to Weber's distinction between "rents" and "profits." See Vilfredo Pareto, *The Mind and Society* (New York: Dover, 1935), Vol. 2, p. 1558 ff.

CHAPTER THREE
THE ECONOMY AND POLITICS

1. Stinchcombe argues that "the book [*Economy and Society*] is a detailed statement of the conditions under which the classical model of the economy works"; see Arthur Stinchcombe, "Review of Max Weber's *Economy and Society*," p. 286 in *Stratification and Organization* (Cambridge: Cambridge University Press, 1986).

2. Max Weber, "Diskussionsrede zu W. Sombarts Vortrag über Technik und Kultur. Erste Soziologentagung Frankfurt 1910," p. 456 in *Gesammelte Aufsätze zur Soziologie und Sozialpolitik* (Tübingen: J.C.B. Mohr, 1988); the translation comes from Reinhard Bendix and Guenther Roth, *Scholarship and Partisanship: Essays on Max Weber* (Berkeley: University of California Press, 1971), p. 242. Weber made the same point in 1904 when he wrote, "The so-called 'materialist conception of history' . . . as a formula for the causal analysis of historical reality is to be rejected most emphatically." See Weber, "'Objectivity' in Social Science and Social Policy," p. 68 in *The Methodology of the Social Sciences* (New York: Free Press, 1949), or "Die 'Objektivität' sozialwissenschaftlicher und socialpolitischer Erkenntnis," p. 166 in *Gesammelte Aufsätze zur Wissenschaftslehre* (Tübingen: J.C.B. Mohr, 1988).

3. Talcott Parsons has aptly summarized Weber's position in the following way:

As contrasted with the utilitarian tradition it is first notable that Weber never dealt with economic problems without careful attention to their political context. Of course, in many organizational contexts, the degree of independence of economic processes and interests, on the one hand from conditioned and diffuse *Gemeinschaft* structures, on the other from political authority, is low. Weber was, however, particularly interested in the situations and conditions where this independence did develop and this was to him a primary aspect of modern capitalism. (Talcott Parsons, "Value-freedom and Objectivity," p. 43 in Otto Stammer, ed., *Max Weber and Sociology Today* [New York: Harper Torchbacks, 1972]).

To this should be added that to Weber personally, politics should have precedence over economics. This is clear from many of his writings, including his inaugural speech at Freiburg University and the pamphlet on the stock exchange.

4. Max Weber in a letter to Mina Tobler, dated January 17, 1919, as cited in Weber, *Zur Neuordnung Deutschlands. Schriften und Reden 1918–1920. Max Weber Gesamtausgabe I/16* (Tübingen: J.C.B. Mohr, 1988), p. 19 n. 53. For a summary of Weber's political involvements, see, e.g., p. 3 ff. in Wolfgang Mommsen, *The Political and Social Theory of Max Weber* (Cambridge: Polity Press, 1989), p. 7.

5. Max Weber, *Economy and Society: An Outline of Interpretive Sociology* (Berkeley: University of California Press, 1978), p. 1450, or "Parlament und Regierung im neugeordneten Deutschland," p. 492 in *Gesammelte Politische Schriften* (Tübingen: J.C.B. Mohr, 1988); emphasis added. The closest to a formal definition of politics that can be found in Weber's work is probably the following: "In our terms, then, 'politics' would

mean a striving for a share of power or for influence on the distribution of power, whether it be between states or between the groups of people contained within a single state"; see Weber, "The Profession and Vocation of Politics," p. 311 in *Political Writings* (Cambridge: Cambridge University Press, 1994), or "Politik als Beruf," p. 506 in *Gesammelte Politische Schriften.*

6. E.g., Max Weber, *Wirtschaftsgeschichte* (Berlin: Duncker und Humblot, 1991), pp. 1–2.

7. A "political organization" is a *"Herrschaftsverband"* in the terminology of Part 1 of *Economy and Society* and a *"politische Gemeinschaft"* in the terminology of chapter 9 in the earlier Part 2 of the same work. See Weber, *Economy and Society,* pp. 54, 901 ff., or *Wirtschaft und Gesellschaft,* pp. 29, 514 ff. What people in everyday life refer to as a political organization is, in the terminology of *Economy and Society,* usually a "voluntary organization" (*"Verein"*). See *Economy and Society,* p. 52, or *Wirtschaft und Gesellschaft,* p. 28.

8. Weber, *Economy and Society,* p. 902, or *Wirtschaft und Gesellschaft,* pp. 514–15. Since Weber's argument on this point is rarely mentioned, it is worthwhile to cite his statements in full: "As a separate structure, a political community can be said to exist only if, and in so far as, a community constitutes more than an 'economic group; or, in other words, in so far as it possesses value systems ordering matters other than the directly economic disposition of goods and services"; "a separate 'political' community is constituted where we find . . . social action which is not restricted exclusively to the satisfaction of common economic needs in the frame of a communal economy, but regulates more generally the interrelations of the inhabitants of the territory."

9. Weber, *Economy and Society,* pp. 908–9, or *Wirtschaft und Gesellschaft,* p. 519.

10. *"Gesetzlichkeit"*; see Weber, *Wirtschaftsgeschichte,* p. 1.

11. Weber mentions the following seven topics in §37: (1) the monetary system of the state; (2) ruling political organizations prefer their own subjects as sources of supply; (3) ruling political organizations may conduct a foreign trade policy; (4) ruling political organizations may regulate economic activity; (5) structures of domination and administration have economic consequences; (6) ruling political organizations compete with one another for more power for themselves and economic gains for their inhabitants; and (7) ruling political organizations provide for their own needs in different ways. See Weber, *Economy and Society,* pp. 193–94, or *Wirtschaft und Gesellschaft,* p. 114.

12. Goldscheid had introduced the project of a *Finanzsoziologie* in his work *Staatssozialismus und Staatskapitalismus* from 1917, and Schumpeter's work appeared in 1918; Weber created his sociology of domination during the period 1910–20. See Stefan Breuer, *Max Webers Herrschaftssoziologie* (Frankfurt: Campus Verlag, 1991); Rudolf Goldscheid, *Staatssozialismus oder Staatskapitalismus?* (Vienna: Anzengruber-Verlag Brüder Suschitsky, 1917); and Joseph A. Schumpeter, "The Crisis of the Tax State," pp. 99–140 in *The Economics and Sociology of Capitalism* (Princeton, N.J.: Princeton University Press, 1991).

13. *"Wirtschaft und Herrschaft,"* letter from Max Weber to his publishing house, dated September 25, 1919, as cited in Johannes Winkelmann, *Max Webers hinterlassenes Hauptwerk* (Tübingen: J.C.B. Mohr, 1986), p. 46.

14. Weber, *The Agrarian Sociology of Ancient Civilizations* (London: NLB, 1976), p. 131, or "Agrarverhältnisse im Altertum," p. 82 in *Gesammelte Aufsätze zur Sozial- und Wirtschaftsgeschichte* (Tübingen: J.C.B. Mohr, 1988), p. 82.

15. Weber, *General Economic History* (New Brunswick, N.J.: Transaction Books, 1981), p. 283, or *Wirtschaftsgeschichte,* p. 244.

16. Weber, *Economy and Society,* pp. 194–201, or *Wirtschaft und Gesellschaft,* pp. 114–19. The original titles of these two paragraphs are "§38. The Financing of Political Bodies" and "§39. Repercussions of Public Financing on Private Economic Activity."

17. Weber describes "financing" [*"Finanzierung"*] as "the way in which they [noneconomic organizations] secure the means of carrying on their corporate activity as such; that is, the activity of the administrative staff itself and that which is directed by it." It may be added that two German terms are translated as "financing" in *Economy and Society: "Finanzierung"* and *"Finanzierungsgeschäfte."* The former is used in Weber's fiscal sociology and refers to the financing of an organization, while the latter refers to supplying capital for a profit and similar activities. For *"Finanzierung,"* see Weber, *Economy and Society,* p. 194, or *Wirtschaft und Gesellschaft,* p. 114, and for *"Finanzierungsgeschäfte,"* see *Economy and Society,* p. 161, or *Wirtschaft und Gesellschaft,* p. 93.

18. Paul Veyne, *Bread and Circuses* (London: Penguin Press, 1990), p. 75. Veyne's celebrated work is mainly about "euergetism," which he defines as "private liberality to give" in antiquity. Weber also distinguishes between "class liturgies" (attached to property) and "status liturgies" (involving collective responsibility). See Weber, *Economy and Society,* p. 350, or *Wirtschaft und Gesellschaft,* pp. 208–9.

19. Weber, *Economy and Society,* p. 199, or *Wirtschaft und Gesellschaft,* p. 117.

20. Weber mentions, all in all, the following factors: that the economic policy of the state can have noneconomic goals; that religion and other ethical systems may impede rational capitalism; that science and technology play a role in rationalizing the economy; and that firms and other organizational forms have to be "invented." See Weber, *Economy and Society,* p. 200, or *Wirtschaft und Gesellschaft,* p. 118.

21. The following statements are based on the major sections on the concept of domination in *Economy and Society;* see Weber, *Economy and Society,* pp. 53–54, 212–15, 262–66, and 941–48, or *Wirtschaft und Gesellschaft,* pp. 28–29, 122–24, 153–55, 541–45.

22. There are two definitions of "domination" in *Economy and Society;* one in part 1 (which Weber checked for publication) and one in the manuscripts left behind and later published as part 2 of *Economy and Society.* According to the former, "'Domination' (*Herrschaft*) is the probability that a command with a given specific content will be obeyed by a given group of persons"; and according to the latter, "in our terminology *domination* shall be identical with *authoritarian power of command."* See Weber, *Economy and Society,* pp. 53, 946, or *Wirtschaft und Gesellschaft,* pp. 28, 544.

23. Weber, "The Three Types of Legitimate Rule," p. 6 in Amitai Etzioni, ed., *A Sociological Reader on Complex Organizations* (New York: Holt, Rinehart and Winston, 1969), or "Die drei reinen Typen der legitimen Herrschaft," p. 475 in *Gesammelte Aufsätze zur Wissenschaftslehre.* Weber says similarly that the situation becomes "relatively unstable" when there are only *"purely* material interests" to unite a staff and its chief; see Weber, *Economy and Society,* p. 213, or *Wirtschaft und Geellschaft,* p. 122.

24. The three major versions of Weber's sociology of domination can be found in the following places in his work: in Part 1 of *Economy and Society;* in the second part of *Economy and Society;* and in a draft that was located among Weber's effects. A fourth—very brief—discussion of domination can also be found in the last few pages of Weber's introduction ("Einleitung") to his collected essays in the sociology of religion. See Weber, *Economy and Society,* pp. 212–301, 941–1211, or *Wirtschaft und Gesellschaft,* pp. 122–76, 541–868; "The Three Types of Legitimate Rule," pp. 6–15 in Etzioni, ed., *A Sociological Reader on Complex Organizations,* or "Die drei reinen Typen der legitimen Herrschaft," pp. 475–88 in *Gesammelte Aufsätze zur Wissenschaftslehre;* and "The Social Psychology of the World Religions," pp. 295–301 in Hans Gerth and C. Wright Mills,

eds., *From Max Weber* (New York: Oxford University Press, 1946), or Weber, "Einleitung," pp. 268–75 in Vol. 1 of *Gesammelte Aufsätze zur Religionssoziologie* (Tübingen: J.C.B. Mohr, 1988). For a good discussion of the differences and similarities between the different versions, see, for example, Breuer, *Max Webers Herrschaftssoziologie.*

25. The German term for "means of administration" is *Verwaltungsmittel.* See, e.g., Weber, *Economy and Society,* pp. 218–19, 980–83, or *Wirtschaft und Gesellschaft,* pp. 126, 566–67; and Weber, "The Profession and Vocation of Politics," pp. 315–16 in *Political Writings,* or "Politik als Beruf," pp. 510–11 in *Gesammelte Politische Schriften.* There is also an economic dimension to the separation of the warrior from the means of warfare; see Weber, *Economy and Society,* pp. 1154–55, or *Wirtschaft und Gesellschaft,* pp. 683–84.

26. Weber, *Economy and Society,* pp. 223, 973, or *Wirtschaft und Gesellschaft,* pp. 128, 561–62. For literature that is critical of Weber's theory of bureaucracy, see chapter 2, n. 100.

27. Weber, *Economy and Society,* pp. 967–68, or *Wirtschaft und Gesellschaft,* p. 558.

28. The most important of these is the firm (which is discussed in chapter 2). Weber notes that all large capitalist firms are examples of bureaucracies, but he says little about their internal structure; for this the reader is referred to such works as Jürgen Kocka, "The Rise of the Modern Industrial Enterprise in Germany," pp. 77–116 in Alfred Chandler and Herman Daems, eds., *Managerial Hierarchies* (Cambridge, Mass.: Harvard University Press, 1980); and the section on Germany in Alfred Chandler, *Scale and Scope: The Dynamics of Industrial Capitalism* (Cambridge, Mass.: Harvard University Press, 1990). The management of firms, according to Weber, follows "laws which . . . are quite different from those obtaining in the sphere of political administration," but, again, he does not spell out which these are; see Weber, "The Profession and Vocation of Politics," p. 316 in *Political Writings,* or "Politik als Beruf," p. 511 in *Gesammelte Politische Schriften.* There is also an interesting analysis in Weber's work of the emergence of discipline in the capitalist firm; see Weber, *Economy and Society,* pp. 1155–56, or *Wirtschaft und Gesellschaft,* pp. 686–87. Weber's contribution to industrial sociology is mentioned in note 159 in the appendix.

29. Jürgen Kocka, "Capitalism and Bureaucracy in German Industrialization before 1914," *Economic History Review* 34 (1981): 453–68.

30. Weber, *Economy and Society,* p. 112, or *Wirtschaft und Gesellschaft,* p. 94.

31. Weber, *Economy and Society,* p. 975, or *Wirtschaft und Gesellschaft,* p. 563.

32. See, e.g., Weber, *Economy and Society,* p. 963, or *Wirtschaft und Gesellschaft,* p. 556. There is also the case, Weber says, that bureaucracy, through its emphasis on following rules, creates problems for choosing the best solution for any individual case; see Weber, *Economy and Society,* pp. 974–75, or *Wirtschaft und Gesellschaft,* p. 562.

33. Weber, *Economy and Society,* pp. 1108–09, or *Wirtschaft und Gesellschaft,* p. 653.

34. Weber, *Economy and Society,* pp. 243, 1115, or *Wirtschaft und Gesellschaft,* pp. 141, 657.

35. Weber, *Economy and Society,* pp. 245, 1113, or *Wirtschaft und Gesellschaft,* pp. 142, 656; emphasis added. In German "anti-economic force" is *die Macht der Unwirtschaftlichkeit.* As an example one could cite the following remark about Jesus: "He carried no purse, for he had no coins and he earned no money"; James M. Robinson, "Foreword," p. xiv in John J. Rousseaud and Rami Arav, *Jesus and His World* (Minneapolis: Fortress Press, 1995).

36. Weber, *Economy and Society,* p. 244, or *Wirtschaft und Gesellschaft,* p. 142; emphasis added. At another place in *Economy and Society* Weber says the same thing,

this time using the word "undignified." See Weber, *Economy and Society,* p. 1113, or *Wirtschaft und Gesellschaft,* p. 655.

37. One of the terms that Weber uses to characterize charisma is *"ausseralltäglich."* See Weber, *Economy and Society,* p. 241, or *Wirtschaft und Gesellschaft,* p. 140. For the quotation in the sentence, see Weber, "The Social Psychology of the World Religions," p. 289 in Gerth and Mills, eds., *From Max Weber,* or "Einleitung," p. 261 in Vol. 1 of *Gesammelte Aufsätze zur Religionssoziologie.* The translation has been changed. It may be noted that the attitudes of Durkheim and Weber toward charisma and the economy are similar. Durkheim contrasts brief periods of "collective effervescence" to periods of low-key everyday life, when economic concerns predominate. See Emile Durkheim, *The Elementary Forms of Religious Life* (New York: Free Press, 1965), p. 245 ff.

38. Weber, *Economy and Society,* p. 1120, or *Wirtschaft und Gesellschaft,* p. 661. The translation has been slightly changed. For the statement that adjustment to the economic forces of everyday life is a more powerful force towards routinization than the problem of succession, see Weber, *Economy and Society,* p. 253, or *Wirtschaft und Gesellschaft,* p. 147.

39. See Weber, *Economy and Society,* pp. 251, 253, or *Wirtschaft und Gesellschaft,* pp. 146, 147. For Weber's doubt about using the term "administration" (*"Verwaltung"*) in the context of pure charisma, see "The Three Types of Legitimate Rule," p. 12, or "Die drei reinen Typen der legitimen Herrschaft," p. 482 in *Gesammelte Aufsätze zur Wissenschaftslehre.*

40. Weber, *Economy and Society,* p. 1118, or *Wirtschaft und Gesellschaft,* p. 659. Weber describes some similar events in his chapter on speculative crises in *General Economic History,* including those involving John Law; see Weber, *General Economic History,* p. 286 ff., or *Wirtschaftsgeschichte,* p. 246 ff. The reader is also reminded of Weber's statement (cited in chapter 2) about "the double nature . . . of the 'spirit of capitalism'."

41. The term "charismatic capitalism" is used in a Weber-inspired study of direct selling organizations (DSOs) by Nicole Woolsey Biggart, who argues that "network DSOs are best understood as charismatic forms of organization and that the practices and arrangements distinctive to the industry [of businesses like Amway, Tuppperware, and Mary Kay Cosmetics] flow from that"; see Nicole Woolsey Biggart, *Charismatic Capitalism: Direct Selling Organizations in America* (Chicago: University of Chicago, 1990), p. 127 and chapter 6 in general. To complete the topic of charisma and economic activities in Weber's thought, the following should be added: all concrete forms of domination consist of a mixture of the three main types; the head of a bureaucracy (including an economic one) can be a charismatic figure; the transformation of charisma in a democratic direction may have a rational impact on the economy; and hunting expeditions were often led by charismatic figures early in history. See Weber, *Economy and Society,* pp. 241, 262–63, 269–70, 1134, or *Wirtschaft und Gesellschaft,* pp. 140, 153–54, 157–58, 670.

42. Weber, *Economy and Society,* p. 1099, or *Wirtschaft und Gesellschaft,* p. 646.

43. The most important exception is that of estate-type domination (*ständische Herrschaft*), in which the administrators control the means of administration. The *Ständestaat* came into being, Weber says, when the existence of fiefs and privileges made the administrative-political structure inflexible; he also adds a few other observations of interest to economic sociology. See, e.g., Weber, *Economy and Society,* p. 1085–88, or *Wirtschaft und Gesellschaft,* pp. 636–38; Weber, "Suffrage and Democracy in Germany," pp. 100–101 in *Political Writings,* or "Wahlrecht und Demokratie in Deutschland," pp. 263–64 in *Gesammelte Politische Schriften.* According to Hintze, Weber's analysis of the *Ständestaat* was incomplete; see Otto Hintze, "The Preconditions of Representative Gov-

ernment," p. 306 in *The Historical Essays of Otto Hintze* (New York: Oxford University Press, 1975). A form of domination that is close to estate-type domination is Western feudalism (discussed later in this chapter).

44. Weber says more precisely that wholesale trade can adapt itself to all conditions and that the formation of trade capital is also possible under "almost all" conditions of domination. See Weber, *Economy and Society*, p. 1095, or *Wirtschaft und Gesellschaft*, p. 643. Weber says something similar about "speculative trade capitalism," which is discussed in chapter 2. Where the line is to be drawn between "trading capitalism" (*"Händler-Kapitalismus"*), as Weber calls the former type of activity, and "speculative trade capitalism" (*"spekulativer Handelskapitalismus"*) is not clear. See Weber, *Economy and Society*, pp. 200, 240, or *Wirtschaft und Gesellschaft*, pp. 119, 139.

45. Weber contrasts Western feudalism (*Lehens-Feudalismus*) with a few other forms of feudalism, of which the most important is prebendal feudalism (*Pfründen-Feudalismus*). See Weber, *Economy and Society*, pp. 255 ff., 259 ff., or *Wirtschaft und Gesellschaft*, pp. 148 ff., 151 ff. Prebendal feudalism lacks the element of fealty and is financed through benefices.

46. Weber, *Economy and Society*, p. 255, or *Wirtschaft und Gesellschaft*, p. 148. According to Otto Hintze, "Max Weber has attempted to explain feudalism in general as the result of the routinization of what he called the type of charismatic domination"; see Otto Hintze, "Wesen und Verbreitung des Feudalismus," p. 87 in Vol. 1 of *Gesammelte Abhandlungen* (Göttingen: Vandenhoeck und Ruprecht, 1970). A fine discussion of Weber's concept of Western feudalism can be found in Stefan Breuer, "Der okzidentale Feudalismus in Max Webers Gesellschaftsgeschiche," pp. 437–75 in Wolfgang Schluchter, ed., *Max Webers Sicht des okzidentalen Christentums* (Frankfurt am Main: Suhrkamp, 1988). In this context see also Gianfranco Poggi, "Max Webers Begriff des okzidentalen Feudalismus," pp. 476–97 in Schluchter, ed., *Max Webers Sicht des okzidentalen Christentums;* and Vatro Murvar, "Some Reflections on Weber's Typology of *Herrschaft*," *Sociological Quarterly* 5 (1964): 374–84.

47. Weber, *Economy and Society*, p. 1106, or *Wirtschaft und Gesellschaft*, p. 651. The translation has been slightly changed.

48. See, e.g., Weber, *Economy and Society*, pp. 233–34, 236, 259–61, 1015–21, 1077–78, 1104–05, or *Wirtschaft und Gesellschaft*, pp. 134–36, 151–53, 586–90, 630–31, 650–51.

49. Weber, *Economy and Society*, p. 1107, or *Wirtschaft und Gesellschaft*, pp. 651–52.

50. See Weber, *Grundriss zu den Vorlesungen über Allgemeine ("theoretische") Nationalökonomie (1898)*, pp. 12–13, 15–16. Weber lectured on the city as part of a more general section on "the historical foundation of the economy." It can also be mentioned that of the four lectures that Weber gave in the fall of 1897 in Mannheim on the theme of "The Course of Economic Development," one dealt explicitly with the city: "Feudalism and the Economy of Cities in the Middle Ages." According to a contemporary account of this lecture, Weber touched on such topics as guilds, trade, and artisans in the medieval city. See Max Weber, "Der Gang der wirtschaftlichen Entwicklung," pp. 842–52 in Vol. 2 of *Landarbeiterfrage, Nationalstaat und Volkswirtschaftspolitik. Max Weber Gesamtausgabe I/4* (Tübingen: J.C.B. Mohr, 1993).

51. Weber, *Economy and Society*, p. 1323, or *Wirtschaft und Gesellschaft*, p. 788. The translation has been slightly changed.

52. For Weber's critique, see *Economy and Society*, pp. 1212–36, or *Wirtschaft und Gesellschaft*, pp. 727–41.

53. Weber, *Economy and Society*, p. 1220, or *Wirtschaft und Gesellschaft*, p. 732; emphasis added.

54. Weber, *Economy and Society*, p. 1219, or *Wirtschaft und Gesellschaft*, p. 731. According to Guenther Roth and Claus Wittich, this critique is aimed exclusively at Gustav Schmoller and not at Karl Bücher; see Weber, *Economy and Society*, pp. 208–9 n. 30. As I noted in chapter 2, I believe that Weber's critique is more general and that it encompasses the very idea of stage theory. In his social and economic history of antiquity from 1909, Weber criticizes, for example, "the currently fashionable enterprise of constructing general schemes of development"; see Weber, *The Agrarian Sociology of Ancient Civilizations*, p. 385, or "Agrarverhältnisse im Altertum," p. 288 in *Gesammelte Aufsätze zur Sozial- und Wirtschaftsgeschichte*.

55. Weber, *Economy and Society*, p. 1295, or *Wirtschaft und Gesellschaft*, p. 774. The section on the patricians' attitude toward entrepreneurship on pages 1293–96 (pages 772–75 in *Wirtschaft und Gesellschaft*) is excellent.

56. Another group of people in antiquity displayed an affinity for rational capitalism, namely the Roman *equites*. See, e.g., Weber, *Economy and Society*, pp. 1358–59, or *Wirtschaft und Gesellschaft*, p. 808. Finley criticizes Weber for characterizing the *equites* as a pure national capitalist class; see M. I. Finley, "The Ancient City: From Fustel de Coulanges to Max Weber and Beyond," *Comparative Studies in Society and History* 19 (1977): 321.

57. Weber, *Economy and Society*, p. 1354, or *Wirtschaft und Gesellschaft*, p. 805.

58. See "Ein Vortrag Max Webers über die Probleme der Staatssoziologie," *Neue Freie Presse (Vienna)*, Nr. 19102 (October 26, 1917), p. 10. The reporter does an excellent job of summarizing Weber's ideas.

59. Weber, *Economy and Society*, p. 1262, or *Wirtschaft und Gesellschaft*, p. 757.

60. Weber, *General Economic History*, p. 337, or *Wirtschaftsgeschichte*, p. 289.

61. For the term "political competition" ("*politische Konkurrenz*") or similar expressions, see, e.g., Weber, *Economy and Society*, p. 354, 1103, or *Wirtschaft und Gesellschaft*, pp. 211, 649; Max Weber, *The Religion of China* (New York: Free Press, 1951), pp. 61–62, or "Konfuzianismus und Taoismus," pp. 348–49 in Vol. 1 of *Gesammelte Aufsätze zur Religionssoziologie*. For arguments using the logic of political competition (but not necessarily the term), see also, e.g., Weber, *Economy and Society*, pp. 165, 1259, or *Wirtschaft und Gesellschaft*, pp. 96, 755; Weber, *General Economic History*, p. 337, or *Wirtschaftsgeschichte*, p. 288–89; and Weber, *The Religion of China*, pp. 84, 103, or "Konfuzianismus und Taoismus," pp. 373, 394 in Vol. 1 of *Gesammelte Aufsätze zur Religionssoziologie*.

62. For mercantilism, see Weber, *General Economic History*, pp. 347–51, or *Wirtschaftsgeschichte*, pp. 296–300; see also *Economy and Society*, pp. 351–54, or *Wirtschaft und Gesellschaft*, pp. 209–11; for imperialism, see Weber, *Economy and Society*, pp. 913–21, or *Wirtschaft und Gesellschaft*, pp. 521–27.

63. Schmoller wrote a few articles on the theme of mercantilism during the years 1884–87; for a translation of one of these, see Gustav Schmoller, *The Mercantile System and Its Historical Significance* (New York: Macmillan, 1902).

64. Wolfgang Mommsen emphasizes the unfinished nature of Weber's theory of imperialism: "He [Weber] did not develop a consistent theory of imperialism [but] he did assemble important elements of such a theory from the sociological point of view." See Wolfgang Mommsen, *Theories of Imperialism* (New York: Random House, 1980), p. 19.

65. See Weber, *Economy and Society*, pp. 910–12, or *Wirtschaft und Gesellschaft*, pp. 520–21. Weber's discussion of imperialism ("The Economic Foundations of 'Imperialism'") contains a much more complex argument than is reproduced in the next passage. Weber, for example, discusses whether the existence of an empire also means that trade increases within its area; whether trade in an area leads to its political unification; and, fi-

nally, how the economic structure of an empire is reflected in its tactics for handling a conquered area economically. See Weber, *Economy and Society,* pp. 913–21, or *Wirtschaft und Gesellschaft,* pp. 521–27.

66. Weber, *Economy and Society,* p. 912, or *Wirtschaft und Gesellschaft,* p. 521.

67. Weber, *Economy and Society,* p. 918, or *Wirtschaft und Gesellschaft,* p. 525. Weber is probably referring to *The Peace* by Aristophanes; see "The Peace," e.g., p. 43 (line 445 ff.) in *The Peace, The Birds, The Frogs* (Cambridge, Mass.: Harvard University Press, 1961).

68. For Lenin, see his *Imperialism, the Highest Stage of Capitalism* (Peking: Foreign Languages Press, 1970); and for Schumpeter, "The Sociology of Imperialisms," pp. 141–219 in *The Economics and Sociology of Capitalism.* Weber probably wrote about imperialism in the early 1910s; Lenin's work was published in 1917 (and translated into German in 1921); Schumpeter's was published in 1918–19.

69. Weber, *Economy and Society,* pp. 162, 166, or *Wirtschaft und Gesellschaft,* pp. 94, 97.

70. G. F. Knapp, *Staatliche Theorie des Geldes* (Leipzig: Duncker und Humblot, 1905), pp. 1, 33. *"Das Geld ist ein Geschöpf der Rechtsordnung"; ". . . . ein Geschöpf der rechtsbildenden Tätigkeit des Staates . . . ."* See also *The State Theory of Money* (London: Macmillan, 1924), pp. 1, 40.

71. Weber, *Economy and Society,* p. 179, or *Wirtschaft und Gesellschaft,* p. 105. According to Mises, writing in the late 1910s, the state theory of money had become "the accepted doctrine" in Germany, Austria, and Russia; see Ludwig von Mises, "On the Classification of Monetary Theories," p. 511 in *The Theory of Money and Credit* (Indianapolis: Liberty Fund, [1924] 1981). Bertram Schefold explains the popularity of Knapp's ideas among German economists on the ground that they saw money as the creation of the state while the gold standard was associated with the supremacy of the London gold market; see Bertram Schefold, "Knapp, Georg Friedrich (1842–1926)," p. 54 in Vol. 3 of John Eatwell, Murray Milgate, and Peter Newman, eds., *The New Palgrave: A Dictionary of Economics* (London: Macmillan, 1987).

72. Knut Wicksell, "Knapps penningteori," *Ekonomisk tidskrift (Sweden)* 9 (1907): 52.

73. Wicksell says that Knapp's many new terms may at first seem puzzling but adds that "on the whole [they] represent a big step forward because, without exception, they constitute real conceptual distinctions . . . which once they have been established through well chosen technical terms, are not so easy to eliminate"; see Wicksell, "Knapps penningteori," *Ekonomisk tidskrift* 9 (1907): 42. Weber commends Knapp for his "courage" to suggest new terms so there would be less reliance on everyday words, which are always easy to misunderstand; see Weber, "Antikritisches zum 'Geist' des Kapitalismus," pp. 155, 176 n. 5 in Weber, *Max Weber, Die protestantische Ethik, II. Kritiken und Antikritiken* (Gütersloh: Gütersloher Verlagshaus Mohn, 1978). Weber also commends Knapp on his "able and valuable attempt to systematize terminology and concepts"; see Weber, *Economy and Society,* p. 78, or *Wirtschaft und Gesellschaft,* p. 40. Schumpeter's verdict, finally, is the following: Knapp "was a master in the art of coining new concepts and naming them felicitously." Schumpeter then adds, tongue in cheek: "It should be observed that the Greek words borrowed for the purpose served very well: the German economists at that time were not as a rule good theorists, but most of them had had a classical education and knew Greek"; see Joseph A. Schumpeter, *History of Economic Analysis* (London: Allen and Unwin, 1954), p. 1091 n. 14.

74. Knapp was a leading member of the *Kathedersozialisten,* whom Mises heartily despised. Mises argued that the state theory of money was a useless doctrine because it ig-

nored the workings of the market and the formation of prices; everything was explained as the result of the activities of the state. See Ludwig von Mises, *The Theory of Money and Credit*, pp. 83–94, 275–76, 503–24. Weber may well have been familiar with Mises's critique of Knapp since it was presented in a useful overview article from 1917–18; see Mises, "On the Classification of Monetary Theories," pp. 503–24 in *The Theory of Money and Credit*. Finally, Schumpeter summed up the impact of Knapp's theory of money in the following way: "It is impossible to deny that in handling what are fundamentally questions of economic theory it [Knapp's theory] went wrong, and that its influence on monetary science in Germany has been, in the main, an unfortunate one"; see Joseph A. Schumpeter, "G. F. Knapp," *Economic Journal* 36 (1926): 514.

75. Weber, *Economy and Society,* p. 78, or *Wirtschaft und Gesellschaft,* p. 40. Weber says that "the formulation of monetary theory which has been most acceptable to the author, is that of von Mises." Although Weber says that he will not discuss monetary theory in *Economy and Society,* he nonetheless devotes a number of pages to Knapp (including a special section on *The State Theory of Money*) but includes nothing whatsoever on Mises's ideas.

76. Weber, *Economy and Society,* p. 184, or *Wirtschaft und Gesellschaft,* p. 109. At another place in his work Weber notes similarly that "with economic policy one does not create a capitalistic economic mentality"; see Weber, *The Religion of China,* pp. 237–38, or "Konfuzianismus und Taoismus," p. 524 in Vol. 1 of *Gesammelte Aufsätze zur Religionssoziologie* (the translation has been changed). In general, Weber felt that the attempts of the state to influence the economy through various interventions would have "unforeseen" and "unintended consequences"; see Weber, *Economy and Society,* p. 994, or *Wirtschaft und Geselschaft,* p. 574.

77. Knapp defines money as "a chartal means of payment"; and Weber defines it in the following way: "'Money' we call a chartal means of payment which is also a means of exchange." See Knapp, *The State Theory of Money,* p. 38; Weber, *Economy and Society,* p. 76, or *Wirtschaft und Gesellschaft,* p. 39. Kurt Singer notes that Weber does not seem to have known that the second edition of Knapp's work (which appeared in 1918) contains a discussion of how the price of money is set in reality; see G. F. Knapp and Friedrich Bendixen, *Zur staatlichen Theorie des Geldes* (Tübingen: J.C.B. Mohr, 1958), p. 235. The addition to the second edition of Knapp's work, which Weber presumably did not read, is entitled "Nachträge und Ergänzungen"; see Knapp, *Staatliche Theorie des Geldes,* 2d ed. (Munich: Duncker und Humblot, 1918), pp. 395–445.

78. Again, the reader may be referred to the debate about economic power and price. At issue was whether the state could set prices or the market should decide the prices. See Eugen von Böhm-Bawerk, "Control or Economic Law?," pp. 139–200 in *Shorter Classics of Eugen von Böhm-Bawerk* (South Holland, Ill.: Libertarian Press, [1914] 1962); Joseph A. Schumpeter, "Das Grundprinzip der Verteilungstheorie," *Archiv für Sozialwissenschaft und Sozialpolitik* 41 (1916–17): 1–88.

79. Other topics of interest in this context are: economics in relation to the separation of powers (*Economy and Society,* pp. 283–84, or *Wirtschaft und Gesellschaft,* pp. 166–67); economics and political representation (*Economy and Society,* pp. 296–97, or *Wirtschaft und Gesellschaft,* p. 174); economic aspects of political parties, such as their financing (*Economy and Society,* p. 286, or *Wirtschaft und Gesellschaft,* p. 168); and the necessity for the parliament to control the budget ("Parliament and Government in Germany under a New Political Order," pp. 142, 165, 226–27 in *Political Writings,* or "Parlament und Regierung im neugeordneten Deutschland," pp. 317, 339, 400 in *Gesammelte Politische Schriften*). I have not found any natural links between Weber and public

choice theory—beyond the fact that Weber viewed modern democracy as a system in which leaders compete for votes (somewhat like Schumpeter), and that he occasionally used a term such as "political entrepreneur" (typically in the sense of the U.S. political boss who controls a number of votes). See, e.g., Weber, "Parliament and Government in Germany under a New Political Order," p. 216, in *Political Writings,* or "Parlament und Regierung im neugeordneten Deutschland," p. 389 in *Gesammelte Politische Schriften;* "The Profession and Vocation of Politics," pp. 344–48 in *Political Writings,* or "Politik als Beruf," pp. 534–41 in *Gesammelte Politische Schriften.*

80. Weber, "On the Situation of Constitutional Democracy in Russia," pp. 68–70 in *Political Writings,* or "Zur Lage der bürgerlichen Demokratie in Russland," pp. 63–64 in *Gesammelte Politische Schriften.*

81. Weber, "Parliament and Government in Germany under a New Political Order," pp. 175–76, 194 in *Political Writings,* or "Parlament und Regierung im neugeordneten Deutschland," pp. 349, 367 in *Gesammelte Politische Schriften;* Weber, *Economy and Society,* pp. 283–84, or *Wirtschaft und Gesellschaft,* pp. 166–67.

82. Weber, "On the Situation of Constitutional Democracy in Russia," p. 68 in *Political Writings,* or "Zur Lage der bürgerlichen Demokratie in Russland," p. 63 in *Gesammelte Politische Schriften.*

83. The German terms are *ökonomisch abkömmlich, leben 'für' die Politik,* and *leben von der Politik [im ökonomischen Sinn des Wortes]*. For "economic availability," see, e.g., Weber, "Suffrage and Democracy in Germany," pp. 109–12 in *Political Writings,* or "Wahlrecht und Demokratie in Deutschland," pp. 272–75 in *Gesammelte Politische Schriften; Economy and Society,* pp. 290–91, or *Wirtschaft und Gesellschaft,* p. 170; and for "living off politics in the economic sense of the word," see, e.g., Weber, "The Profession and Vocation of Politics," p. 318 in *Political Writings,* or "Politik als Beruf," pp. 513–14 in *Gesammelte Politische Schriften;* Weber, "Parliament and Government in Germany under a New Political Order," p. 216 in *Political Writings,* or "Parlament und Regierung im neugeordneten Deutschland," p. 389 in *Gesammelte Politische Schriften.*

84. Weber, "Socialism," p. 276 in *Political Writings,* or "Der Sozialismus," p. 497 in *Gesammelte Aufsätze zur Soziologie und Sozialpolitik* (Tübingen: J.C.B. Mohr, 1988).

85. The closest that Weber comes to a definition of "economic availability" is when he says that "the politician must be economically 'dispensable' or 'available' (*abkömmlich*), which means that his income must not depend on the fact that he personally and constantly devotes all or most of his productive energy and thought to the task of earning a living"; see Weber, "The Profession and Vocation of Politics," pp. 318–19 in *Political Writings,* or "Politik als Beruf," p. 514 in *Gesammelte Politische Schriften.*

86. Weber, "Suffrage and Democracy in Germany," p. 111 in *Political Writings,* or "Wahlrecht und Demokratie in Deutschland," pp. 273–74 in *Gesammelte Politische Schriften.* Weber's term is *"innerliche Abkömmlichkeit";* emphasis has been added and the translation has been changed.

87. Stinchcombe refers in passing to "Weber's old-fashioned treatment of prices under socialism"; see Stinchcombe, "Max Weber's *Economy and Society,*" p. 287 in *Stratification and Organization.* Parsons notes apropos of Weber's statement that rational capital accounting presupposes that money operates efficiently in a way that it is unlikely to do in socialism, that "the principal weight of technical opinion seems at present [in the late 1940s] to take the opposite position from that which Weber defends"; and the current editors of *Economy and Society* apparently agree since they decided to keep Parsons's note. See Weber, *Economy and Society,* pp. 93, 207 n. 17. In a now-famous article from 1936–37, Oskar Lange claimed that the problems of a socialist economy could be solved

through some measure of decentralization of the economy (with decisions about production made at the enterprise level) in combination with a Central Planning Board (which would set "the right equilibrium prices"). See Oskar Lange, "On the Economic Theory of Socialism," p. 89 in B. E. Lippincott, ed., *On the Economic Theory of Socialism* (New York: McGraw-Hill, 1964).

88. Weber, *Economy and Society*, p. 1402, or "Parlament und Regierung im neugeordneten Deutschland," p. 332 in *Gesammelte Politische Schriften*. For a good summary of Weber's view of socialism, see "Socialism, Stagnation and Slavery," pp. 82–89 in David Beetham, *Max Weber and the Theory of Modern Politics* (Cambridge: Polity Press, 1985). Weber discusses a number of different types of socialism in his work and considered them to have the following in common: an opposition to "the anarchy of production," which capitalism entails, and a desire to create an economy without profit, a so-called communal economy (*Gemeinwirtschaft*). See, e.g., Weber, "Socialism," pp. 281–82, 284–85 in *Political Writings*, or "Der Sozialismus," pp. 500, 502 in *Gesammelte Aufsätze zur Soziologie und Sozialpolitik*. When Weber spoke of "socialism," he meant roughly what people today mean when they speak of "state socialism." Communism was in his opinion oriented to consumption; it was indifferent to calculation; and it was based on a feeling of mutual solidarity in work arrangements. He criticized "syndicalism" for being naive and unable to realize that the workers would not be able to take over the running of the factories themselves and that a new bureaucracy would soon emerge. The form of socialism that Weber was most sympathetic to seems to have been a form of consumers' coops ("socialism of the consumers"; "*Konsumentensozialismus*") which he, on the other hand, never considered to be a serious contender for power. For Weber's view of communism, see, e.g., *Economy and Society*, pp. 112, 153–54, or *Wirtschaft und Gesellschaft*, pp. 61, 88–89; for his views of syndicalism and of socialism of the consumers, see, e.g., "Socialism," pp. 296–97, 287 in *Political Writings*, or "Der Sozialismus," pp. 512–13, 504 in *Gesammelte Aufsätze zur Soziologie und Sozialpolitik*.

89. Weber, *The Agrarian Sociology of Ancient Civilizations*, p. 365, or "Agrarverhältnisse im Altertum," p. 277 in *Gesammelte Aufsätze zur Sozial- und Wirtschaftsgeschichte*. The translation has been changed. Also the word "bureaucracy" (in the expression "every bureaucracy") is emphasized in the original.

90. A strong socialist state would exploit weaker socialist states, for example, by forcing them to trade on unfavorable terms. See Weber, *Economy and Society*, pp. 919–20, or *Wirtschaft und Gesellschaft*, pp. 526–27. When Weber discussed workers' having to face a united elite in socialism, he usually had the example of the socialization of the Prussian mines in mind. See e.g., Weber, "Parliament and Government in Germany under a New Political Order," p. 157 in *Political Writings*, or "Parlament und Regierung im neugeordneten Deutschland," p. 332 in *Gesammelte Politische Schriften* (for a critique of Weber on this point, see Beetham, *Max Weber and the Theory of Modern Politics*, pp. 84–85). As to the managers, Weber is talking about tendencies in the long run; in the short run, socialists might be forced to use former managers to run their factories, as the Bolsheviks had done. For Weber's analysis of the Soviet Union, see, e.g., Weber, "Socialism," p. 299 in *Political Writings*, or "Der Sozialismus," p. 514 in *Gesammelte Aufsätze zur Soziologie und Sozialpolitik;* "The Profession and Vocation of Politics," p. 335, or "Politik als Beruf," p. 529 in *Gesammelte Politische Schriften*. See in this context also Stefan Breuer, "Soviet Communism and Weberian Sociology," *Journal of Historical Sociology* 5 (1992): 267–90.

91. Weber, *Economy and Society*, p. 202, or *Wirtschaft und Gesellschaft*, p. 119.

92. So did the Russian economist Boris Brutzkus, according to Hayek. For Hayek's

friendly comments on Weber, see p. 143 ff. in Friedrich von Hayek's "Socialist Calculation, I: *The Nature and History of the Problem*" in *Individualism and Economic Order*
(Chicago: University of Chicago Press, 1948). Keith Tribe agrees with Hayek that Weber
and Mises independently made similar but by no means identical critiques of the economy of socialism. See Keith Tribe, *Strategies of Economic Order* (Cambridge: Cambridge
University Press, 1995), p. 142 ff. Mises's essay was published in the spring of 1920 in the
Archiv für Sozialwissenschaft und Sozialpolitik under the title "Die Wirtschaftsrechnung
im sozialistischen Gemeinwesen" and has been translated as "Economic Calculation in
the Socialist Commonwealth" (pp. 87–130 in Friedrich von Hayek, ed., *Collectivist Economic Planning* [London: George Routledge and Sons, 1948]). The whole debate on socialist economics is succinctly summarized by Lars Udehn in "Central Planning: Post-
script to a Debate," pp. 29–60 in Ulf Himmelstrand, ed., *Spontaneity and Planning in
Social Development* (London: SAGE, 1981). Weber notes in *Economy and Society* that
he only became aware of Mises's essay when Part 1 of *Economy and Society* was already
in print; see Weber, *Economy and Society*, p. 107, or *Wirtschaft und Gesellschaft*, p. 58.
Even if it is correct that Weber's and Mises's articles parallel each other (and that Weber
deserves some of the praise that Mises has received for formulating the first critique of
socialist economics), there is also quite a bit of difference between their approaches.
Weber, for example, made clear that his critique of socialist calculation was made from
the perspective of formal rationality; no distinction between formal and substantive
rationality can be found in Mises.

93. Weber, *Economy and Society*, p. 104, or *Wirtschaft und Gesellschaft*, p. 56.

94. Weber, *Economy and Society*, p. 103, or *Wirtschaft und Gesellschaft*, p. 55. The
translation has been changed; like Keith Tribe, I translate "*kontrolliert*" as "policed." See
Keith Tribe, "The Logical Structure of the Economic World," p. 159 in *Strategies of Economic Order.*

95. Weber, *Economy and Society*, p. 107, or *Wirtschaft und Gesellschaft*, p. 58. The
punctuation has been changed.

CHAPTER FOUR
THE ECONOMY AND LAW

1. Max Weber, *Economy and Society: An Outline of Interpretive Sociology* (Berkeley:
University of California Press, 1978), p. 905, or *Wirtschaft und Gesellschaft. Grundriss
der verstehenden Sociologie* (Tübingen: J.C.B. Mohr, 1972), p. 516. The other two
"*Grundfunktionen*" of the modern state are "the organized armed protection against outside attack (military administration)" and "the cultivation of hygienic, educational, social-
welfare, and other cultural interests (the various branches of administration)". Today one
would probably add a directly economic function, namely to keep the economy growing
and unemployment low.

2. Weber, *Economy and Society*, pp. 336, 329, or *Wirtschaft und Gesellschaft*, pp. 198,
193.

3. Weber, *General Economic History* (New Brunswick, N.J.: Transaction Books,
1981), p. 277, or *Wirtschaftsgeschichte* (Berlin: Duncker und Humblot, 1991), p. 240.
The translation has been changed. For a more extended discussion of the need for a
calculable law in rational captalism, see later in this chapter.

4. Levin Goldschmidt (1829–1897) was professor of commercial law at Berlin Uni-

versity from 1875 until he fell ill in the early 1890s. Toward the end of his career Gold-schmidt wanted Weber to replace him (Guenther Roth, "Between Cosmopolitanism and Ethnocentrism: Weber in the Nineties," *Telos* 96 [1993]: 161n. 31). Before Goldschmidt, little attention had been paid to commercial law as a special field. Goldschmidt empha-sized the special role that the Italian merchants had played during the Middle Ages in laying the foundation for modern commercial legislation; it is to their genius, he often said, that we owe many of the most important innovations in this field. In 1858 Gold-schmidt created *Zeitschrift für das gesammte Handelsrecht* and in 1864–1868 the first edition of his major work, *Handbuch des Handelsrechts,* appeared. A central theme in Goldschmidt's work is that the study of commercial law should draw on both legal sci-ence and economics. To indicate the value of Goldschmidt's work for social science in general, one can cite what economic historian Michael Postan wrote in the 1930s about "the study of the forms and methods of medieval business": "Its progress has largely been due to the activities of legal historians gathered around the late L. Goldschmidt and his *Zeitschrift für das gesammte Handelsrecht.*" Postan then adds that "Goldschmidt's clas-sic [*Universalgeschichte des Handelsrechts,* 1891] still remains the best general treatise on the technique of medieval business." See Michael Postan, "Studies in Bibliography: I. Medieval Capitalism," *Economic History Review* 4 (1933): 220. For a general intro-duction to Goldschmidt's work, see his "Handelsrecht (Geschichtliche Entwickelung)," pp. 316–27 in Vol. 5 of J. Conrad et al., eds., *Handwörterbuch der Staatswissenschaften* (Jena: Gustav Fischer, 1910); and for an introduction to his life, see Max Pappenheim, "Levin Goldschmidt," *Zeitschrift für das gesammte Handelsrecht* 47 (1898): 1–49. Weber's relations to Goldschmidt were not always the best. He was, for example, quite upset by the critique that Goldschmidt directed at his first dissertation in the third edi-tion of *Handbuch des Handelsrecht* (1891) and toyed for a while with the idea of writ-ing an answer.

5. Weber dealt with the law in his two dissertations, his many writings on stock ex-change legislation, and a number of other items, including his critique of Rudolf Stamm-ler's *Wirtschaft und Recht nach der materialistischen Geschichtsauffassung* (Leipzig: Ver-lag von Veit und Comp., 1896; 2d ed. 1906). It was clear from the beginning that the topic of law and economy was to be part of the *Grundriss.* In the proposed table of contents from 1910 Weber had put himself down as the author of an article to be called "The Econ-omy and Law," which was part of a section entitled *Economy and Society* and described as "The Economy and Law (1. Their Fundamental Relationship, 2. Epochs in the De-velopment of Present Conditions)." He had also scheduled a section for one of the vol-umes in the *Grundriss* entitled "Legal Foundations of Modern Capitalism," with one ar-ticle to be called "The Modern Private Legal Order and Capitalism" (to be written by Alexander Leist) and another to be called "The Modern State and Capitalism" (to be writ-ten by Weber himself). In the amended table of contents from 1914 a few changes were introduced, but the overall picture was prettty much the same. Weber was to write an ar-ticle called "The Fundamental Relationship between the Economy and Law"; and there were also to be articles entitled "The Modern Private Legal Order and Capitalism" (by Leist) and "The Modern State Order and Capitalism" (author unknown, but probably not Weber). See Johannes Winkelmann, *Max Webers hinterlassenes Hauptwerk* (Tübingen: J.C.B. Mohr, 1986), pp. 151–52.

6. Weber participated in the debate with a brief article in which he argued that the op-position of Germanic to Roman law was simplistic and that Roman law had become a scapegoat for various economic ills in Germany. See Weber, "'Roman' and 'Germanic'

Law," *International Journal of the Sociology of Law* 13 (1985): 237–46; see also Arie Brand, "Against Romanticism: Max Weber and the Historical School of Law," *Australian Journal of Law and Society* 1 (1982): 87–100.

7. Weber, *Economy and Society*, p. 858, or *Wirtschaft und Gesellschaft*, p. 495.

8. Talcott Parsons, "Value-freedom and Objectivity," p. 40 in Otto Stammer, ed., *Max Weber and Sociology Today* (New York: Harper and Row, 1972).

9. Stephen P. Turner and Regis A. Factor, *Max Weber: The Lawyer as Social Thinker* (London: Routledge, 1994).

10. See, e.g., Julien Freund, "The Sociology of Law," pp. 245–66 in *The Sociology of Max Weber* (Harmondsworth, Eng.: Penguin Books, 1972); and Wolfgang Schluchter, "Types of Law and Types of Domination," pp. 82–138 in *The Rise of Western Rationalism: Max Weber's Developmental History* (Berkeley: University of California Press, 1981).

11. See Max Rheinstein, "Introduction," pp. xvii–lxiv in Max Weber, *On Law in Economy and Society* (Cambridge, Mass.: Harvard University Press, 1954); David Trubek, "Max Weber on Law and the Rise of Capitalism," *Wisconsin Law Review* (1972): 720–53; Anthony Kronman, *Max Weber* (Stanford, Calif.: Stanford University Press, 1983); and Manfred Rehbinder and Klaus-Peter Tieck, eds., *Max Weber als Rechtssoziologe* (Berlin: Duncker und Humblot, 1987).

12. Parsons, "Value-freedom and Objectivity," p. 42. This key consists presumably of the argument that law is central to the normative order, not only in society as a whole but also more specifically in the economy. Kronman, *Max Weber*, p. 118. Johannes Winkelmann, "Max Webers 'Rechtssoziologie,'" pp. 18–19 in Max Weber, *Rechtssoziologie* (Neuwied: Hermann Luchterhand Verlag, 1960).

13. The law and economics field today has a near monopoly on the analysis of the relationship between law and economics. In the United states, for example, there are six journals in law and economics but not one in the sociology of law. Several theoretical perspectives inform the law and economics movement, especially those of Richard Posner and R. H. Coase, but also that of Friedrich Hayek. According to a famous article by Coase, regardless of how rights are allocated, the market will lead to a socially efficient outcome. Posner, in contrast, sees a more active role for the judge: in the common-law tradition, the judge attempts to bring about a socially efficient outcome through his or her actions. Hayek, finally, sees law in a more evolutionary perspective and warns against the tendency of imposing rational models on everything, including law. What Coase thinks of Weber's view of law and economy is not known. Hayek, however, sharply criticized Weber for ignoring the fact that law may emerge spontaneously and that it must not be reduced to something that can be consciously created and imposed: "For Weber [in *Economy and Society*] 'order' is throughout something which is 'valid' or 'binding,' which is to be enforced or contained in a maxim of law. In other words, order exists for him only as organization and the existence of a spontaneous order never becomes a problem." (See F. A. Hayek, p. 170 n. 50 in Vol. 2 of *Law, Legislation and Liberty* [London: Routledge and Kegan Paul, 1982]). Posner, finally, severely criticizes Weber for having a "useless methodology," by which he means that Weber indulges in too many broad historical predictions. "This is a style of prediction alien to most economists," according to Posner, who explains the difference between the economic approach and that of Weber in the following manner:

> Despite the leading role that "ideal types" play in his [Weber's] methodology, his game is not one of trying to control or predict the social or natural environment by isolating

causal relations. An economist who, utilizing the simplified psychology of "economic man," predicts that an increase in cigarette taxes will reduce the output of cigarettes is trying to identify a causal relation that can be manipulated to alter our social environment—for example, in the direction of reducing the amount of cigarette smoking. Weber's goal is different. He seeks to identify and describe grand themes in history, such as the growing disenchantment of the world as rational methods of social organization and endeavour increasingly replace irrational ones. His ideal types are stylized versions of the practices, institutions, and modes of thought that shape the grand themes. (Richard Posner, "The Sociology of the Sociology of Law: A View from Economics," *European Journal of Law and Economics* 2 [1995]: 267–68)

Weber no doubt would agree with Posner that for problems in theoretical economics, model building of the type that Posner talks about (using the imposition of a cigarette tax as his example) is appropriate. When it comes to more complex empirical phenomena, however, Weber and Posner part ways. Posner's perspective on these issues grows out of his suggestion that the judge, in the common-law tradition, acts to bring about a socially effective outcome. Weber, however, attempts to approach empirical problems concerning law and economics from the perspective of action that is driven by interests as well as oriented to the behavior of others.

14. When Marianne Weber and Melchior Palyi included this chapter in the edition of *Economy and Society* from 1922, they used the original title "Die Wirtschaft und die Ordnungen." In later editions the title was changed by Johannes Winkelmann to "Die Wirtschaft und die gesellschaftlichen Ordnungen in ihrer prinzipiellen Beziehung" (4th ed.; 1956) and to "Die Wirtschaft und die gesellschaftlichen Ordnungen" (5th ed.; 1972). According to Winkelmann, Weber wrote at the top of the original manuscript: "I. Die Wirtschaft und die Ordnungen." See Johannes Winkelmann, *Wirtschaft und Gesellschaft. Erläuterungsband* (Tübingen: J.C.B. Mohr, 1976), p. 55.

15. For this passage, see Weber, *Economy and Society,* pp. 29–31, 33–36, or *Wirtschaft und Gesellschaft,* pp. 14–16, 17–19. "An order will be called . . . *law* if it is externally guaranteed by the probability that physical or psychological coercion will be applied by a *staff* of people in order to bring about compliance or avenge violation" (p. 34 or p. 17).

16. See, e.g., Weber, "Diskussionsrede zu dem Vortrag von A. Voigt über 'Wirtschaft und Recht,'" p. 475 in *Gesammelte Aufsätze zur Soziologie und Sozialpolitik* (Tübingen: J.C.B. Mohr, 1988); Weber, *Critique of Stammler* (New York: Free Press, 1977), pp. 101–3, or "R. Stammlers 'Überwindung' der materialistischen Geschichtsauffassung," pp. 325–27 in *Gesammelte Aufsätze zur Wissenschaftslehre* (Tübingen: J.C.B. Mohr, 1988).

17. Weber, *Economy and Society,* p. 33, or *Wirtschaft und Gesellschaft,* p. 17; emphasis in the original.

18. "To the person who finds himself actually in possession of the power to control an object or a person the legal guaranty gives a specific certainty of the durability of such power. To the person to whom something has been promised the legal guaranty gives a higher degree of certainty that the promise will be kept. These are indeed the most elementary relationships between law and economic life." Weber, *Economy and Society,* p. 667, or *Wirtschaft und Gesellschaft,* p. 398.

19. Weber, *Economy and Society,* p. 67, or *Wirtschaft und Gesellschaft,* p. 33.

20. Weber, *Economy and Society,* p. 162, or *Wirtschaft und Gesellschaft,* pp. 94–95.

21. Weber, *Economy and Society,* p. 315, or *Wirtschaft und Gesellschaft,* p. 184. The

reader is reminded of Weber's statement: "To the person who finds himself actually in possession of the power to control an object or a person the legal guaranty gives a specific certainty of the durability of such power. To the person to whom something has been promised the legal guaranty gives a higher degree of certainty that the promise will be kept. These are indeed the most elementary relationships between law and economic life"; Weber, *Economy and Society*, p. 667, or *Wirtschaft und Gesellschaft*, p. 398.

22. Weber, *Economy and Society*, p. 328, or *Wirtschaft und Gesellschaft*, p. 193. Prefiguring to some extent the findings of Stewart Macaulay by several decades, Weber notes that "in most business transactions it never occurs to anyone even to think of taking legal action." See Stewart Macaulay, "Non-Contractual Relations in Business: A Preliminary Study," *American Sociological Review* 28 (1963): 55–67. There exists a huge literature following up on Macaulay's famous article; see especially Peter-Vincent Jones, "Contract and Business Transactions: A Socio-Legal Analysis," *Journal of Law and Society* 16 (1989): 166–86; and, from an economist's perspective, see Benjamin Klein, "Self-Enforcing Contracts," pp. 89–95 in Eirik Furubotn and Rudolf Richter, eds., *The New Institutional Economics* (Tübingen: J.C.B. Mohr, 1991).

23. Weber, *Economy and Society*, p. 331 or *Wirtschaft und Gesellschaft*, p. 194. According to Weber, people may follow the law for many reasons other than just the existence of the law; and he especially mentions utilitarian and ethical motives plus the fear of meeting with disapproval. See Weber, *Economy and Society*, p. 314, or *Wirtschaft und Gesellschaft*, p. 184.

24. Weber, *Economy and Society*, p. 327, or *Wirtschaft und Gesellschaft*, p. 192. Weber's argument on this point is similar to his notion that economic theory does not need to take psychology into account because it does not rest on a psychological foundation. Contemporary economic theory, it may be added, has in some cases moved beyond the point of disregarding the legal system.

25. Weber often debated Stammler and in general took his argument very seriously. Apart from his 1907 critique in *Archiv für Sozialwissenschaft und Sozialpolitik* (known as *Critique of Stammler*) and the section in "The Economy and Social Norms" (which has been given the title "*Excursus* in Response to Rudolf Stammler" in the English translation), there are, e.g., important references to Stammler in Part 1 of *Economy and Society* plus an incomplete draft of an article on Stammler that was found among Weber's effects (see pages 145–82 in *Critique of Stammler*). Stammler answers Weber's critique in the third edition of *Wirtschaft und Recht;* see Stammler, *Wirtschaft und Recht nach der materialistischen Geschichtsauffassung* (Jena: Gustav Fischer, 1914), pp. 670–73 n. 232. For a discussion of Weber's ideas and a defense of Stammler, see also Karl Diehl, "Einwendungen gegen die sozialrechtliche Theorie, besonders die Kritik von Max Weber," pp. 122–39 in *Die sozialrechtliche Richtung in der Nationalökonomie* (Jena: Gustav Fischer, 1941).

26. Weber, *Economy and Society*, pp. 333–37, or *Wirtschaft und Gesellschaft*, pp. 196–98.

27. Stammler's ideas came to constitute the foundation for the so-called School of Social Law in Germany, which held that society was constituted according to legal norms and that law had priority over the economy. Economist Karl Diehl (1864–1943) was a prominent member of this school; and Weber appreciated Diehl's work quite a bit, to judge from his statement in 1918 in connection with the appointment of a professor in economics at the University of Vienna. Weber, however, also felt that Diehl—following Stammler—did not properly separate the perspectives of jurisprudence and economics. See Weber, [Gutachten Max Webers an die Wiener Fakultät] (Merseburg: Deutsches

Zentralarchiv, unpublished document, 1918). For the School of Social Law, see, e.g., Diehl, *Die sozialrechtliche Richtung in der Nationalökonomie;* Harald Winkel, "Die sozialrechtliche Schule," pp. 181–87 in *Die deutsche Nationalökonomie im 19. Jahrhundert* (Darmstadt: Wissenschaftliche Buchgesellschaft, 1977).

28. Weber, *Economy and Society,* p. 882, or *Wirtschaft und Gesellschaft,* pp. 504–5.

29. For the quotation, see Weber, *Economy and Society,* p. 883, or *Wirtschaft und Gesellschaft,* p. 505. Weber uses the word "indirect" to describe the influence that economic conditions have on the evolution of law in a few places in *Economy and Society.* At one point he says that "general economic and social conditions" have only "indirectly" (*"indirekt"*) influenced the rationalization of law. He also notes that "the mode in which the current basic conceptions of the various fields of law have been differentiated from each other has depended largely upon factors of legal technique and of political organization. Economic factors can therefore be said to have had an indirect (*indirekt*) influence only"; see Weber, *Economy and Society,* pp. 776, 654–55, or *Wirtschaft und Gesellschaft,* pp. 456, 395.

30. See Weber, *Economy and Society,* p. 883, or *Wirtschaft und Gesellschaft,* p. 505; and for a stronger statement, see Weber, *The Religion of China* (Glencoe, Ill.: Free Press, 1951), p. 149, or "Konfuzianismus und Taoismus," pp. 437–38 in Vol. 1 of *Gesammelte Aufsätze zur Religionssoziologie* (Tübingen: J.C.B. Mohr, 1988). Weber's notion of "calculable law" is discussed later in this chapter.

31. Weber, *Economy and Society,* p. 687, or *Wirtschaft und Gesellschaft,* pp. 411–12. Weber speaks of "'legal inventions'" at another place in *Economy and Society,* and he similarly argues that industrial and entrepreneurial forms of organization have to be invented; see Weber, *Economy and Society,* pp. 200, 775, or *Wirtschaft und Gesellschaft,* pp. 118, 455.

32. Weber, *Economy and Society,* pp. 656–58, or *Wirtschaft und Gesellschaft,* pp. 396–97.

33. Regarding Mesopotamian law, Weber notes that "the oldest and relatively completely known code, which is in this respect the most unique of all those which have come down to us, i.e., the Code of Hammurabi, allows us to infer with some reasonable degree of certainty that there existed relatively strong commercial interests and that the king wished to strengthen the legal security of commerce for his own political and fiscal purposes." See Weber, *Economy and Society,* pp. 851–52, or *Wirtschaft und Gesellschaft,* p. 490; see also Weber, *The Agrarian Sociology of Ancient Civilizations* (London: New Left Books, 1976), p. 99, or "Agrarverhältnisse im Altertum," p. 58 in *Gesammelte Aufsätze zur Sozial- und Wirtschaftsgeschichte.*

34. The following section on Hindu law draws primarily on the following passages: Weber, *Economy and Society,* pp. 678, 790–92, 816–18, or *Wirtschaft und Gesellschaft,* pp. 405, 459–61, 472–73; Weber, *The Religion of India* (New York: Free Press, 1958), pp. 4, 52–53, 111–12, 143 ff., or "Hinduismus und Buddhismus," pp. 4, 54–55, 109–11, 141 ff. in Vol. 2 of *Gesammelte Aufsätze zur Religionssoziologie* (Tübingen: J.C.B. Mohr, 1988). Although I only discuss Hinduism, Weber also covers Jainism and Buddhism in *The Religion of India.*

35. Weber is here speaking about Hinduism, and the "law" he is referring to is a religious one ("ritual law" or *"Ritualgesetz"*). See Weber, *The Religion of India,* p. 112, or "Hinduismus und Buddhismus," p. 111.

36. The term Weber uses for "caste law" is *"Kastenrecht"*; see Weber, *Religion of India,* p. 111, or "Hinduismus und Buddhismus," p. 110. See also Weber, *Economy and Society,* p. 435, or *Wirtschaft und Gesellschaft,* p. 266.

250

37. The following section on Chinese law draws primarily on the following passages: Weber, *Economy and Society,* pp. 380, 726–27, 818, or *Wirtschaft und Gesellschaft,* pp. 229–30, 437, 473–74; Weber, *General Economic History,* pp. 342–43, or *Wirtschaftsgeschichte,* p. 293; Weber, *The Religion of China,* pp. 80–81, 101–2, 169, or "Konfuzianismus und Taoismus," pp. 368–70, 391–93, 457 in Vol. 1 of *Gesammelte Aufsätze zur Religionssoziologie.* For a critical evaluation of Weber's analysis of Chinese law, including the relationship between law and economy, see Karl Bünger, "Das chinesische Rechtssystem und das Prinzip der Rechtsstaatlichkeit," pp. 134–73 in Wolfgang Schluchter, ed., *Max Webers Studie über Konfuzianismus und Taoismus* (Frankfurt am Main: Suhrkamp, 1983).

38. Weber, *General Economic History,* pp. 342–43, or *Wirtschaftsgeschichte,* p. 293.

39. The following section on Islamic law draws primarily on the following passages: Weber, *Economy and Society,* pp. 790–92, 799–800, 818–22, 976, 1115, or *Wirtschaft und Gesellschaft,* pp. 459–61, 466, 474–76, 563, 657. For an interesting analysis of Weber's analysis of Islamic law, including the relationship between law and economy, see Patricia Crone, "Max Weber, das islamische Recht und die Entstehung des Kapitalismus," pp. 294–333 in Wolfgang Schluchter, ed., *Max Webers Sicht des Islams* (Frankfurt am Main: Suhrkamp, 1987). See also the chapter entitled "Weber, Law and Islam," pp. 107–21 in Bryan Turner, *Weber and Islam* (London: Routledge and Kegan Paul, 1974).

40. The most formal definition of *quadi* justice that can be found in Weber's work speaks of "informal judgments rendered in terms of concrete ethical or other practical valuations"; Weber also adds that *quadi* justice "knows no rational rules of decision." See Weber, *Economy and Society,* p. 976, or *Wirtschaft und Gesellschaft,* p. 563. The concept of *quadi* justice plays practically no role in the most complete analysis of Islamic law that can be found in Weber's work; and Weber also made a distinction between the *quadi* as a historical figure and *quadi* justice as a general concept. In general, Weber says, he used the expression of *quadi* in *quadi* justice "in the usual European sense." See Weber, *Economy and Society,* pp. 493, 818–22, 1115, or *Wirtschaft und Gesellschaft,* pp. 300, 474–76, 657; Weber, *The Religion of India,* p. 9, or "Hinduismus und Buddhismus," p. 12 in Vol. 2 of *Gesammelte Aufsätze zur Religionssoziologie.* For a recent description of the *quadi,* see chapter 4 in Noel Couldson, *Conflict and Tension in Islamic Jurisprudence* (Chicago: University of Chicago Press, 1969). Though Coulson's analysis of the *quadi* is made from a different perspective than that of Weber, it is by no means incompatible with Weber's interpretation.

41. Weber, "Parliament and Government in Germany under a New Political Order," p. 148 in *Political Writings* (Cambridge: Cambridge University Press, 1994), or "Parlament und Regierung im neugeordneten Deutschland," p. 323 in *Gesammelte Politische Schriften* (Tübingen: J.C.B. Mohr, 1988). It should be noted that Weber did not view Islamic law as a legal system dominated by *quadi* justice. Islamic law helped to obstruct the emergence of rational capitalism, as Weber saw it, but this was more because of the irrationality at the top of society than at the local level, where the *quadi* or religious judge was active.

42. The following section on Jewish law draws primarily on the following passages: Weber, *Economy and Society,* pp. 412–13, 615–23, 823–28, 1203, or *Wirtschaft und Gesellschaft,* pp. 253, 370–74, 477–80, 721; Weber, *Ancient Judaism* (New York: Free Press, 1952), pp. 61–89, or "Das antike Judentum," pp. 76–99 in Vol. 3 of *Gesammelte Aufsätze zur Religionssoziologie* (Tübingen: J.C.B. Mohr, 1988).

43. Weber, *Economy and Society,* p. 827, or *Wirtschaft und Gesellschaft,* p. 429. For a more affirmative statement on this point, see the same work, p. 613 or p. 368. For

Weber's analysis of Sombart, see *Economy and Society*, pp. 826, 1203, or *Wirtschaft und Gesellschaft*, pp. 479, 721. See especially the legal institutions discussed in chapter 6 of Werner Sombart, *The Jews and Modern Capitalism* (New Brunswick, N.J.: Transaction Books, [1911] 1982).

44. The following section on canon law draws primarily on *Economy and Society*, pp. 828–31, 1186, or *Wirtschaft und Gesellschaft*, pp. 480–82, 708.

45. Weber, *Economy and Society*, pp. 583–89, or *Wirtschaft und Gesellschaft*, pp. 352–55. "It is true that a formal suspension of the prohibition [of usury] was never decreed [by the Catholic Church], but in the course of the 19th century ecclesiastic depositions repeatedly recognized as legal the taking of interest under specified conditions"; Weber, *General Economic History*, pp. 270–71, or *Wirtschaftsgeschichte*, p. 237.

46. The following section on Roman law draws primarily on the following passages: Weber, *Economy and Society*, pp. 682, 686–88, 792–802, 849–55, 977–78, or *Wirtschaft und Gesellschaft*, pp. 408, 411–12, 461–67, 489–93, 563–64.

47. Weber, *Economy and Society*, pp. 683 (for the quotation), 709, or *Wirtschaft und Gesellschaft*, pp. 409 (for the quotation), 426. The translation of the quotation has been changed.

48. The following section on medieval law draws primarily on the following passages: Weber, *Economy and Society*, pp. 379, 688, 853–55, 1237–45, 1325, or *Wirtschaft und Gesellschaft*, pp. 229, 412, 491–93, 741–46, 789–90; Weber, *General Economic History*, pp. 204–6, 341–42, or *Wirtschaftsgeschichte*, pp. 182–84, 292.

49. Weber, *Economy and Society*, p. 855 or *Wirtschaft und Gesellschaft*, p. 493.

50. Weber, "Parliament and Government in Germany under a New Political Order," p. 149 n. A in *Political Writings*, or "Parlament und Regierung im neugeordneten Deutschland," p. 323 in *Gesammelte Politische Schriften*. Weber's statements about medieval law are otherwise scattered throughout his work, including *Economy and Society*. Weber's statement in "Parliament and Government" can be compared with the following statement from *General Economic History*:

> In fact all the characteristic institutions of modern capitalism have other origins than Roman law. The annuity bond, whether arising out of a personal debt or a war loan, came from medieval law, in which German legal ideas played their part. Similarly, the stock certificate arose out of medieval and modern law and was unknown to the law of antiquity. Likewise the bill of exchange, to the development of which Arabic, Italian, German, and English law contributed. The commercial company is also a medieval product; only the commenda enterprise was current in antiquity. So also the mortgage, with the security of registration, and the deed of trust, as well as the power of attorney, are medieval in origin and do not go back to antiquity. (Weber, *General Economic History*, pp. 341–42, or *Wirtschaftsgeschichte*, p. 292)

For an introduction to the commercial law of the Middle Ages, see, e.g., Harold Berman, "Mercantile Law," pp. 332–56 in *Law and Revolution* (Cambridge, Mass.: Harvard University Press, 1983).

51. The following section on natural law draws primarily on the following passages: Weber, *Economy and Society*, pp. 597–601, 865–80, 883, 1209–10, or *Wirtschaft und Gesellschaft*, pp. 360–62, 496–503, 505, 725–26; Weber, "Rede auf dem ersten Deutschen Soziologentage in Frankfurt 1910. Diskussionsrede zu E. Troeltschs Vortrag über 'Das stoisch-christliche Naturrecht,'" pp. 462–70 in *Gesammelte Aufsätze zur Soziologie und Sozialpolitik*; Weber, *The Religion of India*, pp. 143–46, or "Hinduismus und Buddhismus," pp. 141–46; Weber, *The Religion of China*, pp. 147–50, or "Konfuzianis-

mus und Taoismus," pp. 435–39; Weber, "On the Situation of Constitutional Democracy in Russia," pp. 69–70 in *Political Writings*, or "Zur Lage der bürgerlichen Demokratie in Russland," pp. 63–64 in *Gesammelte Politische Schriften*. According to Paul Honigsheim, Weber was fascinated by the history of natural law; Honigsheim also notes that "Weber's sociology of law makes contact with his sociology of economics." See Paul Honigsheim, *On Max Weber* (New York: Free Press, 1968), pp. 53, 112, 117.

52. Georg Jellinek (1851–1911) was a brilliant jurist whose pamphlet on the origin of the Rights of Man had inspired Weber to his famous thesis in *The Protestant Ethic*. Jellinek does not say much about the relationship between economy and law in *The Declaration of the Rights of Man and of Citizens* (1895), and neither does the secondary literature on Jellinek's work. One of Jellinek's points—that the British tradition of the rights of man empowers and singles out the individual in a very radical manner—is, however, of interest in this context. A work such as Charles Beard's *An Economic Interpretation of the Constitution of the United States* (1913) approaches the relationship between economy and law in the Rights of Man from a very different angle.

53. Weber, *Economy and Society*, p. 1209, or *Wirtschaft und Gesellschaft*, p. 726.

54. Weber, *Economy and Society*, p. 872, or *Wirtschaft und Gesellschaft*, p. 500.

55. Weber, *Religion of India*, p. 4, or "Hinduismus und Buddhismus," p. 4; *Economy and Society*, pp. 872–73, or *Wirtschaft und Gesellschaft*, p. 501.

56. "The dominance of law that has been stereotyped by religion constitutes one of the most significant limitations on the rationalization of the legal order and hence also on the rationalization of the economy"; see Weber, *Economy and Society*, p. 577, or *Wirtschaft und Gesellschaft*, p. 349. See also, for example, the discussion of hierocracy and law in the same works on page 1185, or page 708.

57. These three legal prerequisites are to some extent explicitly spelled out in Part 1 of *Economy and Society*. As earlier noted, for example, Weber argues in §31 that for there to be a maximum degree of formal rationality in capital accounting there has to be "substantive freedom of contract," "complete calculability of . . . the legal order," and "a reliable, purely formal guarantee of all contracts by the public authority." (See Weber, *Economy and Society*, p. 162, or *Wirtschaft und Gesellschaft*, p. 94.) Mostly, however, the three prerequisites remain implicit but are fully discussed elsewhere in Weber's work.

58. Weber, "Forms of Creation of Rights," pp. 666–752 in *Economy and Society*, or pp. 397–440 in *Wirtschaft und Gesellschaft*. See also Weber's discussion of the contract in the section on natural law; Weber, *Economy and Society*, pp. 865–80, or *Wirtschaft und Gesellschaft*, pp. 496–503. For Weber on the labor contract, see his 1902 review of Philipp Lotmar's *Der Arbeitsvertrag* in *Archiv für Sozialwissenschaft und Sozialpolitik*.

59. Weber, *Economy and Society*, pp. 671, 677, or *Wirtschaft und Gesellschaft*, pp. 401, 404.

60. Weber, *Economy and Society*, pp. 668, 683, or *Wirtschaft und Gesellschaft*, pp. 398, 409. The key passage on page 668 is difficult to penetrate, but its translation can be improved by referring to the concept of "power of control and disposal" (*"Verfügungsgewalt"*). This concept, to recall, plays an important role in Weber's economic sociology, as outlined in chapter 2 of *Economy and Society*.

61. Weber, *Economy and Society*, p. 673, or *Wirtschaft und Gesellschaft*, p. 402.

62. *"Kontraktgesellschaft"*; see Weber, *Economy and Society*, pp. 669, 691, or *Wirtschaft und Gesellschaft*, pp. 399, 414. One consequence of this fact was expressed in the following manner by Sir Henry Maine: "It is certain that the science of Political Economy . . . would fail to correspond with the facts of life if it were not true that Imperative Law had abandoned the largest part of the field it once occupied, and had left men to set-

tle rules of conduct for themselves with a liberty [through Contract] never allowed to them till recently"; Henry Maine, *Ancient Law* (London: Everyman's Library, [1861] 1977), p. 179.

63. Weber's analysis of the contract differs to a large extent from that of Emile Durkheim. One of these differences concerns how the history of the contract is portrayed. Alan Hunt notes—correctly in my opinion—that "his [Weber's] treatment of the evolution of contract is very markedly 'economic' and this constitutes the major difference between his treatment and Durkheim's who failed to situate his discussion in an economic content"; Alan Hunt, *The Sociological Movement in Law* (London: Macmillan, 1978), p. 128. For a critique of the tendency to reduce Weber's analysis of the contract to the relationship between the contract and capitalism, see Jean-Guy Belley, "Max Weber et la théorie du droit des contrats," *Droit et Société* 9 (1988): 281–99. Durkheim's analysis of the contract is primarily to be found in Emile Durkheim, *The Division of Labor in Society* (New York: Free Press, [1893] 1984), pp. 79–80, 158–64, and in the sections on the contract on pp. 171–220 in Durkheim, *Professional Ethics and Civic Morals* (Westport, Conn.: Greenwood Press, 1983).

64. Weber, *Economy and Society*, p. 674, or *Wirtschaft und Gesellschaft*, p. 403.

65. Weber, *Economy and Society*, p. 680, or *Wirtschaft und Gesellschaft*, pp. 406–7. Another example, which comes from Roman law during the first two centuries AD and which is told by Paul Veyne, is the following. Assume that someone breaks into your house, kills your slaves, and takes over your property. In order to be compensated, you would first have to seize the offender yourself, bring him to court, and get a positive verdict. You would not get your property back through the court, however; you would have to seize the offender's property yourself, sell it at an auction, and keep a sum that was equal to the value of your house. See Paul Veyne, "The Roman Empire," p. 166–67 in Vol. 1 of Paul Veyne ed., *A History of Private Life* (Cambridge, Mass.: Harvard University Press, 1987).

66. The author of this section, jurist Alexander Leist (1862–1918), died before he had completely finished his contribution to the *Grundriss* (which nonetheless was published in a patched-up version). Weber would presumably have adjusted his sociology of law to this fact when he rewrote it for the new version of *Economy and Society*. See Alexander Leist (ed. Hans Nipperdey), "Die moderne Privatrechtsordnung und der Kapitalismus," pp. 28–48 in Carl Brinkmann et al. eds., *Spezifische Elemente der modernen kapitalistischen Wirtschaft. Grundriss der Sozialökonomik. Abt. IV. I. Teil* (Tübingen: J.C.B. Mohr, 1925).

67. See Karl Marx, *Capital: A Critique of Political Economy* (New York: Modern Library, [1867] 1906), pp. 195–96. Marx associates the contract with the sphere of circulation ("there alone rule Freedom, Equality, Property and Bentham"), which he contrasts to the sphere of production, where surplus value is being produced. The parallels between Marx and Weber on this point have not been noticed by Marxist writers on law and capitalism; see, e.g., Michael Tigar, *Law and the Rise of Capitalism* (New York: Monthly Review Press, 1977).

68. Weber, *Economy and Society*, pp. 730–31 or *Wirtschaft und Gesellschaft*, p. 440.

69. Weber, *Economy and Society*, p. 730, or *Wirtschaft und Gesellschaft*, p. 440. The translation has been slightly changed.

70. Weber, *Economy and Society*, p. 707, or *Wirtschaft und Gesellschaft*, pp. 424–25.

71. For the former, see especially the section entitled "Associational Contracts—Juristic Personality," pp. 705–29 in *Economy and Society*, or pp. 423–39 in *Wirtschaft und Gesellschaft*. Weber's discussion of the firm's evolution as a more specific economic orga-

nization can be found in many places of his work; see especially the following: Weber, "The Disintegration of the Household: The Rise of the Calculative Spirit and the Modern Capitalist Enterprise," pp. 375–80 in *Economy and Society*, or pp. 226–30 in *Wirtschaft und Gesellschaft;* "Forms of Commercial Enterprise" and "The External Facts in the Evolution of Capitalism," pp. 223–29, 279–85 in *General Economic History*, or pp. 198–203, 240–46 in *Wirtschaftsgeschichte*.

72. Weber, *The Religion of India*, p. 52, or "Hinduismus und Buddhismus," p. 54.

73. Weber, *Economy and Society*, pp. 380, 726–27, or *Wirtschaft und Gesellschaft*, pp. 229–30, 437–38.

74. Weber at one point calls these corporations "state capitalist associations"; see Weber, *Economy and Society*, pp. 380, 687, or *Wirtschaft und Gesellschaft*, pp. 230, 411.

75. James Coleman sets 1243 as the symbolic birthdate for the concept of the organization or for the "fictitious person" (*"persona ficta"*); and he adds that "through the law of limited liability [the idea of a fictitious person] became the vehicle that created the modern corporation." See James Coleman, "The Rational Reconstruction of Society," *American Sociological Review* 58 (1993): 2. The person who invented the notion of "fictitious person" or "juristic personality" was an Italian jurist named Sinibald Fieschi (who lived from the end of the twelfth century to 1254), who later became Pope Innocent IV. See in this context Gierke's discussion of the discovery of the notion of *persona ficta,* which is the one that Coleman relies on, in Otto von Gierke, *Political Theories of the Middle Age* (Boston: Beacon Press, 1958), pp. xviii–xix.

76. Weber, *Economy and Society*, p. 379, or *Wirtschaft und Gesellschaft*, p. 229. In *General Economic History* the birth of separate corporate property is dated to early fourteenth-century Florence and the notion of *corpo della compagnia;* se Weber, *General Economic History*, p. 229, or *Wirtschaftsgeschichte*, p. 228.

77. *"Berechenbares Recht"*; see Weber, *Economy and Society*, pp. 847, 855, or *Wirtschaft und Gesellschaft*, pp. 487, 493; Weber, *General Economic History*, p. 277, or *Wirtschaftsgeschichte*, p. 240.

78. Weber, *Economy and Society*, p. 847, or *Wirtschaft und Gesellschaft*, p. 487. The emphasis in the text can be found in the original but not in the translation into English. Businessmen, Weber also says, typically develop a "rationalism of a more practical sort." See Weber, "The Social Psychology of World Religions," pp. 279, 284 in H. H. Gerth and C. Wright Mills, eds., *From Max Weber* (New York: Oxford University Press, 1946), or "Einleitung," pp. 251, 256 in Vol. 1 of *Gesammelte Aufsätze zur Religionssoziologie* (Tübingen: J.C.B. Mohr, 1988).

79. For Weber's use of the term "legal interests" (*"Rechtsinteresse"*), see *Economy and Society*, p. 814, or *Wirtschaft und Gesellschaft*, p. 471.

80. Weber, *Economy and Society*, p. 855, or *Wirtschaft und Gesellschaft*, p. 493. The translation has been slightly changed.

81. Trubek cites a working paper by a graduate student that highlights "the England Problem" and appeared the same year as Trubek's article: The main thesis in this paper is the following: "The hypothesis briefly stated is that in the absence of a systematic legal code rational capitalism will only develop in those systems where the legal order has been structurally or institutionally differentiated from the traditional or anti-modernist elements in the society. And further, this differentiated and autonomous legal system is available for capture and manipulation by the capitalist strata of the developing nation"; Jerold Guben, "'The England Problem' and the Theory of Economic Development" (Yale Law School, Program in Law and Modernization, Working Paper #9, 1972), pp. 1, 14. It may

be added that Max Rheinstein—many years before Trubek and Guben—pointed out that Weber was well aware that English law did not develop along the same lines as those of other countries, but that England nonetheless developed a rational form of capitalism. See Rheinstein, "Introduction," p. lviii in Weber, *On Law in Economy and Society.*

82. Trubek, "Max Weber on Law and the Rise of Capitalism," p. 746.

83. According to Trubek, Weber says that "England was unique in that it achieved capitalism 'not because but rather in spite of its judicial system.'" What Weber actually says is that "England achieved capitalistic supremacy among the nations not because but rather to some extent (*zum Teil*) in spite of its judicial system"; Weber, *Economy and Society,* p. 814, or *Wirtschaft und Gesellschaft,* p. 471. Weber's third argument, according to Trubek, why it had been possible to introduce capitalism into England, was that its legal system was "sufficiently calculable to support capitalism since judges were favorable to capitalism *and* adhered to precedent"; see Trubek, "Max Weber on Law and the Rise of Capitalism," pp. 747, 748.

84. See Hunt, *The Sociological Movement in Law,* pp. 122–28; Maureen Cain, "The Limits of Idealism: Max Weber and the Sociology of Law," *Research in Law and Sociology* 3 (1980): 70–76; Kronman, *Max Weber,* pp. 120–24; Bryan Turner, *For Weber* (London: Routledge and Kegan Paul, 1981), pp. 319–51; Hubert Treiber, "'Elective Affinities' between Weber's Sociology of Religion and Sociology of Law," *Theory and Society* 14 (1985): 839–47; Michel Coutu, "Les transformations du droit et l'emergence du capitalisme: Le problème anglais," *Les Cahiers du Droit* 33 (1992): 71–113; Sally Ewing, "Formal Justice and the Spirit of Capitalism: Max Weber's Sociology of Law," *Law and Society Review* 21 (1987): 487–512.

85. This is the argument of Bryan Turner, who on the whole follows Trubek's position. Turner also argues that England's legal backwardness was in fact an advantage when it came to the introduction of capitalism. See Turner, *For Weber,* pp. 329–30, 250–51.

86. E.g., Coutu, "Les transformations du droit," pp. 71–73. See in this context also Ewing's interesting argument that modern capitalism, according to Weber, needs a "formal rational administration of justice" rather than a logically formal kind of justice; Ewing, "Formal Justice and the Spirit of Capitalism," p. 487.

87. Weber, *The Religion of China,* p. 102, or "Konfuzianismus und Taoismus," p. 393; emphasis in the original text, but not in the English translation. Weber also notes elsewhere that English common law was calculable. See, e.g., Weber, "Parliament and Government in Germany under a New Political Order," p. 148 in *Political Writings,* or "Parlament und Regierung im neugeordneten Deutschland," p. 323 in *Gesammelte Politische Schriften;* Weber, *Economy and Society,* p. 787, or *Wirtschaft und Gesellschaft,* p. 457. Weber's statements about formal legal rationality creating the highest degree of calculability are often made in his discussion of formal and substantive rationalization. It is also clear that Weber espoused a theory of Western rationality that is close to a philosophy of history and of less relevance to his middle-range discussion of law and economy.

88. That Weber himself was well aware of this is clear from his references to Lord Mansfield (who was a key figure in introducing the law merchant into English common law) and from Levin Goldschmidt's discussion of this issue in *Handbuch des Handelsrechts.* See Levin Goldschmidt, *Handbuch des Handelsrechts* (Erlangen: Verlag von Ferdinand Enke, 1874), Vol. 1, pp. 265–69. For a contemporary discussion of the introduction of the law merchant into English law, see, e.g., J. H. Baker, "The Law Merchant and the Common Law before 1700," *Cambridge Law Journal* 38 (November 1979): 295–322; Bruce Carruthers, *City of Capital* (Princeton, N.J.: Princeton University Press, 1996), pp.

127–31; David Lieberman, "Property, Commerce, and the Common Law: Attitudes to Legal Change in the Eighteenth Century," pp. 144–58 in John Brewer and Susan Staves, eds., *Early Modern Conceptions of Property* (London: Routledge, 1995).

89. This is forcefully argued by Harold Berman and Charles Reid, "Max Weber as Legal Historian" (Emory University, unpublished paper, 1996), pp. 14–15. See also Harold Berman and Charles Reid, "The Transformation of English Legal Science: From Hale to Blackstone," *Emory Law Journal* 45 (1996): 437–522.

CHAPTER FIVE
THE ECONOMY AND RELIGION

1. Marianne Weber, *Max Weber: A Biography* (New York: John Wiley and Sons, 1975), p. 335; emphasis in the original. It can be added that even though Weber was always interested in religion he nonetheless considered himself "unmusical" in religious matters. See Weber's famous letter to Ferdinand Tönnies, dated February 19, 1909, in Weber, *Briefe 1909–1910. Max Weber Gesamtausgabe II/6* (Tübingen: J.C.B. Mohr, 1994), p. 65. It may also be noted that from early on Weber's interest in religion extended to its economic dimension. On this score Weber was possibly inspired by what Knies had to say about economy and religion in the course titled "Allgemeine Volkswirtschaftslehre (theoretische Nationalökonomie)" that Weber attended in the summer semester of 1883. For Knies on religion and economy, see Karl Knies, *Die politische Oekonomie vom geschichtlichen Standpunkte* (Leipzig: Hans Buske [1883] 1930), pp. 110–26.

2. It is not clear whether Weber had originally intended to include a section on religion in his contribution to the *Grundriss*, but in the outline from 1914 he had assigned himself the following topic: "Religious Communities: Religion as Conditioned by Class; Religions from Different Cultures and Economic Mentality." After Weber's death, a few hundred pages of writings on religion were found among his belongings, and it was decided that these had been written for the *Grundriss*. Today these can be found in *Economy and Society* in the form of two long chapters: "Religious Groups (The Sociology of Religion)" (part 2, chap. 6; 236 pp.) and "Political and Hierocratic Domination" (part 2, chap. 15; 54 pp.). For religion in the different versions of the *Grundriss,* see Johannes Winkelmann, *Max Webers hinterlassenes Hauptwerk* (Tübingen: J.C.B. Mohr, 1986), pp. 151, 169.

3. Friedrich Wilhelm Graf, who kindly answered my questions about this term, has told me that he is not sure when *Heilsgüter* (goods of salvation) was first used or by whom, but that it was mainly used in Lutheran and Calvinist theology from the late sixteenth and seventeenth centuries. "I suspect," Graf says, "Weber has taken the term from the works of Matthias Schneckenburger and Karl Bernhard Hundeshagen which he had read very carefully for his work on the protestant ethics" (letter to the author, October 7, 1996). The term is not used in today's theological discourse, at least not by Protestant theologians. For information on Schneckenburger and Hundeshagen, see Friedrich Wilhelm Graf, "The German Theological Sources and Protestant Church Politics," pp. 27–49 in Hartmut Lehmann and Guenther Roth, eds., *Weber's Protestant Ethic* (Cambridge: Cambridge University Press, 1993).

4. Parsons as well as Roth-Wittich translate *Heilsgüter* as "religious benefits," and according to Martin Risebrodt "the translation 'religious benefits' seems to express the meaning quite appropriately, although 'religious goods' would be possible too" (letter to the author, November 18, 1996). The term "religious benefits" is introduced in chapter

1 of *Economy and Society* ("§17. Political and Hierocratic Organizations"); see Weber, *Economy and Society: An Outline of Interpretive Sociology* (Berkeley: University of California Press, 1978), pp. 54–56, or *Wirtschaft und Gesellschaft. Grundriss der verstehenden Soziologie* (Tübingen: J.C.B. Mohr, 1972), pp. 29–30). The reader may recall that the term "goods" (*Güter*) is defined as part of "utility" in Weber's economic sociology, as presented in chapter 2 of *Economy and Society* and discussed in chapter 2 of this book. More precisely, Weber defines "economically oriented action" as a search for the "satisfaction of a desire for 'utilities' (*'Nutzleistungen'*)"—with "'utilities'" consisting of "services" as well as of "goods" (cf. Weber, *Economy and Society*, pp. 68–69, or *Wirtschaft und Gesellschaft*, pp. 34–35). While it can be discussed whether the notion of "religious benefits" constitutes *the* key concept in Weber's sociology of religion as a whole, I would argue that it represents an interesting point of departure for his analysis of the relationship between the economy and religion.

5. See, for example, Weber's statement in "The Protestant Sects and the Spirit of Capitalism" (1920) that "it is not the ethical *doctrine* of a religion, but that form of ethical conduct upon which *premiums* are placed that matters. Such premiums operate through the form and the condition of the respective goods of salvation (*Heilsgüter*)"; Weber, "The Protestant Sects and the Spirit of Capitalism," p. 321 in Hans Gerth and C. Wright Mills, eds., *From Max Weber* (New York: Oxford University Press, 1946), or "Die protestantischen Sekten und der Geist des Kapitalismus," pp. 234–35 in Vol. 1 of *Gesammelte Aufsätze zur Religionssoziologie* (Tübingen: J.C.B. Mohr, 1988).

6. See, e.g., Weber, *Economy and Society*, pp. 399–400, 527, or *Wirtschaft und Gesellschaft*, pp. 245, 320. See also Weber, "The Social Psychology of the World Religions," pp. 277–78 in Gerth and Mills, eds., *From Max Weber*, or "Einleitung," p. 249 in Vol. 1 of *Gesammelte Aufsätze zur Religionssoziologie;* Weber, *Ancient Judaism* (Glencoe, Ill.: Free Press, 1952), pp. 197–98, 233, 370, or "Antike Judenthum," pp. 211, 250, 385 in Vol. 3 of *Gesammelte Aufsätze zur Religionssoziologie*.

7. Weber, *Ancient Judaism*, p. 223, or "Antike Judenthum," p. 238 in Vol. 3 of *Gesammelte Aufsätze zur Religionssoziologie*.

8. Weber, *Economy and Society*, p. 406, or *Wirtschaft und Gesellschaft*, p. 249. Early religion, magic, and hierocracy, Weber says, typically lead to a "stereotyping" of the economy. See, e.g., Weber, *Economy and Society*, pp. 129–30, 151, 405–6, 577–79, 1185, or *Wirtschaft und Gesellschaft*, pp. 72–73, 87, 249, 348–49, 708; Weber, *General Economic History* (New Brunswick, N.J.: Transaction Books, 1981), pp. 123, 361, or *Wirtschaftsgeschichte* (Berlin: Duncker und Humblot), pp. 117, 308. A number of other phenomena—such as law, patrimonialism, and political capitalism—can also lead to a stereotyping of the economy; see, e.g., Weber, *Economy and Society*, pp. 199, 254, 759, 1038, or *Wirtschaft und Gesellschaft*, pp. 117, 148, 444, 602. According to Weber, "stereotyping" also means that decisions that are seen as *not* falling under its categories can be made arbitrarily. See, e.g., Weber, *Economy and Society*, pp. 1185–86, or *Wirtschaft und Gesellschaft*, p. 708.

9. The modern notion of a stereotype—as a preconceived and oversimplified notion of another person—comes from Walter Lippmann's *Public Opinion* (1922). I am grateful to Robert K. Merton for setting me straight on this issue.

10. Weber, *Economy and Society*, p. 424, or *Wirtschaft und Gesellschaft*, p. 259. Weber speculates that the need for benefits in the next world would initially have been especially strong among the wealthy: "In keeping with the law of marginal utility, a certain concern for one's destiny after death would generally arise when the most essential earthly needs have been met, and thus this concern is [originally] limited primarily to the

circles of the noble and the well-to-do"; see Weber, *Economy and Society*, p. 520, or *Wirtschaft und Gesellschaft*, p. 316.

11. For "impersonality," see, e.g., Gerth and Mills, eds., *From Max Weber*, p. 371; Weber, *Economy and Society*, pp. 584–85, 600, 1186–87, or *Wirtschaft und Gesellschaft*, pp. 353, 361, 708–9; Weber, "Religious Rejections of the World and Their Directions," p. 331 in Gerth and Mills, eds., *From Max Weber*, or "Zwischenbetrachtung," p. 544 in Vol. 1 of *Gesammelte Aufsätze zur Religionssoziologie*; Weber, *General Economic History*, pp. 357–58, or *Wirtschaftsgeschichte*, p. 305. Weber uses the term *Unpersönlichkeit* early on in his work, such as in his pamphlet on the stock exchange from 1894 to 1896. See, e.g., Weber, "Die Börse," pp. 267, 271 in *Gesammelte Aufsätze zur Soziologie und Sozialpolitik* (Tübingen: J.C.B. Mohr, 1988). Weber occasionally uses the term *Versachligung* as a complement to *Unpersönlichkeit*; see, e.g., Weber, *Economy and Society*, p. 585, or *Wirtschaft und Gesellschaft*, p. 353.

12. Weber, *Economy and Society*, pp. 581–85, or *Wirtschaft und Gesellschaft*, pp. 351–53. For charity, see, e.g., Weber, *Economy and Society*, pp. 579–83, or *Wirtschaft und Gesellschaft*, pp. 350–52; see also Weber, *The Religion of China* (Glencoe, Ill.: Free Press, 1951), pp. 209–10, or "Konfuzianismus und Taoismus," p. 495 in Vol. 1 of *Gesammelte Aufsätze zur Religionssoziologie*.

13. Weber, *Economy and Society*, p. 54, or *Wirtschaft und Gesellschaft*, p. 29. A "theocracy" is a hierocracy in which a high priest is the political ruler; "caesaropapism" is the belief that the priestly power is completely subordinate to the political power. See Weber, *Economy and Society*, pp. 1159–63, or *Wirtschaft und Gesellschaft*, pp. 689–92.

14. Weber, *Economy and Society*, p. 1186, or *Wirtschaft und Gesellschaft*, p. 708.

15. Weber discusses usury quite a bit, but less so the notion of a just price. See, e.g., Weber, *Economy and Society*, pp. 562–63, 583–89, 1188–90, or *Wirtschaft und Gesellschaft*, pp. 340, 352–55, 710–11; Weber, *General Economic History*, pp. 267–71, or *Wirtschaftsgeschichte*, pp. 234–37; Weber, *The Protestant Ethic and the Spirit of Capitalism* (London: Allen and Unwin, 1930), pp. 200–201, 203–4, or "Die protestantische Ethik," pp. 56–57 in Vol. 1 of *Gesammelte Aufsätze zur Religionssoziologie*. On usury, see, e.g., Benjamin Nelson, *The Idea of Usury: From Tribal Brotherhood to Universal Otherhood* (Chicago: University of Chicago Press, 1969). Raymond De Roover, an expert on medieval finance, has charged Weber and many other economic historians with idealizing the notion of the just price; and the modern consensus is apparently that religious medieval thought was much more favorable to the idea of free competition than was earlier thought. See, e.g., Gabriel Le Bras, "Conceptions of Economy and Society," p. 563 in Vol. 3 of *The Cambridge Economic History of Europe* (Cambridge: Cambridge University Press, 1963). According to De Roover, Weber and many other economic historians closely followed Roscher's 1874 account of the theories of Henry of Langenstein the Elder (1325–1397) in their view of the just price. According to Langenstein, the producer could set his own price when the authorities failed to set a fair price, but he must not exceed what was needed to maintain his own and his family's normal lifestyle. But the ideas of Langenstein were exceptions rather than the rule during the Middle Ages, according to De Roover, and most medieval scholastic doctors simply equated the just price with the market price (with one exception: when the market failed, the authorities had the duty to step in and regulate the price). See Raymond De Roover, "Economic Thought, I: Ancient and Medieval Thought," p. 433 in Vol. 4 of David L. Sills, ed., *International Encyclopaedia of the Social Sciences* (New York: Macmillan, 1968); see also Raymond De Roover, "The Concept of the Just Price: Theory and Economic Policy," *Journal of Economic History* 18 (1958): 418–38.

16. Weber, *Economy and Society*, p. 1190, or *Wirtschaft und Gesellschaft*, pp. 711–12.

17. One of the few commentators on Weber's work who has studied this issue, Stephen A. Kent, notes that the Quakers' policy on fixed prices was indeed based on their opinion that the seed of God existed in each and every person and that all customers should therefore be treated alike. He also cites a publication from 1655 by a Quaker who notes that "his business suffered from his refusal either to haggle with customers or to show them 'civil respect' by removing his hat and bowing to them when they entered his shop." See Stephen A. Kent, "The Quaker Ethic and the Fixed Price Policy: Max Weber and Beyond," *Sociological Inquiry* 53 (1983): 19; see in this context also Balwant Nevaskar, "Economic Ethic of Quakers," pp. 118–38 in *Capitalists without Capitalism* (Westport, Conn.: Greenwood, 1971). For Weber on sects, see "'Churches' and 'Sects' in North America: An Ecclesiastical Socio-Political Sketch," *Sociological Theory* 3 (Spring 1985): 7–13, or "'Kirchen' und 'Sekten' in Nordamerika," *Die christliche Welt* 20 (1906): 558–62 (which in its turn was a somewhat revised version of "'Kirchen' und 'Sekten,'" *Frankfurter Zeitung*, April 13 and 15, 1906); Weber, "The Protestant Sects and the Spirit of Capitalism," pp. 302–22 in Gerth and Mills, eds., *From Max Weber*, or "Die protestantische Sekten und der Geist des Kapitalismus," pp. 207–36 in Vol. 1 of *Gesammelte Aufsätze zur Religionssoziologie*.

18. For the monastic orders, see Weber, *Economy and Society*, pp. 1166–70, or *Wirtschaft und Gesellschaft*, pp. 694–97.

19. Weber, *Economy and Society*, p. 1169, or *Wirtschaft und Gesellschaft*, p. 696; see also Weber, *General Economic History*, pp. 364–65, or *Wirtschaftsgeschichte*, p. 311 (where Weber emphasizes asceticism—not religious enthusiasm—as the driving force behind the Tibetan achievements).

20. See, e.g., Weber, *Economy and Society*, pp. 483, 491–92, or *Wirtschaft und Gesellschaft*, pp. 294, 299–300. For the terms "theodicy of good fortune" and "theodicy of suffering," see Weber, "The Social Psychology of the World Religions," pp. 271, 273 in Gerth and Mills, eds., *From Max Weber*, or "Einleitung," pp. 242, 244 in Vol. 1 of *Gesammelte Aufsätze zur Religionssoziologie*. Weber's discussion of the relationship of privileged and nonprivileged groups to religion may well have its roots in Nietzsche's work, such as *The Genealogy of Morals* (1887). I am gratfeul to Ralph Schroeder for pointing this out to me.

21. Weber, *Economy and Society*, p. 491, or *Wirtschaft und Gesellschaft*, p. 299.

22. In his debate at the German Sociological Society in 1910 Weber said, for example, "We should not yield to the opinion . . . that one might view religious developments as a reflex of something else, of some economic situation. In my opinion this is unconditionally not the case." See Weber, "Max Weber on Church, Sect, and Mysticism," *Sociological Analysis* 34 (1973): 143.

23. "The nature of a stratum's religiosity has nowhere been solely determined by economic conditions"; Weber, *The Religion of China*, p. 196, or "Konfuzianismus und Taoismus," pp. 480–81 in Vol. 1 of *Gesammelte Aufsätze zur Religionssoziologie*.

24. For the religious propensity of these two groups, see Weber, *Economy and Society*, pp. 476–77, 484–86, or *Wirtschaft und Gesellschaft*, pp. 290–91, 295–96; Weber, "The Social Psychology of the World Religions," p. 283 in Gerth and Mills, eds., *From Max Weber*, or "Einleitung," p. 255 in Vol. 1 of *Gesammelte Aufsätze zur Religionssoziologie*.

25. Weber, *Economy and Society*, p. 528, or *Wirtschaft und Gesellschaft*, p. 321.

26. "The psychological effect of the confessional was everywhere to relieve the individual of responsibility for his own conduct, that is why it was sought, and that weakened

the rigorous consistency of the demands of asceticism"; Weber, *The Protestant Ethic,* p. 250 n. 149, or "Die protestantische Ethik und der Geist des Kapitalismus," p. 144 n. 1 in Vol. 1 of *Gesammelte Aufsätze zur Religionssoziologie.* In making this argument Weber subscribes to a psychological theory according to which a believer will change his or her behavior only if there is no other way out. He similarly points out that Egyptian religion failed to affect the behavior of its believers by allowing people to have a scarabee placed on their bodies when they were buried, thereby tricking the gods into believing that they had committed no sins. See Weber, *Ancient Judaism,* pp. 144, 199, 249, or "Antike Judenthum," pp. 156, 213, 265 in Vol. 3 of *Gesammelte Aufsätze zur Religionssoziologie.*

27. That Weber first lectured on the main thesis of *The Protestant Ethic* in 1898 is important because it is often argued that Weber got his ideas on this score from Werner Sombart's *Der moderne Kapitalismus* (1902). According to an authority on Weber's sociology of religion, "there are at present no legitimate grounds for doubting this [that in 1898 Weber lectured on the main thesis of *The Protestant Ethic*]." See Friedrich Wilhelm Graf, "Friendship between Experts: Notes on Weber and Troeltsch," p. 223 in W. J. Mommsen and Jürgen Osterhammel, eds., *Max Weber and His Contemporaries* (London: Unwin Hyman, 1987). For Weber's own assertion of having lectured on the main thesis in *The Protestant Ethic* in 1898, see "Antikritisches zum 'Geist' des Kapitalismus," p. 150 in Max Weber, *Die protestantische Ethik II* (Gütersloh: Gütersloher Verlagshaus Mohn, 1978). A much more important source of inspiration than *Der moderne Kapitalismus* was a small work by Weber's friend and colleague Georg Jellinek, who argued that human rights had their origin in Puritan ideas and not in political thought. See Georg Jellinek, *The Declaration of the Rights of Man and of Citizens* (New York: Henry Holt, [1895] 1901). For different views of the relationship of Weber to Sombart as it concerns *The Protestant Ethic,* see Michael Appel, *Werner Sombart* (Marburg: Metropolis Verlag, 1992), pp. 121–27; Hartmut Lehmann, "The Rise of Capitalism: Weber versus Sombart," pp. 195–208 in Lehmann and Roth, eds., *Weber's Protestant Ethic;* and Friedrich Lenger, *Werner Sombart 1863–1941* (Munich: C. H. Beck, 1994), pp. 129–35.

28. As part of his argument Weber also discusses the educational achievements of Catholic and Protestant students, in the course of which he cites some figures that contain a numerical error, as pointed out by Kurt Samuelsson. Weber uses a study by Martin Offenbacher, and "through a typographical or arithmetical error, Offenbacher . . . made the proportion of Protestants in the *Realgymnasien* 69% instead of 59%; Weber later took over and used this incorrect figure [in the table on page 189 in *The Protestant Ethic*]." See Kurt Samuelsson, *Religion and Economic Action* (London: Heinemann, 1961), p. 140.

29. Weber, *The Protestant Ethic,* pp. 39–40 n. 20, p. 191, or "Die protestantische Ethik," pp. 22–23, 27–28 n. 3 in Vol. 1 of *Gesammelte Aufsätze zur Religionssoziologie.* Weber argues (1) that politically excluded minorities tend to compensate by advancing in the economic sphere (e.g., the Huguenots in France or the Jews in all countries); and (2) that migrant workers typically break with their earlier traditionalism when they begin to work in different surroundings.

30. Weber, *The Protestant Ethic,* p. 64, or "Die protestantische Ethik," p. 49 in Vol. 1 of *Gesammelte Aufsätze zur Religionssoziologie.* The German original reads: "*Geist des (modernen) Kapitalismus.*"

31. Quoted in Weber, *The Protestant Ethic,* pp. 50, 49, 53, or "Die protestantische Ethik," pp. 32, 31, 36 in Vol. 1 of *Gesammelte Aufsätze zur Religionssoziologie.* The exclamation mark was added by Weber. For the correct wording of the quotation about "a Man diligent in his Calling," see Benjamin Franklin, *The Autobiography of Benjamin Franklin* (New Haven, Conn.: Yale University Press, 1964), p. 144.

32. The German term for "the instinct of acquisition" or "impulse to acquisition" is *Erwerbstrieb,* and it was used, for example, by Schmoller in *Grundriss der Allgemeinen Volkswirtschaftslehre* (1900–1904) and by Sombart in *Der moderne Kapitalismus* (1902). Both Schmoller and Sombart were critical of using this concept biologically, as some economists did, and insisted that the *Erwerbstrieb* changed with social and historical circumstances. According to Weber, writing in the mid-1910s on *Economy and Society,* *Erwerbstrieb* was nonetheless "a concept . . . which is wholly imprecise and better not used at all"; see Weber, *Economy and Society,* pp. 1190–91, or *Wirtschaft und Gesellschaft,* p. 712. Weber also directs harsh criticism at the idea that the instinct of acquisition had led to the creation of capitalism ("it should be taught in the kindergarten of cultural history that this naive idea of capitalism must be given up once and for all"; Weber, *The Protestant Ethic,* p. 17, or "Vorbemerkung," p. 4 in Vol. 1 of *Gesammelte Aufsätze zur Religionssoziologie*). Nonetheless, Weber occasionally uses the term himself, roughly in the sense of a biological impulse or drive that can be formed by the resistance it meets in a personality (see Weber, *Economy and Society,* pp. 617–18, or *Wirtschaft und Gesellschaft,* p. 371; Weber, *General Economic History,* p. 356, or *Wirtschaftsgeschichte,* p. 303). I have been unable to trace the history of the concept of *Erwerbstrieb.* One possible origin may have been German psychology, another Adam Smith's famous quip about "the propensity" or "the disposition" to "truck, barter, and exchange" in *The Wealth of Nations.* See Gustav von Schmoller, "Der Erwerbstrieb und die wirtschaftlichen Tugenden," pp. 33–41 in Vol. 1 of *Grundriss der Allgemeinen Volkswirtschaftslehre* (Leipzig: Duncker und Humblot, 1900); Werner Sombart, "Das Erwachsen des kapitalistischen Geistes," pp. 378–90 in Vol. 1 of *Der moderne Kapitalismus* (Leipzig: Duncker und Humblot, 1902); and Adam Smith, *An Inquiry into the Nature and Causes of the Wealth of Nations* (Oxford: Oxford University Press, 1976), pp. 25, 30.

33. Weber, *The Protestant Ethic,* p. 58, or "Die protestantische Ethik," p. 43 in Vol. 1 of *Gesammelte Aufsätze zur Religionssoziologie.* See also *The Protestant Ethic,* pp. 69, 76, or "Die protestantische Ethik," pp. 53–54, 61.

34. Weber used the concept of adventurers' capitalism in the early 1900s, when *The Protestant Ethic* was published, but also some ten or fifteen years later, around the time that he wrote chapter 2 of *Economy and Society.* See Weber, *The Protestant Ethic,* pp. 20, 25, or "Vorbemerkung," pp. 7, 11 in Vol. 1 of *Gesammelte Aufsätze zur Religionssoziologie;* Weber, "Parliament and Government in Germany under a New Political Order," p. 148 in *Political Writings,* or "Parlament und Regierung im neugeordneten Deutschland," p. 323 in *Gesammelte Politische Schriften* (Tübingen: J.C.B. Mohr, 1988). For Weber's typology of capitalism in §31 in chapter 2, see Weber, *Economy and Society,* pp. 164–66, or *Wirtschaft und Gesellschaft,* pp. 95–97.

35. Weber alternatively uses the term "traditionalism." See, e.g., Weber, *The Protestant Ethic,* pp. 58–60, 65, or "Die protestantische Ethik," pp. 43–44, 50 in Vol. 1 of *Gesammelte Aufsätze zur Religionssoziologie.*

36. Weber, *The Protestant Ethic,* pp. 64, 67, or "Die protestantische Ethik," pp. 50, 51 in Vol. 1 of *Gesammelte Aufsätze zur Religionssoziologie.*

37. In his famous description of what drives the entrepreneur, Schumpeter mentions "the dream and the will to found a private kingdom, . . . the will to conquer, [and] finally, there is the joy of creating, of getting things done or simply of exercising one's energy and ingenuity." Schumpeter also states that being an entrepreneur cannot be a "vocation" because it is not of a routine character. To this should be added that although Schumpeter is talking about the entrepreneur in a modern capitalist system in general, Weber is discussing the entrepreneur in the transition to such a system. See Joseph A. Schumpeter,

The Theory of Economic Development (Cambridge, Mass.: Harvard University Press, 1934), pp. 77, 92–94. Schumpeter's work on the entrepreneur, *Theorie der wirtschaft-ichen Entwicklung,* appeared a few years after *The Protestant Ethic* (1904–5) in 1911; Weber's personal, annotated copy of Schumpeter's work still exists.

38. Weber, *The Protestant Ethic,* p. 91, or "Das protestantische Ethik," p. 83 in Vol. 1 of *Gesammelte Aufsätze zur Religionssoziologie.* The German term for "formation" is *Prägung;* emphasis added.

39. In the first version of *The Protestant Ethic,* Weber mainly relied on the concept of "psychological impulses" (*"psychologische Antriebe"*; translated by Parsons as "religious sanctions"); in the revised edition he also used the concept of "psychological premiums" (*"psychologische Prämien"*). Around the same time that he revised *The Protestant Ethic,* Weber summarized his approach in this study in the following manner: "It is not the eth-ical *doctrine* of a religion that matters, but that form of ethical conduct upon which *pre-miums* are placed." See Weber, "The Protestant Sects and the Spirit of Capitalism," p. 321 in Gerth and Mills, eds., *From Max Weber,* or "Die protestantischen Sekten und der Geist des Kapitalismus," pp. 234–35 in Vol. 1 of *Gesammelte Aufsätze zur Religionssozi-ologie.* It may be added that Weber devised his own terminology with concepts such as "psychological impulses" because he did not think that there existed adequate terms in the psychology of his day.

40. Weber, *The Protestant Ethic,* p. 155, or "Die protestantische Ethik," p. 163 in Vol. 1 of *Gesammelte Aufsätze zur Religionssoziologie.*

41. Weber, *The Protestant Ethic,* p. 162, or "Die protestantische Ethik," pp. 175–76 in Vol. 1 of *Gesammelte Aufsätze zur Religionssoziologie.* The translation has been changed.

42. Weber, *The Protestant Ethic,* pp. 176–77, or "Die protestantische Ethik," pp. 198–99 in Vol. 1 of *Gesammelte Aufsätze zur Religionssoziologie.* The translation has been changed.

43. In this context see also the following statement by Weber from a few years later:

We want to reiterate as clearly as possible that, as far as the modern industrial work-force is concerned, religion as such no longer creates differences in the way in which this seems to have been true for the bourgeoisie in the era of early capitalism. Rather, the intensity of religious influence, whether Catholic or Protestant, on conduct is im-portant. Contemporary Catholicism, which differs so much in its thrust from medieval Catholicism, is today as useful a means of domestication as any kind of 'Protestant as-ceticism.' (Max Weber "Zur Psychophysik der industriellen Arbeit," pp. 239–40 n. 1 in *Gesammelte Aufsätze zur Soziologie und Sozialpolitik.* The translation is from Guen-ther Roth, "Global Capitalism and Multiethnicity: Max Weber Then and Now," un-published paper, p. 9.)

44. In being asked by Benjamin Nelson in the mid-1970s why he had chosen to trans-late *"ein stahlhartes Gehäuse"* in *The Protestant Ethic* (1930) as "iron cage"—a term that has become very famous—Parsons gave the following answer:

I cannot remember clearly just how and why I decided when more than 35 years ago I was translating Weber's *Protestant Ethic* essay to introduce the phrase 'iron cage' . . . I think 'iron cage' was a case of rather free translation. I do not remember being aware at the time of the use of the phrase by John Bunyan. However, as you know, I was brought up deeply steeped in a puritan background, and whether or not I intention-ally adopted the term from Bunyan seems to me probably secondary. The most likely explanation of my choice is that I thought it appropriate to the puritan background of Weber's own personal engagement in the Puritan Ethic problem.

See the letter by Talcott Parsons to Benjamin Nelson, dated January 24, 1975, in the Harvard University Archives (HUG[FP]42.8.8, Box 10); Weber, *The Protestant Ethic,* p. 181, or "Die protestantische Ethik," p. 203 in Vol. 1 of *Gesammelte Aufsätze zur Religionssoziologie.* For Parsons's translation of *The Protestant Ethic,* see also Peter Ghosh, "Some Problems with Talcott Parsons' Translation of 'The Protestant Ethic,'" *Archives Européennes de Sociologie* 30 (1994): 104–23.

45. Weber, *The Protestant Ethic,* p. 182, or "Die protestantische Ethik," p. 204 in Vol. 1 of *Gesammelte Aufsätze zur Religionssoziologie.*

46. In this context see also the evocative remarks that Weber made at the 1910 meeting of the German Sociological Society: "Max Weber on Church, Sect, and Mysticism," *Sociological Analysis* 34 (1973): 140–49. In general, the influence of ascetic Protestantism on U.S. society has been surprisingly neglected in social science; for an exception, see Seymour Martin Lipset's work, e.g., "Culture and Economic Behavior: A Commentary," *Journal of Labor Economics* 11 (1993): S330–47; and Seymour Martin Lipset, *American Exceptionalism: A Double-Edged Sword* (New York: W. W. Norton, 1996).

47. Two additional places are Weber's contribution to the debate surrounding *The Protestant Ethic* (discussed later in this chapter) and the section in *Economy and Society* entitled "The Reformation and Its Impact on Economic Life." See Weber, *Economy and Society,* pp. 1196–1200, or *Wirtschaft und Gesellschaft,* pp. 716–17.

48. Parsons uses the term "double ethic" (for "*Aussenmoral*") in *The Protestant Ethic;* see Weber, *The Protestant Ethic,* p. 57, or "Die protestantische Ethik," p. 43 in Vol. 1 of *Gesammelte Aufsätze zur Religionssoziologie.*

49. A recent article in the *Economist* said, for example: "Perhaps the oldest school [in culture and the economy] holds that cultural values and norms equip people—and, by extension, countries—either poorly or well for economic success. The archetypal modern pronouncement of this view was Max Weber's investigation of the Protestant work ethic"; "Cultural Explanations," *Economist,* November 9, 1996, p. 26.

50. Barrington Moore, Jr., *Injustice: The Social Bases of Obedience and Revolt* (White Plains, N.Y.: M. E. Sharpe, 1978), p. 466 n. 7. Barrington Moore is referring to Weber's thesis about the origin of the work ethic.

51. I have been unable to find a single full analysis by an economist of Weber's argument in *The Protestant Ethic.* One reason for this is probably that economic theory does not address questions of this type; or, to cite Nicholas Kaldor, "economic speculation [that is, economic theory] here trespasses on the fields of sociology and social history; and the most that an economist can say is that there is nothing in economic analysis as such which would dispute the important connection, emphasised by economic historians and sociologists, between the rise of Protestant ethic and the rise of Capitalism"; Nicholas Kaldor, "The Relation of Economic Growth and Cyclical Fluctuations," *Economic Journal* 64 (1954): 67. There exist, however, some minor references to Weber's thesis in works by such well-known economists as Kenneth Boulding (positive), Albert O. Hirschman (positive), Paul Samuelson (negative), Joseph Schumpeter (negative), and Jacob Viner (negative). See Kenneth Boulding, "Religious Foundations of Economic Progress," *Public Affairs* 14 (1952): 3; Albert O. Hirschman, *The Passions and the Interests* (Princeton, N.J.: Princeton University Press, 1977), pp. 9–12; Gaston Rimlinger, "Review of Jacob Viner, *Religious Thought and Economic Society,*" *Journal of Economic History* 39 (1979): 834; Paul Samuelson, *Economics* (New York: McGraw-Hill, 1970), p. 747; and Jacob

Viner, *Religious Thought and Economic Society: Four Chapters of an Unfinished Work* (Durham, N.C.: Duke University Press, 1978). Schumpeter's critique of *The Protestant Ethic* is worth citing:

> Some economists, among whom it must suffice to mention Max Weber, have felt the need of explaining the rise of capitalism by means of a special theory. But the problem such theories have been framed to solve is wholly imaginary and owes its existence to the habit of painting unrealistic pictures of a purely feudal and a purely capitalist society, which then raises the question what it was that turned the tradition-bound individual of the one into the alert profit hunter of the other. According to Weber, it was the religious revolution that, changing humanity's attitude toward life, produced a new spirit congenial to capitalist activity. We cannot go into the historical objections that may be raised against this theory. It is more important that the reader should realize that there is no problem. (Schumpeter, "Capitalism," p. 191 in *Essays* [New Brunswick, N.J.: Transaction Books, 1989])

For a similar statement by Schumpeter, see Vol. 1, p. 228 of *Business Cycles* (New York: McGraw-Hill, 1939). A number of contemporary economists—including Kenneth Arrow, Amartya Sen, Albert O. Hirschman, and Robert Solow—also discuss their relationship to Weber in Richard Swedberg, *Economics and Sociology* (Princeton, N.J.: Princeton University Press, 1990). Recently a few articles in mainstream economic journals have argued that Weber's idea of a capitalist spirit is a useful antidote to the current notion in economic theory that wealth is only as valuable as its implied consumption. See, e.g., Gurdip S. Bakshi and Zhiwu Chen, "The Spirit of Capitalism and Stock-Market Prices," *American Economic Review* 86 (1996): 133–57; and Heng-fu Zou, "'The Spirit of Capitalism' and Long-Run Growth," *European Journal of Political Economy* 10 (1994): 279–93. For an attempt to model the work ethic, see Roger Congleton, "The Economic Role of a Work Ethic," *Journal of Economic Behavior and Organization* 15 (1991): 365–85. The general attitude of economists toward Weber is also discussed in section IV of the appendix, entitled "Weber's Work in Economics as Seen by Economists, Economic Historians, and Sociologists."

52. Weber, "Kritische Bemerkungen zu den vorstehenden 'Kritischen Beiträgen,'" pp. 29–31 in *Die protestantische Ethik II*. The Calvinist Afrikaners, for example, failed for a long time to develop a thriving capitalism. See, e.g., Francis Fukuyama, *Trust* (London: Penguin Books, 1995), p. 44.

53. Weber, "Kritische Bemerkungen zu den vorstehenden 'Kritischen Beiträgen,'" p. 28, in *Die protestantische Ethik II*.

54. Weber, "Kritische Bemerkungen zu den vorstehenden 'Kritischen Beiträgen,'" pp. 30, 32 in *Die protestantische Ethik II*. Jacob Fugger II, also called Jacob the Rich, was the leading figure in a banking and mercantile family that dominated Europe in the fifteenth and sixteenth centuries. For a good study of the Fuggers, which appeared in 1896 and with which Weber no doubt was familiar, see Richard Ehrenberg, *Capital and Finance in the Age of the Renaissance: A Study of the Fuggers and Their Connections* (Fairfield, N.J.: A. M. Kelley, 1985).

55. Weber, "Bemerkungen zu den vorstehenden 'Replik,'" p. 55 in *Die protestantische Ethik II*. Sombart had argued in *Der moderne Kapitalismus* (1902) that "the capitalist spirit" constituted "an organizational unity" of "economic rationalism" and "the instinct of acquisition." See Sombart, *Der moderne Kapitalismus*, Vol. 1, p. 391.

56. There is no current, thorough analysis of the debate on *The Protestant Ethic*. For a good introduction to the debate, however, see Gordon Marshall, *In Search of the Spirit*

of Capitalism: An Essay on Max Weber's Protestant Ethic Thesis (London: Hutchinson, 1982). For an attempt to see how *The Protestant Ethic* has fared in sociology as well as in other social sciences, see the chapter devoted to *The Protestant Ethic* in Peter Hamilton, *The Social Misconstruction of Reality* (New Haven, Conn.: Yale University Press, 1996). Two good collections of texts (which, however, do not cover the developments since the early 1970s) are Philippe Besnard, ed., *Protestantisme et capitalisme. La controverse post-weberiènne* (Paris: Colin, 1970); and Robert W. Green, ed., *Protestantism, Capitalism, and Social Science: The Weber Thesis Controversy* (Lexington, Mass.: D. C. Heath, 1973). Stephen Kalberg has also recently surveyed the way *The Protestant Ethic* has fared in the U.S. debate among sociologists; see Stephen Kalberg, "On the Neglect of Weber's *Protestant Ethic* as a Theoretical Treatise: Demarcating the Parameters of Postwar American Sociological Theory," *Sociological Theory* 14 (1996): 49–70. For some recent interesting contributions to the religious side of the argument in *The Protestant Ethic*, see, e.g., the articles by Friedrich Wilhelm Graf, Kaspar von Greyerz, and Malcolm MacKinnon in Lehmann and Roth, eds., *Weber's Protestant Ethic*. Richard Hamilton also discusses the way Protestant theologians have viewed Weber's work in *The Social Misconstruction of Reality*. Unfortunately there is not enough space to mention the most important contributions to the debate of *The Protestant Ethic* or to comment on the neglected but important discussion of a Weber-derived *problematique*—namely, the structure and nature of the work ethic in Western countries and elsewhere. For two of the most interesting contributions to the post–World War II debate on *The Protestant Ethic*, see Christopher Hill, "Protestantism and the Rise of Capitalism," pp. 15–39 in F. J. Fisher, ed., *Essays in the Economic and Social History of Tudor and Stuart England* (Cambridge: Cambridge University Press, 1961); and Michael Walzer, "Puritanism as a Revolutionary Ideology," *History and Theory* 3 (1964): 59–90. For the debate on the work ethic, see, e.g., Fukuyama, *Trust*, pp. 43–8; Adrian Furnham, "The Protestant Work Ethic and Attitudes towards Unemployment," *Journal of Occupational Psychology* 55 (1982): 277–85; Ronald Inglehart, *Culture Shift* (Princeton, N.J.: Princeton University Press, 1990); Seymour Martin Lipset, "The Work Ethic, Then and Now," *Journal of Labor Research* 13 (1992): 45–54; Daniel Yankelovich and John Immerwahr, "The Work Ethic and Economic Vitality," pp. 144–70 in Michael Wachter and Susan Wachter, eds., *Removing Obstacles to Economic Growth* (Philadelphia: University of Pennsylvania Press, 1984); Daniel Yankelovich et al., *The World at Work* (New York: Octagon Books, 1985).

57. See James Coleman, "Social Theory, Social Research, and a Theory of Action," *American Journal of Sociology* 91 (1986): 1309–35; see also James Coleman, *Foundations of Social Theory* (Cambridge, Mass.: Harvard University Press, 1990), pp. 1–23.

58. Weber uses the term "lifestyle" ("*Lebensstil*," "*Lebensführung*") explicitly. See Weber, *The Protestant Ethic*, pp. 52, 55, 58, or "Die protestantische Ethik," pp. 33, 37, 43 in Vol. 1 of *Gesammelte Aufsätze zur Religionssoziologie*. I discuss Coleman's interpretation of Weber at some length in "Analyzing the Economy: On the Contribution of James S. Coleman," pp. 313–28 in Jon Clark, ed., *James S. Coleman* (London: Falmer Press, 1996). It should also be mentioned that Gudmund Hernes has challenged Coleman's argument that Weber does not provide a solution to "the problem of transformation." See the excellent article by Gudmund Hernes entitled "The Logic of *The Protestant Ethic*," *Rationality and Society* 1 (1989): 123–62 (as well as the debate with James Coleman in the same volume). Hernes argues that Weber explains Step 3 in the following manner: the ascetic Protestant merchant helped to introduce a fierce form of competition into traditional capitalism through a kind of positive prisoner's dilemma. All the ascetic merchants felt that they had to outdo the other merchants in order to produce the

high profits that were a sign that they were among the elect. Coleman's argument that Hernes ignores barriers to entry is countered by Hernes's argument that the ascetic Protestant merchant had the moral stamina to put up with the kind of resistance and hostility that tends to emerge when economic traditionalism is challenged.

59. Gordon Marshall, "The Dark Side of the Weber Thesis: The Case of Scotland," *British Journal of Sociology* 31 (1980): 420; see also Gordon Marshall, "The Weber Thesis and the Development of Capitalism in Scotland," *Scottish Journal of Sociology* 3 (1979): 173–211; and Gordon Marshall, "Mad Max True?," *Sociology* 17 (1983): 569–73.

60. See the excellent discussion of this problem in Marshall's two books: Gordon Marshall, *Presbyteries and Profits: Calvinism and the Development of Capitalism in Scotland, 1560–1707* (Oxford: Oxford University Press, 1971), pp. 58–59; and Gordon Marshall, *In Search of the Spirit of Capitalism*, pp. 58–59, 64–68, 113. Weber tends to equate the two terms "economic form" ("*Form*," "'*kapitalistische' Form*") and "economic system" ("*Wirtschaftssystem*"; e.g., "*Kapitalismus als Wirtschaftssystem*"). In my mind it would have been preferable to make a distinction between the two; let "economic form" be identical to "economic organization," and let "economic system" be broader in scope and include the judicial system, labor, and the like. For Weber's use of "capitalism as an economic system" and similar expressions, see, e.g., Weber, *Die protestantische Ethik II*, pp. 28, 47, 167, 170–72; and for "economic form" and similar expressions, see, e.g., Weber, *Die protestantische Ethik II*, pp. 28, 171, and *The Protestant Ethic*, pp. 64–65, 67, or "Die protestantische Ethik," pp. 49–51 in Vol. 1 of *Gesammelte Aufsätze zur Religionssoziologie*.

61. Marshall, *In Search of the Spirit of Capitalism*, p. 13.

62. Drawing on his analysis in *Presbyteries and Profits*, Marshall concludes that both a Protestant ethic and a spirit of capitalism existed in Scotland—but that the evidence for the former's causing the latter is less strong. See Marshall, *Presbyteries and Profits*, p. 261. Marshall's other empirical examples include seventeenth-century Scottish political economists and the activities of one particular capitalist, Sir John Clerk of Penicuik (1649–1722). See Marshall, "The Weber Thesis and the Development of Capitalism in Scotland"; and Marshall, "The Dark Side of the Weber Thesis," pp. 419–40.

63. Conversation with Marshall in Stockholm on April 29, 1996.

64. Weber, *The Protestant Ethic*, p. 183, or "Die protestantische Ethik," p. 205 in Vol. 1 of *Gesammelte Aufsätze zur Religionssoziologie*. The translation has been changed.

65. H. Stuart Hughes, *Consciousness and Society: The Reorientation of European Social Thought, 1890–1930* (New York: Vintage Books, 1958), pp. 322–23. Friedrich Tenbruck argues that it is wrong to view the studies in *The Economic Ethic of the World Religions* as "hypothesis and control evidence" for the thesis in *The Protestant Ethic* and that Weber in his later works wanted "to show . . . how and through what forces, there emerged in the world religions a dominant economic ethic"; see Friedrich Tenbruck, "The Thematic Unity in the Works of Max Weber," *British Journal of Sociology* 31 (1980): 327–28. Tenbruck, it seems to me, has a point but overdoes it by not stressing Weber's concern with rational capitalism in his studies of world religions and their economic ethics.

66. As mentioned earlier, the most reliable description of Weber's proposed studies in economic ethics is an announcement from Weber's publisher for a set of books entitled *Gesammelte Aufsätze zur Religionssoziologie*, written by Weber himself and published in 1919. For a translation, see pp. 424–25 in Wolfgang Schluchter, *Rationalism, Religion, and Domination* (Berkeley: University of California Press, 1989), pp. 424–25. The col-

lected essays in the sociology of religion were scheduled to appear in four volumes and to include a history of the European bourgeoisie in antiquity and the Middle Ages.

67. *"Wirtschafts-Soziologie."* See Weber, "Die Wirtschaftsethik der Weltreligionen," p. 237 n. 1 in Vol. 1 of *Gesammelte Aufsätze zur Religionssoziologie.* (This note was left out of the English translation; see Weber, "The Social Psychology of the World Religions," p. 267 in Gerth and Mills, eds., *From Max Weber).* Weber uses exactly the same expression and says the same thing about economic sociology in the first version of this article. See Weber, "Die Wirtschaftsethik der Weltreligionen. Religionssoziologische Skizzen. Einleitung," *Archiv für Sozialwissenschaft und Sozialpolitik* 41 (1915–16): 1 n. 1.

68. All of these concepts are used in *Economy and Society* but not defined in chapter 2 on economic sociology. Weber had already spoken of "ideal" and "material needs" in his lectures on economics in the 1890s; see Weber, *Grundriss zu den Vorlesungen über Allgemeine ("theoretische") Nationalökonomie (1898),* p. 29.

69. See the discussion of the concept of economic sphere in chapters 1 and 2 plus the section on this topic in Weber, "Religious Rejections of the World and Their Directions," pp. 331–33 in Gerth and Mills, eds., *From Max Weber,* or "Zwischenbetrachtung," pp. 544–46 in Vol. 1 of *Gesammelte Aufsätze zur Religionssoziologie.* For the concept of "Eigengesetzlichkeit," see also "Religious Rejections of the World," pp. 339, 340, or "Zwischenbetrachtung," pp. 552, 554. In translating the concept of "Eigengesetzlichkeit" as "limited autonomy," I follow Robert K. Merton. See Robert K. Merton, *Science, Technology and Society in Seventeenth Century England* (New York: Harper and Row, [1938] 1970), pp. ix–x. Weber furthermore says that each sphere has a certain "inner logic" (*"Eigenlogik,"*). (I thank Ralph Schroeder for this information.)

70. Weber, "The Social Psychology of the World Religions," p. 280 in Gerth and Mills, eds., *From Max Weber,* or "Einleitung," p. 252 in Vol. 1 of *Gesammelte Aufsätze zur Religionssoziologie.* Little attention has been paid in the secondary literature to Weber's concepts of ideal and material interests. For an exception, see Stephen Kalberg's article on this topic; there are also scattered remarks in Wolfgang Schluchter's work. See Stephen Kalberg, "The Role of Ideal Interests in Max Weber's Comparative Historical Sociology," pp. 46–67 in Robert J. Antonio and Ronald M. Glassman, eds., *A Weber-Marx Dialogue* (Lawrence: University of Kansas Press, 1985); and, e.g., Wolfgang Schluchter, *The Rise of Western Rationalism* (Berkeley: University of California Press, 1981), pp. 25–27, 34.

71. Weber, "The Social Psychology of the World Religions," p. 280 in Gerth and Mills, eds., *From Max Weber,* or "Einleitung," p. 252 in Vol. 1 of *Gesammelte Aufsätze zur Religionssoziologie.* The term Weber uses is *"Weltbild"* (world picture).

72. The term *Wirtschaftsethik* seems to have been common in Weber's day and was used, for example, by Heinrich Dietzel in the 1890s and by Ernst Troeltsch some years later. See Heinrich Dietzel, *Theoretische Sozialökonomik* (Leipzig: Winter'sche Verlagshandlung, 1895), pp. 30–35; Ernst Troeltsch, *Die Soziallehren der christlichen Kirchen und Gruppen,* Vol. 1 of *Gesammelte Schriften* (Tübingen: J.C.B. Mohr, [1912] 1923), pp. 955–57. The term "moral economy" was introduced by E. P. Thompson in the 1970s and has often been used to make the point that people's attitudes toward their work and livelihood are not just "rational" and driven by hunger and the like, but also infused by distinct values, especially what is fair. Weber's concept of economic ethic is, however, both broader and more differentiated than moral economy; hence, it is also, in my opinion, preferable. There is an interesting link between Weber's concept of depersonaliza-

tion and his notion of economic ethic; the economic ethic of modern capitalism is extremely hard to influence from the outside. For the notion of moral economy, see especially E. P. Thompson, "The Moral Economy of the English Crowd in the Eighteenth Century," *Past and Present* 50 (1971): 76–136; see also James C. Scott, *The Moral Economy of the Peasant* (New Haven, Conn.: Yale University Press, 1976); Peter Swenson, *Fair Shares: Unions, Pay and Politics in Sweden and West Germany* (London: Adamente Press, 1989), 11 ff.; and (for a critique of the moral economy argument) Samuel Popkin, *The Rational Peasant* (Berkeley: University of California Press, 1979), pp. 1–82.

73. For the former opinion, see Charles Camic, "Weber and the Judaic Economic Ethic: A Comment on Fahey," *American Journal of Sociology* 89 (1984): 411; and for the latter opinion, see R. H. Tawney, *Religion and the Rise of Capitalism* (New York: Mentor, [1926] 1952), pp. 27, 29 ff., 39, 53. Tawney does not refer to Weber's concept of economic ethic but uses the term for his own purposes in his debate of Weber's work.

74. Marianne Weber, *Max Weber*, pp. 331–32.

75. Weber, "The Social Psychology of the World Religions," p. 267 in Gerth and Mills, eds., *From Max Weber*, or "Einleitung," p. 238 in Vol. 1 of *Gesammelte Aufsätze zur Religionssoziologie*.

76. Weber, "The Social Psychology of the World Religions," p. 268 in Gerth and Mills, eds., *From Max Weber*, or "Einleitung," p. 238 in Vol. 1 of *Gesammelte Aufsätze zur Religionssoziologie*.

77. Weber writes specifically about "'Wirtschaftsethik' einer Religion," but the English translators of this text did not notice Weber's distinction between an economic ethic in general and the economic ethic of a religion. See Weber, "The Social Psychology of the World Religions," p. 267 in Gerth and Mills, eds., *From Max Weber*, or "Einleitung," p. 238 in Vol. 1 of *Gesammelte Aufsätze zur Religionssoziologie;* emphasis added.

78. Weber, "The Social Psychology of the World Religions," p. 269 in Gerth and Mills, eds., *From Max Weber*, or "Einleitung," p. 240 in Vol. 1 of *Gesammelte Aufsätze zur Religionssoziologie*.

79. Weber does not use the concept "economic ethic" (*Wirtschaftsethik*) in the first version of *The Protestant Ethic* from 1904–5, but adds it in the revised version.

80. Weber, "The Social Psychology of the World Religions," p. 268 in Gerth and Mills, eds., *From Max Weber*, or "Einleitung," in Vol. 1 of *Gesammelte Aufsätze zur Religionssoziologie*, p. 238.

81. In the main text I follow Weber's key argument in *The Religion of China*. The passages in this work that are of particular interest to economic sociology are the following: Weber, *The Religion of China*, pp. 3–12 (money and monetary policy), 50–62 (taxation), 226–49 (Confucianism and Puritanism, including personalism and impersonality in the economy), or "Konfuzianismus und Taoismus," pp. 276–90, 335–49, 512–36 in Vol. 1 of *Gesammelte Aufsätze zur Religionssoziologie*. Weber also mentions the role of rotating credit associations in China; see *The Religion of China*, pp. 209, 292–93 n. 40, or "Konfuzianismus und Taoismus," p. 494 n. 1. Literature that evaluates Weber's analysis of China is presented later.

82. Weber, *The Religion of China*, p. 100, or "Konfuzianismus und Taoismus," p. 100 in Vol. 1 of *Gesammelte Aufsätze zur Religionssoziologie*. The translation has been changed. In a letter to Robert Liefmann, dated March 9, 1920, Weber writes, "The modern economy does not only presuppose the rational . . . state but also rational technology (science) and a specific type of rational lifestyle. Why else would not capitalism have emerged in China? It had several thousands of years of time to do so!"

83. Weber, *The Religion of China,* p. 249, or "Konfuzianismus und Taoismus," p. 536 in Vol. 1 of *Gesammelte Aufsätze zur Religionssoziologie.*

84. In the main text I follow Weber's key argument in *The Religion of India: The Sociology of Hinduism and Buddhism* (New York: Free Press, 1958). The passages in this work that are of particular interest to economic sociology are the following: Weber, *The Religion of India,* pp. 111–17 (the caste system and the economy), 193–204 (the Jains, a sect similar in many ways to ascetic Protestantism), 216–19 (the economic ethic of Buddhism), 270–82 (capitalism and Japan), or pp. 203–17, 234–37, 295–309 in Vol. 2 of *Gesammelte Aufsätze zur Religionssoziologie.* I have chosen not to discuss the economic ethic of Buddhism in the main text because I find Weber's analysis rather sketchy (see in this context also "The Other-Worldliness of Buddhism and Its Economic Consequences," pp. 627–30 in *Economy and Society,* or *Wirtschaft und Gesellschaft,* pp. 377–78). Randall Collins claims that Weber seriously underestimated the economic role of Buddhism in China and that there existed a strong "Buddhist capitalism," particulary during the early Chinese Middle Ages and through the early T'ang. See Randall Collins, *Weberian Sociological Theory* (Cambridge: Cambridge University Press, 1986), pp. 58–73. Further literature that evaluates Weber's analysis of India is cited later. It should be noted that the translation of *The Religion of India* is poor.

85. Weber, *The Religion of India,* p. 4, or "Hinduismus und Buddhismus," p. 4 in Vol. 2 of *Gesammelte Aufsätze zur Religionssoziologie.* The translation has been changed.

86. Weber, *The Religion of India,* p. 112, or "Hinduismus und Buddhismus," pp. 110, 111 in Vol. 2 of *Gesammelte Aufsätze zur Religionssoziologie.*

87. In the main text I follow Weber's key argument in *Ancient Judaism.* The passages in this work that are of particular interest to economic sociology are the following: Weber, *Ancient Judaism,* pp. 28–57 (plebeian strata in early Palestine), 61–89 (social laws in Judaism), 252–54 (Egyptian and Israeli economic ethic), 255–63 (charity), 342–45 (dualistic economic ethic plus a comparison of Judaism to ascetic Protestantism), 400–403 (the economic ethic of pharisaical Judaism), pp. 406–11 (the anti-economic mentality of the Essenes), or pp. 34–66, 66–98, 269–71, 271–80, 419–21, 423–29 in Vol. 3 of *Gesammelte Aufsätze zur Religionssoziologie.* In this context see also the discussion of Jewish economic ethic in *Economy and Society;* see especially "Judaism and Capitalism," "Jewish Rationalism versus Puritan Asceticism," and "Hierocracy and Economic Ethos in Judaism," pp. 611–15, 615–23, 1200–04 in *Economy and Society,* or *Wirtschaft und Gesellschaft,* pp. 367–70, 370–74, 719–21. Literature that evaluates Weber's analysis of Judaism is cited later.

88. In Weber's definition of pariah people in *Economy and Society,* he notes that a further characteristic is "a far-reaching distinctiveness in economic functioning." The full definition is the following:

> In our usage, 'pariah people' denotes a distinctive hereditary social group lacking autonomous political organization and characterized by internal prohibitions against commensality and intermarriage originally founded upon magical, tabooistic, and ritual injunctions. Two additional traits of a pariah people are political and social disprivilege and a far-reaching distinctiveness in economic functioning. (Weber, *Economy and Society,* p. 493, or *Wirtschaft und Gesellschaft,* p. 300)

There exists a debate around Weber's concept of the Jews as a pariah people; for an introduction, see, e.g., Arnaldo Momigliano, "A Note on Max Weber's Definition of Judaism as a Pariah-Religion," *History and Theory* 19 (1980): 313–18.

89. For Weber's polemic against Sombart's argument that it was the Jews who had cre-

ated modern (rational) capitalism, see Weber, *Economy and Society,* pp. 611–15, or *Wirtschaft und Gesellschaft,* pp. 367–70; Weber, *General Economic History,* pp. 358–61, or *Wirtschaftsgeschichte,* pp. 406–11. "Pariah capitalism" is a general category and refers to more than just the Jewish people. Gary Hamilton, for example, defines it in the following manner: "The essence of pariah capitalism . . . is a structure of power asymmetry which enables an elite group to control and prey upon the wealth generated by a pariah group." See Gary Hamilton, "Pariah Capitalism: A Paradox of Power and Dependence," *Ethnic Groups* 2 (1979): 3.

90. This is how I interpret Weber's argument in the introduction to *The Economic Ethics of the World Religions.* See Weber, "The Social Psychology of the World Religions," pp. 268–69 in Gerth and Mills, eds., *From Max Weber,* or "Einleitung," pp. 239–40 in Vol. 1 of *Gesammelte Aufsätze zur Religionssoziologie.*

91. Weber, "The This-Worldliness of Islam and Its Economic Ethics," pp. 623–27 in *Economy and Society,* or *Wirtschaft und Gesellschaft,* pp. 375–76. One can also find many important comments on Christianity—but fewer on its economic ethic.

92. For a solid introduction to the discussion of the patrimonial structure of the Islamic state, its cities, and similar issues, see Wolfgang Schluchter, "Hindrances to Modernity: Max Weber on Islam," pp. 105–78 in *Paradoxes of Modernity* (Stanford, Calif.: Stanford University Press, 1996).

93. For a discussion of the concept of predestination in Islam, see Weber, *Economy and Society,* pp. 572–76, or *Wirtschaft und Gesellschaft,* pp. 346–48.

94. Emil Lederer, "Max Weber," *Archiv für Sozialwissenschaft und Sozialpolitik* 48 (1920/21): iii.

95. One of these was to lump together all non-Western countries and analyze them in terms of "traditionalism"; another to view the reasons why these countries had not followed the same course of socio-economic development as the West in social-psychological terms. Modernization theorists have also attempted to find ethics analogous to ascetic Protestantism in various countries. Some of the modernization studies that were inspired or influenced by Weber are of excellent quality, however, and represent model studies of "economic ethic." See especially Robert Bellah, *Togugawa Religion* (Glencoe, Ill.: Free Press, 1957); Robert Bellah, "Reflections on the Protestant Ethic Analogy in Asia," *Journal of Social Issues* 19 (1963): 52–60; Clifford Geertz, "Religious Belief and Economic Behavior in a Central Javanese Town," *Economic Development and Cultural Change* 4 (1956): 134–58; S. M. Lipset, "Values and Entrepreneurship in the Americas," pp. 77–140 in *Revolution and Counterrevolution* (New Brunswick, N.J.: Transaction Books, [1970] 1988). See also the fine collection of articles in S. N. Eisenstadt, ed., *The Protestant Ethic and Modernization* (New York: Basic Books, 1968).

96. One commentator writes, for example, "I have imagined a number of times that the good German professor [Weber] would come back to life today, say on top of a high-rise office building in downtown Taipei, that he would take one look out the window and say, 'Well, I was wrong!'"; Peter Berger, "An East Asian Development Model?," p. 7 in Peter Berger and Hsin-Huang Michael Hsiao, eds., *In Search of an East Asian Development Model* (New Brunswick, N.J.: Transaction Books, 1988). For a similar attitude, see also Fukuyama, *Trust,* pp. 326, 350, 416–17 n. 1; and for a critique of this type of argument, see Gary Hamilton and Cheng-Shu Kao, "Max Weber and the Analysis of East Asian Industrialization," *International Sociology* 2 (1987): 289–300.

97. A version of this can be found in *The Structure of Social Action* by Parsons, but I cite one of Parsons's unpublished papers from the 1940s because it contains a more force-

ful and clear statement. Parsons says that the argument in *The Economic Ethics of the World Religions* is very similar to that of *The Protestant Ethic*:

> Weber isolated the influence of the religious ethic by a rough, but for his broadest purposes, adequate method. What he attempted to do was to judge whether at the time preceding the emergence of the religious movement in question the general character of the social structure apart from religion was more or less 'favorable' to the development of the institutional patterns characteristic among the western world. In the two cases most fully worked out—namely, China and India—his conclusion was that at comparable stages—that is, comparable to Europe on the eve of the reformation—the situation was in all the relevant respects at least as favorable as it was in western Europe. (Weber, Paper for Barnes Symposium—unpublished, p. 19; Harvard University Archives, HUG(FP) 42.42, Box 2)

See also Talcott Parsons, *The Structure of Social Action* (Glencoe, Ill.: Free Press, 1949), pp. 539–42. For a critique of this type of reasoning as applied to China, see Gary Hamilton, "Why No Capitalism in China? Negative Questions in Historical Comparative Research," *Journal of Developing Societies* 1 (1985): 192–93.

98. Weber, "Einleitung," p. 237 n. 1 in Vol. 1 of *Gesammelte Aufsätze zur Religionssoziologie*.

99. See especially the work of Mark Elvin, Gary Hamilton, and Randall Collins in this context. Elvin both confronts Weber's thesis of why rational capitalism did not spontaneously emerge in China and evaluates Weber's research on a number of topics. Capitalism did not emerge in China, Elvin claims, because of what he calls a high-level equilibrium trap, meaning by this that a variety of noncultural factors prevented demand and supply forces from working out freely. This trap became especially strong in the early 1800s. As to Weber's opinion on separate economic topics in *The Religion of China*—such as money and monetary policy, the tax system, and the regulation of rivers—Elvin mostly finds Weber wrong or confusing. Gary Hamilton argues that Weber misunderstood the nature of Chinese patriarchal domination and also that "negative questions" such as "Why is there no capitalism in China?" invite misleading answers because they project Western experience onto China. Hamilton adds that Weber did not grasp the important role of merchants' associations in China. Randall Collins shows, among other things, with the help of the work of Joseph Needham, how Weber's view of Chinese science and technology is outmoded. For a general analysis of Chinese economic history, see Mark Elvin, *The Pattern of the Chinese Past* (London: Eyre Methuen, 1973); and for his detailed critique of Weber's *The Religion of China*, see Elvin, "Why China Failed to Create an Endogenous Industrial Capitalism: A Critique of Max Weber's Explanation," *Theory and Society* 13 (1984): 379–91. For Gary Hamilton's work on Weber and China, see especially, Gary Hamilton, "Why No Capitalism in China? Negative Questions in Historical Comparative Research," *Journal of Developing Societies* 1 (1985): 187–211; and Gary Hamilton, "Patriarchalism in Imperial China and Western Europe: A Revision of Weber's Sociology of Domination," *Theory and Society* 13 (1984): 393–425. For Collins's views, see especially Randall Collins, *Weberian Sociological Theory*, pp. 58–72; in this context see also N. Sivin, "Max Weber, Joseph Needham, Benjamin Nelson: The Question of Chinese Science," pp. 37–49 in E. V. Walter et al. eds., *Civilizations East and West: A Memorial Volume for Benjamin Nelson* (Atlantic Highlands, N.J.: Humanities Press, 1985). It is obvious that Weber was not aware of the advances in the Chinese coal and iron industry in the eleventh century, as documented by Robert Hartwell (from 1966 to 1971) and

summarized by William McNeill, *The Pursuit of Power* (Chicago: University of Chicago Press, 1982). (See, however, Weber's statement in *General Economic History* that despite the "enormous armies" of China and the arms they needed, "no impulse toward a capitalistic development followed from the fact"; Weber, *General Economic History*, pp. 308–9, or *Wirtschaftsgeschichte*, pp. 265–66.)

100. The secondary literature on Weber's analyses of Islamic society, Indian society, and Jewish "pariah capitalism" is stronger on assertions than on references to current works in economic history. For two interesting general introductions to the secondary literature on *The Religion of India* (with some relevant information on economic issues), see Detlef Kantowsky, ed., *Recent Research on Max Weber's Studies of Hinduism* (Munich: Weltforum Verlag, 1986); and David Gellner, "Max Weber, Capitalism and The Religion of India," *Sociology* 16 (1982): 526–43. For some general introductions to economy and religion in Islamic society, which do not make much use of the existing literature on the economic history of Islam, see Bryan Turner, "Islam, Capitalism and the Weber Theses," *British Journal of Sociology* 25 (1974): 230–43; Bryan Turner, *Weber and Islam* (London: Routledge and Kegan Paul, 1974); Maxime Rodinson, *Islam and Capitalism* (London: Allen Lane, 1974); and Maxime Rodinson, "Islamischer Patrimonialismus—ein Hindernis für die Entwicklung des modernen Kapitalismus?," pp. 180–89 in Wolfgang Schluchter, ed., *Max Webers Sicht des Islams* (Frankfurt am Main: Suhrkamp Verlag, 1987). An innovative attempt to look at the relationship between economics and religion from the point of view of preference falsification can be found in Timur Kuran, "Islam and Underdevelopment: An Old Puzzle Revisited," *Journal of Institutional and Theoretical Economics* 153 (1997): 41–71. For an attempt to confront Weber's notion of "pariah capitalism" with findings in economic history, see Hans Liebeschütz, "Max Weber's Historical Interpretation of Judaism," *Year Book of the Leo Baeck Institute* 9 (1964): 51–52.

101. Schluchter, *Rationalism, Religion, and Domination*, pp. 114–15.

Chapter Six
Epilogue: Weber's Vision of Economic Sociology

1. The reader may wish to consult the appendix for a full discussion of what Weber meant by social economics or *Sozialökonomik*.

2. Weber also looks at the relationship of the economy to kinship groups, ethnic groups, and population. Weber's views on economic policy, it may be added, deserve a book-length study of their own. For an interesting study of how Weber viewed the relationship between the economy and ethnic groups, see Guenther Roth, "Global Capitalism and Multiethnicity: Max Weber Then and Now" (1996, unpublished paper).

3. "Die materiale ökonomische Kultursoziologie"; Max Weber, "Vorwort," p. vii in *Wirtschaft und Wirtschaftswissenschaft. Grundriss der Sozialökonomik. I. Abteilung* (Tübingen: J.C.B. Mohr, 1914). That this pamphlet was to have contained a discussion of art and science, among other things, seems clear from Weber's reference in an early section of *Economy and Society* to "the relationship between the economy and the specific areas of culture (literature, art, science, etc.)." See Weber, *Economy and Society: An Outline of Interpretive Sociology* (Berkeley: University of California Press, 1978), p. 356, or *Wirtschaft und Gesellschaft. Grundriss der verstehenden Soziologie* (Tübingen: J.C.B. Mohr, 1972), p. 212 (the translation has been changed). In his 1910 outline for the *Grundriss*, Weber had scheduled himself for a section entitled "Wirtschaft und Kultur (Kritik

des historischen Materialismus)," so perhaps Weber's pamphlet would have contained a critique of Marxism as well. In a letter from Weber to his publishing company dated December 30, 1912, he also mentions his "sociology of culture"; here, however, he says that it will contain "art, literature, world views"; see Johannes Winkelmann, *Max Webers hinterlassenes Hauptwerk* (Tübingen: J.C.B. Mohr, 1986), p. 36.

4. Weber, "'Objectivity' in Social Science and Social Policy," p. 65 in *The Methodology of the Social Sciences* (New York: Free Press, 1949), or "Die 'Objektivität' sozialwissenschaftlicher und sozialpolitischer Erkenntnisse," p. 163 in *Gesammelte Aufsätze zur Wissenschaftslehre* (Tübingen: J.C.B. Mohr, 1988). This rather feeble relationship between art and economy is characteristic for a situation where art has become its own sphere in society ("the esthetic sphere"), while at an earlier stage the relationship could be more direct and powerful. A natural economy, for example, would typically develop a "strongly stylized culture" because a large part of its surplus could be used for artistic purposes as long as the everyday needs of the people remained simple. See Weber, *Economy and Society*, p. 89, or *Wirtschaft und Gesellschaft*, p. 47. For a discussion of the esthetic sphere, see Weber, "Religious Rejections of the World and Their Direction," pp. 340–43 in H. H. Gerth and C. Wright Mills, eds., *From Max Weber* (New York: Oxford University Press, 1946), or "Zwischenbetrachtung," pp. 554–56 in Vol. 1 of *Gesammelte Aufsätze zur Religionssoziologie* (Tübingen: J.C.B. Mohr, 1988).

5. Weber, *The Protestant Ethic and the Spirit of Capitalism* (London: Allen and Unwin, 1930), p. 169, or "Die protestantische Ethik und der Geist des Kapitalismus," pp. 187–88 in Vol. 1 of *Gesammelte Aufsätze zur Religionssoziologie*.

6. Weber, *The Rational and Social Foundations of Music* (Carbondale, Ill.: Southern Illinois University Press, 1958), p. 124, or "Die rationalen und soziologischen Grundlagen der Musik," p. 928 in *Wirtschaft und Gesellschaft* (Tübingen: J.C.B. Mohr, 1956).

7. The first quotation in this sentence comes from Weber, *General Economic History* (New Brunswick, N.J.: Transaction Books, 1981), p. 306, or *Wirtschaftsgeschichte* (Berlin: Duncker und Humblot, 1991), p. 263, and the second from Weber, *Economy and Society*, p. 1194, or *Wirtschaft und Gesellschaft*, p. 714.

8. Weber, "Anticritical Last Word on *The Spirit of Capitalism*," *American Journal of Sociology* 83 (1978): 1129, or *Die Protestantische Ethik. II. Kritiken und Antikritiken* (Gütersloh: Gütersloher Verlagshaus Mohn, 1987), pp. 324–25; similarly *General Economic History*, p. 368, or *Wirtschaftsgeschichte,* p. 314. In this context see especially the debate over the relationship between religion and science in *Past and Present* during 1964–65 as well as the work of Robert K. Merton, e.g. "Puritanism, Pietism and Science" and "Science and Economy in 17th Century England," pp. 620–60 and 661–81 in *Social Theory and Social Structure* (New York: Free Press, 1968).

9. Weber, "Debattereden auf der Tagung des Vereins für Sozialpolitik in Wien 1909 zu den Verhandlungen über die Produktivität der Volkswirtschaft," pp. 422–23 in *Gesammelte Aufsätze zur Soziologie und Sozialpolitik* (Tübingen: J.C.B. Mohr, 1988).

10. Weber, *Economy and Society*, p. 67, or *Wirtschaft und Gesellschaft,* p. 33.

11. Weber, *General Economic History*, p. 305, or *Wirtschaftsgeschichte*, p. 263.

12. Weber made this clear in an often cited statement that he made in a debate in 1910 at a meeting of the German Sociological Society (and which is cited in full at the beginning of chapter 3 in this book); see Weber, "Diskussionsrede zu W. Sombarts Vortrag über Technik und Kultur. Erste Soziologentagung Frankfurt 1910," p. 456 in *Gesammelte Aufsätze zur Soziologie und Sozialpolitik.*

13. Weber, *General Economic History*, p. 302, or *Wirtschaftsgechichte*, pp. 259–60. In

Economy and Society, Weber emphasizes a mixture of social and technological criteria in his definition of the factory. See Weber, *Economy and Society,* p. 117, or *Wirtschaft und Gesellschaft,* p. 64.

14. The first use of the term Industrial Revolution that has been established is from France in the 1830s. It was popularized through Arnold Toynbee's *Lectures on the Industrial Revolution in England* (1884), which Weber had read and also recommended to his students when he taught economics in the 1890s. See Weber, *Grundriss zu den Vorlesungen über Allgemeine ("theoretische") Nationalökonomie (1898)* (Tübingen: J.C.B. Mohr, 1990), pp. 15, 18. For the history of the term and for the current state of the debate, see, e.g., D. C. Coleman, *Myth, History and the Industrial Revolution* (London: Hambledon Press, 1992); Joel Mokyr, ed., *The British Industrial Revolution* (Boulder, Colo.: Westview Press, 1993); and S. G. Checkland, "Industrial Revolution," pp. 811–15 in Vol. 2 of John Eatwell, Murray Milgate, and Peter Newman, eds., *The New Palgrave: A Dictionary of Economics*(London: Macmillan, 1987).

15. Weber, "Anticritical Last Word on *The Spirit of Capitalism,*" p. 1128, or *Das protestantische Ethik.II,* p. 323.

16. According to Guenther Roth and Wolfgang Schluchter, "Weber originally had planned to write this section [the section on economy and race] himself, and the chapter on ethnic groups in *Economy and Society* [pp. 385–98] may be a version of what he had in mind." See Guenther Roth and Wolfgang Schluchter, *Max Weber's Vision of History* (Berkeley: University of California Press, 1979), p. 173 n. 16. Wolfgang Mommsen argues more generally that Weber "enlisted him [Michels] as an author in the *Grundriss*" in order to help Michels in his career. See Wolfgang Mommsen, *The Political and Social Theory of Max Weber* (Cambridge: Polity Press, 1989), p. 89.

17. The section on degeneration problems (which was not included in the final volume that appeared in 1929) was entitled: "Capitalism and Quality of Population (Modern Degeneration Problems insofar as They are Related to the Singularity of Capitalism)." No potential author was cited. "Degeneration problems" also played a role in Weber's work on the psychophysics of labor. See Wolfgang Schluchter and Sabine Frommer, "Einleitung," pp. 66–67 in Max Weber, *Zur Psychophysik der industriellen Arbeit. Schriften und Reden 1908–1912. Max Weber Gesamtausgabe I/11* (Tübingen: J.C.B. Mohr, 1995).

18. The best introduction to Weber's opinion on race (including race and economy) is still Ernst Moritz Manasse, "Max Weber on Race," *Social Research* 14 (1947): 191–221. The reader may also want to consult Weber's debate with Alfred Ploetz in 1910 at the German Sociological Society: Max Weber, "Diskussionsrede dortselbst zu dem Vortrag von A. Ploetz über 'Die Begriffe Rasse und Gesellschaft,'" pp. 456–62 in *Gesammelte Aufsätze zur Soziologie und Sozialpolitik,* or "Max Weber on Race and Society," *Social Research* 38 (1971): 30–41; and Weber, "Max Weber, Dr. Alfred Ploetz, and W.E.B. Du Bois (Max Weber on Race and Society II)," *Sociological Analysis* 34 (1973): 308–12. Weber makes a quick reference to the influence of race on the economy (but no more) in his outline for lectures in economics from the 1890s; see Weber, *Grundriss zu den Vorlesungen über Allgemeine ("theoretische") Nationalökonomie (1898),* p. 29.

19. Even though Weber speaks freely about race in his inaugural address, it should be noted that he makes qualifications when he uses it as an explanation. At one point he says that "something . . . is either natural to the Slav race or has been bred into it in the course of its history." See Weber, "The Nation State and Economic Policy," p. 8 in *Political Writings* (Cambridge: Cambridge University Press, 1994), or "Der Nationalstaat und die Volkswirtschaftspolitik," p. 6 in *Gesammelte Politische Schriften* (Tübingen: J.C.B. Mohr,

1988). By 1904, Weber emphasized the social rather than the racial factor when he looked at the same problem: "It is not natural differences in the physical and chemical qualities of the soil, or differences in the economic talent of the races, but the historically established economic *milieu* that is the determining factor in the difference in the results of peasant agriculture." See Weber, "Capitalism and Rural Society in Germany," pp. 378–79 in Gerth and Mills, eds.,), *From Max Weber.*

20. Weber, "'Objectivity'," p. 69 in *The Methodology of the Social Sciences,* or "Die 'Objektivität'," pp. 167–68 in *Gesammelte Aufsätze zur Wisssenschaftslehre.*

21. See Weber, *The Protestant Ethic,* p. 199 n. 17, or "Die protestantische Ethik," pp. 46–47 n. 1 in Vol. 1 of *Gesammelte Aufsätze zur Religionssoziologie.*

22. For an exception, see *General Economic History,* where Weber argues that American blacks were for a long time unsuitable for factory work, and adds: "Here is one case in economic history where tangible racial distinctions are present." See Weber, *General Economic History,* p. 379 n. 2, or *Wirtschaftsgeschichte,* p. 257 n. 1. Some doubts about the authenticity of this note has been expressed by Ernst Moritz Manasse, "Max Weber on Race," *Social Research,* 14 (1947): 210 n. 41. Weber, however, also mentions the problems of American blacks in factory work elsewhere; see Weber, "Zur Psychophysik der industriellen Arbeit," p. 125 in *Gesammelte Aufsätze zur Soziologie und Sozialpolitik;* and Weber, "Research Strategy for the Study of Occupational Careers and Mobility Patterns," p. 126 in *The Interpretation of Social Reality* (London: Nelson, 1971), or "Methodologische Einleitung für die Erhebungen des Vereins für Sozialpolitik über Auslese und Anpassung (Berufswahlen und Berufsschicksal) der Arbeiterschaft der geschlossenen Grossindustrie (1908)," p. 27 in *Gesammelte Aufsätze zur Soziologie und Sozialpolitik.*

23. Weber, *Economy and Society,* pp. 387, 342, or *Wirtschaft und Gesellschaft,* pp. 235–36, 201.

24. Weber, *Economy and Society,* pp. 38–40, or *Wirtschaft und Gesellschaft,* pp. 20–21.

25. Social Darwinism also represents an attempt to introduce values into science. See, e.g., Weber, "'Energetic' Theories of Culture," *Mid-American Review of Sociology* 9 (1984): 34, or "'Energetische' Kulturtheorien", p. 401 in *Gesammelte Aufsätze zur Wisssenschaftslehre.*

26. Aptitude ("*Angepasstheit*")—see Weber, *Economy and Society,* pp. 150–53, or *Wirtschaft und Gesellschaft,* pp. 86–88.

27. Weber discusses this issue in his work on the psychophysics of labor; see, e.g., Weber, "A Research Strategy for the Study of Occupational Careers and Mobility Patterns," p. 133 in *The Interpretation of Social Reality,* or "Methodologische Einleitung," p. 35; "Zur Psychophysik der industriellen Arbeit," pp. 155–57 in *Gesammelte Aufsätze zur Soziologie und Sozialpolitik.* It is sometimes claimed that it was Weber—rather than American social scientists in the late 1920s and 1930s—who discovered that workers often have a norm for how much to produce that must not be exceeded. In this context see, e.g., Anthony Oberschall, *Empirical Social Research in Germany 1848–1914* (New York: Basic Books, 1965), pp. 120–21. Weber also touches on similar issues elsewhere in his work. In *The Protestant Ethic,* for example, he mentions that Methodist workers in eighteenth-century England were discriminated against by other workers because of their willingness to work very hard; and in *Economy and Society* he mentions that workers in a socialist society would use "restrictions of production" as a weapon to force a change in the working conditions. See Weber, *The Protestant Ethic and the Spirit of Capitalism* (London: Allen and Unwin, 1930), p. 63, or "Die protestantische Ethik und der

Geist des Kapitalismus," p. 47 in Vol. 1 of *Gesammelte Aufsätze zur Religionssoziologie* (Tübingen: J.C.B. Mohr, 1988); Weber, *Economy and Society*, p. 203, or *Wirtschaft und Gesellschaft*, p. 119.

28. Weber, "A Research Strategy for the Study of Occupational Careers and Mobility Patterns," p. 134, or "Methodologische Einleitung," pp. 36–37; see also Marianne Weber, *Max Weber* (New York: Wiley and Sons, 1975), pp. 330–31.

29. Weber, "A Research Strategy for the Study of Occupational Careers and Mobility Patterns," p. 129, or "Methodologische Einleitung," p. 31; emphasis added.

30. Weber, *Economy and Society*, p. 149, or *Wirtschaft und Gesellschaft*, pp. 85–86; for the information in the next sentence, see Weber, *General Economic History*, p. 354, or *Wirtschaftsgeschichte*, pp. 301–2.

31. He says that climate has also affected people's attitudes, and much of what is often explained by race should rather be explained by climate. See especially Weber, *The Agrarian Sociology of Ancient Civilizations*, p. 357, or "Agrarverhältnisse im Altertum," p. 270; Weber, *General Economic History*, pp. 130–31, or *Wirtschaftsgeschichte*, pp. 124–25; and Weber, "Anticritical Last Word on *The Spirit of Capitalism*," *American Journal of Sociology* 83 (1978): p. 1128.

32. See, e.g., Weber, *General Economic History*, pp. 353–54, or *Wirtschaftsgeschichte*, pp. 301–2.

33. See, e.g., Weber, *Economy and Society*, pp. 971–72, 1261, or *Wirtschaft und Gesellschaft*, pp. 560, 756; see also Weber, *The Agrarian Sociology of Ancient Civilizations*, pp. 38, 84, 157, or "Agrarverhältnisse im Altertum," pp. 2, 46, 102 in *Gesammelte Aufsätze zur Sozial- und Wirtschaftsgeschichte;* and Weber, *General Economic History*, pp. 56–57, 321, or *Wirtschaftsgeschichte*, pp. 64, 275–76. For China, see, e.g., Weber, *The Religion of China* (New York: Free Press, 1951), pp. 16, 20–21, 31, 64, 136, 272–73 n. 14, or "Konfuzianismus und Taoismus," pp. 294, 298, 311–12, 351 n. 1, 425, 360 n. 1 in Vol. 1 of *Gesammelte Aufsätze zur Religionssoziologie*.

34. A careful assessment of Weber's ideas on the relationship between control of irrigation and despotism can be found in an article by Stefan Breuer, which discusses contemporary research on the territorial states in ancient Mesopotamia and Phoenicia. See Stefan Breuer, "Stromuferkultur und Küstenkultur. Geographische und ökologische Faktoren in Max Webers 'ökonomischer Theorie der antiken Staatenwelt,'" pp. 111–50 in Wolfgang Schluchter, ed., *Max Webers Sicht des antiken Christentums* (Frankfurt am Main: Suhrkamp, 1985). Commenting on Weber's analysis of water control in China, Mark Elvin says that Weber is not wrong but that he overemphasizes the role of the state; see Mark Elvin, "Why China Failed to Create an Endogenous Industrial Capitalism: A Critique of Max Weber's Explanation," *Theory and Society* 13 (1984): 386. Karl Wittfogel's thesis of "oriental despotism," which is far more coarse and mechanical than Weber's argument, is generally regarded as wrong. See Karl Wittfogel, *Oriental Despotism: A Comparative Study of Total Power* (New York: Vintage Books, 1981); for a critique of Wittfogel's ideas, see the literature cited in Anne Bailey and Josep Llobera, "Karl A. Wittfogel and the Asiatic Mode of Production: A Reappraisal," *Sociological Review* 27 (1979): 558 n. 56.

35. A few first editions were split into two volumes in the second edition, usually in order to let some author of a major contribution—such as Gottl-Ottlilienfeld or von Wieser—appear in a volume of his own.

36. Friedrich von Hayek, "Hayek on Wieser," p. 563 in Henry William Spiegel, ed., *The Development of Economic Thought* (New York: Wiley and Sons, 1952); Joseph A. Schumpeter, *History of Economic Analysis* (London: Allen and Unwin, 1954), p. 891.

37. That Schumpeter was a contributor to the *Grundriss* is well known; that Hayek was also one is less well known. Hayek was asked in the 1920s to prepare a volume on money and credit for the *Grundriss*—presumably the contribution on "Geld und Kredit; Kapitalmarkt; Notenbanken" for Book II, which is devoted to the economic dimension of capitalism. Hayek, who had many other responsibilities at the time, succeeded in completing four chapters. These deal with money and monetary theory from 1650 to 1850 and were published for the first time in 1991 in Vol. 3 of Hayek's collected works. See Friedrich von Hayek, *The Trend of Economic Thinking* (London: Routledge, 1991), pp. 127–244.

38. The information that Lederer took over the editorship of the *Grundriss* comes from two sources: Johannes Winkelmann, who has studied the correspondence of the publisher, the Siebeck family (see Winkelmann, *Max Webers hinterlassenes Hauptwerk*, p. 91), and a letter to the author, dated October 17, 1996, from Georg Siebeck, the great-grandson of Paul Siebeck, who was Weber's publisher. I have, however, been unable to verify this information in the secondary literature on Lederer.

39. *Wirtschaft und Wirtschaftswissenschaft. Grundriss der Sozialökonomik. I. Abteilung* (Tübingen: J.C.B. Mohr, 1914); and *Die natürlichen und technischen Beziehungen der Wirtschaft. Grundriss der Sozialökonomik. II. Abteilung* (Tübingen: J.C.B. Mohr, 1914).

40. Karl Bücher, "Volkswirtschaftliche Entwicklungsstudien," pp. 1–18; Joseph Schumpeter, "Epochen der Dogmen- und Methodengeschichte," pp. 19–124; and Friedrich von Wieser, "Theorie der gesellschaftlichen Wirtschaft," pp. 125–443. The size of each volume in the *Grundriss* is approximately that of a volume in the *Encyclopaedia Britannica*, which means that there is much more text on one page than would normally appear in a regular-sized book.

41. Alfred Hettner, "Die geographischen Bedingungen der menschlichen Wirtschaft," pp. 1–31; Paul Mombert, "Wirtschaft und Bevölkerung, I: Bevölkerungslehre," pp. 32–96; Robert Michels, "Wirtschaft und Bevölkerung, II: Wirtschaft und Rasse," pp. 97–102; Karl Oldenberg, "Die Konsumtion," pp. 103–64; Heinrich Herkner, "Arbeit und Arbeitsteilung," pp. 165–98; and Friedrich Gottl-Ottlilienfeld, "Wirtschaft und Technik," pp. 199–381.

42. The three sections were called "Volkswirtschaftlehre," "Finanzwissenschaft," and "Verwaltungslehre." The first section contained a mixture of economic theory and accounts for different branches of the economy; the second was centered on the finances of the state; and the third had articles on statistics, the police system, and poor-law administration. This account is based on the first edition of the *Handbuch*, which appeared in 1882. For a discussion of the different editions of Schönberg's work, see Max Weber, *Briefe 1909–1910. Max Weber Gesamtausgabe II/6* (Tübingen: J.C.B. Mohr, 1994), pp. 15–16.

43. Weber, "Vorwort," p. viii in *Wirtschaft und Wirtschaftswissenschaft. Grundriss der Sozialökonomik. I. Abteilung*.

44. For the titles of all the contributions to the first and the second editions of the *Grundriss*, see Richard Swedberg, "Max Weber's Handbook in Economics: *Grundriss der Sozialökonomik*," *Working Paper Series Work-Organization-Economy*, Department of Sociology, Stockholm University, 1997. Weber himself oversaw the production of most of Book I, and the end product and the original design are very similar. See *Grundriss der Sozialökonomik. Erstes Buch. Grundlagen der Wirtschaft. I. Abteilung. Wirtschaft und Wirtschaftswissenschaft* (Tübingen: J.C.B. Mohr, 1914); *Grundriss der Sozialökonomik. II. Abteilung. Die natürlichen und technischen Beziehungen der Wirtschaft*

(Tübingen: J.C.B. Mohr, 1914); and *Grundriss der Sozialökonomik. III. Abteilung. Wirtschaft und Gesellschaft.* (Tübingen: J.C.B. Mohr, 1921–22). In 1921 the following two parts of *Wirtschaft und Gesellschaft* appeared: 1. Lieferung (Erster Teil), Die Wirtschaft und die gesellschaftlichen Ordnungen und Mächte, Kapitel I–IV, 1–180; and 2. Lieferung (Zweiter Teil), Typen der Vergemeinschaftung, Kapitel I–IV, 181–356. In 1922 the following two parts appeared: 3. Lieferung (Zweiter Teil, Kapitel IV/Schluss–VIII, 357–600); and 4. Lieferung (Dritter Teil, Typen der Herrschaft, Kapitel I–IX, 603–817, Register). All four parts were bound together in one volume in 1922. Second editions include I. Abteilung (1924, in 2 different volumes), II. Abteilung (1923, in two different volumes) and III. Abteilung (Weber's *Wirtschaft und Gesellschaft;* 1925).

45. See Werner Sombart, "Prinzipielle Eigenart des modernen Kapitalismus," pp. 1–26; Alexander Leist (bearbeitet von Hans Nipperday), "Die moderne Privatrechtordnung und der Kapitalismus," pp. 27–48; and Carl Brinkmann, "Die moderne Staatsordnung und der Kapitalismus," pp. 49–67 in *Grundriss der Sozialökonomik. Zweites Buch. Spezifische Elemente der modernen kapitalistischen Wirtschaft. IV. Abteilung. I. Teil* (Tübingen: J.C.B. Mohr, 1925).

The essay on price formation was written by Franz Eulenberg and entitled "Die Preisbildung in der modernen Wirtschaft" (pp. 258–315). Book II appeared five years after Weber died and is quite similar to the one Weber designed. No second edition ever appeared.

46. The two parts of Book V appeared in 1926–1927 and contain more or less what Weber had planned: *Grundriss der Sozialökonomik. Das soziale System des Kapitalismus. IX. Abteilung. I. Teil. Die gesellschaftliche Schichtung im Kapitalismus* (Tübingen: J.C.B. Mohr, 1926); and *Grundriss der Sozialökonomik. IX. Abteilung. II. Teil. Die autonome und staatliche soziale Binnenpolitik im Kapitalismus* (Tübingen: J.C.B. Mohr, 1927). No second editions appeared.

47. Weber himself oversaw the production of three of the five volumes in the first edition. There are a few minor discrepancies between Weber's plan and what was eventually produced. See *Grundriss der Sozialökonomik. V. Abteilung. Die einzelnen Erwerbsgebiete in der kapitalistischen Wirtschaft und die ökonomische Binnenpolitik im modernen Staate. I. Teil. Handel 1.2* (Tübingen: J.C.B. Mohr, 1918); *Grundriss der Sozialökonomik. V. Abteilung. Die einzelnen Erwerbsgebiete in der kapitalistischen Wirtschaft und die ökonomische Binnenpolitik im modernen Staate. II. Teil. Bankwesen* (Tübingen: J.C.B. Mohr, 1915); *Grundriss der Sozialökonomik. V. Abteilung. Handel, Transportwesen, Bankwesen. III. Teil. Transportwesen* (Tübingen: J.C.B. Mohr, 1930); *Grundriss der Sozialökonomik. VI. Abteilung. Industrie, Bergwesen, Bauwesen* (Tübingen: J.C.B. Mohr, 1914); and *Grundriss der Sozialökonomik. VII. Abteilung. Land- und forstwirtschaftliche Produktion. Versicherungswesen. I* (Tübingen: J.C.B. Mohr, 1914). The following volumes appeared in a second edition: V. Abteilung. I. Teil (1925), V. Abteilung. II. Teil (1925), VI. Abteilung (1923), VII. Abteilung (1922).

48. See Alfred Weber, "Industrielle Standortslehre (Allgemeine und kapitalistische Theorie des Standortes)," pp. 54–82; and Friedrich Leitner, "Betriebslehre der kapitalistischen Grossindustrie," pp. 83–135, both in *Grundriss der Sozialökonomik. VI. Abteilung. Industrie, Bergwesen, Bauwesen* (Tübingen: J.C.B. Mohr, 1914). Eugen von Philippovich points out the innovative nature of Leitner's article in his review of two volumes in the *Grundriss;* and according to Carl Friedrich (who translated *The Theory of the Location of Industries* [1909] into English), Alfred Weber's contribution to the *Grundriss* contains "an outline" of the much awaited realistic theory of location. See Eugen von Philippovich, "Ein neuer 'Grundriss der Sozialökonomik [Review of Abt. 2

and 6]," *Archiv für Sozialwissenschaft und Sozialpolitik* 39 (1914): 829; Carl Friedrich, "Introduction," p. 11 n. 9 of Alfred Weber, *Alfred Weber's Theory of the Location of Industries* (Chicago: University of Chicago Press, 1929). According to Mark Blaug, "Weber's book must be regarded as the first successful treatise on location theory in the sense of inspiring ongoing interest and ongoing inquiry into location theory as a specialised branch of economcis"; see Mark Blaug, "Weber, Alfred (1868–1958), p. 266 in *Great Economists before Keynes* (Atlantic Highlands, N.J.: Humanities Press, 1986). After completing his famous work on the theory of location, Alfred Weber left economics and turned to sociology. Alfred Weber was a much more creative economist than his brother Max—and a much less creative sociologist. For Alfred Weber's life and work, see, e.g., Edgar Salin, "Weber, Alfred," pp. 491–93 in Vol. 16 of David L. Sills, ed., *International Encyclopaedia of the Social Sciences* (New York: Macmillan, 1968); Martin Green, "Alfred," pp. 225–36 in *The von Richthofen Sisters* (New York: Basic Books, 1974); and Wolfgang Schluchter, "Max Weber und Alfred Weber. Zwei Wege von der Nationalökonomie zur Kultursoziologie," pp. 199–221 in Hans G. Nutzinger, ed., *Zwischen Nationalökonomie und Universalgeschichte* (Marburg: Metropolis-Verlag, 1995).

49. Weber called this book *Kapitalistische Weltwirtschaftsbeziehungen und äussere Wirtschafts- und Sozialpolitik im modernen Staate*. The volume that was produced covered most of this topic and consists of a 300-page essay by Franz Eulenberg entitled "Aussenhandel und Aussenhandelspolitik (Die internationalen Wirtschaftsbeziehungen)." See *Grundriss der Sozialökonomik. Aussenhandel und Aussenhandelpolitik. (Die internationalen Wirtschaftsbeziehungen). VIII. Abteilung* (Tübingen: J.C.B. Mohr, 1929).

50. That this was true in Weber's day is clear from the following quote from Werner Sombart: "Despite the fact that capitalism tends to become the sole subject matter of economics, neither the term nor the concept has as yet been universally recognized by representatives of academic economics. . . . The term is not found in Gide, Cauwes, Marshall, Seligman or Cassel, to mention only the best known texts." Werner Sombart, "Capitalism," p. 195 in Vol. 3 of Edwin R. A. Seligman and Alvin Johnson, eds., *Encyclopaedia of the Social Sciences* (New York: Macmillan, 1930).

51. Georg von Below, "Review of *Grundriss der Sozialökonomik* [Abt. 1, 2 and 6]," *Vierteljahrschrift für Sozial- und Wirtschaftsgeschichte* 13 (1916): 213–24.

52. Eugen von Philippovich, "Ein neuer 'Grundriss der Sozialökonomik' [Review of Abt. 2 and 6]," *Archiv für Sozialwissenschaft und Sozialpolitik* 39 (1914): 819–20.

53. Robert Liefmann, "Review of *Grundriss der Sozialökonomik*, Abt. 1, 2 and 6," *Zeitschrift für Politik* 8 (1915): 586–99.

54. Margrit Schuster and Helmuth Schuster, "Industriesoziologie im Nationalsozialismus," *Soziale Welt* 35 (1984): 101. The authors of this article reviewed the correspondence between Weber and Gottl and note that Weber took his editorial duties very seriously, suggesting to Gottl numerous ways to improve his contribution to the *Grundriss*. Emil Lederer and Jakob Marschak's article "Der neue Mittelstand" for the *Grundriss* (1926) was translated by the sociologists at Columbia University in the late 1930s, which is a sign of appreciation. See Emil Lederer and Jakob Marschak, "The New Middle Class" (Columbia University, unpublished manuscript, 1936).

55. Letter from Georg Siebeck to the author, dated October 17, 1996. Georg Siebeck is the great-grandson of Paul Siebeck (1855–1920), who persuaded Max Weber to become editor for the *Grundriss*, and the grandson of Oskar Siebeck (1880–1936), during whose time as head of the publishing house the *Grundriss* was completed. During its first twenty-five years, *Wirtschaft und Gesellschaft* sold fewer than 2,000 copies. See Guen-

ther Roth, "'Value-Neutrality' in Germany and the United States," p. 43 in Reinhard Bendix and Guenther Roth, *Scholarship and Partisanship* (Berkeley: University of California Pres, 1971).

56. See especially Alfred Amonn, "Wieser's 'Theorie der gesellschaftlichen Wirtschaft', I–II," *Archiv für Sozialwissenschaft und Sozialpolitik* 53 (1924–25): 289–369, 653–701. For the English translation of von Wieser's book, see the next note.

57. *Theory of the Social Economy* is the literal translation; when von Wieser's work was translated in 1927 it was given the shorter and more catchy title *Social Economics*. The translation was made by A. Ford Hinrichs, assistant professor of economics at Brown University. See Friedrich von Wieser, *Social Economics* (London: Allen and Unwin, 1927). According to Robert Liefmann, "the title [of von Wieser's work] shall perhaps be seen as a concession to the sociological viewpoint"; see Robert Liefmann, "*Grundriss der Sozialökonomik*, Abt. I, II, VI," *Zeitschrift für Politik* 8 (1915): 589.

58. Friedrich von Wieser, "Theorie der gesellschaftlichen Wirtschaft," p. 138 in *Wirtschaft und Wirtschaftswissenschaft. Grundriss der Sozialökonomik. I. Abteilung.*

59. Friedrich von Hayek, "Friedrich von Wieser (1851–1926)," p. 119 in *The Fortunes of Liberalism* (London: Routledge, 1992); Wesley Clair Mitchell, "Foreword," p. ix in von Wieser, *Social Economics;* Oscar Morgenstern, "Friedrich von Wieser, 1851–1926," p. 68 in Vol. 1 of Stephen Littlechild, ed., *Austrian Economics* (Aldershot, Eng.: Edward Elgar, 1990); Joseph A. Schumpeter, "Friedrich von Wieser, 1851–1926," p. 162 in *Ten Great Economists* (New York: Oxford University Press, 1951).

60. Letter from Max Weber to his publisher, dated April 2, 1914, as cited in Winkelmann, *Max Webers hinterlassenes Hauptwerk*, p. 38.

61. Von Wieser had told Weber that he considered this transition very important but also "very difficult." See the letter from Friedrich von Wieser to Max Weber, dated July 15, 1909, in Max Weber, *Briefe 1909–1910. Max Weber Gesamtausgabe II/6* (Tübingen: J.C.B. Mohr, 1994), p. 183. For Weber's conception of von Wieser's contribution to the *Grundriss*, see also his 1909–10 plan (where Weber says that the author of the section assigned to von Wieser was to use the principle of "decreasing abstraction" to approach "empirical reality"); see Winkelmann, *Max Webers hinterlassenes Hauptwerk*, p. 151. The section where von Wieser goes from "the simple economy" to "the social economy" is on pages 149–67 in *Social Economics.*

62. In the original edition of his work (1914), von Wieser cites only the following sources for his sociological notes: Albert Schäffle, Adolph Wagner, Gustav von Schmoller, Carl Menger, Eugen von Philippovich, and himself. In the second (unchanged) edition from 1924, however, von Wieser adds, among others, Ferdinand Tönnies, Georg Simmel, and Max Weber.

63. For Schumpeter's use of the terms "*Soziologie*" and "*ökonomische Soziologie*," see, e.g., Josph A. Schumpeter, "Epochen der Dogmen- und Methodengeschichte," pp. 37, 70, 72 in *Wirtschaft und Wirtschaftswissenschaft. Grundriss der Sozialökonomik. I. Abteilung.* To Schumpeter, at this stage of his thought, sociology represented "deeper insight into society" and was characterized as "a satisfactory theory of social institutions and principles of social organization" (p. 72).

64. An attempt to trace this theme in Schumpeter's work can be found in Richard Swedberg, *Schumpeter—A Biography* (Princeton, N.J.: Princeton University Press, 1991).

65. Schumpeter, *History of Economic Analysis*, pp. 12–24.

66. Joseph A. Schumpeter, *Economic Doctrine and Method* (London: Allen and Unwin, 1954), p. 173.

67. See Harvey Leibenstein, "Bandwagon, Snob and Veblen Effects in the Theory of Consumers' Demand," *Quarterly Journal of Economics* 64 (May 1950): 183–207; Thomas Schelling, *Micromotives and Macrobehavior* (New York: W. W. Norton, 1978).

68. Weber uses the idea of social mechanisms in his work, but not the term. See Peter Hedström and Richard Swedberg, "Social Mechanisms," *Acta Sociologica* 39 (1996): 281–308.

69. For more details on the history of economic sociology, see the article by Richard Swedberg, "Economic Sociology: Past and Present," *Current Sociology* 35 (Spring 1987): 1–221.

70. See especially Harrison White, "Where Do Markets Come From?," *American Journal of Sociology* 87 (1981): 517–47; Arthur Stinchcombe, *Economic Sociology* (New York: Academic Press, 1983); James Coleman, "Introducing Social Structure into Economic Analysis," *American Economic Review* 74, no. 2 (1985): 84–88.

71. The monographs include Mark Granovetter, *Getting a Job* (Cambridge, Mass.: Harvard University Press, 1974); Viviana Zelizer, *Morals and Markets* (New York: Columbia University Press, 1979); Nicole Woolsey Biggart, *Charismatic Capitalism* (Chicago: University of Chicago Press, 1989); Fred Block, *Postindustrial Possibilities* (Berkeley: University of California Press, 1990); Neil Fligstein, *The Transformation of Corporate Control* (Cambridge, Mass.: Harvard University Press, 1990); Ronald Burt, *Structural Holes: The Social Structure of Competition* (Cambridge, Mass.: Harvard University Press, 1992); Frank Dobbin, *Forging Industrial Policy* (Cambridge: Cambridge University Press, 1994). The readers in economic sociology include Roger Friedland and A. F. Robertson, eds., *Beyond the Marketplace* (New York: Aldine de Gruyter, 1990); Sharon Zukin and Paul DiMaggio, eds., *Structures of Capital* (Cambridge: Cambridge University Press, 1990); Mark Granovetter and Richard Swedberg, eds., *The Sociology of Economic Life* (Boulder, Colo.: Westview Press, 1992); and Richard Swedberg, ed., *Explorations in Economic Sociology* (New York: Russell Sage Foundation, 1993). See also Neil Smelser and Richard Swedberg, eds., *Handbook of Economic Sociology* (New York: Princeton University Press and Russell Sage Foundation, 1994); Richard Swedberg, "New Economic Sociology: What Has Been Accomplished, What Is Ahead?," *Acta Sociologica* 40 (1997): 161–82.

72. Mark Granovetter, "Economic Action and Social Structure: The Problem of Embeddedness," *American Journal of Sociology* 91 (1985): 504.

73. For an attempt to combine an interest-driven approach with the concept of embeddedness, see "Introduction," pp. 1–26 in Granovetter and Swedberg, eds., *The Sociology of Economic Life*.

74. See especially Mark Granovetter, "Economic Institutions as Social Constructions: A Framework for Analysis," *Acta Sociologica* 35 (1992): 3–11.

75. Coleman, "Introducing Social Structure into Economic Analysis," p. 84.

76. Mark Granovetter, "Economic Decisions and Social Structure: The Problem of Embeddedness" (1982, unpublished paper), p. 2. For a much more concentrated statement, see the final version, "Economic Action and Social Structure: The Problem of Embeddedness," *American Journal of Sociology* 91 (1985): 506.

77. The term New Economic Sociology (coined by Granovetter in the mid-1980s) roughly covers what in this chapter is referred to as contemporary economic sociology. See Mark Granovetter, "The Old and the New Economic Sociology: A History and an Agenda," pp. 89–112 in Friedland and Robertson, eds., *Beyond the Marketplace*. Old Economic Sociology is the sociology that some industrial sociologists as well as Parsons and Smelser worked with in the 1950s and 1960s.

78. For a similar argument, see Marshall Meyer, "The Weberian Tradition in Organizational Research," pp. 191–215 in Craig Calhoun et al., eds., *Structures of Power and Consent* (Cambridge: Cambridge University Press, 1990).

79. The two sources on bureaucracy that are usually cited in mainstream sociology are chapters 3 and 11 in *Economy and Society.* The section entitled "Bureaucracy" in *From Max Weber,* comes, for example, from chapter 11. See Max Weber, in Gerth and Mills, eds., *From Max Weber,* pp. 196–244; Weber, *Economy and Society,* pp. 956–1005, or *Wirtschaft und Gesellschaft,* pp. 551–79.

80. Weber discusses this topic as well as the birth of the organization in general in his sociology of law; see chapter 4 in this volume.

81. See Viviana Zelizer, *Morals and Markets;* and Viviana Zelizer, *Pricing the Priceless Child* (New York: Basic Books, 1985). In another book, Zelizer analyzes the social dimension of money and squarely opposes the tendency of most sociological theorists, including Weber, to view money as something "impersonal" and thereby nonsocial. See Viviana Zelizer, *The Social Meaning of Money* (New York: Basic Books, 1994).

82. Weber, *The Protestant Ethic and the Spirit of Capitalism* (London: Allen and Unwin, 1930), p. 17, or "Vorbemerkung," p. 4 in Vol. 1 of *Gesammelte Aufsätze zur Religionssoziologie* (Tübingen: J.C.B. Mohr, 1988).

83. It would be interesting to compare the idea of rent-seeking and Weber's concept of political capitalism in order to find out to what extent they differ and perhaps also complement each other. Whereas rent-seeking has primarily dealt with contemporary times and modern liberal capitalism, Weber's analysis of political capitalism is usually focused on antiquity and pre-industrial profit-making. Weber's analysis of capitalism furthermore looks at concrete historical examples, while the literature on rent-seeking typically attempts to produce general models. Apart from what Weber has to say about political capitalism, the notion of "rent" plays an important role in his economic sociology. Rent, according to Weber, is connected to wealth and householding, not to capital and profit-making, and it generally has a conservative effect on the rest of the economy (see figure 2.10)

84. Weber, "The Nation State and Economic Policy," p. 15 in *Political Writings,* or "Der Nationalstaat und die Volkswirtschaftspolitik (1895)," pp. 12–13 in *Gesammelte Politische Schriften;* emphasis added.

APPENDIX
THE EVOLUTION OF WEBER'S THOUGHT ON ECONOMICS

1. Mark Blaug, ed., *Who's Who in Economics* (Cambridge, Mass.: MIT Press, 1986), p. 872. Similar opinions are cited in the last section of this appendix. I would agree with the following statement by Keith Tribe about Weber and sociology: "Weber did not regard his project as an essentially sociological one, but it was to this discipline that his work was principally assigned after his death. The fit, however, is not a good one, leading to an overemphasis on some aspects of Weber's programme and a total neglect of some others"; Keith Tribe, "Translator's Introduction," pp. 2–3 in Wilhelm Hennis, *Max Weber* (London: Allen and Unwin, 1988). For a bibliographical list of works on Weber's economic sociology, see Richard Swedberg, "Max Weber's Economic Sociology: A Bibliography," *Working Papers Work-Organization-Economy,* Department of Sociology, Stockholm University, 1998.

2. "Weber began as an economist, and always remained a political economist"; Ralf

Dahrendorf, "Max Weber and Modern Social Science," p. 574 in Wolfgang Mommsen and Jürgen Osterhammel, eds., *Max Weber and His Contemporaries* (London: Unwin Hyman, 1987). See also Weber, "Science as a Vocation," p. 129 in Hans Gerth and C. Wright Mills, eds., *From Max Weber* (New York: Oxford University Press, 1946), or "Wissenschaft als Beruf," p. 582 in *Gesammelte Aufsätze zur Wissenschaftslehre* (Tübingen: J.C.B. Mohr, 1988); in articles from 1908 and 1909 as well as in a letter to Brentano dated April 13, 1909, Weber refers to economics as "our discipline"; cf. Max Weber, "Marginal Utility Theory and 'The Fundamental Law of Psychophysics' (1908)," *Social Science Quarterly* 56 (1975): 31, or "Die Grenznutzlehre und das 'psychophysische Grundgesetz' (1908)," p. 393 in *Gesammelte Aufsätze zur Wissenschaftslehre;* Max Weber, "'Energetic' Theories of Culture (1909)," *Mid-American Review of Sociology* 9 (1984): 42, or "'Energetische' Kulturtheorien (1909)," p. 413 in *Gesammelte Aufsätze zur Wissenschaftslehre;* and Max Weber, *Briefe 1909–1910. Max Weber Gesamtausgabe II/6* (Tübingen: J.C.B. Mohr, 1994), p. 93. In his inaugural lecture in Freiburg from 1895, Weber proclaimed himself to be a disciple of the Historical School; see Max Weber, "The Nation State and Economic Policy," p. 19 in *Political Writings* (Cambridge: Cambridge University Press, 1994), or "Politik als Beruf," p. 16 in *Gesammelte Politische Schriften* (Tübingen: J. C. B. Mohr, 1988).

3. Karl Jaspers, *On Max Weber* (New York: Paragon House, 1989), p. 98 (the translation has been slightly changed); Marianne Weber, *Max Weber: A Biography* (New York: John Wiley and Sons, 1975), p. 423.

4. On cameralism and early German economics in general, see the fine study by Keith Tribe, *Governing the Economy: The Reformation of German Economic Discourse, 1750–1840* (Cambridge: Cambridge University Press, 1988). For an introduction to the history of economic thought in nineteenth-century Germany, see Harald Winkel, *Die deutsche Nationalökonomie im 19. Jahrhundert* (Darmstadt: Wissenschaftliche Buchgesellschaft, 1977).

5. Wilhelm Roscher, *Grundriss zu Vorlesungen über die Staatswirtschaft. Nach geschichtlicher Methode* (Göttingen: Verlag der Dieterischen Buchhandlung, 1843), p. v. An English translation of the preface to this book (by W. J. Ashley) has been published as "Roscher's Programme of 1843," *Quarterly Journal of Economics* 9 (1894–95): 99–105. Friedrich Karl von Savigny (1779–1861) was the founder of the German Historical School of Law; and one of his main ideas was that law was not the creation of reason but the result of a nation's experience. Karl Friedrich Eichhorn (1781–1854) was a leading figure in the German Historical School of Law.

6. Roscher, *Principles of Political Economy* (New York: Henry Holt, 1878), Vol. 1, p. 111.

7. Roscher, *Grundriss,* pp. iv, 3, 4.

8. This theme is discussed in Karl Knies's major work from 1853 and even more so in its second, enlarged edition from 1883. See Karl Knies, *Die politische Oekonomie vom Standpunkte der geschichtlichen Methode* (Braunschweig: G. A. Schwetschke und Sohn, 1853), pp. 89–109; and Karl Knies, *Die politische Oekonomie vom geschichtlichen Standpunkte* (Leipzig: Hans Buske [1883] 1930), pp. 106–41.

9. The quotation comes from "Schmoller on Roscher," p. 365 in Henry William Spiegel, ed., *The Development of Economic Thought* (New York: John Wiley and Sons, 1952).

10. Gustav von Schmoller, *Über einige Grundfragen der Sozialpolitik und der Volkswirtschaftslehre* (Leipzig: Dunckerund Humblot, 1898), p. 338.

11. Schumpeter, *History of Economic Analysis* (London: Allen and Unwin, 1954),

p. 802. See also, e.g., Abraham Asher, "Professors as Propagandists: The Politics of the Kathedersozialisten," *Journal of Central European Affairs* 23 (1963): 282–302.

12. This section is based on Gustav von Schmoller, "Volkswirtschaft, Volkswirtschafts- lehre und -methode," pp. 527–63 in Vol. 6 of J. Conrad et al., eds., *Handwörterbuch der Staatswissenschaften* (Jena: Gustav Fischer, 1894).

13. Edwin Gay, "Tasks of Economic History," p. 411 in Frederic Lane and Jelle Riemersma, eds., *Enterprise and Secular Change* (London: Allen and Unwin, 1953), p. 411. Gay had studied with Schmoller in Berlin. The original text reads: "Aber, meine Her- ren, es ist alles so unendlich compliziert."

14. Carl Menger, *Die Irrthümer des Historismus in der deutschen Nationalökonomie* (Vienna: Alfred Hölder, 1884), p. 46. Schmoller's statement about one little room in the big house of economics comes from his "Der Methodologie der Staats- und Sozialwis- senschaften," *Jahrbuch für Gesetzgebung, Verwaltung und Volkswirtschaft* 7 (1883): 251.

15. Carl Menger, *Investigations into the Method of the Social Sciences with Special Reference to Economics* (New York: New York University Press, [1883] 1985), pp. 139–59. That Menger had influenced Weber in this regard is clear, I would argue, from the fol- lowing well-known statement about "the fundamental problem of economics" in *Roscher and Knies* (1903–1906): "the fundamental substantive and methodological problem of economics is constituted by the question: how are the origins and persistence of the in- stitutions of economic life to be explained, institutions which were *not* purposefully cre- ated by collective means, but which nevertheless—from our point of view—function pur- posefully?" See Weber, *Roscher and Knies: The Logical Problems of Historical Economics* (New York: Free Press, 1975), p. 80, or "Roscher und Knies und die logischen Probleme der historischen Nationalökonomie," p. 29 in *Gesammelte Aufsätze zur Wissenschafts- lehre.*

16. Hayek writes: "Menger was greatly interested in history and the genesis of insti- tutions, and he was anxious mainly to emphasize the different nature of the task of the- ory and the task of history proper and to prevent a confusion of their methods. The dis- tinction, as he elaborated it, considerably influenced the later work of Rickert and Max Weber." See Friedrich von Hayek, *The Fortunes of Liberalism* (London: Routledge, 1992), p. 78 n. 49.

17. Max Weber, "Debattereden auf der Tagung des Vereins für Sozialpolitik in Wien 1909 zu den Verhandlungen über die Produktivität der Volkswirtschaft," p. 419 in *Gesammelte Aufsätze zur Soziologie und Sozialpolitik* (Tübingen: J.C.B. Mohr, 1988). In this context, see also Wilhelm Hennis, "The Pitiless 'Sobriety of Judgment': Max Weber between Carl Menger and Gustav von Schmoller—The Academic Politics of Value Free- dom," *History of the Human Sciences* 4 (1991): 28–59.

18. Schumpeter, *History of Economic Analysis*, pp. 21, 819. On page 21, Schumpeter uses the term *Sozialökonomie* and translates it as "social economics."

19. Jean-Baptiste Say, *Cours complet d'économie politique pratique* (Paris: Rapilly, Li- braire, 1828), Vol. 1, p. 2. Maxime Leroy claims that it was Destutt de Tracy who first used the term (in the early 1820s) and that Sismondi then popularized it; see Maxime Leroy, *Histoire des idées sociales en France* (Paris: Librairie Gallimard, 1962), Vol. 2, p. 163. The term used by the German translator of Say for "*économie sociale*" was, however, "*die gesellschaftliche Staatswirthschaft,*" not "*Sozialökonomik.*" The first recorded use of "*Sozialökonomik*" (or a similar term) in Germany is to be found in a noneconomic work from 1846 ("Social-Ökonomie"); and the first time it was used in an economic work was in 1848 (in a book by Bruno Hildebrand, entitled *Die Nationalökonomie der Gegenwart und Zukunft*). For the information on the translation of Say, see Jean-Baptiste Say, *Hand-*

buch der practischen National-Oekonomie oder der gesammten Staatswirthschaft für Staatsmänner, Gutsherren, Gelehrte, Kapitalisten, Landwirthe, Fabrikanten, Handelsherren und alle denkende Staatsbürger, trans. F. A. Rüder (Leipzig: C.H.F. Hartmann, 1829), Vol. 1, p. 1; see also F. Lifschitz, "J. B. Says Methodologie der Wirtschaftswissenschaft," *Jahrbücher für Nationalökonomie und Statistik* 28 (1904): 614–24. For the information on the first recorded uses of "Sozialökonomik" (and similar terms) in Germany, see L. H. Adolph Geck, *Über das Eindringen des Wortes* **Sozial** *in die deutsche Sprache* (Göttingen: Otto Schwartz, 1963), pp. 38, 41. For some additional information on the history of this term, see also Richard Swedberg, "Schumpeter's Vision of Socioeconomics," *Journal of Socio-Economics* 24 (1995): 525–44.

20. Mill himself saw "social economy" as the science that deals with "every part of man's nature, in so far as influencing the conduct or condition of man in society." See John Stuart Mill, "On the Definition of Political Economy; and on the Method of Investigation Proper to It (1838)," p. 136 in *Essays on Some Unsettled Questions of Political Economy* (London: John W. Parker, 1844).

21. Note that an effort has been made to track down the various editions of a work that uses the term "social economics" because the term made a new appearance, so to speak, in each edition. The dates refer to the following works: Bruno Hildebrand, *Die Nationalökonomie der Gegenwart und Zukunft* (1848) as cited in Geck, *Über das Eindringen des Wortes* **Sozial** *in die deutsche Sprache,* p. 48; Wilhelm Roscher, *Die Grundlagen der Nationalökonomie. Ein Hand- und Lesebuch für Geschäftsmänner und Studierende* (Stuttgart: J. G. Cott'scher Verlag, 1854), p. 24 (reference to Say and others' "*économie sociale*"); Albert Schäffle, *Das gesellschaftliche System der menschlichen Wirtschaft* (Tübingen: J.C.B. Mohr: H. Laupp'sche Buchhandlung, 1867), p. 3 ("Socialökonomie"); Eugen Dühring, *Cursus der National- und Socialökonomie einschliesslich der Hauptpunkte der Finanzpolitik* (Berlin: Verlag von Theobald Grieben, 1873); Eugen Dühring, *Cursus der National- und Socialökonomie,* 2d ed. (Leipzig: Fues's Verlag, 1876), p. 3; and Karl Knies, *Die politische Oekonomie* ([1883] 1930), p. 3 ("*sociale Oekonomie*"). The term "*Socialwirtschaftslehre*" was used for "*économie sociale*" by Heinrich Dietzel in 1882 and 1883; see Heinrich Dietzel, *Ueber das Verhältnis der Volkswirtschaftslehre zur Socialwirtschaftslehre* (Berlin: Puttkammer und Mühlbrecht, 1882), and Heinrich Dietzel, "Der Ausgangspunkt der Socialwirtschaftslehre und ihr Grundbegriff," *Zeitschrift für die gesamte Staatswissenschaft* 39 (1883): 1–80. Carl Menger uses "*sociale Oekonomie*" (referring explictly to Say's "*économie sociale*") in *Untersuchungen* (1883); cf. Carl Menger, *Untersuchungen über die Methode der Socialwissenschaften, und der Politischen Oekonomie* (Leipzig: Duncker und Humblot, 1883), p. 251. See also Werner Sombart, *Die römische Campagna. Eine sozialökonomische Studie* (Leipzig: Duncker und Humblot, 1888). Given the number of economists who used the term "social economics" *before* or simultaneously with Dietzel there is no reason to believe, as Hennis and Winkelmann do, that Weber got the term from Dietzel; cf. Johannes Winkelmann, *Max Webers hinterlassenes Hauptwerk* (Tübingen: J.C.B. Mohr, 1986), p. 12 n. 21; Wilhelm Hennis, "A Science of Man: Max Weber and the Political Economy of the German Historical School," p. 53 n. 23 in Mommsen and Osterhammel, eds., *Max Weber and His Contemporaries.* Hennis is convinced that Weber read the 1883 edition of Knies's textbook (where "*sociale Oekonomie*" appears) and says that it was published "in the very same semester as that in which Weber finally realized the quality of his teacher"; cf. Hennis, "A Science of Man," p. 41). Weber also refers to the 1883 edition in his reading guide in economics from 1898; cf. Max Weber, *Grundriss zu den Vorlesungen über Allgemeine ("theoretische") Nationalökonomie (1898)* (Tübingen: J.C.B. Mohr, 1990), p. 5. Knies, like Say, affirms that

economics means an analysis of society; "Let it suffice for us to indicate that the phrase 'political economy' must likewise mean 'social economy'" (*Die politische Oekonomie*, p. 3).

22. To Dietzel, however, *Socialökonomik* is the science that focuses on those social phenomena that result from actions by individuals. See Dietzel, *Theoretische Socialökonomik* (Leipzig: C. F. Winter'sche Verlagshandlung, 1895), Vol. 1, pp. 27–28. Léon Walras also initiated a new use of *"économie sociale"* when he defined it as "the science of distribution of social wealth"; cf. Léon Walras, *Elements of Pure Economics or the Theory of Social Wealth* (London: Allen and Unwin, [1874] 1954), p. 79. Someone who explicitly followed Walras on this point is Knut Wicksell, who also added that *"socialekonomi"* was the same as "economic policy"; see Knut Wicksell, *Föreläsningar i nationalekonomi* (Lund: Gleerups, [1901] 1966), Vol. 1, p. 6.

23. Schmoller objected in particular to Heinrich Dietzel's use of the term, according to which the state was not part of the "social economy." See Gustav von Schmoller, "Volkswirtschaft, Volkswirtschaftslehre und -methode," p. 429 in Vol. 8 of Conrad et al. eds., *Handwörterbuch der Staatswissenschaften* (Jena: Gustav Fischer, 1911). In a book from the same year, Alfred Amonn says that "when this name ['*Volkswirtschaftslehre*'] was not felt to be totally 'right,' an attempt was made with 'Sozialwirtschaftslehre'; and also 'Sozialökonomie' and 'Sozialökonomik.'" See Alfred Amonn, *Objekt und Grundbegriffe der Theoretischen Nationalökonomie* (Leipzig: Franz Deuticke, 1911), p. 440.

24. Schumpeter, *History of Economic Analysis*, p. 535.

25. Given the fact that Marshall was so concerned with the question of what term to use instead of the outmoded "political economy," it may be of some interest to note that the well-known sentence in *Principles of Economics* stating that the analysis of economic phenomena "is better described by the broad term 'Economics' than by the narrower term 'Political Economy'" had the following wording in the 3d and the 4th editions: the analysis of economic phenomena "is better described as *Social Economics,* or as *Economics* simply, than as *Political Economy.*" See Alfred Marshall, p. 43 in Vol. 1 and p. 159 in Vol. 2 of the variorum edition of *Principles of Economics* (London: Macmillan, 1961). I thank Patrik Aspers for drawing my attention to this passage in Marshall.

26. That the first recorded use of the term "economic sociology" was by Jevons in 1879 (in the preface to the second edition of *The Principles of Economics*) is an opinion I share with Jean-Jacques Gislain and Philippe Steiner; see their *La sociologie économique 1890–1920* (Paris: Presses Universitaires de France, 1995), pp. 10–11. Jevons saw sociology in a Spencerian light and defined economic sociology as *"[the] science of the development of economic forms and relations"*; W. Stanley Jevons, "Preface to the Second Edition (1879)," p. xvi in *The Theory of Political Economy* (New York: Augustus M. Kelley [1905] 1965). Like Menger, Jevons wanted to improve economics by introducing a firm division of labor into economics itself, with "economic sociology" separated from, e.g., "fiscal science," "commercial statistics," "systematic and descriptive economics," and "the mathematical theory of economics"; see W. Stanley Jevons, "The Future of Political Economy (1876)," pp. 185–206 in *The Principles of Economics* (London: Macmillan, 1905) and Jevons, "Preface to the Second Edition (1879)," p. xvii in *The Theory of Political Economy*. For a critical view of Jevons's notion of economic sociology, see Thomas Edward Cliffe Leslie's review of Jevons's work from 1879, pp. 157–62 in Vol. 7 of R. D. Collison Black, ed., *Papers and Correspondence of William Stanley Jevons* (London: Macmillan, 1981). In France, Durkheim proposed a *"sociologie économique"* in the mid-1890s; see, e.g., the section entitled "Sociologie Economique" in *L'Année Sociologique* 1 (1896/1897).

27. See the statement that "economics belongs . . . to the realm of sociology" in Franz

Oppenheimer, "Ökonomie und Soziologie," *Monatsschrift für Soziologie* 1 (1909): 607. Around this time, the Austrian economist Friedrich von Wieser was also becomming interested in sociology. For Wieser and economic sociology, see the discussion of *Grundriss der Sozialökonomik* in chapter 6 of this work.

28. Schmoller, "Volkswirtschaft" (1894), p. 539.

29. See on this point Schumpeter's statement in *History of Economic Analysis* that "the Schmollerian economist was in fact a historically minded sociologist in the latter term's widest meaning" (p. 812). According to Schmoller's successor in Berlin, "Schmoller was first of all a sociologist"; see Heinrich Herkner, "Gustav Schmoller als Soziologe," *Jahrbücher für Nationalökonomie und Statistik* 118 (1922): 3 (with references to others who shared this opinion, such as Carl Brinkmann and Georg von Below). According to French sociologists Emile Durkheim and Paul Fauçonnet, Schmoller's *Grundriss* (1900–1904) contains "toute une sociologie, vue du point de vue économique"; cf. Emile Durkheim and Paul Fauçonnet, "Sociologie et sciences sociales," *Revue philosophique* 55 (January–June 1903): 496.

30. The two chairs in "economics and sociology" were given to Franz Oppenheimer (University of Frankfurt am Main) and Leopold von Wiese (University of Cologne). During the years 1919–1933, forty appointments to professorships with *Soziologie* in the title were made in Germany, and thirteen of these were in "economics and sociology." The exact titles of the chairs varied; Adolf Löwe, for example, was in 1926 appointed to a chair in "Wirtschaftstheorie und Soziologie" at the University of Kiel, and Fritz Karl Mann to a chair in "Nationalökonomie und Soziologie" in 1932, also at the University of Kiel. See Dirk Käsler, *Die frühe deutsche Soziologie 1909 bis 1934 und ihre Enstehungsmilieus. Eine wissenschaftssoziologische Untersuchung* (Opladen: Westdeutscher Verlag, 1984), pp. 626–28.

31. According to an analysis of the subjects published in economics journals in Germany during the years 1900–1930, "sociology and philosophy" made up 6–10 percent of the articles in *Schmollers Jahrbuch;* 15–20 percent in *Archiv für Sozialwissenschaft und Sozialpolitik;* 5–10 percent in *Zeitschrift für Sozialwissenschaft;* and about 10 percent in *Zeitschrift für die gesamte Staatswissenschaft;* see Erhard Stölting, *Akademische Soziologie in der Weimarer Republik* (Berlin: Duncker und Humblot, 1986), pp. 148–59.

32. Only parts of *The Philosophy of Money* is of a sociological character; see esp. pp. 170–90 in Georg Simmel, *The Philosophy of Money* (London: Routledge, [1906] 1978). Simmel's work on money was favorably reviewed by Schmoller and G. F. Knapp; Menger was profoundly critical. According to Schmoller, Simmel's work was of a "sociological-philosophical character," and according to Knapp, Simmel's book "rather deals with the sociological side of the money economy" than with economic theory; for Schmoller, see David Frisby, "The Works," p. 197 in Vol. 1 of David Frisby, ed., *Georg Simmel: Critical Assessments* (London: Routledge, 1994); and for Knapp, see David Frisby, *Simmel and Since* (London: Routledge, 1992), p. 84. For other works in economic sociology from this time, see, for example, the following: Karl Wasserrab, *Soziologische Nationalökonomie* (Munich: Duncker und Humblot, 1917); Rudolf Goldscheid, *Staatssozialismus oder Staatskapitalismus. Ein finanzsoziologischer Beitrag zur Lösung des Staatsschulden-Problems* (Vienna: Anzengruber-Verlag Brüder Suschitsky, 1917); Joseph A. Schumpeter, *Die Krise des Steuerstaates* (Graz: Leuschner und Lubensky, 1918); Joseph A. Schumpeter, *Zur Soziologie der Imperialismen* (Tübingen: J.C.B. Mohr, 1919); Robert Wilbrandt, *Oekonomie. Ideen zu einer Philosophie und Soziologie der Wirtschaft* (Tübingen: J.C.B. Mohr, 1920). For Sombart's speculation whether the second edition of *Der moderne Kapitalismus* is a work in "Wirtschaftssoziologie . . . or something similar," see

Werner Sombart, *Der moderne Kapitalismus* (Munich: Deutscher Taschenbuch Verlag [1916] 1987), p. xvii. Finally, as a curiosity it can be mentioned that Carl Menger's attempt to recast his economic theory during the last few decades of his life (he died in 1921) supposedly went in an economic sociological direction; see especially the material and argument presented in Kiichiro Yagi, "Carl Menger after 1871" (1988, unpublished manuscript). Menger himself did not call what he did "sociology," but his assistant Felix Somary did, and it seems clear that Menger showed some interest in comparative, ethnographic studies during this part of his life. The general impression one gets from Yagi, however, is that much more research needs to be done on Menger's papers before it is possible to establish what Menger tried to accomplish, and whether it reasonably can be said to constitute economic sociology.

33. According to a letter to his mother dated May 2, 1882, Weber found Knies's lectures "boring"; and in a letter to his father dated February 23, 1883, he stated that "even if [Knies's lectures] are not interesting, something which probably the topic prevents, it is in any case treated in a thorough manner." The positive opinion of Knies's lectures is to be found in a letter from Weber to his father, dated May 5, 1883. See Weber, *Jugendbriefe* (Tübingen: J.C.B. Mohr, 1936), pp. 41, 71, 74; see also Marianne Weber, *Max Weber*, p. 65. According to information that has kindly been supplied to me by the Archive of the University of Heidelberg, Weber took a course from Knies called "General Economics (Theoretical Economics)" (Allgemeine Volkswirtschaftslehre [theoretische Nationalökonomie]) during the summer semester of 1883. In 1882 he attended only one lecture by Knies. I also thank Wilhelm Hennis for help with understanding Weber's relationship to Knies.

34. Weber, *Jugendbriefe*, p. 74. In the fall of 1883 Weber also read Gustav von Schmoller's essays on political economy in *Preussische Jahrbücher*. But even though Weber began reading economics literature seriously in 1883, he would say four years later, "As a political economist I am still poorly informed." See Max Weber, letters to his father (September 3, 1883) and to Hermann Baumgarten (September 30, 1887) in *Jugendbriefe*, pp. 75, 273.

35. See Hennis, "A Science of Man," pp. 25–58 in Mommsen and Osterhammel, eds., *Max Weber and His Contemporaries*.

36. The main challenge to Hennis has come from Martin Riesebrodt; see Martin Riesebrodt, "From Patriarchalism to Capitalism: The Theoretical Context of Max Weber's Agrarian Studies (1892–3)," p. 144 in Keith Tribe, ed., *Reading Weber* (London: Routledge, 1989). For Hennis's answer to Riesebrodt (that no real evidence for the influence of Schmoller has been produced), see Hennis, "The Pitiless 'Sobriety of Judgment,'" *History of Human Sciences* 4(1991), p. 191 n. 5. Bertram Schefold also mentions Knies as a major influence on Weber; see Bertram Schefold, "Knies, Karl Gustav Adolf (1821–1898)," p. 55 in Vol. 3 of John Eatwell, Murray Milgate and Peter Newman, eds., *The New Palgrave: A Dictionary of Economics* (London: Macmillan, 1987).

37. Alexander von Schelting, "Die logische Theorie der historischen Kulturwissenschaft von Max Weber und im besonderen sein Begriff des Idealtypus," *Archiv für Sozialwissenschaft und Sozialpolitik* 49 (1922): 705.

38. For "one-third economist," see Weber's letter to Hermann Baumgarten, dated January 3, 1891, in *Jugendbriefe*, p. 327.

39. Jürgen Backhaus has argued that "Weber carefully avoided studying with all the major economists in Berlin, like Schmoller and Wagner." This is correct on a general level, even though it should be noted that Weber did take a course from Wagner while in Berlin, probably in political science ("*staatswissenschaftliche Vorlesungen*"). See Backhaus, as

cited in Harald Hagemann, "How Well Has Werner Sombart's Scholarship Stood Up in the Applied Fields?," p. 149 in Vol. 1 of Jürgen Backhaus, *Werner Sombart (1863–1941), Social Scientist* (Marburg: Metropolis-Verlag, 1996). For the teachers Weber had as a student, see the account of his life that Weber attached to his first dissertation and which is reprinted in Johannes Winkelmann, "Max Webers Dissertation," p. 12 in René König and Johannes Winkelmann, eds., *Max Weber zum Gedächtnis* (Cologne: Westdeutscher Verlag, 1963).

40. Marianne Weber, *Max Weber,* p. 115.

41. The title of the dissertation was *Entwickelung des Solidarhaftprinzips und des Sondervermögens der offenen Handelsgesellschaft aus den Haushalts- und Gewerbegemeinschaften in den italienischen Städten (The Principle of Joint Liability and the Separate Fund in Business Partnerships: Their Development out of the Household and Trade Communities in the Italian Cities).* The thesis constitutes part 3 of a larger work: Max Weber, "Zur Geschichte der Handelsgesellschaften im Mittelalter (1889)," pp. 312–443 in *Gesammelte Aufsätze zur Sozial- und Wirtschaftsgeschichte* (Tübingen: J.C.B. Mohr, 1988). Although part 3 constituted the thesis, technically speaking, Weber himself nonetheless referred to the whole book as his thesis ("my as-doctoral-dissertation-functioning book"); see Weber's letter to Hermann Baumgarten, dated July 30, 1889, in Weber, *Jugendbriefe,* p. 312.

42. Max Weber, *Die römische Agrargeschichte in ihrer Bedeutung für das Staats- und Privatrecht (1891). Max Weber Gesamtausgabe I/2* (Tübingen: J.C.B. Mohr, 1986).

43. Marianne Weber, *Max Weber,* p. 124; letter to Hermann Baumgarten, dated January 3, 1891, in Weber, *Jugendbriefe,* p. 327.

44. Max Weber, *Die Lage der Landarbeiter im ostelbischen Deutschland. 1892. Max Weber Gesamtausgabe I/3* (Tübingen: J.C.B. Mohr, 1984), pp. 18–1057.

45. G. F. Knapp, "Referat," p. 7 in Verein für Sozialpolitik, *Verhandlungen der am 20. und 21. März 1893 in Berlin abgehaltenen Generalversammlung des Vereins für Sozialpolitik* (Leipzig: Duncker und Humblot, 1893).

46. The expression is from Weber's inaugural lecture in Freiburg; see Max Weber, "The Nation State and Economic Policy," p. 8 in *Political Writings,* or "Der Nationalstaat und die Volkswirtschaftspolitik," p. 7 in *Gesammelte Politische Schriften.*

47. It has been argued in recent studies of Weber's early works that the concept of *"Arbeitsverfassung"* is a key to his approach. It is also often noted that this term is hard to translate. According to Lawrence Scaff, for example, *"Arbeitsverfassung"* is "a shorthand way of characterizing the historically given 'constitution,' or 'organization' of labor, or labor relations"; and Keith Tribe notes that "there is some difficulty with the term *'Arbeitsverfassung,'* which is frequently used by Weber. . . . The problem here is that *'Verfassung'* means literally 'constitution' as in the 'British Constitution,' and is used by Weber and others to denote the ensemble of legal, economic, and political conditions governing the employment of labour and the relation of labourers to specified persons." See Lawrence Scaff, "The Problem of Thematic Unity in the Works of Max Weber," p. 44 in Tribe, ed., *Reading Weber;* and Tribe, p. 185, "Translator's Note" in *Reading Weber.*

48. Weber, *Die Lage der Landarbeiter im ostelbischen Deutschland. 1892. Max Weber Gesamtausgabe I/3,* pp. 920–21.

49. Weber, "Die deutschen Landarbeiter (1894)," p. 66 as cited in Scaff, "Weber before Weberian Sociology," pp. 27–28 in Tribe, ed., *Reading Weber.*

50. Philippovich had first recommended Friedrich von Wieser, followed by Max Sering. Why this list was not followed is not clear; in any case, Weber was number one on Philippovich's second list, followed by Carl Johannes Fuchs (who later replaced Weber

in Freiburg) and Walter Lotz; see Keith Tribe, *Strategies of Economic Order: German Economic Discourse, 1750–1950* (Cambridge: Cambridge University Press, 1995), p. 82. According to a notice in *Journal of Political Economy* of 1893, the departure of Philippovich had hurt Freiburg quite a bit because it was "already weakened by the loss of Professor Holst"; see *Journal of Political Economy* 1 (1893): 264. For a sense of the courses and seminars that were given in Freiburg in the 1890s, see the list for the winter semester of 1889–1890 and the summer semester of 1890 in (no author), "Instruction in Public Law and Political Economy in German Universities," *Annals of the American Academy in Political and Social Science* 1 (1890–91): 81, 87, 274, 277.

51. Marianne Weber, *Max Weber*, p. 200. The translation has been changed. The three areas to which economics, according to Weber, led directly are "Kultur- und Ideengeschichte [und] philosophische Probleme." The comment of Ludwig von Mises, who detested historical economics, on Weber's appointment at Freiburg is worth citing: "He was appointed professor of economics without having dealt with this science before, which was a customary procedure at the time." See Ludwig von Mises, *A Critique of Interventionism* (New Rochelle, N.Y.: Arlington House, [1929] 1977), p. 103.

52. For Weber at Freiburg, see also Tribe, *Strategies of Economic Order*, p. 84. In Weber's day the two basic courses in economics at German universities were "General Theoretical Economics" (*Allgemeine theoretische Nationalökonomie*) and "Practical Economics" (*Praktische Nationalökonomie*); and at Freiburg, Weber shared the responsibility for teaching them with Gerhart von Schulze-Gaevernitz. All in all, Weber taught the following courses while in Freiburg: winter semester of 1894–95: "General Theoretical Economics" and "Finance"; summer semester of 1895: "Practical Economics (Economic Policy)," "The German Labor Question in the City and in the Countryside," and a seminar or course called "Agrarian Policy"; winter semester of 1895–96: "General Theoretical Economics" and "Money, Banking, and the Stock Market"; summer semester of 1896: "General Theoretical Economics" and "History of Economics"; and the winter semester of 1896–97: "Finance" and "The Stock Market and Its Legal Regulation." Together with his colleague Schulze-Gaevernitz, Weber also each term taught "a cameralistic seminar." See Wolfgang J. Mommsen and Rita Aldenhoff, "Einleitung," p. 41 in Vol. 1 of *Landarbeiterfrage, Nationalstaat und Volkswirtschaftspolitik. Max Weber Gesamtausgabe I/4* (Tübingen: J.C.B. Mohr, 1993). It may be added that the winter semester typically started mid-October and lasted until mid-March; the summer semester began mid-April and ended by mid-August; see H. R. Seager, "Economics at Berlin and Vienna," *Journal of Political Economy* 1 (1893): 239. (These were the official dates, but "the semester actually opens a week or ten days later than announced, and closes a week or ten days earlier"; no author, "Instruction in Public Law and Political Economy in German Universities. II," *Annals of the American Academy in Political and Social Science* 1 [1890–1891]: 272). Weber's notes for his courses in economics will eventually be published in the *Gesamtausgabe* and should provide a more complete picture of Weber's view of economics than the one that is currently possible.

53. Marianne Weber, *Max Weber*, p. 202; cf. p. 228. I have only been able to locate two other accounts of Weber as a teacher in Freiburg: those of Robert Liefmann, who described Weber's lectures as "rather unsystematic," and Hermann Schumacher, who described them as "unfinished." See Robert Liefmann, "Robert Liefmann," pp. 157–58 in Felix Meiner, ed., *Die Volkswirtschaftslehre der Gegenwart in Selbstdarstellungen* (Leipzig: Felix Meiner, 1924); and Hermann Schumacher, "Weber, Max," p. 598 in *Deutsches Biographisches Jahrbuch* (Berlin: Deutsche Verlags-Anstalt Stuttgart, 1928).

54. Marianne Weber, *Max Weber*, p. 216.

55. "The Nation State and Economic Policy," p. 12, or "Der Nationalstaat und die Volkswirtschaftspolitik," p. 10 in "Der Nationalstaat und die Volkswirtschaftspolitik." Weber would later say that he did not any longer "identify" with what he had said in 1895 "on several important points." See Weber, "Gutachten zur Werturteilsdiskussion im Ausschuss des Vereins für Sozialpolitik," p. 127 in Eduard Baumgarten, *Max Weber. Werk und Person* (Tübingen: J.C.B. Mohr, 1964).

56. Max Weber, "The Nation State and Economic Policy," pp. 17, 21, 18 in *Political Writings*, or pp. 15, 18, 16 in "Der Nationalstaat und die Volkswirtschaftspolitik."

57. Max Weber, "The Social Causes of the Decay of Ancient Civilization," *Journal of General Education* 5 (1949–51): 75–88. Another, but less skillful translation can be found in Max Weber, *The Agrarian Sociology of Ancient Civilizations* (London: New Left Books, 1976), pp. 387–411.

58. Max Weber, "Die Börse," pp. 322, 321 in *Gesammelte Aufsätze zur Soziologie und Sozialpolitik*.

59. G. F. Knapp, followed by Karl Bücher, had originally been placed ahead of Weber by the Faculty of Philosophy in Heidelberg; see Tribe, *Strategies of Economic Order*, p. 85. The documents relating to Weber's appointment in Heidelberg do not exist any longer, according to information I have received from the University Archives at the Ruprecht-Karls-Universität Heidelberg. (I gratefully acknowledge the helpfullness of Prof. Wolgast in this matter.) See the Faculty of Philosophy in a memorandum dated November 1896 as cited in Tribe, *Strategies of Economic Order*, p. 85.

60. During seminars, students wrote papers under the supervision of their professor. Seminars typically took place in a special room with a library that was available to the students. For the role of the seminar in German economics, see S. M. Wickett, "Political Economy at German Universities," *Economic Journal* 8 (1898): 148–50, and Seager, "Economics at Berlin and Vienna," *Journal of Political Economy* 1 (1893), pp. 245–48.

61. For these and the few other details that are known, see Mommsen and Aldenhoff, "Einleitung," pp. 45–46 in Vol. 1 of *Landarbeiterfrage, Nationalstaat und Volkswirtschaftspolitik. Max Weber Gesamtausgabe I/4.*

62. Weber and Emanuel Leser were responsible at Heidelberg for teaching general theoretical economics and practical economics. In addition, Weber taught the following courses and lecture series: summer semester of 1897: "General (Theoretical) Economics" and "Seminar in Economics"; winter semester of 1897–98: "Practical Economics: Trade Policy, Industrial Policy, and Infrastructure Policy," and "Agrarian Policy"; summer semester of 1898: "General (Theoretical) Economics, excluding History of Economics" and "The Social Question and the Labor Movement"; winter semester of 1898–99: "Seminar in Economics" and "Practical Economics (excluding Money and Banking), the General Part: Population Policy, Trade Policy, Industrial Policy, Infrastructure Policy, and Agrarian Policy"; and winter semester of 1899–1900: "Agrarian Policy" (not completed). Many more courses were announced but not given because of Weber's illness. See Mommsen and Aldenhoff, "Einleitung," p. 42 in Vol. 1 of *Landarbeiterfrage, Nationalstaat und Volkswirtschaftspolitik. Max Weber Gesataugabe I/4.*

63. Marianne Weber, *Max Weber*, p. 228.

64. Mommsen and Aldenhoff, "Einleitung," p. 45 n. 171 in Vol. 1 of *Landarbeiterfrage, Nationalstaat und Volkswirtschaftspolitik. Max Weber Gesamtausgabe I/4.*

65. The first version from 1897 was eighteen pages long; the seocnd version from 1898 was twenty-nine pages long; and the book-length study appeared in 1909. See Max Weber, "Agrarverhältnisse im Altertum," pp. 1– in Supplementary Volume 2 of J. Conrad et al., eds., *Handwörterbuch der Staatswissenschaften,* (Jena: Gustav Fischer, 1897);

"Agrargeschichte. I. Agrarverhältnisse im Altertum", pp. 57–85 in Vol. 1 of J. Conrad et al, eds., *Handwörterbuch der Staatswissenschaften*, 2d ed. (Jena: Verlag von Gustav Fischer, 1898); and *The Agrarian Scoiology of Ancient Civilizations,* trans R. I. Frank (London: New Left Books, [1909] 1976).

66. The course was entitled "Der Gang der wirtschaftlichen Entwicklung" and was delivered in four installments (November 19 and 26 and December 3 and 10, 1897). The titles of the lectures were: "The Emergence of Private Property and the Agrarian Foundation of the European Economy," "Feudalism and the City Economy in the Middle Ages," "The Development of the National Economy and the Mercantilistic System," and "The Social Situation of Modern Capitalism." For more information, see Weber, Vol. 2 of *Landarbeiterfrage, Nationalstaat und Volkswirtschaftspolitik. Max Weber Gesamtausgabe I/4,* pp. 842–52.

67. Little is known about this textbook. Marianne Weber writes, "For his great course on theoretical political economy [in Heidelberg] he gave his students a printed outline that he intended to expand into a textbook." See Marianne Weber, *Max Weber,* p. 228. According to Lawrence Scaff, drawing on some unpublished correspondence, Weber wrote to his mother on July 23, 1899, that "he wants to have the 'Grundriss' in manuscript form next year and available as a book the year afterward"—a plan that Weber's illness, if nothing else, prevented. See Lawrence Scaff, *Fleeing the Iron Cage: Culture, Politics, and Modernity in the Thought of Max Weber* (Berkeley: University of California Press, 1989), p. 33 n. 33. It is generally assumed that Weber's textbook would have been structured as his reading guide.

68. Weber, *Grundriss zu den Vorlesungen über Allgemeine ("theoretische") Nationalökonomie (1898).* The title of the booklet is identical to the title of the reading guide, while the notes for the students have as a title *Erstes Buch. Die begrifflichen Grundlagen der Volkswirtschaftslehre.* According to the introduction, written by the editors of the *Gesamtausgabe,* the reading guide was in all likelihood prepared for Weber's course in general economic theory in the summer semester of 1898. A date for the notes is not given, but the editors point out some discrepancies between the reading guide and the notes, and the reader is left with the impression that the notes must have been prepared for one of the other times Weber taught this course, perhaps for the summer semester of 1897 in Heidelberg (but conceivably also for the winter semesters 1894–95 or 1895–96 or the summer semester of 1896). No thorough analysis has been made of the *Outline,* even if it is generally recognized as an important document for the understanding of Weber as an economist and as a social scientist more generally. For some interesting comments, see Scaff, *Fleeing the Iron Cage,* pp. 32–33, 43, 134–35; and Tribe, "Introduction," p. 4 ff. in *Reading Weber.*

69. It is reasonable to assume that Weber also discussed Marx in his lectures at Freiburg. Exactly when Weber began studying Marx's work is not known. The first time he mentions Marx is, as far as I know, in a letter from 1892. See Tribe, ed., *Reading Weber,* p. 155 n. 10. The notes that Weber made on Marx's work for the *Outline* of 1898 are still in existence at the Max Weber Arbeitsstelle in Munich; they indicate, according to Lawrence Scaff, that Weber intended to include "a comprehensive critique of Marx's value theory in the context of socialist thought." See Scaff, *Fleeing the Iron Cage,* p. 43 n. 19.

70. Weber, *Grundriss,* pp. 29, 30. The second citation as translated by Tribe, "Introduction," p. 6 in *Reading Weber.*

71. "Economic action" ("*Wirtschaften*"), "power of control and disposal" ("*Verfügungsgewalt*"), "opportunity" ("*Chance*") and "struggle" ("price struggle," "struggle be-

tween competitors," etc.), (*"Kampf," "Preiskampf," "Konkurrenzkampf"*). Many other terms and concepts that became part of Weber's economic sociology in *Economy and Society* are also to be found in the *Outline*, including "utility" (*"Nutzleistungen"*), "market situation" (*"Marktlage"*), and "domination (in the economy)" (*"Herrschaft"*).

72. See Weber, *Grundriss zu den Vorlesungen über Allgemeine ("theoretische") Nationalökonomie (1898)*, pp. 47, 51–52, 53. In his views of the theoretical formation of prices, Weber followed Austrian economics. For a succinct presentation of the Austrian theory of price formation, see Schumpeter, *History of Economic Analysis*, pp. 912–17, 920–24.

73. Frank H. Knight, *Risk, Uncertainty and Profit* (Chicago: University of Chicago Press, [1921] 1985), pp. 76–79. See in this context also Joseph Persky, "Perspectives: The Ethology of *Homo Economicus,*" *Journal of Economic Perspectives* 9 (1995): 221–31.

74. Marianne Weber, *Max Weber*, pp. 251, 253.

75. Weber worked hard to get Sombart to replace him in Freiburg as well as in Heidelberg; see Tribe, *Strategies of Economic Order*, p. 87; Marianne Weber, *Max Weber*, p. 242. Karl Rathgen (1856–1921) stayed in Heidelberg until 1907, when he moved to the German Colonial Institute in Hamburg.

76. Eberhard Gothein (1853–1923) specialized in nineteenth-century economic history and also did work in cultural history.

77. Weber, "Between Two Laws," p. 78 in *Political Writings*, or "Zwischen zwei Gesetzen," p. 144 in *Gesammelte Politische Schriften*. This article appeared in 1916.

78. V. I. Lenin, "Lecture on the 1905 Revolution," p. 251 in Vol. 23 of *Collected Works* (Moscow: Progress Publishers, 1964). Lenin wrote this article in 1917, but it was not published until 1925.

79. Weber in a letter to Schmoller, dated June 23, 1908, in *Briefe 1906–1908. Max Weber Gesamtausgabe II/5* (Tübingen: J.C.B. Mohr, 1990), p. 595.

80. Weber, "Marginal Utility Theory and 'The Fundamental Law of Psychophysics,'" *Social Science Quarterly* 56 (June 1975): 33, or "Die Grenznutzenlehre und das 'psychophysische Grundgesetz,'" p. 396 in *Gesammelte Aufsätze zur Wissenschaftslehre*, p. 396. For Weber's positive attitude toward Menger in his response to Brentano, see also his letter to Brentano of October 30, 1908, in *Briefe 1906–1908*, pp. 688–89. Weber here says that Menger was right in the *Methodenstreit* "when it comes to *the key issue* on the most important points." By "key issue" Weber undoubtedly meant whether it was correct to let economic history replace economic theory, as Schmoller for all practical purposes wanted.

81. Weber, "Debattereden auf der Tagung des Vereins für Sozialpolitik in Wien 1909 zu den Verhandlungen über die Produktivität der Volkswirtschaft," p. 419 in *Gesammelte Aufsätze zur Soziologie und Sozialpolitik;* emphasis added.

82. Edgar Jaffé, Werner Sombart, and Max Weber, "Geleitwort," *Archiv für Sozialwissenschaft und Sozialpolitik* 19 (1904): v.; emphasis in the original.

83. Weber, "'Objectivity' in Social Science and Social Policy," p. 63 (cf. p. 58) in *The Methodology of the Social Sciences* (New York: Free Press, 1949), or "Die 'Objektivität' sozialwissenschaftlicher und sozialpolitischer Erkenntnis," p. 160 (cf. p. 155) in *Gesammelte Aufsätze zur Wissenschaftslehre*.

84. Weber, "Objectivity," p. 63, or "Objektivität," p. 161.

85. Weber, "Objectivity" pp. 63–67, or "Objektivität," p. 161–66. The exact definition is the following: "Most roughly expressed, the basic element in all those phenomena which we call, in the widest sense, 'social-economic' is constituted by the fact that our physical existence and the satisfaction of our most ideal needs are everywhere confronted

with the quantitative limits and the qualitative inadequacy of the necessary external means, so that their satisfaction requires planful provision and work, struggle with nature and the association (*Vergesellschaftung*) of human beings" (pp. 63–64 or p. 161).

86. Weber, "Objectivity," p. 64, or "Objektivität," p. 161. For Weber's statement that social economics is a "science of reality" ("*Wirklichkeitswissenschaft*"), see "Objectivity," p. 72, or "Objektivität," p. 170.

87. Weber, "Objectivity," pp. 65–66, or "Objektivität," p. 163–64.

88. Weber, "Objectivity," pp. 64–65, or "Objektivität," p. 162.

89. Weber, "Objectivity," p. 64, or "Objektivität," p. 162.

90. Weber, "Objectivity," p. 65, or "Objectivität," p. 162.

91. As an example of this, the reader is referred to the analysis of the effects of "financing" on political organizations in chapter 3 of this volume. Weber does not seem to use the terms "economic phenomena," "economically relevant phenomena," and "economically conditioned phenomena" in his later work.

92. Weber, "Objectivity," pp. 69–71, or "Objektivität," pp. 168–70. Schumpeter's often cited statement that "the whole of Max Weber's facts and arguments [in *The Protestant Ethic*] fits perfectly into Marx's system" fails to take into account Weber's notion that causality goes in both directions. See Joseph A. Schumpeter, *Capitalism, Socialism and Democracy* (New York: Harper and Row, 1975), p. 11.

93. Weber, "Objectivity," pp. 89–90, or "Objektivität," p. 190. In an essay written a few years later, Weber adds: "The law of marginal utility uses the fiction of a purely quantifiable measurability of needs and . . . methodologically this is fully justifiable"; Weber, "'Energetic' Theories of Culture," *Mid-American Review of Sociology* 9 (1984). p. 53 n. 2, or "'Energetische' Kulturtheorien," p. 403 n. 1 in *Gesammelte Aufsätze zur Wissenschaftslehre*.

94. Weber, "Objectivity," p. 90, or "Objektivität" p. 190.

95. Weber, "Objectivity," pp. 90, 88, or "Objektivität," pp. 190, 188.The translation has been slightly changed. Weber's formulation is no doubt witty. In hindsight, however, it is perfectly clear that he was wrong in hinting that marginal utility economics had exhausted its potential in 1904.

96. Weber, "Marginal Utility Theory and 'The Fundamental Law of Psychophysics,'" *Social Science Quarterly* 56 (1975): 32, or "Die Grenznutzlehre und das 'psychophysiche Grundgesetz,'" p. 394 in *Gesammelte Aufsätze zur Wissenschaftslehre*.

97. Weber, "Marginal Utility Theory," p. 33, or "Grenznutzlehre," p. 395.

98. See Weber, *The Agrarian Sociology of Ancient Civilizations*, p. 358, or *Agrarverhältnisse im Altertum*, p. 271 in *Gesammelte Aufsätze zur Sozial- und Wirtschaftsgeschichte*. The translation has been slightly changed.

99. Weber, *The Agrarian Sociology of Ancient Civilizations*, p. 45, or *Agrarverhältnisse im Altertum*, p. 10.

100. The example has to do with the reasons for the increasing difficulty of the lower classes to lease land and the accompanying fall in their population. Weber, *The Agrarian Sociology of Ancient Civilizations*, p. 253, or *Agrarverhältnisse in Altertum*, p. 185.

101. In his copy of *Untersuchungen über die Methode der Socialwissenschaften* (1883), where Menger argues that one should not attempt to develop an economic theory for each stage of economic development, Weber wrote, "Why not?" See Carl Brinkmann, *Gustav Schmoller und die Volkswirtschaftslehre* (Stuttgart: Verlag W. Kohlhammer, 1937), pp. 135–36.

102. Weber, "Methodological Introduction for the Survey of the Society for Social Policy Concerning Selection and Adaptation (Choice and Course of Occupation) for the

Workers of Major Industrial Enterprises," p. 155 in Max Weber, *The Interpretation of Social Reality* (New York: Schocken Books, 1980), or "Methodologische Einleitung für die Erhebung des Vereins für Sozialpolitik über Auslese und Anpassung (Berufswahl und Berufsschicksal) der Arbeiterschaft der geschlossenen Grossindustrie," p. 60 in *Gesammelte Aufsätze zur Soziologie und Sozialpolitik.*

103. Max Weber, *The Protestant Ethic and the Spirit of Capitalism* (London: Allen and Unwin, 1930), p. 277, or "Die protestantische Ethik und der Geist des Kapitalismus," p. 191 in Vol. 1 of *Gesammelte Aufsätze zur Religionssoziologie* (Tübingen: J.C.B. Mohr, 1988).

104. In one of his essays from this period, Weber writes: "The fact that the *different* disciplines should be confronted with and cross each other with respect to their objects of study is certainly self-evident. This happens in economics (*Nationalökonomie*), for example, just as soon as it emerges from 'pure' theory." See Weber, "'Energetic' Theories of Culture," p. 41, or "'Energetische' Kulturtheorien," p. 413 in *Gesammelte Aufsätze zur Wissenschaftslehre.* The translation has been changed.

105. Unofficial version for the Verein from 1913 and the slightly expanded public version from 1917. Max Weber, "Max Weber," pp. 147–86 in Heino Henrich Nau, *Der Werturteilsstreit* (Marburg: Metropolis, 1996); Weber, "The Meaning of 'Ethical Neutrality' in Sociology and Economics," pp. 1–47 in *The Methodology of the Social Sciences,* or "Der Sinn der 'Wertfreiheit' der soziologischen und ökonomischen Wissenschaften," pp. 489–540 in *Gesammelte Aufsätze zur Wissenschaftslehre.* Nau's book also contains the other contributions that were prepared in 1913 for the 1914 meeting of the Verein.

106. Weber, *The Protestant Ethic and the Spirit of Capitalism,* p. 27, or "Vorbemerkung," p. 12 in Vol. 1 of *Gesammelte Aufsätze zur Religionssoziologie.*

107. According to Gustav Stolper, it was Friedrich von Wieser who succeeded in getting Weber to Vienna; see Gustav Stolper, "Max Weber" (1920), p. 58 in König and Winkelmann, eds., *Max Weber zum Gedächtnis.* In the end, Weber did not want to accept the chair Philippovich had once had. When he was later asked to judge the candidates that had applied for the same chair, he set Schumpeter first, followed by Johann Plenge and Ladislaus von Bortkiewics in shared second place, and Othmar Spann and Karl Diehl in shared third place. While Weber bent over backward to be objectivein judging Spann, for example, he was harsh toward Arthur Spiethoff, who in his eyes represented the kind of scholar Schmoller had been: too much mixed up with the politics of the state. See Weber, [Gutachten an die Wiener Fakultät 1918] and for a comment, Hennis, "The Pitiless 'Sobriety of Judgment,'" p. 49 ff.

108. "Wirtschaft und Gesellschaft (Positive Kritik der materialistischen Geschichtsauffassung)"; Weber also taught a "Soziologisches Kolloquium" while at Vienna—all according to information that the Archive of the University of Vienna kindly has supplied me. According to the same source, other material on Weber at the University of Vienna was in all likelihood destroyed during World War II together with most of the records of the Faculty of Law. Marianne Weber says that "under the title 'A Positive Critique of the Materialistic View of History', he [Weber] presented his research on the sociology of religion as well as his sociology of the state"; see Marianne Weber, *Max Weber,* p. 604. According to Mommsen and Schluchter, Weber lectured directly from his contribution to the *Grundriss;* see Wolfgang J. Mommsen and Wolfgang Schluchter, "Einleitung," pp. 20–21 in Weber, *Wissenschaft als Beruf. 1917/1919. Politik als Beruf. 1919. Max Weber Gesamtausgabe I/17* (Tübingen: J.C.B. Mohr, 1992)

109. See, e.g., Hayek, *The Fortunes of Liberalism,* p. 144.

110. Hayek continues: "I in fact got a half-promise from my father that after getting

my degree at Vienna I might go for a year to Munich [to study with Weber]"; Friedrich Hayek, *Hayek on Hayek* (London: Routledge, 1994), p. 64. Hayek's statement comes from a series of interviews conducted during 1984–1988. Hayek also mentions Weber in Vienna in *The Fortunes of Liberalism*, p. 186.

111. See Franz J. Bauer, ed., *Die Regierung Eisner 1918/19. Ministerratsprotokolle und Dokumente* (Düsseldorf: Droste Verlag), pp. 309–13. Gerhart Schulze-Gaevernitz (1864–1943) was active as a politician as well as an economist; and in the latter capacity he was especially interested in the economy of England. Moritz Julius Bonn (1873–1965) is a little-known economist who later emigrated to the United States, where he taught at several universities.

112. Ulrich Linse, "Hochschulrevolution. Zur Ideologie und Praxis sozialistischer Studentengruppen während der deutschen Revolutionszeit 1918/19," *Archiv für Sozialgeschichte* 14 (1974): 11 ff.

113. Marianne Weber, *Max Weber*, p. 646.

114. Wilhelm Hennis, "'Die Volle Nüchternheit des Urteils,'" p. 107 n. 4 in Gerhard Wagner and Heinz Zipprian, eds., *Max Webers Wissenschaftslehre* (Frankfurt am Main: Suhrkamp, 1994).

115. "Outline of Universal Social and Economic History" (winter term 1919–20). Weber also taught: "The General Categories of Social Science" (summer term 1919), "Socialism" (summer term 1920), and "General Theory of the State and Politics (Sociology of the State)" (summer term 1920); see Mommsen and Schluchter, "Einleitung," p. 21 n. 82 in Weber, *Wissenschaft als Beruf. 1917/1919. Politik als Beruf. 1919. Max Weber Gesamtausgabe I/17*. The courses of the summer term of 1920 were not completed; see S. Hellmann and Melchior Palyi, p. [xviii] in *Wirtschaftsgeschichte* (Berlin: Duncker und Humblot, 1991). See, finally, M. Rainer Lepsius, "Max Weber in München. Rede anlässlich einer Gedanktafel," *Zeitschrift für Soziologie* 6 (1977): 91–118.

116. For the story of how Weber's *Economy and Society* was written, see especially Wolfgang Schluchter, "Economy and Society: The End of a Myth," pp. 433–63 in *Rationalism, Religion, and Domination: A Weberian Perspective* (Berkeley: University of California Press, 1989); Winkelmann, *Max Webers hinterlassenes Hauptwerk;* and Wolfgang Mommsen, "Die Siebecks und Max Weber," *Geschichte und Gesellschaft* 22 (1996): 19–30.

117. Weber in a letter to Siebeck, dated December 26, 1908, as cited in Weber, *Briefe 1906–1908*, p. 705. Weber repeats this statement nearly verbatim in a letter to Siebeck from mid-April 1909; see Weber, *Briefe 1909–1910*, p. 106. The theory section, according to the 1910 plan for the *Grundriss*, was to by "decreasing abstraction be directed toward empirical reality"; see Weber, *Briefe 1909–1910*, p. 767.

118. Marianne Weber, *Max Weber*, pp. 331, 418. Marianne Weber says this twice, using the very same words.

119. These articles were the following: "Economy and Race"; "The Object and the Logical Nature of the Central Questions [in Economics]"; "The Modern State and Capitalism"; "The General Importance of Modern Transportation Links and Communication Services for the Capitalist Economy"; "The Limits to Capitalism in the Agrarian Economy"; "Types and Scope of the Restraints, Reactions, and Set-Backs of the Capitalist Economy"; "Agrarian Capitalism and Population Groups" (together with Schwiedland); "Policy Measures to Protect the Middle Class (Industrial Corporate Policy in the Widest Sense of the Term; Retailer Policy; Farmers' Corporate Policy: Policy for Incorporation and Limits to Debts; Farmers' Estates)"; "Positive Middle Class Policy Measures. a). Domestic Colonization Policy," "The So-Called New Middle Class (Mittelstand)"; "The Na-

ture and Social Position of the Working Class (a. The Concept of 'Workers,' Material Class Position and Material Class Interests. b. The Social Position of the Proletariat)"; and (possibly, together with Alfred Weber) "The Tendencies toward Internal Reorganization in Capitalism. (Monopolistic, Collectivistic and Bureaucratic Developmental Tendencies in the Context of Their Social Effects; Rents [das Rentnertum]; Tendencies toward Social Regrouping)." See Weber, "Stoffverteilungsplan für das 'Handbuch der politischen Ökonomie,' Mai 1910," pp. 766–74 in Max Weber, *Briefe 1909–1910.*

120. Marianne Weber, *Max Weber*, p. 419.

121. Weber in a letter to Paul Siebeck, dated December 30, 1913, and translated by Guenther Roth, "Introduction," pp. xxv–xxvi in Wolfgang Schluchter, *The Rise of Western Rationalism: Max Weber's Developmental History* (Berkeley: University of California Press, 1981). It is unclear when Wieser's manuscript arrived, but it was probably early 1914. In April 1914, Weber says that Wieser's contribution disregarded certain "sociological problems" and that he felt that he had to make further changes. See Winkelmann, *Max Webers hinterlassenes Hauptwerk* p. 38. According to a letter to the author from Wolfgang Schluchter, dated September 9, 1996, Weber however had made no changes in response to von Wieser before World War I broke out.

122. Johannes Winkelmann cites a letter from Weber to Paul Siebeck, dated March 22, 1912, in which Weber says that the term "*Sozialökonomik*" is not only the most modern but also "the best name for the discipline [of economics]"; Weber adds "*Volkswirtschaftslehre*" as a possible alternative. See Winkelmann, *Max Webers hinterlassenes Hauptwerk*, pp. 12, 25. In a letter to the author dated May 29, 1985, Winkelmann writes that "The term *Sozialökonomik* emphasizes in particular the social preconditions and effects of economic action." In August 1909, Weber had suggested to Paul Siebeck that *Siebeck's Handbuch der Sozialökonomik* would be a suitable title for the work, but added: "Or, in God's name [use] 'Pol[itical] economy'"; see Weber to Paul Siebeck, letter dated August 20, 1909, in *Briefe 1909–1910*, p. 230. According to the editors of Weber's *Briefe 1909–1910*, "Weber wanted [in the *Grundriss*] to offer an overall presentation of economics which could tie together both the theoretical and the historical school in the economics of those days and which would relate it to society, state, law, technology and art. For this conception Weber chose the expression *Sozialökonomik*"; see M. Rainer Lepsius and Wolfgang J. Mommsen, "Einleitung," pp. 2–3 in Weber, *Briefe 1909–1910.*

123. The plan for the *Grundriss* from 1914 can be found (in German as well as in English) in Schluchter, *Rationalism, Religion, and Domination*, p. 467. It should be mentioned that around this time Weber also played with the idea of naming his work "The Social Conditions of the Economy" ("*Gesellschaftliche Bedingungen der Wirtschaft*"). See the letter from Weber to Siebeck, dated March 18, 1914, as cited in Winkelmann, *Max Webers hinterlassenes Hauptwerk*, p. 76. The words "The Economy and the Social Orders and Powers" were printed on the title page of Part 1 of *Economy and Society* from 1921, which Weber had personally inspected. The title pages of this edition reads:

GRUNDRISS
DER
SOZIALÖKONOMIK
III. Abteilung
Wirtschaft und Gesellschaft
I
Die Wirtschaft und die gesellschaftlichen
Ordnungen und Mächte

The section called *Economy and Society* was also to include a contribution called "The Course of Development of the Systems and Ideals of Economic and Social Policy," which had been an independent section in the plan from 1910. In the 1956 and 1972 editions (edited by Johannes Winkelmann), "Die Wirtschaft und die gesellschaftlichen Ordnungen und Mächte" became the title of Part 2. It is also the title of Part 2 of the English edition, where it is translated as "The Economy and the Arena of Normative and De Facto Powers."

124. The exact titles of the three sections from the 1910 plan are: "Economy and Law (1. Fundamental Relationship, 2. Epochs in the Development of Present Conditions)," "Economy and Social Groups (Family and Community Associations, Status Groups and Classes, State)," and "Economy and Culture (Critique of Historical Materialism)." According to the 1914 plan, Weber's contribution—"The Economy and the Social Orders and Powers," Part I of "Economy and Society" in Book I of the *Grundriss*—was to have the following structure: "1. Categories of the Social Orders. The Fundamental Relationship between Economy and Law. The Economic Relations of the Associations in General," "2. The Household, Oikos and Enterprise," "3. The Neighborhood Association, Sib and Community," "4. Ethnic Community Relations," "5. Religious Communities. The Conditioning of Religion by Class Constellations; Cultural Religions and Economic Attitudes," "6. Market Relationships (Marktvergemeinschaftung)," "7. The Political Association. The Developmental Conditions of Law. Status Groups, Classes, Parties. The Nation," and "Domination (Die Herrschaft). a) The Three Types of Legitimate Domination, b) Political and Hierocratic Domination, c) Non-Legitimate Domination. The Typology of Cities, d) The Development of the Modern State, e) Modern Political Parties." See the 1910 plan prepared in 1909 as well as the 1914 plan in Schluchter, *Rationalism, Religion, and Domination*, pp. 466–67

125. Letter to Paul Siebeck, dated October 27, 1919, as cited in Winkelmann, *Max Webers hinterlassenes Hauptwerk*, p. 46.

126. In his correspondence and footnotes Weber always referred to his manuscript as *Wirtschaft und Gesellschaft,* and this is also the title that is used in Weber's contract with his publisher from 1919. While it for some time has been the consensus among scholars that *The Economy and the Social Orders and Powers* is the correct title, Wolfgang Mommsen has recently argued that Weber at the very end of his life preferred *Economy and Society.* See Schluchter, *Rationalism, Religion, and Domination,* pp. 459–60; Mommsen, "Die Siebecks und Max Weber," p. 30. The current subtitle of *Wirtschaft und Gesellschaft,* "Grundriss der verstehenden Soziologie," was not part of the original title but was added in the 1956 edition by Johannes Winkelmann (and reproduced in the current English translation as "An Outline of Interpretive Sociology").

127. According to the index to *Wirtschaft und Gesellschaft. Grundriss der verstehenden Soziologie,* the term *Sozialökonomik* appears only three times in this work. See Max Weber, *Economy and Society: An Outline of Interpretive Sociology* (Berkeley: University of California Press, 1978), pp. 311–12, 336, 635, or *Wirtschaft und Gesellschaft. Grundriss der verstehenden Soziologie* (Tübingen: J.C.B. Mohr, 1972), pp. 181, 197, 382. The term also appears during this period in, for example, "Some Categories of Interpretive Sociology (1913)," *Sociological Quarterly* 22 (1981): 152, or "Ueber einige Kategorien der verstehenden Soziologie," p. 429 in *Gesammelte Aufsätze zur Wissenschaftslehre.* The most interesting reference is where Weber writes: "*Sozialökonomik* . . . considers actual human activities as they are conditioned by the necessity to take into account the facts of economic life" (*Economy and Society,* pp. 311–12). My interpretation of this passage is that it does not constitute a definition and that Weber mainly wanted to contrast

the approach of economics to that of jurisprudence. A different opinion is expressed by Guenther Roth in a work from the late 1960s: "When Weber wrote the first pages of *Economy and Society* for the series [*Grundriss der Sozialökonomik*, according to the table of contents from 1909–1910] he defined *Sozialökonomik* as a field that 'considers actual human activities as they are conditioned by the necessity to take into account the facts of economic life'"; Guenther Roth, "'Value-Neutrality' in Germany and the United States," p. 38 in Reinhard Bendix and Guenther Roth, *Scholarship and Partisanship* (Berkeley: University of California Press, 1971).

128. See Weber, "The Meaning of 'Ethical Neutrality'" (1917)," p. 45 in *The Methodology of the Social Sciences,* or "Der Sinn der 'Wertfreiheit'," p. 538 in *Gesammelte Aufsätze zur Wissenschaftslehre.* In chapter 2 of *Economy and Society* Weber also explicitly speaks of "economic history," "economic sociology," and "economic theory." See Weber, *Economy and Society,* pp. 63, 79, 89, or *Wirtschaft und Gesellschaft,* pp. 31, 41, 47. See note 131 for the term "economic sociology" in Weber's work from this period.

129. Weber, "Some Categories of Interpretive Sociology," *Sociological Quarterly* 22 (1981): 151–80, or "Über einige Kategorien der verstehenden Soziologie," *Logos* 4 (1913): 427–74.

130. Acccording to Wolfgang Schluchter, in a letter to the author dated September 9, 1996, "Chapter 2 ['Sociological Categories of Economic Action' in *Economy and Society*] was mainly written in 1919–1920 but is based on manuscripts written earlier, even as early as the turn of the century." According to Guenther Roth, in a letter to the author dated March 12, 1985, "The second chapter in the new part of ES [*Economy and Society*] was written only after 1918, when Weber made a major effort to catch up with the literature. Before 1914 (and thus in the old version of ES) there was no major chunk that deserved a separate name as 'soc. of the economy.'"

131. See, for example, the following usages: "Wirtschafts-Soziologie" (1916; repeated in 1920); "Soziologie der Wirtschaft" (1917); "eine Soziologische Theorie der Wirtschaft" (1918–1920); "Wirtschafts*soziologie*" (1918–1920); and "Wirtschafts-*Soziologie*" (1920). The sources for these statements are, in chronological order: "Die Wirtschaftsethik der Weltreligionen. Religionssoziologische Skizzen. Einleitung," *Archiv für Sozialwissenschaft und Sozialpolitik* 41 (1915–1916): 1 n. 1 and the revised 1920 version of this article in Vol. 1 of *Gesammelte Aufsätze zur Religionssoziologie,* p. 237 n. 1; "The Meaning of 'Ethical Neutrality,'" p. 45, or "Der Sinn der 'Wertfreiheit,'" p. 538; *Economy and Society,* pp. 68, 79, or *Wirtschaft und Gesellschaft,* pp. 34, 41; letter to Robert Liefmann, dated March 9, 1920, as cited in Hennis, "'Die volle Nüchternheit des Urteils,'" p. 107 in Wagner and Zipprian, eds., *Max Webers Wissenschaftslehre.* In 1910 Weber also referred to "ökonomisch-soziologischen Gesichtspunkten" in one of his contributions to the debate around *The Protestant Ethic;* see Max Weber, "Antikritsches zum 'Geist' des Kapitalismus," p. 150 in Weber, *Die Protestantische Ethik, II. Kritiken und Antikritiken.*

132. Max Weber, "[Geschäftsbericht], p. 42 in *Verhandlungen des Ersten Deutschen Soziologentages* (Frankfurt am Main: Verlag Sauer und Auvermann Kg, [1911] 1969).

133. See Edgar Jaffé, "Das theoretische System der kapitalistischen Wirtschaftsordnung," *Archiv für Sozialwissenschaft und Sozialpolitik* 44 (1917): 1–2; Werner Sombart and Max Weber, "Erklärung," *Archiv für Sozialwissenschaft und Sozialpolitik* 44 (1917): 348.

134. Weber wrote to Robert Liefmann in a letter dated December 12, 1919: "I regret myself that I have been able to do so little, or virtually nothing, for theory. But one cannot do everything. I do not hold theory in any less esteem. The other things also need to be done"; as cited in Hennis, "A Science of Man," p. 54, n. 26 in Mommsen and Oster-

hammel, eds., *Max Weber and His Contemporaries.* (Liefmann had written his doctoral dissertation for Weber in Freiburg and also dedicated a major work in economics [1917–1919] to Weber, despite differences between the two on economics; see Hennis, "The Pitiless 'Sobriety of Judgment,'" pp. 54–55 n. 9.) According to von Mises, "Just before his untimely death Weber regretted that his knowledge of modern theoretical economics and the classical system was too limited. He mentioned his fear that time would not permit him to fill these regrettable gaps"; see Mises, *A Critique of Interventionism,* p. 103.

135. Weber, in a letter to Robert Liefmann dated March 3, 1920, as cited in Hennis, "The Pitiless 'Sobriety of Judgment,'" p. 29. (The translation has been slightly changed.) That other people thought Weber had a low opinion of economic theory is clear not only from Edgar Jaffé's 1917 article (see earlier in the text), but also from a comment that can be found in Schumpeter's *History of Economic Analysis.* Schumpeter here says that he, like von Wieser, was invited to participate in the *Grundriss* with the motivation that "he [Weber] saw no objection of principle to what economic theorists actually did, though he disagreed with them on what they thought they were doing, that is, on the epistemological interpretation of their procedure"; see Schumpeter, *History of Economic Analysis,* p. 819. Schumpeter, it can be added, must have cited from memory when he wrote these lines in the 1940s because he does not seem to have brought Weber's letter with him to the United States, where he emigrated in 1932.

136. This is, for example, the case with the otherwise interesting work of Hinnerk Bruhns, Simon Clarke, and Robert Holton and Bryan Turner; see Hinnerk Bruhns, "Max Weber, l'économie et l'histoire," *Annales. Histoire, Sciences Sociales* 51 (1996): 1273; Simon Clarke, *Marx, Marginalism and Modern Sociology: From Adam Smith to Max Weber* (London: Macmillam, 1982), pp. 166–70; and Robert J. Holton and Bryan Turner, *Max Weber on Economy and Society* (London: Routledge, 1989), pp. 39, 55–65. According to Yuichi Shionoya, economist and Schumpeter expert, "Even though Weber sometimes uses the word 'Sozialökonomik' . . . , he nonetheless did not develop the content and method relating to this concept"; see Yuichi Shionoya, "Max Webers soziologische Sicht der Wirtschaft," p. 109 in K. H. Kaufhold, G. Roth, and Y. Shionoya, eds., *Max Weber und seine "Protestantische Ethik"* (Munich: Duncker und Humblot, 1992). The economist who has come the closest to what Weber meant with *Sozialökonomik* is, in my opinion, Arthur Schweitzer. See Arthur Schweitzer, "Max Weber's *Economy and Society*: A Review Article," *Journal of Economic Literature* 8 (1970): 1203–09.

137. These people include Robert Liefmann, Alexander von Schelting, and Leopold von Wiese. See in particular Robert Liefmann, "Review of *Grundriss der Sozialökonomik,* Abt. I, II, VI," *Zeitschrift für Politik* 8 (1915): 586–99; Leopold von Wiese, "Soziologie," pp. 379–83 in Vol. 3 of Ludwig Elster, ed., *Wörterbuch der Volkswirtschaft* (Jena: Gustav Fischer, 1933); and Alexander von Schelting, "Eine Einführung in die Methodenlehre der Nationalökonomie," *Archiv für Sozialwissenschaft und Sozialpolitik* 54 (1925), p. 216.

138. What I say here is not based on a systematic study of histories of economic thought but on an impressionistic view of the literature. Among well-known works with references to Weber, see, e.g., Mark Blaug, *Economic Theory in Retrospect* (Cambridge: Cambridge University Press, 1983), pp. 708, 712; T. W. Hutchison, *A Review of Economic Doctrines 1870–1929* (Oxford: Clarendon Press, 1953), pp. 186, 298–302; Karl Pribram, *A History of Economic Reasoning* (Baltimore: Johns Hopkins University Press, 1983), pp. 227–29; Eric Roll, *A History of Economic Thought* (London: Faber and Faber, 1960), pp. 460–61; Ben S. Seligman, *Main Currents in Modern Economics: Economic Thought since*

1870 (New York: Free Press, 1962), pp. 22–31; Othmar Spann, *The History of Economics* (New York: Arno Press, [1926] 1972), pp. 242–43, 277–78; Henry William Spiegel, *The Growth of Economic Thought* (Englewood Cliffs, N.J.: Prentice-Hall, 1971), pp. 429–31; Sidney Weintraub, ed., *Modern Economic Thought* (Oxford: Basil Blackwell, 1977), p. 13. There is no mention of Weber at all in, e.g., Jürg Niehans, *A History of Economic Theory: Classic Contributions, 1720–1980* (Baltimore: Johns Hopkins University Press, 1990), or Vincent Bladen, *From Adam Smith to Maynard Keynes: The Heritage of Political Economy* (Toronto: University of Toronto Press, 1974). For a thorough study of this theme, one would have to systematically consult many of the works listed in Richard S. Howey, *A Bibliography of General Histories of Economics, 1692–1975* (Lawrence: Regents Press of Kansas, 1982).

139. Adolf Weber, "Der Anteil Deutschlands an der nationalökonomischen Forschung seit dem Weltkrieg," p. 27 in Vol. 2 of M. J. Bonn and M. Palyi, eds., *Die Wirtschaft nach dem Kriege. Festschrift für Lujo Brentano zum 80. Geburtstag* (Munich: Duncker und Humblot, 1925). Bertram Schefold has argued that Weber is ignored in contemporary German economics. See Bertram Schefold, "Max Webers Werk als Hinterfragung der Ökonomie," pp. 6–7 in Bertram Schefold et al., *Max Weber und seine 'Protestantische Ethik'* (Düsseldorf: Verlag Wirtschaft und Finanzen Gmbh, 1992).

140. Joseph A. Schumpeter, "Deutschland," p. 17 in Vol. 1 of Hans Mayer et al., eds., *Die Wirtschaftstheorie der Gegenwart* (Vienna: Julius Springer, 1927). Schumpeter chose one hundred articles in recent economic journals and among other things made a rough content analysis, according to which 36 percent of the articles were in economic theory, 16 percent on "sociological" topics, 39 percent on "practical, purely historical, etc." matters, and 9 percent on methodology. Referring to the postwar generation of German economists, Mises noted that "they were dilettants in everything they undertook"; see Ludwig von Mises, *Notes and Recollections* (South Holland, Ill.: Libertarian Press, 1978), p. 102.

141. I have been unable to locate any references in the work of Carl Menger (1840–1921) to Weber; it also seems that Menger had none of Weber's works in his enormous library of economic literature. (I gratefully acknowledge a letter from Katsuyoshi Watarai, dated July 19, 1995, in which he says that "the Menger collection at our center [the Hitotsubashi University, where Menger's library can be found today] contains none of Max Weber's work"; see also Handels-Universität Tokio, *Katalog der Carl Menger-Bibliothek in der Handels-Universität Tokio,* I–II [Tokyo: Handelsuniversität Tokio, 1926–1955]). As to Böhm-Bawerk (1851–1914), I have not been able to find more than one reference to Weber's work, more precisely to Weber's article on marginal utility (see note 150 below). See Eugen von Böhm-Bawerk, *Capital and Interest. Volume II: The Positive Theory of Capital* (South Holland, Ill.: Libertarian Press, 1959), pp. 430–31 n. 81. Although von Wieser (1851–1926) knew Weber personally and made an important contribution to the *Grundriss der Sozialökonomik* in 1914 (for more details, see chapter 6 in this volume), it is my strong impression that he was not very interested in Weber's work. The only reference to Weber in von Wieser's work that I have been able to locate is a mention of *Wirtschaft und Gesellschaft* in the second edition of von Wieser's *Theorie der gesellschaftlichen Wirtschaft* (1924). See von Wieser, "Theorie der gesellschaftlichen Wirtschaft," p. 108 in *Grundriss der Sozialökonomik. Abteilung I. II. Teil* (Tübingen: J.C.B. Mohr, 1924).

142. That Weber's methodology was one of the favorite topics at the Mises Seminar (where Alfred Schutz was also present) comes from Gottfried Haberler, "A Vienna Seminarian Remembers," p. 51 in John L. Andrews, ed., *Homage to Mises* (Hillsdale, Mich.:

Hillsdale College Press, 1981). Haberler writes, "The seminar met twice a month, on Fridays at 7:00 P.M. in Mises' office in the Chamber of Commerce; Mises sat at his desk, and the members of the group around him. The meeting would begin with a talk by Mises himself or with a paper by another member on some problem of economic theory, economic policy, sociology, or methodology; the *verstehende Soziologie* of Max Weber and related problems were favorite topics." For the links between Weber and Austrian economists, see the following two studies: Robert J. Holton and Bryan Turner, "Max Weber, Austrian Economics, and Liberalism," pp. 30–67 in *Max Weber on Economy and Society;* and Christopher Prendergast, "Alfred Schutz and the Austrian School of Economics," *American Journal of Sociology* 92 (1986): 1–26. See also Helmut Wagner, *Alfred Schutz: An Intellectual Biography* (Chicago: University of Chicago Press, 1983), e.g., pp. 12–13.

143. According to Talcott Parsons (who translated Part I of *Economy and Society* in 1947), Hayek wrote to him in early 1939 that a young economist by the name of A. M. Henderson had made a draft translation of the first two chapters of *Wirtschaft und Gesellschaft* under his direction and asked Parsons if he would review them. See Talcott Parsons, letter to Frank Knight, dated May 17, 1939 (Harvard University Archives); and Talcott Parsons, "The Circumstances of My Encounter with Max Weber," p. 42 in Robert K. Merton and Matilda White Riley, eds., *Sociological Traditions from Generation to Generation* (Norwood, N.J.: Ablex, 1980). For Machlup, see, e.g., Fritz Machlup, "The Ideal Type: A Bad Name for a Good Construct (1978)," pp. 211–21 in *Methodology of Economics and Other Social Sciences* (New York: Academic Press, 1978). Machlup invited Afred Schutz to lecture to his economics students in 1949; see Wagner, *Alfred Schutz,* p. 167. Another avenue into U.S. economics for Weber's ideas on economics, one might have thought, would have been through Frank Knight, who translated Weber's *Wirtschaftsgeschichte* into English in the 1920s. But according to a letter to the author (dated March 22, 1988) from Edward Shils (who knew Knight well and participated in a seminar on Weber in the mid-1930s, arranged by Knight), this did not happen: "Max Weber's ideas had no impact whatsoever on economics in the United States (and none on Knight's own work)." See also Edward Shils, "Tradition, Ecology, and Institution in the History of Sociology," *Daedalus* 99 (Fall 1970): 823 n. 21.

144. Alfred Schutz (1899–1959) is today mostly known as a social philosopher and phenomenologist but also had important links to economics in his life. He had, for example, a degree in law, with economic aspects of international law as his specialty (his most important teachers in economics were Mises and Wieser); he worked for some time for the Austrian Bankers' Association; and he earned his living working in international banking until becoming a full-time professor at the New School of Social Research in the mid-1950s. Schutz was a good friend of Hayek as well as of Machlup and published an important paper on rationality in *Economica* in 1943. See Wagner, *Alfred Schutz,* pp. 9 ff., 52, 69 ff., 166–68. See also the review of *The Phenomenology of the Social World* (by Alfred Stonier and Karl Bode) in *Economica* (1937); Prendergast, "Alfred Schutz and the Austrian School of Economics"; Bruce Pietrykowski, "Alfred Schutz and the Economists," *History of Political Economy* 28 (1996): 219–44; and the January 1993 issue of *Rationality and Society,* which is devoted to a discussion of a "rational choice reconstruction of the theory of action of Alfred Schutz." According to Schutz's biographer, "Schutz could sit for hours in order to think out the meanings and the implications of formulations that occurred in one dense paragraph of *Wirtschaft und Gesellschaft*"; Wagner, *Alfred Schutz,* p. 15.

145. Mises argued that Weber's notion of ideal type and marginal utility theory were

not compatible, while Schutz took the opposite position (referring to Weber's later formulations). At issue in this debate were not so much Weber's ideas per se as the status of marginal utility theory and economic theory more generally. For an excellent discussion of the positions of Menger, Mises, Schutz, and Weber, see Prendergast, "Alfred Schutz and the Austrian School of Economics." For Mises's position, see Ludwig von Mises, "Sociology and History," pp. 68–129 in *Epistemological Problems of Economics* (Princeton, N.J.: D. Van Nostrand Company, [1929] 1960); and for Schutz's position, see Alfred Schutz, *The Phenomenology of the Social World* (London: Heinemann, 1967), pp. 241–49.

146. Some members of what is sometimes called modern Austrian economics or neo-Austrian economics have also paid attention to Weber, especially Ludwig Lachmann and Israel Kirzner. Lachmann, who has been interested in Weber's methodology as well as his economic sociology, is the first Austrian economist to have produced a major study of Weber. See Ludwig Lachmann, *The Legacy of Max Weber* (London: Heinemann, 1970). See also Lachmann's essay "Socialism and the Market: A Theme of Economic Sociology Viewed from a Weberian Perspective," *South African Journal of Economics* 60 (1992): 24–43. For Israel Kirzner, see, e.g., *The Economic Point of View* (Kansas City, Mo.: Sheed and Ward, 1976), pp. 157–59; and Israel Kirzner, "Philosophical and Ethical Implications of Austrian Economics," pp. 76–78 in Edwin Dolan, ed., *The Foundations of Modern Austrian Economics* (Kansas City, Mo.: Sheed and Ward, 1976).

147. Ludwig von Mises, *Critique of Interventionism*, pp. 102–3. For other versions of this theme, see the following works: Ludwig von Mises, "Sociology and History," p. 74 in *Epistemological Problems of Economics;* and Ludwig von Mises, *Human Action: A Treatise on Economics* (New Haven, Conn.: Yale University Press, 1949), p. 126. The citation from Schumpeter comes from *History of Economic Analysis*, p. 819. Schumpeter here also mentions "[Weber's] almost complete ignorance of economic theory." In an article written just after Weber's death, Schumpeter expressed a slightly different opinion: "He [Weber] was an economist only indirectly and secondarily"; see Joseph Schumpeter, "Max Weber's Work," p. 225 in *The Economics and Sociology of Capitalism* (Princeton, N.J.: Princeton University Press, 1991).

148. According to Gunnar Myrdal, "Weber was more of a sociologist than an economist"; and according to Ben Seligman, Weber "was not really an economist in the analytical sense." Seligman elaborates: "While he [Weber] developed an institutional framework for economic action, he seldom inquired into what an economist would consider to be the really substantive issues. In his analysis of capitalism, for example, there is not much that one can find on business cycles. Whatever theory he used, he took from the Austrians." See Gunnar Myrdal, *The Political Element in the Development of Economic Thought* (London: Routledge and Kegan Paul, [1930] 1953), p. 13; Ben Seligman, *Main Currents in Modern Economics* (New York: Free Press, 1962), p. 23. As another example of what distinguished Weber's sociological mode of analysis from that of economics, one might cite Frank Knight's critique of the concept of ideal types in a letter to Parsons, dated February 7, 1935: "I do not think that the general notions of economic behaviour and the perfect market are 'ideal types,' in Max Weber's sense. They are essentially mechanical, of the nature of mathematical maxima, and I do not think that is what Max Weber meant by an ideal type" (Harvard University Archives).

149. I have been unable to find any references to Weber in the works of Marshall, Wicksell, Pareto, and Keynes. As to Pareto, Edward Shils writes, "Pareto never referred to him [Weber]"; Shils, "Tradition, Ecology, and Institution in the History of Sociology," p. 783. (In 1907, however, Pareto included a translation of Weber's second dissertation

in *Biblioteca di Storia Economica,* which he edited together with Ettore Ciccotti. See on this point also chap. 6 in Alan Sica, *Weber, Irrationality and Social Order* [Berkeley: University of California Press, 1968].) According to Norbert Wiley, in a study comparing the ideas of Keynes and Weber, "The two theorists do not cite each other in their writings, and Keynes (1883–1946) being nineteen years younger than Weber (1864–1920) and from a different tradition in economics, they have little historical connection. The closest they ever came to a meeting was at the Versailles Conference, in 1919, when both were serving on their national delegations." Norbert Wiley, "The Congruence of Weber and Keynes," p. 48 n. 1 in Randall Collins, ed., *Sociological Theory, 1983* (San Francisco: Jossey-Bass, 1983).

150. George Stigler, "The Development of Utility Theory. II," *Journal of Political Economy* 58 (1950): 377; Friedrich von Hayek, *The Trend of Economic Thinking* (London: Routledge, 1991), p. 360; Paul Rosenstein-Rodan, "Marginal Utility (1927)," p. 204 in Israel M. Kirzner, ed., *Classics in Austrian Economics* (London: William Pickering, 1994); and Lionel Robbins, *An Essay on the Nature and Significance of Economic Science* (London: Macmillan, 1984), p. 85. Böhm-Bawerk also mentions Weber's article, but mixes praise with criticism, noting that "certain statements of Weber's [about the opposition of economic theory and psychology] may definitely be said to overshoot the mark." See Böhm-Bawerk, *Capital and Interest. Volume II: Positive Theory of Capital,* pp. 430–31 n. 81.

151. For an account of Weber's argument, see chapter 4 in this volume. For the argument itself, see Weber, *Economy and Society,* p. 327, or *Wirtschaft und Gesellschaft,* p. 192.

152. See, e.g., Roll, *A History of Economic Thought,* p. 461; Robbins, *The Nature and Significance of Economic Science,* pp. xxxviii–xxxix, 2.

153. For the opinions of some prominent economists on *The Protestant Ethic,* see note 51 in chapter 5.

154. Arthur Scheitzer, "Frank Knight's Social Economics," *History of Political Economy* 7 (1985): 279.

155. Economic historians have made less use of *Economy and Society.* When a new edition of the English translation was reviewed in the prestigous *Journal of Economic History,* it was noted that when the first edition of the translation appeared in 1968, "it was not reviewed in this journal or in the economic journals." The reviewer then asks, "Now that we have it, it is not easy to know what to do with it"; see Karl de Schweinitz, "Review of Max Weber, *Economy and Society,*" *Journal of Economic History* 39 (1979): 834–35. As far as I know, no attempt has been made to evaluate Weber's general influence on and importance for economic history. An article that covers some aspects of this task is Paul Honigsheim, "Max Weber as Historian of Agriculture and Rural Life," *Agricultural History* 23 (1949): 179–213. How economic historians view *The Protestant Ethic* is also discussed in Richard Hamilton, *The Social Misconstruction of Reality* (New Haven, Conn.: Yale University Press, 1996), pp. 90–91, 243–44 n. 71.

156. Rondo Cameron, *A Concise Economic History of the World: From Paleolithic Times to the Present,* 2d ed. (New York: Oxford University Press, 1993); Fernand Braudel, *Afterthoughts on Material Civilization and Capitalism* (Baltimore: Johns Hopkins University Press, 1977), p. 66. The whole section reads as follows: "For Max Weber, capitalism in the modern sense of the word was no more and no less than a creation of Protestantism or, to be even more accurate, of Puritanism. All historians have opposed this tenuous theory, although they have not managed to be rid of it once and for all. Yet it is clearly false" (pp. 65–66). For a less blunt position, see Braudel, *The Wheels of Commerce* (London: Fontana Press, 1985), p. 566 ff.

157. Raymond Aron, *German Sociology* (New York: Free Press, [1936] 1963), p. 67; see M. I. Finley, "The Ancient City: From Fustel de Coulanges to Max Weber and Beyond," *Comparative Studies in Societies and History* 19 (1977): 318; Arnaldo Momigliano, "The Instruments of Decline," *Times Literary Supplement* 3917 (April 8, 1977): 435–36. See in addition the use made of Weber's study in Douglass C. North, *Structure and Change in Economic History* (New York: W. W. Norton, 1981), pp. 99, 102, 107.

158. Eli Hecksher, *Industrialismen. Den ekonomiska utvecklingen sedan 1750* (Stockholm: Kooperativa förbundets bokförlag, 1938), p. 346; A. P. Usher, "Review of *General Economic History,*" *American Economic Review* 18 (1928): 105. The quotation from Heckscher is a one-line summary of *General Economic History;* but see also his statement in another article: "The reader finds geniality on nearly every page [of *General Economic History*]"; cf. Eli Heckscher, "Den ekonomiska historiens aspekter," *Historisk tidskrift,* 50 (1930): 20. One of Usher's students, Frank Knight, translated *Wirtschaftsgeschichte* into English and notes in the preface: "My former teacher in the field of economic history, Professor A. P. Usher, has kindly answered questions and given valuable advice and suggestions." See Frank Knight, "Translator's Preface," p. xvi in *General Economic History* (New York: Greenberg, 1927). On the subject of Harvard economic historians, Talcott Parsons has reported that according to E. F. Gay, Weber was "one of the few most stimulating minds and fruitful minds of the field of economic history." See Talcott Parsons, *The Structure of Social Action* (New York: Free Press, [1949] 1968), Vol. 2, p. 501.

159. Sociologists have of course made some use of Weber's economic sociology, but often within the framework of later subfields of sociology. Ralf Dahrendorf has, for example, argued that Weber's work on industrial workers around the turn of the century qualifies him as the founder of "industrial sociology"; see Ralf Dahrendorf, *Industrie- und Betriebssoziologie* (Berlin: Walter de Gruyter, 1956), p. 24. Weber's industrial sociology, however, covers only a minor part of his economic sociology; more precisely (as Gert Schmidt has argued), his methodological essay for the Verein from 1908, his work on the psychophysics of labor (1908–9), and his review of a book by Adolf Levinstein in the *Archiv* from 1909. See Gert Schmidt, "Max Weber and Modern Industrial Sociology: A Comment on Some Recent Anglo-Saxon Interpretations," *Social Analysis and Theory* 6 (1976): 47–73; and Gert Schmidt, "Max Webers Beitrag zur empirischen Industrieforschung," *Kölner Zeitschrift für Soziologie und Sozialpsychologie* 32 (1980): 76–92. Weber's three works are the following: Max Weber, "Methodological Introduction for the Survey of the Society for Social Policy Concerning Selection and Adaptation (Choice and Course of Occupation) for the Workers of Major Industrial Enterprises," pp. 103–55 in J.E.T. Eldridge, ed., *The Interpretation of Social Reality* (London: Nelson, 1971); Max Weber, "Zur Psychophysik der industriellen Arbeit (1908–09)," pp. 61–255 in *Gesammelte Aufsätze zur Soziologie und Sozialpolitik;* and Max Weber, "On the Method of Social-Psychological Inquiry and Its Treatment (Review of Works by Adolf Levenstein)," *Sociological Theory* 13 (1995): 100–106.

310

Grundriss zu den Vorlesungen über Allgemeine ("theoretische") Nationalökonomie (1898). See under Weber, Max. Works
guilds, 13, 15, 210n.10

Haberler, Gottfried, 204
Hamilton, Gary, 270nn.89 and 96, 271nn.97 and 99
Hayek, Friedrich von, 80, 154, 160, 176, 198, 204, 205, 246n.13, 295n.110, 302n.143
Heckscher, Eli, 9, 17, 206, 305n.158
Heilsgüter. See religious benefits
Hellmann, Siegmund, 208n.1
Henderson, A. M., 302n.143
Hennis, Wilhelm, 181, 288nn.33 and 36
Herkner, Heinrich, 196
Hernes, Gudmund, 265n.58
Herrschaft. See domination
heterocephalous organizations, 41
heteronomous organizations, 41
Hildebrand, Bruno, 45, 174, 177
Hinduism, 139–40. *See also* Weber, Max. Works: *The Religion of India*
Hintze, Otto, 208n.4
Hirschman, Albert O., 3, 263n.51
Historical School of Economics, 155, 161, 174–77, 186–87, 190, 193, 282n.2
Holton, Robert, 302n.142
homo economicus, 185, 187
hope for compensation, 113–14, 116
household and householding, 11, 16, 30–31, 52, 200
Hume, David, 5
Hutchison, T. W., 300n.138
"hydraulic" bureaucracy, 12, 71, 153

ideal interests. *See* interests
ideal type, 193–94, 203, 204, 205, 216n.15, 303n.148
imperialism, 75–76, 79
imperialist capitalism, 75–76. *See also* imperialism
impersonality, 43–44, 111, 227n.107, 257n.11, 267n.72, 268n.81
incentives, 262n.39
income distribution, 39, 150, 157, 224n.83
India. *See* Hinduism; Indian law; Weber, Max. Works: *The Religion of India*
Indian law, 92
individualism, 77. *See also* methodological individualism
industrial location theory, 157–58, 278n.48
Industrial Revolution, 149–50

industrial sociology, 152, 236n.28, 275n.27, 279n.54, 281n.77, 305n.159
industry, 12–14, 39, 278nn.47 and 48, 291n.62. *See also* Industrial Revolution
inflation, 76–77
inheritance, 92, 94, 95, 101, 224n.85
instinct of acquisition. *See* acquisitive drive or instinct
institutions, 15, 17, 39–45, 90, 160, 167, 176, 192, 249n.31, 284n.15
insurance, 155, 278n.47
interest on loans, 141–42. *See also* usury
interests, 3–6, 23–25, 77, 87, 100, 109–11, 133–34, 163, 164, 207n.5, 267n.70. *See also* cognitive interest; uniformities determined by self-interest
iron cage metaphor, 50–51, 196, 262n.44
Islam, 133, 142–43, 270n.92. *See also* Islamic law; *quadi*
Islamic law, 93–94, 98

Jaffé, Edgar, 190, 192, 203
Jains, 249n.34, 269n.84
Japan, 75, 269n.84, 270n.95
Jellinek, Georg, 96, 252n.52, 260n.27
Jevons, William Stanley, 179, 185, 286n.26
Jewish law, 94, 98
Jewish people and the economy, 15, 17–18, 19–20, 94. *See also* Jewish law; Judaism; pariah capitalism
joint liability, 92, 93, 102, 103–4,
joint-stock corporation, 102–4
Jones, Bryn, 216n.16
Judaism, 19–20, 94, 140–42. *See also* Weber, Max. Works: *Ancient Judaism*
jurisprudence, 88, 227n.110, 248n.27
juristic personality, 16, 102, 169, 254n.75
just price, 55, 97, 112, 258n.15

Kalberg, Stephen, 216n.16
Kaldor, Nicholas, 263n.51
Kampf. See struggle
Kantowsky, Detlef, 272n.100
Kaufmann, Felix, 219n.33
Keynes, John Maynard, 205, 303n.149
Kirzner, Israel, 303n.146
Knapp, G. F., 76–77, 175, 181–82, 240n.73, 291n.59
Knies, Karl, 174, 175, 180–81, 184, 185, 187, 256n.1, 288n.33
Knight, Frank H., 187, 205, 216n.16, 218n.22, 302n.143, 303n.148
Kocka, Jürgen, 63, 170

purposive contract. *See* contract
putting-out system, 13–14, 122

quadi, 93–94, 250n.40
Quakers, 113, 197, 259n.17

race and the economy, 35–36, 150–51, 152, 200, 274nn.16–19 and 41, 270n.95, 296n.116
Rathgen, Karl, 189, 293n.75
rational action, 26–30
rational capitalism, 17–20, 46–49, 50–51, 59–61, 65–70, 86, 88, 90–91, 97–98, 99–107, 203, 212n.36, 231n.141
rationality: empirical existence of, 36, 167, 171, 255n.87; formal and substantive, 36–39, 70, 76, 87–88, 102, 221n.51; as a method in sociology and economics, 28, 164. *See also* calculation; rational action; rational capitalism
regulation, 42–43, 47, 87–88, 188
religion and the economy, 18–20, 108–45, 262n.43. *See also* Calvinism; canon law; Catholicism; Islam; Judaism; Lutheranism; Methodism; mysticism and the economy; religious benefits; salvation and the economy; Weber, Max. Works: *The Economic Ethics of the World Religions*, *The Protestant Ethic and the Spirit of Capitalism*, and "The Protestant Sects and the Spirit of Capitalism"
religious benefits, 109–11, 125, 134, 256nn.3 and 4
rent, 31, 50, 52, 78, 232n.151. *See also* rent-seeking
rent-seeking, 51, 53, 172, 282n.83
Riesebrodt, Martin, 256n.4
rights, 39, 96–97
Rights of Man, 96
risk, 218n.22
Robbins, Lionel, 205
Rodbertus, Karl, 220n.29
Roll, Eric, 300n.138
Roman law, 82, 95–96, 98, 103, 245n.6, 251n.50
Rome, 48, 59, 74, 183–84, 185, 195–96. *See also* Roman law
Roscher, Wilhelm, 174, 177, 185, 192, 193, 204
Rosenstein-Rodan, Paul, 204, 205
rotating credit associations, 268n.81
Roth, Guenther, 46, 208n.4, 231n.146, 299n.130
routinization of charisma, 64, 65, 69

salvation and the economy, 116–19, 125

Samuelson, Paul, 263n.51
Samuelsson, Kurt, 260n.28
Savigny, Friedrich Karl von, 174
saving, 37
Say, Jean-Baptiste, 177
Scaff, Lawrence, 289n.47, 292nn.67–69
scarcity of means, 29, 37, 163, 164, 192, 195, 223n.70, 293n.85
Schäffle, Albert, 177, 179
Schefold, Bertram, 288n.36, 301n.139
Schelling, Thomas, 3–4, 53, 162
Schelting, Alexander von, 181, 216n.16
Schluchter, Wolfgang, 143, 274n.17, 296n.116, 297n.121, 299n.131
Schmidt, Gert, 305n.159
Schmoller, Gustav von, 45–46, 70–71, 155, 158, 161, 176, 177, 179, 180, 181, 182, 185, 190, 204
Schönberg, Gustav, 154–55, 157, 199
Schroeder, Ralph, 259n.20, 267n.69
Schulze-Gaevernitz, Gerhart von, 199, 290n.52, 296n.111
Schumacher, Hermann, 290n.53
Schumpeter, Joseph, 58, 75, 155–56, 160–61, 165, 171, 177, 180, 190, 199, 204, 261n.37, 263n.51
Schutz, Alfred, 204–5, 302n.144
Schweitzer, Arthur, 300n.136
science and the economy, 18, 19, 146–48, 271n.99. *See also* technology
Scotland, 132
sect, 111, 113, 115, 126, 128–29, 263n.46, *See also* Weber, Max. Works: "The Protestant Sects and the Spirit of Capitalism"
selection, 34
self-interest. *See* interests; uniformities determined by self-interest
Seligman, Ben, 300n.138
Sen, Amartya, 3, 264n.51
sensuality and the economy, 147
services, 29
Shils, Edward, 216n.16, 302n.143
Shionoya, Yuichi, 300n.136
Sica, Alan, 208n.4
Siebeck, Georg, 159, 296n.116
Siebeck, Oskar, 279n.55, 296n.116
Siebeck, Paul, 279n.55, 296n.116
Simmel, Georg, 160, 287n.32
slaves, 13, 48, 63, 95, 111, 183–84
Smelser, Neil, 165
Smith, Adam, 39, 181
social action, 23–25. *See also* economic action
social constitution. *See* constitution
Social Darwinism, 151, 275n.25

ABOUT THE AUTHOR

Richard Swedberg is Professor of Sociology at Stockholm University.
He is the author of several works in the field of economic sociology and of
Joseph A. Schumpeter: A Biography (Princeton). With Neil Smelser,
he edited *The Handbook of Economic Sociology* (Princeton).